Social Morality

Saint Alberto Hurtado, S.J.

TRANSLATED AND

EDITED BY

Scott FitzGibbon

Fernanda Soza

CONVIVIUMPRESS

SERIES MARTYRIA

2018

Social Morality

http://www.conviviumpress.com
sales@conviviumpress.com
ventas@conviviumpress.com
convivium@conviviumpress.com

7661 NW 68th St, Suite 108
Miami, Florida 33166. USA
Phone: +1 (305) 8890489
Fax: +1 (305) 8875463

Edited *and* Translated *by* Scott FitzGibbon
and Fernanda Soza
Designed *by* Eduardo Chumaceiro d'E
Series: *Martyria*

ISBN: 978-1-934996-73-7

Printed in Colombia
Impreso en Colombia
Panamericana Formas e Impresos, S.A.

Convivium Press
Miami, 2018

Social Morality

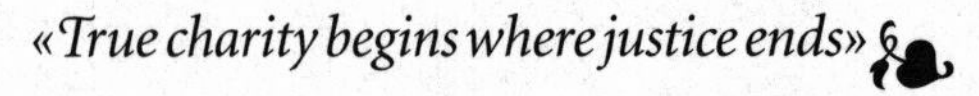
«True charity begins where justice ends»

We dedicate this book to Alberto Hurtado Fuenzalida, chemical engineer and entrepreneur, whose philanthropic work in recent years reflected his belief that education is a foundation for the well-being and fulfillment of each human being, as well as a catalyst for social change. Alberto Hurtado Fuenzalida's efforts in such matters began with his support for and active participation in the directive council of the Alberto Hurtado University of Chile, created in 1997 by the Society of Jesus; a university educational project based on the Jesuit tradition that welcomes and integrates students from different sectors of Chilean society.

Alberto Hurtado Fuenzalida was the second-degree nephew of San Alberto Hurtado, to whom he owed his name and much of his upbringing and training. When he was only 15 years old, his mother María Fuenzalida became widowed and Father Alberto Hurtado became a second father figure and important role model for him and his five brothers. The importance of education and social action was always emphasized in his home and inculcated the Ignatian spirit that has been part of his professional and personal journey.

Respect, integrity, dedication and generosity in all ventures are the set of values that characterize Alberto Hurtado Fuenzalida and that reflect a legacy that inspires his family in the same way that Father Alberto Hurtado inspired him.

Contents

Biographical Introduction by John Gavin, S.J. PAGE 20

Editors' and Translators' Introduction PAGE 56

Glossary PAGE 60

Acknowledgements PAGE 62

PART ONE

1

Introduction. Individual and Social Morality PAGE 64

1. *Catholic Social Morality* PAGE 68

1.1. RIGHT OF THE MAGISTERIUM OF THE CHURCH IN THE SOCIAL FIELD PAGE 68

1.2. DIFFERENT FORMS OF ECCLESIASTICAL MAGISTERIUM PAGE 71

1.3. SECULAR SOURCES OF CATHOLIC SOCIAL MORALITY PAGE 72

2. *Historical Summary of the Development of Catholic Social Morality* PAGE 73

2.1. THE PATRISTIC AGE (FIRST TO NINTH CENTURIES) PAGE 73

2.2. THE MIDDLE AGES PAGE 75

2.3. THE MODERN ERA PAGE 77

2.4. FROM THE FRENCH REVOLUTION TO THE PRESENT PAGE 80

2.5. THE ACTION OF THE SOVEREIGN PONTIFFS PAGE 91

2.6. CATHOLIC EPISCOPAL ACTION PAGE 94

2

Social Life and Natural Societies PAGE 97

1. *Man's Tendency to Live in Society* PAGE 99

2. *Concept of Society* PAGE 100

3. *The Origin of Human Society* PAGE 101

4. *Social Groups that Form Human Society* PAGE 102

5. *Supernatural Society* PAGE 104

6. *Harmony of the Social Structure* PAGE 105

3

The Family: Mission and Constitution of the Family. The Education of Children *PAGE 107*

1. *The Mission of Family* PAGE 109
2. *The Constitution of the Family* PAGE 110
3. *The Rights of the Child* PAGE 113
4. *Who is Responsible for the Protection of the Rights of the Child* PAGE 114
   - 4.1. FAMILY AND EDUCATION PAGE 114
   - 4.2. THE CHURCH AND EDUCATION PAGE 115
   - 4.3. THE STATE AND EDUCATION PAGE 116
   - 4.4. THE CRAFTS PAGE 119
5. *The Patrimonial Rights of the Family* PAGE 119
   - 5.1. THE ECONOMIC PROBLEM PAGE 119
   - 5.2. THE FAMILY WAGE PAGE 120
   - 5.3. PENSIONS. SAVINGS. SOCIAL INSURANCE. DOMESTIC EDUCATION PAGE 121
   - 5.4. THE FAMILY DWELLING PAGE 123
   - 5.5. HOME OWNERSHIP PAGE 125
   - 5.6. THE TWO PILLARS OF HOME OWNERSHIP PAGE 128
   - 5.7. THE FEMINIST PROBLEM PAGE 128

4

Civil Society. The State *PAGE 137*

1. *Elements of the State* PAGE 139
2. *The Nature of the State* PAGE 139
3. *The State's Personality* PAGE 140
4. *Origin of the State* PAGE 141
5. *Authority in Society* PAGE 143
6. *Position with Respect to Established Power* PAGE 145
7. *Theories as to the Immediate Origin of Power in Society* PAGE 145
   - 7.1. THEORY OF HISTORICAL-LEGAL EVENTS PAGE 146
   - 7.2. THEORY OF THE SOCIAL PACT PAGE 146

8. *The Mission of Authority* PAGE 147

9. *Legislative, Executive and Judicial Powers* PAGE 151

9.1. PENALTIES. THE DEATH PENALTY PAGE 151

9.2. LEGISLATIVE POWER. THE FORCE OF THE LAW PAGE 152

9.3. THE OBLIGATION OF UNJUST LAWS PAGE 153

9.4. CRIMINAL LAWS PAGE 154

10. *State Intervention in Social Problems* PAGE 157

10.1. RIGHT OF THE STATE TO INTERVENE PAGE 157

10.2. THE FIELD OF STATE INTERVENTION PAGE 159

10.3. THE STATE AND WEAK AND INDIGENT PEOPLE PAGE 162

10.4. THE STATE AND PRIVATE PROPERTY PAGE 163

10.5. THE STATE AND COMMERCE PAGE 165

10.6. THE STATE AND SOCIAL EVILS PAGE 166

10.7. THE STATE: AN EXAMPLE OF PRUDENT AND SOBER ADMINISTRATION PAGE 166

10.8. THE DUTY TO RESPECT AND SUPPORT SPIRITUAL VALUES PAGE 167

10.9. FRUITS OF CATHOLIC DOCTRINE ON STATE INTERVENTION PAGE 167

11. *Civic Duties* PAGE 169

11.1. PATRIOTISM PAGE 169

11.2. PARTICIPATION IN PUBLIC LIFE PAGE 170

11.3. POLITICAL PARTIES PAGE 171

11.4. YOUNG PEOPLE AND POLITICS PAGE 175

11.5. TAXES. MILITARY SERVICE PAGE 176

11.6. CONSCIENTIOUS OBJECTION PAGE 177

11.7. THE RIGHT OF REBELLION PAGE 177

5

Social Classes PAGE 179

1. *Characteristics of Social Classes* PAGE 181

2. *The Harmony of Classes* PAGE 182

3. *Occupations* PAGE 184

6
International Society *PAGE 189*

1. *Existence of an International Society* PAGE 191
2. *Towards a Society of Nations* PAGE 192
3. *The Problem of War* PAGE 193
4. *To Live in Peace* PAGE 194

7
The Social Disorder. The Social Question *PAGE 197*

1. *Meaning of the Social Question* PAGE 199
2. *Is a Perfect Social Order Possible?* PAGE 199
3. *General Causes of the Social Question* PAGE 200
4. *Aspects of the Social Question* PAGE 202
5. *The Social Problem in Our Days* PAGE 203
   - 5.1. MILITARY CONFLICTS PAGE 203
   - 5.2. THE SPECTER OF ANOTHER WAR PAGE 204
   - 5.3. THE CLASS STRUGGLE PAGE 205
   - 5.4. UNEMPLOYMENT AND STRIKES PAGE 206
   - 5.5. DIFFICULTIES OF NATIONAL AND INTERNATIONAL TRADE PAGE 207
   - 5.6. INFLATION OF STATE BUDGETS PAGE 208
   - 5.7. DISORDER AND PARASITISM IN DISTRIBUTION PAGE 208
   - 5.8. FREQUENT DECREASE IN THE PURCHASING POWER OF SALARY PAGE 208
   - 5.9. INTERVENTION WITH SOCIAL SECURITY MEASURES PAGE 209
   - 5.10. RURAL EXODUS AND CITY HAZARDS PAGE 209
   - 5.11. UNJUST DISTRIBUTION OF WEALTH PAGE 210
   - 5.12. SOCIAL DISORIENTATION PAGE 214

8 System for Resolving the Social Question *PAGE 215*

1. *Liberalism* PAGE 217

1.1. ABSOLUTE LIBERALISM PAGE 217

1.2. MITIGATED LIBERALISM PAGE 219

1.3. THE TOLERANCE OF THE CHURCH PAGE 221

1.4. ECONOMIC LIBERALISM PAGE 223

1.5. ECONOMIC NEOLIBERALISM PAGE 224

1.6. CONCLUSIONS OF THE POPES AS TO ECONOMIC LIBERALISM PAGE 227

2. *Capitalism* PAGE 230

2.1. WHAT IS CAPITALISM? PAGE 230

2.2. A CAPITALIST CREATION: THE CORPORATION PAGE 231

2.3. CONCENTRATION OF POWER: FRUIT OF CAPITALISM PAGE 234

2.4. ASSESSMENT OF CAPITALISM PAGE 237

3. *Socialism* PAGE 239

3.1. DIVERSITY OF TRENDS PAGE 239

3.2. MAN, THE CENTER PAGE 240

3.3. THE PRIMACY OF SOCIETY OVER THE INDIVIDUAL PAGE 240

3.4. PRESENT DIRECTIONS OF SOCIALISM PAGE 243

3.5. THE CHURCH'S CONCLUSION AS TO SOCIALISM PAGE 244

4. *Marxism* PAGE 247

4.1. MARX'S SYSTEM PAGE 247

4.2. CONTEMPORARY MARXISM PAGE 254

4.3. CHURCH'S OPINION ON ATHEISTIC COMMUNISM PAGE 255

4.4. MAIN COUNTERPOSITIONS TO CATHOLICISM PAGE 257

4.5. ATTITUDE OF CATHOLICS VIS-A-VIS COMMUNISM PAGE 259

4.6. JUDGMENT OF THE FACTS PAGE 260

PART TWO

9 Foundations of Catholic Social Morality *PAGE 263*

1. *God* *PAGE 265*
2. *Man* *PAGE 267*
3. *Consequences of the Dignity of the Human Person* *PAGE 269*
   - 3.1. THE PRIMACY OF MAN OVER MATTER *PAGE 269*
   - 3.2. PROPERTY AT THE SERVICE OF MAN *PAGE 270*
   - 3.3. RESPECT FOR THE AUTONOMY OF THE HUMAN PERSON AND HIS ULTIMATE ORIENTATION *PAGE 271*
   - 3.4. THE SUBSTANTIAL EQUALITY OF HUMAN NATURE AND THE NECESSARY INEQUALITY OF CONDITIONS *PAGE 271*
   - 3.5. THE DUTY TO IMPROVE ONE'S CHARACTER *PAGE 271*
   - 3.6. PONTIFICAL TEACHING ON THE CONSEQUENCES OF THE DIGNITY OF THE HUMAN PERSON *PAGE 272*

10 Principles of Catholic Social Morality *PAGE 275*

1. *Justice* *PAGE 277*
   - 1.1. DIFFERENT KINDS OF JUSTICE *PAGE 278*
   - 1.2. GENERAL, LEGAL OR SOCIAL JUSTICE *PAGE 280*
2. *Charity* *PAGE 284*
3. *Equity* *PAGE 285*
4. *The Common Good* *PAGE 286*
   - 4.1. THE COMMON GOOD AND INDIVIDUAL GOOD *PAGE 287*

11

Work and Economic Life *PAGE 289*

1. *The Meaning of Work* PAGE 291
2. *The Mystique of Work* PAGE 292
3. *The Personal Obligation of Work* PAGE 293
4. *The State and Obligatory Labor* PAGE 294
5. *Working Regimes* PAGE 294
6. *The Employment Contract* PAGE 301
7. *Lease of Services or Partnership?* PAGE 302
8. *Projects to Reform the Company* PAGE 303
9. *The Amount of Wages* PAGE 304
   - 9.1. FIRST POINT TO CONSIDER RELATED TO WAGES: THE SUBSISTENCE OF THE WORKER AND HIS FAMILY PAGE 305
   - 9.2. SECOND POINT: THE SITUATION OF THE COMPANY PAGE 308
   - 9.3. THIRD POINT: THE COMMON GOOD AND ITS DEMANDS PAGE 308
   - 9.4. FOURTH POINT: CATEGORIES OF WORK PAGE 311
   - 9.5. FIFTH POINT: MARKET CONDITIONS PAGE 312

12

Rights and Duties of Workers *PAGE 313*

1. *Duties of the Laborer* PAGE 315
2. *Duties of Employers* PAGE 316
3. *Rights of Workers* PAGE 316
4. *Respect for the Dignity of Labor* PAGE 319
5. *The Work of Women* PAGE 320
6. *The Work of Minors* PAGE 321

13

The Organized Occupation. Trade Unionism. Corporatism *PAGE 323*

1. *What is a Union?* PAGE 325
2. *The Right to Organize* PAGE 327
3. *Unionism and Social Peace* PAGE 331
4. *Confessionality of Unions* PAGE 332
5. *History of the Trade Union Movement* PAGE 332
   - 5.1. THE FIRST ASSOCIATIONS PAGE 332
   - 5.2. MEDIEVAL GUILDS PAGE 333
   - 5.3. ABOLITION OF THE GUILDS PAGE 336
   - 5.4. TRADE UNIONISM IN THE MODERN ERA PAGE 337
6. *The Mission of Trade Unionism according to Various Social Schools* PAGE 338
   - 6.1. REVOLUTIONARY TRADE UNIONISM PAGE 338
   - 6.2. REFORMIST TRADE UNIONISM PAGE 344
   - 6.3 OPPORTUNISTIC TRADE UNIONISM PAGE 345
   - 6.4 REALISTIC TRADE UNIONISM PAGE 347
7. *The Great Principles of Realistic Trade Unionism* PAGE 348
   - 7.1. AT THE SERVICE OF MAN PAGE 348
   - 7.2. IN AN AUTHENTIC DEMOCRACY PAGE 349
   - 7.3. FAITHFUL TO JUSTICE PAGE 349
   - 7.4. THE TIRELESS DEFENSE OF VESTED RIGHTS PAGE 350
   - 7.5. TO ELIMINATE THE CAUSE OF THE CLASS STRUGGLE: NOT TO EXACERBATE THE SOCIAL EVIL PAGE 351
   - 7.6. TO ACHIEVE THE COMMON GOOD AND TO SEEK NATIONAL GREATNESS PAGE 354
8. *Relations of the Trade Union with other Societies* PAGE 355
   - 8.1. THE TRADE UNION AND THE STATE PAGE 355
   - 8.2. THE TRADE UNION AND POLITICS PAGE 356
   - 8.3. THE TRADE UNION AND RELIGION PAGE 357
9. *Three Basic Problems: Freedom to Create Various Trade Unions; Freedom of Unions to Federate; and Free Versus Compulsory Organization* PAGE 357
   - 9.1. TRADE UNION UNITY OR PLURALITY PAGE 358
   - 9.2. INTERNATIONAL NORMS ON FREE TRADE UNIONISM PAGE 360
   - 9.3. POSITION OF THE CHURCH TOWARDS TRADE UNION PLURALITY PAGE 364
   - 9.4. THE FREEDOM OF TRADE UNIONS TO FORM FEDERATIONS PAGE 366

9.5. FREE OR COMPULSORY ORGANIZATION *PAGE* 367

9.6. THE UNITY OF THE WORKING CLASS *PAGE* 367

10. *Trade Unions' Means of Action* *PAGE* 368

10.1. PEACEFUL MEANS *PAGE* 368

10.2. VIOLENT MEANS *PAGE* 371

10.3. IS THE STRIKE LEGITIMATE? *PAGE* 372

10.4. CONCILIATION AND ARBITRATION *PAGE* 375

11. *Corporative Association* *PAGE* 375

11.1. THE CORPORATIVE ASSOCIATION'S CHARACTERISTICS *PAGE* 376

11.2. MISSION OF THE CORPORATIVE ASSOCIATION *PAGE* 376

14

Private Property *PAGE* 379

1. *The Notion of Private Property* *PAGE* 381

2. *Various Forms of Property* *PAGE* 381

3. *Doctrines about Property* *PAGE* 383

4. *The Catholic Doctrine of Property* *PAGE* 384

4.1. THE FOUNDATIONS OF PROPERTY RIGHTS *PAGE* 384

4.2. THE DIVINE SANCTION *PAGE* 386

4.3. THE FUNCTIONS OF PRIVATE PROPERTY *PAGE* 386

4.4. CONCRETE WAYS OF REALIZING THE SOCIAL FUNCTION OF PROPERTY *PAGE* 388

5. *State Intervention in Private Property* *PAGE* 392

6. *Legal Titles and Property Acquisition* *PAGE* 399

6.1. OCCUPATION *PAGE* 399

6.2. WORK *PAGE* 399

6.3. PRESCRIPTION *PAGE* 400

6.4. INHERITANCE *PAGE* 400

6.5. CONTRACTS *PAGE* 401

7. *Contemporary Evolution of and Opinions about Forms of Property* *PAGE* 401

8. *General Conclusions* *PAGE* 404

15
Commercial Life PAGE 407

1. *Purchase and Sale* PAGE 409
2. *Just Price* PAGE 411
3. *Just Profit* PAGE 412
4. *Consequences of the Legality of «Individual Benefit» and Competition* PAGE 414
5. *Some Sales Procedures that are Used in Our Days* PAGE 416

16
Currency and Business PAGE 419

1. *Currency* PAGE 421
2. *Banking Morality* PAGE 422
3. *Some Aspects of Stock Market Morality* PAGE 425
4. *Gambling and Speculation* PAGE 427

17
Loans with Interest PAGE 429

1. *The Current Frequency of Loan* PAGE 431
2. *The Concept and the Use of Money in the Precapitalist Era* PAGE 431
3. *Lending at Interest in the Capitalist Era* PAGE 433
4. *Interest Rates* PAGE 435

18

Social Reform PAGE 437

1. *The Urgency of a Social Reform* PAGE 439
2. *Moral and Religious Reform* PAGE 439
   - 2.1. EVANGELICAL LIFE PAGE 441
   - 2.2. CHRISTIAN LOVE PAGE 442
   - 2.3. HUNGER AND THIRST FOR JUSTICE PAGE 444
   - 2.4. SOBRIETY OF LIFE PAGE 445
   - 2.5. SPIRIT OF POVERTY PAGE 445
   - 2.6. PRAYER AND PENANCE PAGE 447
   - 2.7. SOCIAL FORMATION PAGE 449
   - 2.8. SOCIAL ACTION PAGE 449
   - 2.9. ACTION OF THE PRIEST PAGE 450
   - 2.10. WORK OF CATHOLIC ACTION PAGE 455
3. *Economic and Social Action* PAGE 457
4. *Political Action* PAGE 458
5. *Joint Action by All Men of Good Will* PAGE 460

19

Supernatural Life PAGE 463

1. *The Church* PAGE 465
2. *The Communion of Saints* PAGE 466

Index PAGE 469

Biographical Introduction

John Gavin, s.j.[1]

A saint of our time, Alberto Hurtado balanced a rigorous political analysis with an intense spiritual life and personal dedication to the service of the poor. His thought emerged from the intellectual and political currents of his time, yet his writings foreshadow the papal and Society documents on social justice that form the basis of our ministries today.

1
A New Jesuit Saint

On October 23, 2005, I had the great privilege of being in Rome for the canonization of a Jesuit saint: Alberto Hurtado, S.J. Prior to the canonization, Hurtado was not much more than a name to me, a founder of institutions for the poor in Chile during the first half of the twentieth century. As the day approached for the canonization in St. Peter's Square, I read some brief biographies that recounted his sanctity, his tireless efforts for the poor, his inspiring preaching, and his promotion of the Church's social teachings. I found him to be an impressive figure and a fine example of our Jesuit charism.

Yet, it was the arrival of some Chilean guests in the community that truly piqued my interest. Among the pilgrims who came for the canonization, I met two Jesuits who had personally known Alberto Hurtado as a spiritual director. They spoke of a man burning with the love of Jesus, who inflamed others with the desire to transform the world for Christ. «He was a tough director!» said one of the guests. «But his first desire was always to lead us to do great things for Christ». The enthusiasm of those spiritual sons of St. Alberto would be confirmed by Pope Benedict XVI in his canonization homily.

> «You shall love the Lord your God with your whole heart… You shall love your neighbor as yourself» (Matt. 22: 37, 39). This was the program of life of St. Alberto Hurtado, who wished to identify himself with the Lord and to love the poor with this same love. The formation received in the Society of Jesus, strengthened by prayer and adoration of the Eucharist, allowed him to be won over by Christ, being a true contemplative in action. In love and in the total gift of self to God's will, he found strength for the apos-

1 From John Gavin, S.J., «*True Charity Begins where Justice Ends*», *The Life and Teachings of Saint Alberto Hurtado*, S.J., 43 STUDIES IN THE SPIRITUALITY OF JESUITS (2011). Reprinted with the author's permission.

tolate… In his priestly ministry he was distinguished for his simplicity and availability towards others, being a living image of the Teacher, «meek and humble of heart». In his last days, amid the strong pains caused by illness, he still had the strength to repeat: «I am content, Lord», thus expressing the joy with which he always lived.

Unfortunately this saint, revered in Chile for his works and teachings, remains a rather obscure figure in the English-speaking world. His writings, a rich mine of spiritual guidance and profound theological thinking, have remained untranslated, and his primary social apostolate, *El Hogar de Cristo*, though present in the U.S., has not achieved the fame it holds in Spanish-speaking nations.

My hope, in this brief essay, is to present the example and teachings of St. Alberto Hurtado as an inspiration for Jesuits reflecting upon the complex challenges that our mission for faith and justice poses to us today. The example manifested in Hurtado's life found its foundation in a supernatural outlook that can be summarized in three points: the link between the social apostolate and the deification of the human person in Christ; the social apostolate as a participation in the Mystical Body of Christ; and the essential relation between the virtues of justice and charity. I would like to begin, therefore, with the life of Alberto Hurtado as an illustration of these doctrines in action, followed by a closer examination and analysis of these foundational points. The turbulent world of St. Alberto —a period of history that included the Great Depression, the Second World War, and the constant threat of class conflicts and growing poverty— reflects many of the fears and horrors that Jesuits confront around the world today. This remarkable priest and religious, who strove to be «an image of the Teacher», has much to offer his brothers laboring in the contemporary fields for Christ.

2
The Man and His Works

2.1. THE YEARS OF PREPARATION

Luis Alberto Miguel Hurtado Cruchaga was born in Viña del Mar, Chile, on January 22, 1901. His father, Alberto Hurtado Larraín, a minor land owner, died when Alberto was only four years old, leaving the family in serious financial straits. His mother, Ana, moved the family to Santiago, where they depended upon various relatives for housing and support.

Though Hurtado's family had to suffer some early years of financial instability, as a child he enjoyed the love and support of family and community. He began studies in the Colegio San Ignacio in Santiago in 1909, where he came to know the Jesuits. During these years of study and work, he exhibited a strong desire for forming a Christian character and for knowing God's will for his life.

After graduating from San Ignacio, he studied law in the Catholic University and graduated in 1921, having written a thesis titled «The Regulation of Child Labor». One friend during this period described the remarkable character of young Hurtado.

> The virtues were flourishing and solidifying in him, shining forth. Above all, one could note his charity and his unquenchable zeal, which he had to moderate repeatedly in order not to arrive at the point of exaggeration. He could not see someone in pain without seeking a remedy, someone in need without seeking a solution[2].

During these university years he discerned his vocation, considering both marriage and religious life. In the end, however, the call to serve under the banner of Christ in the Society of Jesus would prove to be God's will. He delayed entry for two years, however, in order to settle the financial problems of his mother. At last, in 1923, he entered the novitiate in Chillán. In a letter composed during his second year of the novitiate to his friend Larraín Errázuriz, Hurtado expressed his joy in being a Jesuit at last.

> Finally I am a Jesuit, happier and more content than anyone could be on earth. I am overflowing with joy and I do not tire giving thanks to our Lord for having led me to this paradise, where one is able to dedicate his life to Him twenty-four hours a day, serving Him and loving Him at all hours. Here all action bears fruit through the act of obedience. You cannot understand the state of my soul during these days. I could tell you that I almost cried with joy. The life of a Jesuit novice is, speaking in a Christian manner, the most heavenly in this world[3].

2 A. Lavín, S.J., M. Holley, and M. Larraín, eds. *Biografía y testimonios del Padre Alberto Hurtado* (Santiago, Chile: Editorial Salesiana, 2005), 27.

3 Alberto Hurtado, *Cartas* (Santiago, Chile: Editorial Salesiana, 2003), 35.

The novitiate was followed by the juniorate in Córdoba, Argentina (1925-27) and further studies in the Colegio Maximo in Barcelona, Spain (1927-31). The declaration of the Second Spanish Republic in April 1931 and the subsequent anti-Catholic attacks in the country, forced his transfer to Louvain in order to complete his theology studies (1931-33). During these years of intensive study, Hurtado developed a reputation for his joyful character, his love of prayer and Eucharistic adoration, and his great devotion to Mary. In the words of one contemporary: «I met him again in Barcelona in 1931, and after a few hours of welcomed company, I was able to contemplate the transfiguration of Alberto Hurtado into a true saint, both as a religious and future priest»[4].

The years in Louvain also proved decisive in the formation of Hurtado for his future work as an educator and promoter of Catholic social justice. His rector, the future Superior General Jean Baptiste Janssens, S.J., told the zealous student, «You must take interest in the problems of the world in which you are going to work»[5]. The young Jesuit took these words to heart and made sure that his intellectual formation received in the walls of the theologate would feed his reflection upon the critical social issues of the day. He found particular inspiration for his growing desires in such papal encyclicals as *Divini illius magistri* (1929) and *Quadragesimo anno* (1931), as well as in the theology of the Mystical Body as developed in the work of Emile Mersch, S.J. Through prayer and labor he acquired a thirst to translate his faith into great deeds that would give witness to Christ and transform the world into the Teacher's image. In a letter on the Sacred Heart, composed during this period, Hurtado expressed this need to realize the power of Christian love and devotion through concrete acts of charity.

> I believe that we must live the devotion to the Sacred Heart on the basis of a charity without limits, of a charity refined from every angle. It must make our brothers feel good in the presence of brothers and must make others feel moved not by our words, but by our human-divine charity for and with them. For this charity must be human, if it wants to be divine. In this age of skepticism that now reigns, I do not believe that there is any other medium, humanly speaking, to preach Jesus Christ among those who do not believe other than that of the charity which is of Christ[6].

4 *Biografía y testimonios*, 37.
5 José María Guerrero, S.J., «El P. Alberto Hurtado: Un gigante de la justicia y la caridad», Folletos con Él 259 (Sept. 2005).
6 Hurtado, Cartas, 43.

In this brief reflection one sees already the distinct character of Hurtado's future work in the social apostolate: the desire to incarnate the love of Christ, to draw all into the life of the Mystical Body, to give life to the world through the pulse of the Sacred Heart. «For this charity must be human, if it wants to be divine». Or in the words of Ignatius, «Love ought to manifest itself more by deeds than by words»[7].

On August 24, 1933, Hurtado was ordained to the priesthood in Louvain. The joy of the new priest is palpable in a letter to a brother Jesuit, Sergio Salas.

> Now I am a priest of the Lord! You will well understand my immense happiness and with all sincerity I can tell you that I am *fully* happy. God has granted me a great grace since I have lived contentedly in all the houses through which I have passed and in all the companions that I have had. I consider this a grace. But now, in receiving priestly ordination *in aeternum*, my joy has arrived at its peak, or as we might say in philosophy, potency has arrived at act. Now I desire nothing more than to exercise my ministry with the greatest plenitude possible in the interior life and to have an exterior activity compatible with the former. The secret of this adaptation and of its success is devotion to the Sacred Heart of Jesus, that is, to the overflowing Love of Our Lord that Jesus, as God and man, holds for us and which shines forth in His entire life[8].

His ordination gave the final form to his unfolding vocation. From that point on, Alberto Hurtado desired that all his actions might flow from the grace of his priesthood. As a Jesuit he would imitate the self-emptying of Christ the priest through an outpouring of love incarnated in words and deeds.

Hurtado stayed on in Belgium for two more years in order to complete his doctorate in education at the University of Louvain, writing a thesis on the American pragmatist John Dewey (1935). While working on his dissertation, he received a commission from the Chilean government to study European educational institutions. This gave him the opportunity to visit —in addition to Belgium— Italy, France, Germany, and England. His observations made during this period, combined with his experience in Chile, would eventually lead him to advocate an educational reform, rooted in Christian principles, that promoted the formation of character in youth. Modern education, in his analysis, had

7 *Spiritual Exercises*, no. 230.
8 Hurtado, *Cartas*, 42.

adopted the reigning perception of man as a mere cog in a social machine, failing to form the person for the common good. The disorder and injustice found in so many nations emerged from the failure to educate *persons* for a higher end. «The cause of the actual crisis is neither economic nor political. It is above all *moral* and comes from a general lack of education. Wealth and pleasure govern a world of universal irresponsibility and ferocious individualism. It is time to form militias of upright persons, armed with solid principles and completely resolved to form men!»[9]

2.2. TEACHING AND CATHOLIC ACTION

He returned to Chile in 1935, after an eight-year absence. Now a priest and a fully formed Jesuit, he poured all of his reflection and training into confronting the spiritual and material malaise in his homeland. There was much to do. Though a stable constitution had been in place since 1925, the state was fractured between left-wing forces of Marxist inspiration, which had entered into the government in 1938, and a conservative party which considered itself the authentic voice of the Catholic Church and yet shunned the teachings found in the Church's social doctrines. The civil instability also divided Catholic voices in the public square, even leading to a division within the conservative party (the creation of the Falange Nacional)[10]. Finally, Chile faced enormous social problems, including acute poverty, moral laxity, worker exploitation, a rising number of abortions, and family break-down[11].

Though he would hold a variety of positions in his short life as an active Jesuit in Chile, one can perceive a common thread that would unite all of Hurtado's ministries: the desire for the salvation of souls and unity with the Incarnate Word, Jesus Christ. He believed that the struggle for a just social order, rooted in Christian principles, gave witness to this truth and, through the grace of Christ, invested the natural with the supernatural gift of charity. Thus Hurtado sought to incarnate the interior gifts that he received in his spiritual and sacramental life through service to the Church, while striving to lead others to

9 Alberto Hurtado, *Una verdadera educación* (Santiago, Chile: Editorial Salesiana, 2005), 76.

10 Jaime Castellón, S.J., *Padre Alberto Hurtado, S.J.: Su espiritualidad* (Santiago, Chile: Editorial Don Bosco, 1998), 35-36.

11 In writing on the issue of clandestine abortions, Hurtado spoke of the growing problem *worldwide*. «The number of declared abortions is alarming. This crime of homicide, as real as any other form of homicide, occurs hundreds of thousands of times a year» (Alberto Hurtado, *¿Es Chile un país Católico?* [Santiago, Chile: Editorial Splendor, 1941], 18).

the same outpouring of grace upon a creation yearning for union with God. He wrote concerning a «healthy Christian spirituality»:

> A healthy spirituality is one that consists not only in pious practices or in sentimentalisms, but in allowing oneself to be entirely taken up by Christ, who fills his life. It is a spirituality that nourishes itself in deep contemplation, in which one learns to know God and his brothers, the men of one's own time. It is a spirituality that will allow the apostolic victories that render the Church a leaven in the world[12].

Every apostolic endeavor undertaken by Hurtado would aim at «rendering the Church a leaven in world» and incarnating the truth of Christ.

Upon his return, Hurtado began teaching in the Catholic University and in the Pontifical Seminary in Santiago (1936-41). His teaching, combined with such other tasks as an examiner of postulants, province treasurer and consultor, and spiritual director to students, stretched him thin. Yet, he seemed to thrive on the intense activity, since at last he could let loose the energy that he had been storing through many years of prayer, study, and reflection. In his spiritual formation of students, he particularly tried to lead them to a fuller living of the Christian moral life through prayer and the virtues.

In 1941, however, he took on a new apostolate that would prove to be the ideal field for his talents and spiritual vigor—the Advisor to Youth in the Catholic Action (C.A.) movement. The Catholic Action movement had been promoted by Pope Pius XI in 1927 as «the participation and collaboration of the laity in the Apostolic hierarchy»[13], and Alberto gladly embraced the task of realizing this goal in Chile. He sought to invest the youth of Catholic Action with a solid spiritual and catechetical formation that would inspire them to transform the world

12 Alberto Hurtado, *La búsqueda de Dios* (Santiago, Chile: Editorial Salesiana, 2005), 34.

13 Pius XI, «*Discourse to Italian Catholic Young Women*», *L'Osservatore Romano* (March 27, 1927): 14. The Pope would repeat this definition in the encyclical *Non abbiamo bisogno* (June 29, 1931), 5, in which he took an anti-Fascist stance and addressed Mussolini's suppression of Catholic Action. «It has been for us an exquisite satisfaction to see the Catholic Action organizations of all countries, both near and far, united round the common Father, inspired by a single spirit of faith, of filial sorrow and of generous impulses, all expressing their astonishment and grief in seeing Catholic Action societies persecuted and assailed here, in the very centre of the Apostolic Hierarchy, where its "raison d'être" is strongest. Here in Italy, as in all parts of the world where Catholic Action exists, Catholic Action is true to its solemn and authentic definition. Obeying Our watchful and assiduous instructions (which you, Venerable Brethren, have so largely seconded), it does not wish to be nor can be anything other than "the participation and the collaboration of the laity with the Apostolic Hierarchy"».

for the Reign of God through direct engagement with societal structures[14]. In short, he desired that they be «contemplatives in action». In a circular letter from 1941, Hurtado outlined his program:

> We do not tire in inculcating in youth who generously interest themselves in the good of Chile, opportunely and inopportunely, this idea: that they will be able to do nothing great if first they do not transform themselves into integral Christians, into men who live fully for Christ and aspire to live life as Christ would live it if he were in their place... The great crisis of our nation is a crisis of moral values, in other words, a crisis of Christianity, and this cannot be solved except through men who maintain the integrity of moral values that express a faith fully known and lived in all circumstances and moments[15].

Hurtado worked to make Catholic Action a true spiritual movement that would take on the debilitating problems in Chilean society. He established C.A. groups throughout the country, gave retreats, and organized congresses. In 1943 he founded Servicio de Cristo Rey for those C.A. members «who aspire, with the grace of God, to live fully their faith and to accept all the sacrifices that the apostolate of Catholic Action requires for the extension of the Reign of God»[16]. Members agreed to attend daily Mass, to do a half hour of spiritual reading and meditation a day, to do a three-day retreat with the *Spiritual Exercises* each year, and to commit themselves to regular confession and spiritual direction. The Eucharist, however, always stood at the heart of their formation. «One who receives the Eucharist strips himself of his ego and comes to have no other life but Jesus, the divine life—and there is nothing greater than this»[17].

His work, however, displeased some, both in and out of the Society of Jesus. Many of his Jesuit brethren accused him of being too worldly in his methods and of acting as a «Lone Ranger» apart from any oversight by superiors[18]. Some

14 This approach reflects Hurtado's basic understanding of the realization of the Reign of God: «The Reign of God, which we are obliged to extend and preach in virtue of our faith and of the explicit commandments of Christ, presupposes two elements for its extension: the grace of the Lord, without which nothing can be done in the supernatural order, and free human cooperation» (Hurtado, *¿Es Chile un país Católico?* 48).

15 Id., *Cartas*, 91-92.

16 *Biografía y testimonios*, 61.

17 Hurtado, *Cartas*, 95.

18 On Hurtado's struggles with brother Jesuits, see M. Ortega, *El Padre Hurtado: Un maestro para nuestro tiempo* (Random House: Santiago, Chile, 2005), 98-99; 202-3.

members of the hierarchy also believed that Hurtado was mixing too much social activism and politics into C.A., especially in support of the recently founded conservative Falange party. He responded to some of these charges in a letter to Bishop Eduardo Larraín Cordovez in 1942.

> In returning to Santiago after a long trip for Catholic Action in the South of the country, I met with Fr. Morales Delpiano in the college of San Ignacio, who, I believe, fulfilled a debt of charity in informing me that some were accusing me of mixing in politics and favoring the *Falange*, and that these rumors had reached your ears… It is completely unfounded that I have engaged in political activities of any kind and that I have done anything to recommend or favor the *Falange*, or even to impede it. I strove to fulfill to the letter the norms of the National Episcopacy over the abstention of clerics from the struggles of party politics… The National Council, under my inspiration as advisor, has sent out a circular letter regarding Catholic Action and politics which offers a summary of the pontifical documents and those of the National Episcopacy on this point[19].

Though Hurtado certainly sought to avoid getting involved with party politics, he did note a tendency in himself toward overwork and excessive activism. His zeal to motivate youth to apply their Christian values to problems in society at times even led to a weakening of his spiritual life. Some years earlier, in 1936, after a retreat, he wrote:

> I'm swept away too much by action, and the result is that I don't pay attention to the interior life, the necessity of which I don't feel except in moments of great silence. I'm tempted to make a renewable vow each month to regulate my time in such a way that I may always do my prayer before the Mass and to say my breviary on my knees before the Blessed Sacrament[20].

To overcome this personal weakness, he developed a particularly rigid spiritual program for himself, rooted in the Eucharist and in prayer[21].

19 Hurtado, *Cartas*, 93.
20 Castellón, *Hurtado*, 60.
21 In a retreat meditation from 1941, Hurtado would write: «Jesus, after thirty years of prayer, goes into the desert and passes many nights in prayer while preparing for *the* day. Woe to the apostle who does not do the same. He will become a vender of human things and of personal passions, under the appearance of spiritual ministry» (Alberto Hurtado, *Un fuego que enciende otros fuegos:*

In the end, however, Hurtado renounced his leadership in Catholic Action in 1944, after losing the support of the General Advisor, Bishop A. Salinas. Salinas feared what he perceived to be a cult of personality surrounding the young Jesuit, as well as an «activist» turn in C.A. that could ultimately lead to factions within the movement. Though some members of the hierarchy sought to dissuade him from his resignation, Hurtado believed strongly that it was time to move on. He wrote to Bishop Salinas: «I came to realize quite some time ago that I cannot count on your confidence "from within", that is, a complete confidence, the only form hat one can accept between one friend and another, as you and I have been and as I desire to continue being». Yet, Hurtado had left his mark on the movement, as one contemporary collaborator in C.A. attested: «Father Hurtado was a man of unity. He formed our great internal communion. He united, in the essentials, thousands of young people who think in many different ways about contingent issues, always teaching them charity, comprehension, and joy»[22].

2.3. CARE OF THE HOMELESS

He would not remain inactive for long. On a rainy night in October 1944, he encountered a homeless man in the street, half frozen and ill. The chance meeting moved him to tears, because there was no Catholic home to which he could bring him. Some days later, on October 18, speaking at a women's retreat, Hurtado described the incident and spontaneously poured out his heart, giving form to what would become his greatest apostolic legacy.

> Christ wanders through our streets in the person of so many poor and ill, those deprived of even a wretched domicile. Christ is huddling underneath the bridges in the person of so many children who have no one to call father, who lack, for many years, the kiss of a mother upon the forehead... Christ has no home! *[¡Cristo no tiene hogar!]* Do we not wish to give Him ours, we who have the happiness of having a comfortable home, abundant food, means to educate and provide for our children?[23]

Páginas escogidas del Padre Alberto Hurtado [Santiago, Chile: Editorial Salesiana, 2005], 30-31). For more on Hurtado's spiritual struggle, see P. Cebollada and C. Coupeau, «La novedad de una tradición: Dos testimonios», *Manresa* 77 (October-November 2005): 387-89.

22 *Biografía y testimonios*, 71.

23 Guerrero, *Un gigante.*

After the service, the women insisted on giving him donations to help the poor in the streets. From that moment, he turned his attention more and more toward the problem of homelessness and poverty, planning a network of services —El Hogar de Cristo— that would not only provide temporary relief for the poor, but also would help bring about concrete solutions. During a six-month tour of the United States in 1945-46, Hurtado was in constant correspondence with collaborators back home regarding the development of El Hogar de Cristo, sharing his observations of programs in the U.S. and suggesting possibilities for Chile. From Washington, D.C., he would write: «When one sees this authentic democracy and thinks of how men, such as Lincoln and the current President of the republic [Truman] came from the lower class of the society, one is encouraged to hope that similar miracles might occur for our people, who have many superior aspects to this one, although in other ways less so»[24].

El Hogar de Cristo would eventually take on various kinds of social apostolates, though all aimed at alleviating poverty and providing the destitute with genuine independence and dignity within society. The genius of Hurtado manifested itself in the collaborative nature of the enterprise: people from all walks of life came to contribute to the efforts and the poor themselves often took on roles of responsibility within the organization. One of the earliest works, a shelter on Chorillos Street in Santiago, eventually grew to about eighty beds. Another dormitory on Tocornal Street provided a home for over a hundred women and children. These «shelters», at Hurtado's insistence, were always to be called «homes», places that would provide an authentic loving and nurturing atmosphere for those so used to rejection and derision. «And like the mustard seed in the Gospel parable, [El Hogar de Cristo] grew in order to give a roof, food, and, above all, love to so many who only had scorn for their milk, misfortune for their bread, and an orphanage for their only family»[25].

As an advisor and spiritual guide to those working for El Hogar de Cristo, Hurtado always taught the importance of combining a solid spiritual life with the apostolate. The spiritual contribution of collaborators shared equal importance with the physical works. In a letter to a sister who was lamenting her failure to give more time to the movement, he described the role of the Communion of the Saints, an essential part of his spirituality.

24 Hurtado, *Cartas*, 145.

25 From the funeral homily for Alberto Hurtado, given by Archbishop Manuel Larraín, in *Biografía y testimonios*, 173.

> Up until now you have helped the children with your work, your lessons, your affection; now you continue helping them with your affection, your patience, your prayer, your very sincere desire to continue doing them good. There is a truly consoling dogma, that of the Communion of Saints. It teaches us that there is not a single one of our actions that lacks a social value. Never do we merit solely for ourselves, since all our actions hold a deep social value. In doing good, in suffering with patience, in praying, we always profit for others, for the entire Church militant on earth, for those waiting in purgatory; we give joy to the just in heaven, and, in a special way, we help those who are most intimately tied to us. In this way you continue working for *Hogar* not only with affection, but also with the same, or even greater, efficacy than before[26].

The ministry to abandoned youth became one of the major contributions of El Hogar de Cristo. Hurtado would often work late into the night gathering children from the streets and bringing them back to one of the homes. Once there, the children would receive housing, food, clothing, and education for future work and independence. The attentiveness of Hurtado to their needs was demonstrated in his establishment of a «receiving house» for the youth. He had noticed that when new children arrived —hungry, dirty and confused— they would often be held in contempt by the older children who had already adapted to their new environment. The «receiving house» served as a transitional center for new members of the community, where they would be welcomed and prepared for full integration into a home[27].

As the network of homes and educational services of El Hogar de Cristo grew, Hurtado noted the hunger of some collaborators for a deeper spirituality and sense of incorporation. In 1950 he founded the Fraternidad del Hogar de Cristo, in which members could make private promises of poverty, chastity, and obedience. The members of the Fraternidad, dedicated to the work of El Hogar de Cristo, were not religious, and thus their promises did not have a juridical weight. Yet, the fraternity did reflect a genuine commitment to a simplicity of life, a faithfulness to the Church, and a desire to deepen one's spiritual life through prayer and acts of charity[28].

Another important initiative was the Acción Sindical Chilena (A.SI.CH.), an organization founded in 1947, with the permission of both Father General

26 Hurtado, *Cartas*, 157.
27 Castellón, *Hurtado*, 103.
28 Ibid. 108-14.

Janssens and of Pope Pius XII, to promote the right to organized labor in Chile. Hurtado attempted to mobilize leaders from among the workers, intellectuals, government representatives, and members of the hierarchy in order to address the abuse of laborers and the need for a more just economic order. Despite resistance from some corners, A.SI.CH. succeeded in bringing the much needed voice of the Church into the debate over the dignity of workers. In a letter to his vice-provincial in 1949, Hurtado described the objectives of A.SI.CH.

> [The objective of A.SI.CH.] is to awaken in Christian workers the awareness of organizing unions, and to gather the Christians who are already unionized in order that, with a full formation, they might struggle within the unions for the implementation of a Christian social order… A.SI.CH. is not a movement of Catholic Action, nor does it claim to be an apostolate for winning individuals for the Church. It is a movement of economic and social action that gathers Catholics, as well as those who desire to implement the social order that the encyclicals envision[29].

During these years of intense apostolic activity, Hurtado also became known as a writer and editor of some importance. Some of his works, such as *¿Es Chile un país Católico?* (1941), *Humanismo social* (1947), *Sindicalismo: historia, teoría, práctica* (1950) and *Moral social* (1952, published posthumously), inspired debate over the Church's role in the social apostolate and politics. Others, such as *La vida afectiva en la adolescencia* (1938) and *Puntos de educacíon* (1942), addressed issues regarding the formation of youth and the moral crisis in Chilean families. These books, along with numerous articles and talks, made him a significant figure both in and out of Catholic circles. In 1951 he also founded *Mensaje*, a «religious-social-philosophical» journal that is still in publication. In his inaugural editorial, Hurtado explained the mission of the new journal. «[The journal] has been baptized *Mensaje*, alluding to the message that the Son of God brought from heaven to earth, the resonances of which our journal desires to prolong and apply to our nation of Chile and to our turbulent times»[30].

In May of 1952 Hurtado's health began to deteriorate, and a visit to the clinic at the Catholic University confirmed the worst —he had pancreatic cancer. In late May and in July he suffered two heart attacks. On August 14, 1952, he wrote a

29 Hurtado, *Cartas*, 231-32.

30 *Biografía y testimonios*, 91. For more on the founding of *Mensaje*, see Hurtado, *Un fuego*, 23-24.

final letter to the community of El Hogar de Cristo from his hospital bed: «Finally, as I return to God my Father, I entrust to you one last desire: that you work to create a climate of true love and respect for the poor, because the poor man is Christ. "That which you do for the least, you do it for me"»[31]. Four days later Alberto Hurtado, at the age of fifty-one, died. During sixteen years of intense activity he had changed thousands of lives and had established a pastoral legacy that continues to serve the Church and the world today.

3
Three Essential Teachings

Alberto Hurtado, above all, taught by example. On the one hand, he diligently prepared himself for his future work through prayer and intense study of the Scriptures, the Tradition, Christian spirituality, and secular disciplines as well. He continued to nourish the fruit of these years of formation through a spiritual life rooted in the Eucharist and daily prayer. On the other hand, he read «the signs of the times» and applied his zeal for Christ to the concrete problems of his day. His interior formation incarnated itself in great deeds. «For this charity must be human, if it wants to be divine».

Three essential doctrines animated Alberto Hurtado's works and thought. These are teachings that made his approach to the social apostolate distinct from any secular struggle for justice and, in the end, made his contributions so significant and long lasting: the deification of the human person, the Mystical Body, and the relationship between justice and charity. These principles provide the spiritual and theological inspiration for Hurtado's remarkable apostolic success.

3.1. THE DEIFICATION OF THE HUMAN PERSON

The doctrine of deification (*theosis* in Greek, *deificatio* in Latin) states nothing less than that the human person has been created to participate in the divine life — the human person has been formed «to become divine». This teaching has received a great deal of attention in recent years in both scholarly works and books of popular spirituality. Long considered to be primarily an Eastern doc-

31 Hurtado, *Cartas*, 319.

trine, more recent scholarship has come to recognize its influence in the Western tradition as well[32].

In the tradition, the Church has come to define this doctrine in terms that avoid falling into the heresies of pantheism or the annihilation of human nature. In general, we can distinguish six points: (1) Deification is realized through the Incarnation of the divine Word. Jesus Christ, in the union of divine and human natures —«without confusion, without change, without division, without separation» (Chalcedon)— is the model and source of the deification of humanity, (2) the deified person does not become God by essence, but by participation or adoption, (3) in the union of deification, the integrity of the two natures, human and divine, remains intact, (4) in deification a genuine and authentic union occurs between God and the human person, (5) the human person cannot realize deification on his own, since it is beyond any natural power. The person requires the deifying power of grace for the elevation to divine union, and (6) God does not force this union upon the human person. Each person must freely cooperate with the action of grace through an abandonment in love to the absolute goodness of God and through growth in virtue. In the words of C. S. Lewis, for God «merely to override the human will ... would be for Him useless. He cannot ravish. He can only woo»[33].

Hurtado's works contain numerous references to this doctrine of the Church, making it an essential part of his apostolic vision. In fact, he regularly emphasized the centrality of deification for understanding the human person in reference to God and Society. He summarizes the teaching in his introduction to *Humanismo social.*

> Christianity, in its foundations, is the message of the deification of man, of his liberation from sin, of his return to grace of his reception of genuine divine sonship... We

32 One may consider the *Catechism of the Catholic Church*, which offers a catena of scriptural and patristic citations on deification: « "The Word became flesh to make us «partakers of the divine nature» (2 Pet. 1:4). "For this is why the Word became man, and the Son of God became the Son of man: so that man, by entering into communion with the Word and thus receiving divine sonship, might become a son of God' (St. Irenaeus). "For the Son of God became man so that we might become God' (St. Athanasius). "The only-begotten Son of God, wanting to make us sharers in his divinity, assumed our nature, so that he, made man, might make men gods' (St. Thomas Aquinas)», CCCG, 460. For two excellent recent introductions see N. Russell, *The Doctrine of Deification in the Greek Patristic Tradition* (Oxford: Oxford University Press, 2004); S. Finlan and V. Kharlamov, eds. *Theosis: Deification in Christian theology* (Eugene, Or.: James Clarke and Co., 2006).

33 C. S. Lewis, *The Screwtape Letters* (New York: Time Inc., 1961), 38.

obtain this noted favor of the elevation of man to the supernatural order because the Son of God, in uniting Himself to human nature, through it elevated all of humankind. Our race is united to the principle of divinity and we reach this through our union with God. Christ is the first born of a multitude of brothers whom God makes participants of his nature and with whom he shares his own divine life. Through grace men come to be what Jesus calls the new commandment. From the moment of the Incarnation and through the Incarnation all of us are united at the right hand of Christ and many have [already] reached there; only the condemned are excluded from this union[34].

Hurtado offers here a succinct statement of the classical doctrine of deification: the elevation of man to the divine, the adoption as sons and daughters of God, the participation in God's very nature, the centrality of the Incarnation, the free acceptance or rejection of the divine gift. What makes this summary so important, however, is its place in one of his most important books, *Humanismo social.* It comes right at the beginning of the work, in which Hurtado establishes the ground for all social morality. Thus «social humanism» demands the comprehension of the human person as a dynamic, free, rational being who is created for a supernatural end—a supernatural end manifested and realized in Jesus[35]. From this foundation, Hurtado draws three important conclusions that remain consistent throughout his works.

First, in responding to the social needs of the human person and in addressing the injustices of society, the Church must always remain conscious of the supernatural end of the human person. At first glance, such a teaching may seem counterproductive. If we focus too much on the «supernatural» end of man, shall we not simply overlook his essential, natural needs, clothing, for example, housing, food, and so forth? Yet, Hurtado insists on the importance of this Christian anthropological vision.

34 Alberto Hurtado, *Humanismo social* (Santiago, Chile: Editorial Salesiana, 2004), 23.

35 In part, Hurtado's understanding of deification emerges from his experience of the Spiritual Exercises. Through the Exercises one seeks to imitate Christ and to incarnate him in one's life, to become like the God-made-man. «Like Ignatius, [Hurtado] synthesized the call of his Lord, who invited him to follow Him in suffering and in glory, to continue His, work, to be always with Him and finally to be as He is» (F. Montes Matte, «Alberto Hurtado: Un modo moderno de vivir la espiritualidad Ignaciana», in *Alberto Hurtado: Memoria y actualidad,* edited by F. L. Fernández [Santiago, Chile: Universidad Alberto Hurtado, 2005], 404).

> The richness of our social doctrine resides entirely in the principle of the dignity of the human person in the natural order, and much more in his elevation to the supernatural order. If this doctrine is a dead letter, we shall have nothing to oppose the consistent teaching of Communism, which is firmly logical, while at the same time departing from an erroneous supposition[36].

A focus upon the supernatural end of man, according to Hurtado, affirms his personal dignity and the dignity of the entire natural order. This principle becomes the essential basis for discernment in the social apostolate.

With this teaching, Hurtado directly contrasts Christian social doctrine with Communism. While Communism envisions a materialist denouement in the classless society, Christianity understands the unfolding natural order within a more comprehensive divine calling. It should be stressed that he includes «the dignity of the human person in the natural order» within this dynamic elevation to the divine. This means that Christianity does not conceive of a clean break between the «natural» and the «supernatural» orders, even though, paradoxically, this divine elevation is a gift that exceeds any created nature. Christian social doctrine, therefore, cannot simply overlook man's natural needs in order to seek divine union, but must understand these needs as an integral part of this vocation. In short, while Communism shapes its ethic according to a truncated version of the human person and creation, Christianity seeks a social order according to a natural human dignity that fully unfolds only in an environment charged by grace.

Only Christianity does justice to the human vocation through its doctrine of deification. The human person has a greater calling than a mere temporal classless society: he is destined for divine union. Each and every human person is a potential «god».

> The plans of God are plans of sanctity, justice and love. To penetrate these plans is to enter not into one, but into the only plan that merits to be called real: into the great, eternal reality of being. In order to make him his son, God creates man; in order to divinize him by grace, in order to speak in him his Word; in order to unite him intimately to the divinity, so that the divine nature could be present in him, as the nature of the Father is in the Son[37].

36 Hurtado, *La búsqueda*, 157.
37 Ibid., 254.

Every person must therefore relate to his neighbor as another person sharing in a common vocation in God. One can never reduce the other to an object, to a service, or to a mere creature passing by. Furthermore, in seeking to form a common civil community, Christians must reflect the freedom and dignity that deification in Christ entails. «Whoever wants to persuade another of something must begin by persuading this "someone" that he is a sincere friend who desires his good. The journey to the head begins in the heart»[38]. A just social order that recognizes the supernatural end of man cannot emerge through totalitarian means or the brutal elimination of recalcitrant citizens, but through free cooperation of citizens aiming at the common good.

Second, the doctrine of deification inspires the Church to form a social order conducive to the personal spiritual growth of the human person. The sanctification of the world is the primary mission of the Church: the Church exists that all persons might be one in Christ[39]. This must always remain at the heart of the Church's identity in the world. Yet, again, this does not mean that the Church looks in on itself, since the human person grows in holiness *within* the world. «One is deceived if he pretends to be a Christian, and "regularly attends the temple", but never goes to the shelter to alleviate the misery of the poor… One is deceived if he regularly thinks of heaven, but forgets the miseries of the earth in which he lives»[40]. Human beings are not angels; they are body and spirit, and therefore live and grow within a community of persons. The Church, therefore, embraces the responsibility to form a just society that allows for dignity and freedom.

The social ills that the Church needs to address are many, and these ills obscure the authenticity and joy of the Christian message. Hurtado looked upon his own times with a critical eye, cataloging the wounds that only the Christian faith could cure.

38 Id., Humanismo social, 148.

39 «The reason for the existence of the Church is the sanctification of the world. It desires to extend itself in order to extend sanctity to persons. There is no other mission of the Church: its mission is not political domination, the construction of impressive buildings, the celebration of grand congresses. All the Church does is only for helping the sanctification of souls, which is the only proper end of the Church» (Hurtado, La búsqueda, 138).

40 Ibid, 130.

It is the misery of the world that gives it such anxiety. The insanity of men, their ignorance, their ambitions, their cowardice; the egoism of peoples, the egoism of classes; the stubbornness of the bourgeoisie who do not understand their moral mediocrity; the ardent and pure call of the masses; the narrow vision and, at times, hate of their bosses; the hatred of justice; the massive ranches and pig farms; the insufficient salaries used so poorly; alcoholism, tuberculosis, syphilis, promiscuity, unclean air; the banal spectacle, the carnal spectacle; so many bars, so many questionable cafes; such necessity to forget, such evasion; so many second jobs, such loss of the forms of life. There is as much mediocrity in the rich, as in the poor[41].

These ills that plague the social order, according to Hurtado, spew forth from the deep wound in the hearts of all men: the wound of sin. «Sin is ugliness: it destroys harmony. The work of God is beauty and harmony; sin is disharmony, a strident note»[42]. The Church brings the only hope for freedom from this horror and so she seeks to enter society in order to reveal the divine. «The Church is conscious of being the manifestation of the supernatural, the manifestation of the divine, the manifestation of sanctity. She is, under the appearance of passing things, the new reality brought to earth by Christ, the divinity that shows itself under a terrestrial cover»[43]. In seeking justice, in promoting the dignity of the human person, in addressing the crises of the times, the Church fulfills her mission of calling all persons to their true vocation: union with God. The transforming presence of the Church in the world adumbrates the wondrous transformation of the person in Christ.

Hurtado promoted a social order that reveals the goodness of God and encourages the free response to the divine invitation to man. It promotes growth in the virtues and the avoidance of vice. Thus excessive wealth and oppressive poverty encourage the vices of greed and pride in the rich, and envy and avarice in the poor. Squalor and overcrowded living conditions lead to sins of immodesty and impurity. Obscene luxury and comfort encourage sloth and spiritual mediocrity. While the social environment cannot be used as an excuse for personal sins, it certainly provides the circumstances for growth in virtue and vice. The doctrine of deification therefore demands that the Church seek to pro-

41 Ibid, 69.

42 Alberto Hurtado, *Un disparo a la eternidad: Retiros espirituales predicados por el Padre Alberto Hurtado* (Santiago, Chile: Editorial Salisiana, 2002), 50.

43 Id., *La búsqueda*, 135.

mote those conditions that best allow for the sanctification of persons: a society that promotes justice and the divinely endowed dignity of man[44].

Finally, the doctrine of deification requires that each person, in cooperation with grace, strive to acquire the «divine» characteristics manifested in the person of Jesus Christ, namely, the virtues expressed in God's love for humanity.[45] Mercy, purity of heart, chastity, and above all charity —all these virtues and more reflect God's image in the human person. Thus, while man depends entirely on grace for his union with God, he must cooperate with God's supernatural aid through the spiritual struggle to grow in virtue and overcome vice.

This *personal* struggle to manifest fully the divine likeness, however, has *social* obligations and consequences. While speaking at a university forum, Hurtado said: «It is essential that every student understand that his acts have repercussions on others in the infinite vibrations of joy or sadness. This fact renders even the smallest action important, right down to the humblest virtue, since it never ceases to have social repercussions»[46]. The failure to grow in holiness ripples out into society: a lack of personal chastity contributes to the exploitation of persons in prostitution and pornography; a personal refusal of mercy manifests itself in unjust structures; personal covetousness contributes to a culture bent on greed and conquest. Thus Hurtado stressed that deification, in its demand for personal cooperation with divine grace and growth in the likeness of Christ, must also be the essential basis for the social transformation of the world.

In conclusion, it should be noted that, regarding deification, Hurtado was no universalist. The doctrine of deification can lead some to the conclusion that, no matter what one does or does not do, he will ultimately be united with the divine. Hurtado did not fall into presumption by teaching that divine union was a *fait accompli* in Christ that now overrides the human freedom to accept or to reject God's invitation. Though he lived a life of hope in Jesus and possessed a truly joyous optimism, he stressed the need for personal conversion and an active faith.

44 On the effects of moral laxity upon the social order, see Hurtado, *Un fuego*, 30-31.

45 «This [imitation of Jesus] does not consist only in a historical "praxis",or in speculation, or in an ethic, or in apostolic activism. Christianity supposes all these dimensions, but surpasses them in a total identification with Christ» (P. Castellón Covarrubias, «La centralidad de Jesucristo», in *Hurtado: Memoria y actualidad*, 363.

46 Hurtado, *Humanismo social*, 171.

On the one hand, in all of his works, he focused upon the beauty of God's plan and the hope for the fullness of life through the transformation in Christ. He encouraged his hearers to dream of the happiness that can only be found in God.

> God, who is beautiful, more than the rising sun; tender, more than the love of a mother; caring, intimate, more than the highest peak of love; strong, robust, magnificent in his greatness. Holy, holy, holy, without stain. What can I dream of in my rapture that is more maddening? This will be the reality in all that possesses beauty, and much more... Understanding, tenderness, intimacy, companionship? ... Yes! I shall have it and without stain![47]

Yet, the human person could, through sin, refuse the gift of divine union. «To sin is to die to all that gives life value, and to die in the state of sin is to die forever! No more happiness, no more reconciliation! The Church has condemned the mitigationists. This game involves everything, forever. It's no joke! One who loses this match, loses everything. To be saved and to see God is to live»[48].

The shocking reminders of God's infinite beauty, love, and mercy, along with the horrifying consequences of freely refusing that love, give further impetus to living out actively one's faith. For one's own salvation and deification and for the salvation of others, one must translate the love of Christ into *deeds* that in turn transform society into a testimony to the wonders that await in divine union.

3.2. THE MYSTICAL BODY OF CHRIST

Hurtado's formative years in the Society witnessed a great flowering in the recovery of the doctrine of the Church as the Mystical Body of Christ. A teaching with Scriptural roots (for example, 1 Cor. 12: 12-15; Eph. 5:23; Col. 2:19), it provided a vision of the Church as a living unity in the person of Christ, a powerful image that responded to a world fragmented by a terrifying war and threatened by a growing technocracy. The Jesuit theologian Émile Mersch's major work, *The Whole Christ: The Historical Development of the Doctrine of the Mystical Body in Scripture and Tradition,* had a great influence on the young Hurtado[49].

47 Id., *Un disparo,* 58-59.

48 Ibid., 54-55.

49 Mersch highlighted the implications for the social apostolate in the doctrine of the Mystical Body. «The precepts of justice, of mutual love, and of sincerity, which enjoin us to treat others as we ourselves would like to be treated and to regard them as other selves, are precepts of union» (Émile Mersch, *The Whole Christ: The Historical Development of the Doctrine of the Mystical*

But it would be Pope Pius XII's encyclical *Mystici Corporis* (1943) that would fully open up the importance of this teaching to a world suffering the horrors of World War II. The Pope sought to correct two problems in contemporary ecclesiology: the tendency to limit the Church to a hierarchical institution and the newer tendency to view her as a mystical entity that required no visible structures. This meant addressing «the so-called *popular naturalism*, which sees and wills to see in the Church nothing but a juridical and social union» and the «false *mysticism* creeping in, which, in its attempt to eliminate the immovable frontier that separates creatures from their Creator, falsifies the Sacred Scriptures»[50].

In the encyclical, the Pope taught that the faithful in the Church are mystically united to Christ, the head, and so form one body in which the members participate in the graces flowing from Jesus. In turn, they also build one another up through the intimate union. In this Mystical Body of the faithful, there are not two Churches, hierarchical and lay, but all share in and contribute to the union formed in Christ.

> One must not think, however, that this ordered or «organic» structure of the body of the Church contains only hierarchical elements and with them is complete; or, as an opposite opinion holds, that it is composed only of those who enjoy charismatic gifts —though members gifted with miraculous powers will never be lacking in the Church. That those who exercise sacred power in this Body are its chief members must be maintained uncompromisingly. It is through them, by commission of the Divine Redeemer Himself, that Christ's apostolate as Teacher, King and Priest is to endure. At the same time, when the Fathers of the Church sing the praises of this Mystical Body of Christ, with its ministries, its variety of ranks, its officers, its conditions, its orders, its duties, they are thinking not only of those who have received Holy Orders, but of all those too, who, following the evangelical counsels, pass their lives either actively among men, or hidden in the silence of the cloister, or who aim at combining the active and contemplative life according to their Institute; as also of those who, though living in the world, consecrate themselves wholeheartedly to spiritual or corporal works of mercy, and of those in the state of holy matrimony[51].

Body in Scripture and Tradition, trans. John R. Kelley [Milwaukee: The Bruce Publishing Company, 1933], 122).

50 Pope Pius XII, *Mystici Corporis*, 9.

51 Ibid., 17.

Since Vatican II, this teaching seems commonplace. Yet, during a brutal period of world conflict, the Pope's words offered an ecclesiology that awakened a new sense of solidarity and active participation among the faithful. *All* the faithful share in the deifying union of the Body, *all* share in the mission of the Church to extend and manifest Christ in the world. «It is the will of Jesus Christ that the whole body of the Church, no less than the individual members, should resemble Him»[52].

Hurtado applied the doctrine of the Mystical Body to his own mission in the social apostolate, demonstrating how the Church's intimate union in Christ required an active participation in the transformation of the world. Above all, he stressed that the Church is a supernatural society, since she receives her life from the Incarnate Word and gives life to human beings for their union with God. The Church must always be understood with this sanctifying mission in mind: she is a society «penetrated and given life through the energies of Jesus»[53].

> In the supernatural order there exists another society, the Church... The highest end of all human life is to enter into possession of the supernatural end, that is, to possess God personally, to know him and to love him for eternity. Everything else is for man nothing but a means and holds a secondary importance before this end. *Seek first the reign of God and his justice, all the rest will be given to you in addition* (Matt. 6:33). The Church is the society instituted by Jesus Christ, the true Son of God, in order to help man to fulfill his mission[54].

52 Ibid., 47. The Pope goes on to note the sacramental and ministerial significance of this union in the Mystical Body. «And we see this realized when, following in the footsteps of her Founder, the Church teaches, governs, and offers the divine Sacrifice. When she embraces the evangelical counsels she reflects the Redeemer's poverty, obedience and virginal purity. Adorned with institutes of many different kinds as with so many precious jewels, she represents Christ deep in prayer on the mountain, or preaching to the people, or healing the sick and wounded and bringing sinners back to the path of virtue—in a word, doing good to all. What wonder then, if, while on this earth she, like Christ, suffers persecutions, insults and sorrows» (ibid., 47).

53 Hurtado, *La búsqueda*, 136.

54 Id., *Moral social*, 51. Here Hurtado anticipates the teaching of *Gaudium et spes*, 45: «While helping the world and receiving many benefits from it, the Church has a single intention: that God's kingdom may come, and that the salvation of the whole human race may come to pass. For every benefit which the People of God during its earthly pilgrimage can offer to the human family stems from the fact that the Church is "the universal sacrament of salvation", simultaneously manifesting and exercising the mystery of God's love».

According to Hurtado, the supernatural society of the Church, whose mission is to elevate creation to the divine, contributes to the reformation of the social fabric of humanity in three ways. First, the Church, as the Mystical Body of Christ, serves as a model for a truly just and moral society. She manifests the joyful and intimate communion that exists among all persons by their common life in Christ, which naturally leads to a new vision of the human community in the civil order. Just as in the Church the individual members seek to contribute to the common good and sanctity of one another, so too in the civil realm the citizens give of themselves for the common good of the society.

> Man enters civil society not immediately as an individual, but through the family of which he forms a part. And he forms part of the international society, through the nation. The comparison that St. Paul gives for the Church can be applied to natural societies as well: they form a great body, constituted by members. Each cell forms one great body, consisting of members. Each cell adheres to the body through the member of which he is a part[55].

The Church's society ideally should stand out as an example to the world. She exhibits a social consciousness, that is, the «spontaneous attitude to react fraternally before others, to place one in the point of view of the other as if it were one's own; to tolerate no abuse before the defenseless; to be indignant when justice is violated»[56]. The teaching role of the Church unfolds not only in her words, but also through her example as a just and sanctifying body in the heart of the world.

Second, the Church as the Mystical Body cannot remain turned in on herself, but must reach out through concrete deeds to the world. Though all are not members of the Church, all persons potentially may share in the saving grace that Christ offers through the Gospel. «The destiny of no man is foreign to a Catholic. The whole world is of interest to him, because the love of Christ is extended to every man: he gives his blood for each one, he desires to see each one of them incorporated into the Church»[57]. Every Catholic —religious, clergy, lay person— must remain conscious of his or her intimate link with every human being. Every action and every prayer may change the lives of many and

55 Hurtado, *Moral social*, 51.
56 Ibid, 205.
57 Id., *La búsqueda*, 137.

bring them to the love of Christ. «My action, my desires can have a divine significance, and change the face of the land... I can be so much if I am in Christ, if I cooperate with Christ»[58]. The building up of the body of Christ requires the cooperation of every member in the giving of him or herself to others.

> We are responsible for the Church as collaborators in the great building of the Body of the Lord, in the redemption and sanctification of humanity, that which gives full meaning to creation... The life in the Church, the unfolding of the faith, the explication of dogma, of its moral import, of its cult, of its right—all is in strict dependence on the personal faith and charity of the members of the Body of Christ[59].

Hurtado constantly reminded his listeners and readers that the fulfillment of the mandate to preach the Gospel and build up the Body required *deeds.* During the economic depression and the cataclysmic conflict of the war, the Church needed to shine as a light through her care of the sick, the poor, and the dying. She needed to immerse herself in the struggle of abused workers, in the pain of broken families, in the dirt and grime of the streets, since the harvest «only grows in the mud of the earth. For us, it is the earth of men where the redeeming plan continues and realizes itself»[60]. The «unfolding of faith, the explication of dogma, of its moral import» occurs through a radical imitation of Jesus in humble service to the least in every culture. «Whoever scorns the poor, scorns Christ... The world is tired of words: it wants deeds. It wants to see Christians fulfilling the dogmas it professes. May the number of those who do so grow day by day through a profound meditation on the social meaning of our faith!»[61]

Finally, the Church as the Body of Christ transforms society and culture through its sacramental life. One may think that the Church's celebration of the sacraments nourishes the faithful alone, with little effect upon those outside of the fold. Yet, the Church is truly a leaven in the world through her *supernatural* life, in particular through the Eucharist and confession. The sacraments form the Body of Christ and nourish the members with divine life, so that the members may in turn bring that life into the world. Thus the sacraments are an es-

58 Id., *Un disparo*, 137.
59 Id., *Humanismo social*, 162.
60 Id., *La búsqueda*, 143.
61 Id., *Humanismo social*, 65.

sential part of the social apostolate, since they «divinize» the members of the Christian society so that they may «go out to preach the good news» in word and deed.

This explains why Hurtado placed the celebration of the Eucharist at the center of any social apostolate, since it transforms those who share in the Communion and unites their individual sacrifices to the redeeming sacrifice of the Cross. «In the Eucharist this change takes place: man is transformed into God, he is assimilated by the divinity which possesses him»[62]. Every celebration of the Eucharist unites the members so intimately with the Head of the Body, that they too become «priests» and «victims» who lift up a fallen world.

> ...in participating personally in the state of the victim of Jesus Christ, we are transformed into the divine victim. As the bread truly transubstantiates into the Body of Christ, so the human priest (and thus, all the faithful, the entire Church) is morally transubstantiated into Jesus Christ, the only and eternal Priest, and so all of us faithful are transubstantiated spiritually into Jesus Christ the victim. Thus, our personal immolations are elevated to be Eucharistic immolations of Jesus Christ, who, as the head, assumes and makes the immolations of his members his own. A resentment, a suffering ... immolated and offered in the Mass, are converted into immolations of Jesus Christ[63].

This passage also demonstrates why, in his principal writings on the social apostolate, Hurtado always dedicated a portion to the need for priests[64]. In fact, in *Humanismo social* he highlights the lack of priests in Chile as one of the major contributors to societal decay. Without priests, the supernatural growth of the Body of Christ is stunted and the gifts that the Body offers to the world cannot flow forth.

> Without priests, there are no sacraments; without sacraments, there is no grace, no deification of man, no heaven. Thus it has been rightly said that nothing is more necessary than the Church and in the Church nothing is more necessary than priests... The Church needs workers in a sufficient number, as the teachings of the Popes have

62 Id., *La búsqueda*, 214.
63 Id., *Un disparo*, 295.
64 For the significance of the priesthood in Hurtado's own Jesuit vocation, see J. Ochagavía, S.J., «La "ignacianidad" del padre Alberto Hurtado», *Manresa* 64 (Oct.- Nov., 1992): 455-56.

> constantly reminded us, echoing the Teacher, who taught us that the Good Shepherd has to know his sheep by name, he has to call them by name, he has to carry them to good pastures and lead them to the sheepfold[65].

The elevated depiction of the priesthood cited above may seem like hyperbole to those of the post-Vatican II generation, perhaps even an affront to the laity and lay religious. Yet, in his zeal Hurtado did not mean to take away from the role of other vocations within the Body of Christ. Rather, he sought to demonstrate that priests make their essential contribution to the social apostolate through their celebration of the sacraments, as well as through their «sacred duty of giving witness to the Christian truth in the social terrain with no less courage than in any other terrain in which supernatural revelation is involved... To preach only resignation and charity before great human sufferings would be to cover over injustice»[66]. Hurtado stressed that the absence of priests causes great social harm through a lack of the sacraments and the disappearance of the—ideally!— courageous priestly witness in word and deed.

Hurtado's application of the doctrine of the Mystical Body of Christ to the social apostolate demands that Christians take the Incarnation seriously. «The Word became flesh, and dwelt among us». And so all Christians must give the Word flesh in their daily lives, in their cultures and in their public witness. «The one who accepts the Incarnation has to accept it with all its consequences and must extend its gift, not only to Jesus Christ, but also to His Mystical Body. To neglect the least of our brothers is to neglect Christ; to alleviate one of them is to alleviate Christ in person»[67].

3.3. THE RELATIONSHIP BETWEEN JUSTICE AND CHARITY

According to Hurtado «true charity begins where justice ends». One cannot fully realize the virtue of charity without striving for justice.

> There are many who are disposed to enact charity, but are not resigned to accomplish justice; they are disposed to give alms, but not willing to pay a just salary. Even if it seems strange, it is much easier to be charitable (obviously only in appearance) than just. Such apparent «charity» is not authentic, because the true charity begins where

65 Hurtado, *Humanismo social*, 66.
66 Id., *La búsqueda*, 105.
67 Id., *Moral social*, 204.

justice ends. Charity without justice will not save us from social ills, but only creates a profound resentment. Injustice causes much greater evils than charity can repair[68].

At first glance this statement may seem problematic. Is not charity, a theological virtue, a «higher» virtue than justice?

While Hurtado certainly did not deny the superiority of charity as a supernatural gift, he did emphasize that charity separated from justice was not authentic charity. According to Hurtado, too many Christians content themselves with giving from their excess, while ignoring gross injustices in their midst. To follow Jesus, however, means to crush one's ego, to put on Christ, and to live in solidarity with those in need. It means to do as he did in «healing the sick, multiplying the bread, offering to relieve a burden and giving peace to spirits», since Jesus «showed himself to be the Son of Man before allowing himself to be known as the Son of God»[69]. Thus justice and charity are complements, the essential virtues of Christian perfection and witness.

> Justice and charity complement one another. A charity which does not have the strength to move us to give to our brothers that which we owe them is not true charity. And a justice that is not animated by charity is, in practice, an empty word. How can we hope that fallen man will come out of himself and give to his brother that which he owes if he is not animated by the fire of charity and the power of grace? In order to fully realize justice toward others, one must put himself in their place, to understand their reasons and needs. This is to understand the Gospel maxim: «Do not do to others what you do not want them to do to you; do to others that which you want them to do to you» (Tob. 4:15; Luke 6:31)[70].

The link between the two virtues manifests itself in Hurtado's own life. Hurtado, in his own apostolic works, was never content to provide a temporary solution to grave social injustices. In his writings he taught that, on the one hand, one must respond immediately with the available resources in order to help alleviate the suffering of the poor and destitute. «A year of silence can seem very brief while one lives in an abundance that meets his needs, but it can seem very long for a class which is suffering. The demon of novelty or haste is very danger-

68 Ibid., 214.
69 Id., *Humanismo social*, 83.
70 Id., *La búsqueda*, 221.

ous, but no less dangerous are the demons of omission, of procrastination, and of waiting indefinitely»[71]. On the other hand, he believed that a series of short-term solutions only allows the misery to continue and hardly constitutes a sufficient Christian witness. Christians must work to change hearts and minds, while also leading society to a more just way of life. They must become leaders in reshaping their cultures and ways of being.

> The misery of the people is of body and soul at the same time. To provide for the immediate essentials is necessary, but it hardly changes the situation if minds are not opened; if wills are not rectified and affirmed; if oppression and injustices are not suppressed, or at least attenuated; if one is not associated with the humble in the progressive acquisition of their happiness[72].

In short, «It is not enough to attack the effects, as to attack the causes. What do we gain by moaning and complaining? One must go head to head with evil!»[73]. The struggle for justice therefore demands a complete gift of self —both immediate and durative— in the name of Jesus. This self-emptying is the true actualization of charity[74].

Regarding economic justice, how did Hurtardo perceive the reigning capitalist system of his time, which was locked in a struggle with competing Socialist and Marxist visions? On the one hand, he criticized severely the Socialist and Marxist systems that tended toward a statism that «took economic activity from the hands of the family, businesses, and professions in order to entrust it directly to State»[75]. In fact, the mission of the state is «to protect private property from every unjust violation»[76]. Citizens have the right to pursue just economic enterprises and to benefit from their earnings.

71 Id., *Humanismo social*, 81.

72 Id., *Moral social*, 61.

73 Ibid., 60.

74 Hurtado always called for an imitation of Jesus' *kenosis* within the social apostolate:

> «To give oneself is to fulfill justice.
> To give oneself is to offer oneself and all that one has.
> To give oneself is to orient all one's capacity for action toward the Lord.
> To give oneself is to widen the heart and to direct firmly one's will toward that One who awaits them.
> To give oneself is to love always and as completely as possible» (Hurtado, *La búsqueda*, 27).

75 Id., *Moral social*, 103.

76 Ibid., 109.

On the other hand, capitalism in itself hardly constituted the basis of a just society. Unregulated capitalism leads to the exploitation of the people, and the accumulation of wealth and power among a small elite.

> The capitalist regime, as it has been lived up to this time, cannot be an admissible solution for the Catholic. The judgments of Popes and prelates establish a clear plebiscite that condemns it. Furthermore, Catholics must seek another system that avoids these errors, or they must purify the capitalist regime of its vices. If capitalism wants to survive, it must avoid the concentration of power with its consequent dehumanization. It must cease from its dominance over work, which is immeasurably more noble: work is something human and divine, despite its humble appearances[77].

This means that a form of limited state intervention is permissible. While Hurtado condemned collectivism and statism, he believed that some state regulation was necessary for a just economy.

> Is a direct and positive intervention of the state in economic life permissible? Is a «directed economy» recommended? If we understand by «directed economy» a detailed organization of the economic activities in every particular, enclosing them in every way within the purview of the government, then this is statism with all its dangers. If we mean that the state, in agreement with professional organizations, directs the general economy of a country, as well as the movement of national and international exchange, and stimulates deficient production, such a system exists within just limits, and, rather than «directed economy», it should be called «an organized economy»[78].

Hurtado's critique and correction of contemporary capitalist societies emerged directly from his reflection upon papal writings such as *Rerum novarum*, as well as a burgeoning dialogue taking place within the Society of Jesus[79]. Ac-

77 Ibid., 173.
78 Ibid., 106.
79 On the Society's growing awareness of the social apostolate, see Jean Baptiste Janssens, «De ministeriis nostris» (1947), *Promotio Iustitiæ*, 73 (May 2000): 7. Hurtado's views would find later vindication in the writings of John Paul II: «… it is right to speak of a struggle against an economic system, if the latter is understood as a method of upholding the absolute predominance of capital, the possession of the means of production and of the land, in contrast to the free and personal nature of human work. In the struggle against such a system, what is being proposed as an alternative is not the socialist system, which in fact turns out to be State capitalism, but rather a society of free work of enterprise and of participation. Such a society is not di-

cording to Hurtado, while the socialist solution leads to state repression, unbridled capitalism results in worker exploitation and class oppression. Yet «an organized economy», directed toward the common good, may produce a just order for the good of the human person.

Yet, Hurtado did not labor under any illusions regarding the establishment of the just society on earth: fallen man is incapable of realizing the perfect society in this age. In fact, the hubris of trying to realize the Kingdom on earth can only result in an even greater oppression. While Christianity does indeed mandate the struggle for justice in this life, it does not see justice as the goal of its earthly pilgrimage. The Church exists to lead men to holiness and divine unity, and the fight for a just society represents a form of concrete witness in the journey to the higher end. Hurtado always sought to ground his vision of justice in the higher end of the human person.

> Is a perfect social order possible?
> The individualists and the collectivists say, «Yes». The former say that the [just] social order will be obtained through the liberty of social factors; the latter believe that social harmony will be the fruit of the general planning with the help of science and technology. The Christian, as a realist, and recognizing the true nature of man, asserts that the [just] social order will always only be approximate... The consequent weaknesses of original sin affect the mind, so that it is not capable of full luminosity, as well as the will, which is weak in its tendency toward the good and in its knowledge and application of the adequate means for perfect social cooperation. Since the first rupture from the state of grace in which God created our parents, the earth has conceded its fruits only through labor, and will produce thorns and burs[80].

In the end, social reform must be the fruit of prayer, inspired by the desire to unite oneself with Christ and lead others to the joy of that unity. «The social action of prayer is the greatest of all, because, as St. Ignatius said, the one who prays works with God, the first cause and universal mover. But, in order that it may be called social, it must be done in a social spirit, thinking not only of one-

rected against the market, but demands that the market be appropriately controlled by the forces of society and by the State, so as to guarantee that the basic needs of the whole of society are satisfied» (John Paul II, *Centesimus annus* [1991], 35).

80 Hurtado, *Moral social*, 133-34.

self, but also of others, desiring for them the bounty of goods that one desires for oneself»[81].

Hurtado's position regarding this relationship between justice and charity has found subsequent support in the Second Vatican Council, the general congregations of the Society of Jesus, and recent papal teaching. A few examples demonstrate how Hurtado anticipated a fundamental principle in contemporary thinking on social justice.

In the Second Vatican Council, the pastoral constitution *Lumen gentium*, in particular, reiterated this teaching regarding the charity that inspires justice. The council fathers directed the Church toward a more active engagement with the world, emphasizing that the faith «needs to prove its fruitfulness by penetrating the believer's entire life, including its worldly dimensions, and by activating him toward justice and love, especially regarding the needy»[82]. The social order must be «founded on truth, built on justice and animated by love»[83]. The Christian seeking the Kingdom of God requires «a stronger and purer love for helping all his brethren and for perfecting the work of justice under the inspiration of charity»[84]. *Lumen gentium* clearly linked justice with charity, with justice as the essential virtue for the structuring of the social order and charity as the theological virtue that animates society.

The Society of Jesus would also develop its own social teachings through an emphasis upon the relationship between justice and charity.

Hurtado's former rector from Louvain, Superior General Jean Baptiste Janssens, decried the indifference that many Jesuits were displaying toward the blatant injustices found among the working poor of the time. «Not a few of Ours, especially among the young, are extremely disturbed when they see that, held back by so many easier and less necessary ministries, we show little concern for those masses for whom hardly anyone cares»[85]. General Congregation 31 (1974-75) responded to these concerns and highlighted the union of justice and charity that would direct the Society's response to the needs of the times: «But the social apostolate strives directly by every endeavor to build a fuller ex-

81 Id., *Humanismo social*, 168. Also see id., *Fuego*, 108: «Prayer, which at times seems useless—how great it becomes when one realizes that it means speaking with and being heard by the creator of all things!»

82 *Gaudium et spes*, 21.

83 Ibid., 26.

84 Ibid., 72.

85 Janssens, *De ministeriis nostris*, 7.

pression of justice and charity into the structures of human life in common. Its goal in this is that every man may be able to exercise a personal sense of participation, skill, and responsibility in all areas of community life»[86]. The more recent *Complementary Norms* also stress the link between social justice and social charity: «Moreover, all should understand that they can and ought to exercise the social apostolate in their spiritual ministries by explaining the social teaching of the Church, by stimulating and directing the souls of the faithful toward social justice and social charity, and, finally, by establishing social projects by means of the members of our organizations»[87].

More recently Pope Benedict XVI formulated this truth in his encyclical *Caritas in veritate* (2009). The Holy Father teaches that «justice is inseparable from charity».

> *Charity goes beyond justice*, because to love is to give, to offer what is «mine» to the other; but it never lacks justice, which prompts us to give the other what is «his», what is due to him by reason of his being or his acting. I cannot «give» what is mine to the other, without first giving him what pertains to him in justice. If we love others with charity, then first of all we are just towards them. Not only is justice not extraneous to charity, not only is it not an alternative or parallel path to charity: justice is inseparable from charity, and intrinsic to it. Justice is the primary way of charity or, in Paul VI's words, «the minimum measure» of it, an integral part of the love «in deed and in truth» (1 John 3:18), to which Saint John exhorts us. On the one hand, charity demands justice: recognition and respect for the legitimate rights of individuals and peoples. It strives to build the *earthly city* according to law and justice. On the other hand, charity transcends justice and completes it in the logic of giving and forgiving. The *earthly city* is promoted not merely by relationships of rights and duties, but to an even greater and more fundamental extent by relationships of gratuitousness, mercy and communion. Charity always manifests God's love in human relationships as well, it gives theological and salvific value to all commitment for justice in the world[88].

86 GC 31, 569.

87 The *Constitutions of the Society of Jesus and Their Complementary Norms* (St. Louis: The Instituite of Jesuit Sources, 1996), 299.

88 Pope Benedict XVI, *Caritas in veritate* (2009), 6.

According to Pope Benedict, one cannot transgress the norms of justice «as the recognition and respect of the rights of individuals and peoples» without undermining the authentic charity that «completes the logic of giving and forgiving».

4
A Life of Generosity

What, in the end, was the inspiration for Alberto Hurtado's remarkable synthesis of the spiritual life and apostolic vigor? Certainly his love for Jesus, his zeal for the salvation of souls, and his desire to give witness to the Gospel drove him to empty himself in the struggle for faith and justice. Yet his Jesuit formation and the influence of St. Ignatius must also be recognized as the major framework for his vision and manner of discernment. He was a true contemplative in action, dedicated to concretizing the Gospel message in word and deed.

Perhaps the characteristic that stands out most of all in his apostolic endeavors is his generosity, the total gift of self in Christ's name. In Hurtado's own words, this generosity was formed through the experience of the Spiritual Exercises.

> Generosity is the great instrument for accepting the Law and going beyond it in the service of God. The *Exercises* were made for generous souls, who have much zeal, who hunger to dedicate themselves in complete service to the Lord… The *Exercises* were not made to create generosity, but to develop it in those who possess it. For this reason St. Ignatius always places the election in our hands and the key meditations always end with three possibilities: the «common» person, the good, and the distinguished (for example, the Meditation on the Kingdom, the Classes of Men, the Three Kinds of Humility)…
>
> Therefore, through the *Exercises*, in our works of education and in spiritual direction, we take advantage of this glorious law of our nature in order to push souls to fly ever higher. We don't multiply the commands, but manifest the ideals that are more valuable in life. Our own age does not lack generous people; rather it lacks internal knowledge of the cause for which it is worth sacrificing one's life[89].

89 Hurtado, *Un Disparo*, 152.

As a Jesuit, Hurtado cultivated and manifested the generosity of his soul in order to become a fruitful witness to the love of Jesus and, in turn, he inspired the generosity of numerous souls even after his death. In his life and works we find the inspiration of a saint, a fiery generosity that should ignite our own souls with apostolic fervor. There is only one cause worth dying for: the love for Jesus Christ in mission. «The Good News, the Gospel, which Christ brought to the world, is the reconciliation of souls to the Father. This Good News, preached and applied, is the apostolate»[90]. This great saint of the Society of Jesus will continue to inspire apostolic zeal for Jesus in the sons of Ignatius and in generous souls of every generation.

90 Ibid., 103.

Editors' and Translators' Introduction

This volume is an annotated translation of St. Alberto Hurtado Cruchaga's work, *Moral Social*[1]. Working late at night during the last years of his life, Hurtado produced the rough typescript of this book, in which condition it remained after his death in 1952 until the Pontificia Universidad Católica de Chile published the first Spanish edition in 2004 and a second edition in 2006[2]. This is the first English translation.

The book is of interest because it is the work of a man who loved the Church, honored and studied her teachings, and suffered with and for the poor, whose pain he observed at first hand and keenly felt. On many pages, the book reports and endorses the disquiet, and even the anger, with which Rome greeted the rise of the large business enterprise and the condition of those who labor in it. Precepts and policies based on traditional Catholic morality are developed and deployed throughout the last portions of the book as at least partial remedies for these ills. Hurtado proposes the promotion of social and economic rights, such as the right to housing, to a family wage, to work and to unionize. His fundamental insight into social justice was simple but profound: true charity only begins where justice ends.

We, the editors and translators, have tried to be as faithful as possible to Hurtado's manuscript, but the task was not easy: Hurtado used a typewriter, pasted many pieces of paper containing portions of his other books and Church documents into it, and also added multiple handwritten comments, some of them directing the copying of passages from the works of other authors or the addition of further information. These handwritten instructions were often confusingly phrased and partially illegible.

Regarding the organization of the book, Hurtado did not clearly identify the numbers of chapters and headings. We have followed his approach as best we could.

Hurtado referred to an immense number of authors, institutions, works, and theories —many of them related to Catholic social thought— especially in the first several pages of the manuscript. The editors have added more than 670 footnotes explaining these references, and in many cases identifying their im-

1 On the title page of the manuscript appear the words «MORAL SOCIAL. *Acción Social*». However, in several letters in which Hurtado referred to this book while he was writing it, he identified it only as «Moral Social».

2 *Moral Social: Obra Póstuma de Alberto Hurtado, S.J., Segunda edición.*

portance and context. Materials (including materials in footnotes) within brackets are written by us; everything not in brackets is by Hurtado.

Hurtado often quoted his book *Order Social Cristiano* (*Social Christian Order*), which contains numerous passages from various encyclicals, letters, speeches and other Church documents. To facilitate smoother reading, we have omitted his references to this book in many cases, setting forth only the passages to which he referred.

In translating, our philosophy has been one of near-literalism, in the belief that Hurtado's voice, his implications, and his cast of mind should be reflected as closely as reasonably possible in the English version. Sometimes —for example when Hurtado's Spanish was awkward or unusual or where no smooth and idiomatic English phrase would be faithful to his words— we have accepted the necessity for some awkwardness in the English as well.

Spanish philosophical vocabulary has remained close to its roots in Scholastic thought. In this it differs from English, with the result that Spanish words often mean something different from English words which look similar. «*Realización*», for example, cannot usually be translated «realization». Spanish abstract terms cannot readily be rendered by English terms which carry largely empirical, concrete meanings. «*Encuadrar*», for example, which roughly means «to put inside a quadrant», cannot be translated «to frame» when «*encuadrar*» refers, as it often does, not to constructing a physical frame around something but to locating it conceptually. We have tried to reflect these linguistic differences in our translation.

Spanish words which refer to business entities and the like, and to the people who own, control, manage or work for them, do not map neatly in most instances onto English vocabulary. Set forth below is a Glossary.

Materials quoted by Hurtado are translated into English by us; sometimes as we did this we consulted the quoted originals. There are three categories of exception, where we have not done our own translation but instead used English translations published by others:

- Passages from Scripture (except as stated just below) are from the The Catholic Study Bible (third edition, Oxford University Press, 2016), which in turn relies on the New American Bible (rev. ed., 2010).

- Passages from encyclicals and other Church documents which are available in English on the Vatican website are taken from that source unless otherwise indicated. Where such passages contain quotations from Scripture, we use the Vatican website translation for those as well.

- Passages from the *Código Social de Malinas* (*Social Code of Malines* or Mechlin) are from the English version: *A Code of Social Principles*, published in 1937 by the International Union of Social Studies.

Glossary

Here is a list of some of the Spanish words relating to business entities and the like and to those who own, manage or work for them. In each instances the Spanish word is followed by one or more of the terms which we have often used to render it in English (Sometimes context required variation).

Asalariado	wage earner; worker; employee
Corporación	corporative association
Directores	directors
Empleado	employee
Empleador/Patrón	employer
Empresas	enterprise; corporation
Gremio	guild; corporative association
Obrero	laborer
Profesiones	occupations
Sindicatos	trade unions
Sociedad anónima	corporation
Trabajador	worker; employee

Acknowledgements

The editors and translators are highly grateful to those individuals and institutions that supported this publication and the 2018 conference on Saint Alberto Hurtado at Boston College: nothing would have been possible without their support.

First, we want to give thanks to Mr. Andrónico Luksic, a Chilean businessman and the Chairman of Quiñenco, a holding of the Luksic group; his donation to Boston College allowed us to work on this project for more than one year. Second, we want to express our gratitude to the family of Mr. Alberto Hurtado Fuenzalida, chemical engineer and entrepreneur, whose donation allowed us to defray some of the major expenses of publication. Third, we are very grateful to Mr. Mario Valdivia, a Chilean businessman and philanthropist who donated money for expenses related to the conference. Finally, we want to thank the Institute for the Liberal Arts of Boston College, which supported our project with its major grant for the 2017-18 academic year.

We also want to acknowledge the support and advice given by the Dean of Boston College School of Theology and Ministry, Fr. Thomas Stegman, S.J., and by the Dean of Boston College Law School, Vincent Rougeau. Our special thanks to professors Hosffman Ospino and Rafael Luciani of the Boston College School of Theology and Ministry, for their constant help and encouragement during times in which the project seemed difficult. Our special recognition to Fr. Samuel Fernandez, Chilean priest and professor at the School of Theology of Universidad Católica, who furnished us with the works of Alberto Hurtado and inspired us to initiate this project, and to Patricio Miranda, the editor of the Spanish edition published by the same university; through him we first developed our acquaintance with the book *Social Morality.* We also express our gratitude to the Padre Hurtado Foundation, which allowed us to access a copy of the original manuscript and other materials related to the saint.

Further thanks are extended to Susan Simone Kang, Director of Graduate Legal Education and International Programs of Boston College Law School, for her energetic and wise counsel and advice, and to Karen Breda, Legal Information Librarian and Lecturer in Law at Boston College Law School, whose diligent and efficient support greatly assisted our work.

I

Chapter 1

Introduction. Individual and Social Morality

The activity of man has two aspects: the individual and the social, depending on whether he looks upon himself or others independently of any social organization or as part of the multiple societies to which man belongs: family, nation, union association, etc.

It is often said that morality has been exclusively individual, and that it has neglected social aspects.

It is true that the individual aspect of morality has long been given preference, and this has been the case for two reasons. First, because morality always refers to the person taken in particular: it is the man, individually considered, who does good or evil; he is the one who has received the lights of reason and revelation; he is the one who has a personal destiny to fulfill. Accordingly, all morality is individual, even in its social applications.

There is a second reason why social morality has taken a long time to emerge as an organized corpus. Morality is eminently concrete: from its general and eternal principles it draws conclusions for the problems that are posed for man at a given time. Currently, morality's social approach is newly developed: it can be said that it coincides with the revolutionary discovery of modern machinery, with the formation of big urban centers and large industries, and with the development of workers' and employers' associations. There has never been a time in which morality has lacked social teachings, but social morality as an independent branch of study is something recent, for the reasons already indicated.

Individual morality studies human acts considering the person individually. Social morality deals with human acts considering man as part of a social organization. The fact that a person is incorporated into social groups forces him to work for the common good of each of the communities he is part of, and to seek to establish stable structures that best achieve the common good.

Therefore, it is absolutely necessary to have a moral doctrine that specifies the rights and duties of man in his family, economic, political and international life; that teaches how man can develop his personality in economic, intellectual and moral areas without harming other people's rights. Accordingly, social morality will be a common set of rules that regulates the moral activities of man within the different communities he belongs to, designating his rights and duties as a member of each of them.

1

Catholic Social Morality

The Church, throughout the centuries, has not ceased to make her voice heard on all the problems that concern moral issues, both at individual and social levels.

Some have tried to deny the right of the Church to act in the social sphere, and want to confine her action only to what directly touches and concerns the altar. The whole history of the Church constitutes a frank repudiation of this curtailment.

1.1. RIGHT OF THE MAGISTERIUM OF THE CHURCH IN THE SOCIAL FIELD

Referring to the social problem, Leo XIII says:

> «We approach the subject with confidence, and in the exercise of the rights which manifestly appertain to Us, for no practical solution of this question will be found apart from the intervention of religion and of the Church. It is We who are the chief guardian of religion and the chief dispenser of what pertains to the Church; and by keeping silence we would seem to neglect the duty incumbent on us. Doubtless, this most serious question demands the attention and the efforts of others besides ourselves —to wit, of the rulers of States, of employers of labor, of the wealthy, aye, of the working classes themselves, for whom We are pleading. But We affirm without hesitation that all the striving of men will be vain if they leave out the Church»[1].

> «In regard to the Church, her cooperation will never be found lacking, be the time or the occasion what it may; and she will intervene with all the greater effect in proportion as her liberty of action is the more unfettered. Let this be carefully taken to heart by those whose office it is to safeguard the public welfare»[2].

Pius XI clearly reaffirms this right:

1 [Leo XIII, Encyclical on Capital and Labor *Rerum Novarum* (15 May 1891) §16, at The Holy See, http://w2.vatican.va/content/leo-xiii/en/encyclicals/documents/hf_l-xiii_enc_15051891_rerum-novarum.html (hereinafter referred to as *Rerum Novarum* or *On the Conditions of Workers*).]

2 [*Rerum Novarum* § 63.]

«Yet before proceeding to explain these matters, that principle which Leo XIII so clearly established must be laid down at the outset here, namely, that there resides in Us the right and duty to pronounce with supreme authority upon social and economic matters. Certainly the Church was not given the commission to guide men to an only fleeting and perishable happiness but to that which is eternal. Indeed "the Church holds that it is unlawful for her to mix without cause in these temporal concerns"[3]; however, she can in no wise renounce the duty God entrusted to her to interpose her authority, not of course in matters of technique for which she is neither suitably equipped nor endowed by office, but in all things that are connected with the moral law. For as to these, the deposit of truth that God committed to Us and the grave duty of disseminating and interpreting the whole moral law, and of urging it in season and out of season, bring under and subject to Our supreme jurisdiction not only social order but economic activities themselves.

Even though economics and moral science employs each its own principles in its own sphere, it is, nevertheless, an error to say that the economic and moral orders are so distinct from and alien to each other that the former depends in no way on the latter. Certainly the laws of economics, as they are termed, being based on the very nature of material things and on the capacities of the human body and mind, determine the limits of what productive human effort cannot, and of what it can attain in the economic field and by what means. Yet it is reason itself that clearly shows, on the basis of the individual and social nature of things and of men, the purpose which God ordained for all economic life.

But it is only the moral law which, just as it commands us to seek our supreme and last end in the whole scheme of our activity, so likewise commands us to seek directly in each kind of activity those purposes which we know that nature, or rather God the Author of nature, established for that kind of action, and in orderly relationship to subordinate such immediate purposes to our supreme and last end. If we faithfully observe this law, then it will follow that the particular purposes, both individual and social, that are sought in the economic field will fall in their proper place in the universal order of purposes, and We, in ascending through them, as it were by steps, shall

3 [This quoted phrase is the official Vatican English version of language in *Quadragesimo Anno.* The phrase is quoted by that encyclical from § 65 of Pius XI's encyclical *Ubi Arcano* (23 December 1922), at The Holy See, http://w2.vatican.va/content/pius-xi/en/encyclicals/documents/hf_p-xi_enc_19221223_ubi-arcano-dei-consilio.html (hereinafter referred to as *Ubi Arcano.*) The official English translation of that phrase in *Urbi Arcano*, on that Vatican website, is: «The Church does not desire, neither ought she to desire, to mix up without a just cause in the direction of purely civil affairs».]

attain the final end of all things, that is God, to Himself and to us, the supreme and inexhaustible Good»[4].

Pius XII returns to this same doctrine and says:

«The Church would be untrue to herself, ceasing to be a mother, if she turned a deaf ear to her children's anguished cries, which reach her from every class of the human family. She does not intend to take sides for any of the particular forms in which the several peoples and States strive to solve the gigantic problems of domestic order or international collaboration, as long as these forms conform to the law of God. But on the other hand, as the "Pillar and Ground of Truth"[5] and guardian, by the will of God and the mandate of Christ, of the natural and supernatural order, the Church cannot renounce her right to proclaim to her sons and to the whole world the unchanging basic laws, saving them from every perversion, frustration, corruption, false interpretation and error.

This is all the more necessary for the fact that from the exact maintenance of these laws, and not merely by the effort of noble and courageous wills, depends in the last analysis the solidity of any national and international order, so fervently desired by all peoples»[6].

In 1946 Pius XII alludes again to the same subject:

«The Church must today, more than ever, live her own mission; she must reject with greater energy than ever that false and narrow conception of her spirituality and of her inner life that would like to confine her, blind and silent, in the retreat of the sanctuary.

4 [Pius XI, Encyclical on Reconstruction of the Social Order *Quadragesimo Anno* (15 May 1931) §§ 41, 42 and 43, at The Holy See, http://w2.vatican.va/content/pius-xi/en/encyclicals/documents/hf_p-xi_enc_19310515_quadragesimo-anno.html, (hereinafter referred to as *Quadragesimo Anno.*)]

5 [The English version of the document which Hurtado is here quoting does not contain an internal citation here. In the Spanish version of that document relied upon by Hurtado, the Spanish equivalent of «Pillar and Ground of Truth» («columna y fundamento de la verdad») appears within quotation marks: «1 Tm 3,15».]

6 [Pius XII, *The Internal Order of States and People: Christmas Message of 1942* (24 December 1942) (hereinafter referred to as *Christmas Message of 1942*). This message is available in an English translation on an Eternal Word Television Network site: http://www.ewtn.com/library/papaldoc/p12ch42.htm. Italian and Portuguese versions, as well a Spanish version which differs somewhat from the one Hurtado used, are available at the Vatican website: https://w2.vatican.va/content/pius-xii/es/speeches/1942/documents/hf_p-xii_spe_19421224_radiomessage-christmas.html.]

The Church cannot, isolating herself in the secret of her temples, defect from her divinely providential mission of forming the whole man and thus collaborate tirelessly in the constitution of the solid foundation of society. This mission is essential for her»[7].

1.2. DIFFERENT FORMS OF ECCLESIASTICAL MAGISTERIUM

The Roman Pontiffs clearly affirm their direct magisterium in all matters directly revealed, reserving an indirect magisterium for all matters that relate to dogma or Christian morality, such as human labor, the right of association, the right to strike, fair salary, speculation and hoarding. The Church may rightfully pronounce a decision on many other moral issues when she deems it appropriate. However, the Roman Pontiff himself declares that technical issues are outside the field of the Church's teaching: for example, the preferability of a given method of mining or the organization of economic relations. If a given statement by the Church is not clear as to its technical or moral character, the Church herself is the one who should indicate its nature, and she cannot be subjected to any extraneous judgment.

The Church intervenes to put the faithful on guard against certain errors. The Church also intervenes to recall, in a positive way, the eternal principles of morality and to draw some applications, ordinarily conditioned by those specific circumstances that move the magisterium to teach.

The magisterium of the Church takes on an extraordinarily grave character when either a Council or the Roman Pontiff declares *ex cathedra* that a truth is part of the depository of revelation: to deny such a statement would amount to the sin of heresy. The ordinary magisterium is articulated by the Roman Pontiff, with universal reach, through his encyclicals, addresses and actions, either personal or through the Roman Congregations. In addition, the ordinary magisterium is exercised by bishops in their dioceses, addressing the members of the respective diocese. These acts of the magisterium are not guaranteed to be infallible, but they are part of the universal jurisdiction of the Roman Pontiff or of the diocesan jurisdiction of the Bishop, and they are of a doctrinal or disciplinary order. The faithful must not only externally submit to such declara-

7 [Pius XII, Address to the New Cardinals on the Supranationality of the Catholic Church *L'Elevatezza* (20 February 1946) §§19-20, http://w2.vatican.va/content/pius-xii/es/speeches/1946/documents/hf_p-xii_spe_19460220_la-elevatezza.html. This document is only in Italian and Spanish at that website. The quoted passage is translated by the editors of this book.]

tions, but they must also adhere internally with their intelligence and will to the statements given if they call for intellectual assent rather than the simple accomplishment of an order. Teachings of these kinds can be reformed.

Also, it is good to remember that the Vatican Council teaches expressly (De fide c. 3)[8] that the ordinary teaching of the Roman Pontiff, when he expressly wishes it, or the collective and uniform teaching of the Bishops scattered throughout the world and in conformity with the Roman Pontiff, may suffice to let us know that the doctrine contained in their statements is part of the Catholic faith.

Faced with the teachings of the magisterium of the Church, a member of the faithful must be consistent with himself and abide those teachings with a spiritual disposition: this is the logical consequence of his belonging to the Church and of his faith in the Holy Spirit who rules and governs the Church.

The Church will never intervene with her magisterium except when divine revelation made by Jesus and the Prophets and sealed with the death of the Redeemer is involved. The Church has the promise of being assisted by the Holy Spirit in the teaching of this revelation. The certainty of the magisterium is not bound by the reasons that may be invoked by the Roman Pontiff or a council for their statements. The only thing that becomes part of our faith is the statement itself.

1.3. SECULAR SOURCES OF CATHOLIC SOCIAL MORALITY

In addition to revelation, social morality is also based on reason and experience. Reason presents us the principles of natural law that tell us the order of things established by God. Revelation confirms and completes these matters, and adds positive prescriptions of divine law, particularly moral teachings of the Gospel. Experience intervenes to propose those immediate solutions that seem most apt for application. This experience is the whole history of humankind, and sometimes it has the character of a technically performed experiment. A true Catholic moral science will avoid the pitfalls of theoretical apriorism or of a pragmatism that looks only at results without worrying about foundations.

8 [First Vatican Council, Dogmatic Constitution of the Catholic Faith (24 April 1870), at The Holy See, http://w2.vatican.va/content/pius-ix/it/documents/constitutio-dogmatica-dei-filius-24-aprilis-1870.html. There is no official translation at the Vatican website. An English version can be found at the Eternal Word Television Network website: https://www.ewtn.com/library/councils/v1.htm#4.]

Catholic social morality is not satisfied only with establishing what is lawful and unlawful, but also looks further and aspires to ground our human relations in justice, charity and equity.

Techniques: Catholic social morality requires that *techniques* be put into practice for the realization of its principles: without them, the best doctrines become worthless.

Some moralists are overly simplistic. They affirm that the social question is a moral problem; that it is enough to live the Gospel or create encyclicals to solve it, causing immense damage by these affirmations. The least we can reproach them for is their simplicity.

Social problems are moral ones, but they are not only moral: they also embody technical problems that have to be solved to enable the reasonable application of the principles. If wages are not enough to live on, morality teaches that they have to be made sufficient. But, by what means? Producing deflation or inflation, providing more jobs, opening new industries or fixing prices of products? All these measures should be studied from a technical and effectiveness point of view. The Gospel is indispensable; without it there is no solution, but Jesus never taught that men were exempt from the study of prudential solutions: rather the opposite, He urged them with rare vehemence and He will hold us accountable in proportion to our ability to discover them. It seems important to insist on this point, since the sin of sloth is frequent. Teams of men, well formed in their principles and no less prepared in techniques to solve the complicated problems of a growing world, are needed everywhere. Catholic sociologists may rest in the certainty of their principles and in the help of the grace that will give them strength to put them into effect; but they must collaborate in an effort of invention and application up to the level of their faith.

2 *Historical Summary of the Development of Catholic Social Morality*

2.1. THE PATRISTIC AGE (FIRST TO NINTH CENTURIES).

The mission of the Church is not the secular government of men. She is called to continue Jesus' work of salvation. That is why no one can be surprised that the Gospel and the Church do not present a complete plan of social reform, for example about slavery, but only present the basic moral doctrines on the dignity of man, the nature of the family, of society, etc., and on corresponding actions. Jesus entrusted to us the seed of true love, which time will cause to sprout. This law of love dominates the development of Christian communities: St. Paul gave advice on submission to the established power, rules for masters and slaves. James and John, in their epistles, gave advice on the treatment of the poor and the duty of almsgiving. Special treatises on social themes were rare: their teaching was normally given in preaching and commentary on the Holy Scriptures, and therefore had an oratorical rather than a didactic tone and were directed towards immediate action. In these documents we must look more to their spirit than to legal formulas, which they have never intended to give. The sermons of the Fathers of the Church, that were always addressed to the concrete problems of their audience, must be read with this criterion in mind: to apply them literally to today's problems would be to do violence to their meanings. What really matters is to see the spirit that dominates the whole teaching of the Fathers of the Church.

Especially noteworthy, among the documents of this early period, are: *The Didache* or *The Teaching of the Apostles*[9], from the end of the first century, with its precious passages about mutual love; *The Shepherd of Hermas*[10], from the second century, that urges the mutual help of the rich and the poor; and the writings of Clement of Alexandria: *Paedagogus*[11], and *Who is the Rich Man that Shall Be Saved?*[12], on property and the use of wealth. St. Cyprian[13] (third century) spoke especially of alms; Tertullian[14] of marriage and social life; St. Basil[15] of

9 [*The Didache*, also known as *The Teaching of the Twelve Apostles*, is a brief anonymous early treatise. It is considered to be the product of the group of second-generation Christians known as the Apostolic Fathers.]

10 [Ποιμὴν τοῦ Ἑρμᾶ (*The Shepherd of Hermas*) is an important work attributed to Hermas and written in Rome.]

11 [Clement of Alexandria, *Paedagogus* (*The Instructor*) (c. 182-202). This is the second in the great trilogy in which Saint Clement develops a Christian ethic. The first book deals with the religious basis of Christian morality, the second and third with specific cases.]

12 [Clement of Alexandria, *Quis Dives Salvetur?* (*Who is the Rich Man that Shall Be Saved?*) (c. second century.)]

13 [Cyprian of Carthage (c. 200-258), Bishop of Carthage and a notable early Christian writer. One of his treatises is *De opere et eleemosynis* (*On Works and Alms*).]

14 [Tertullian (c. 155 - c. 240), was based in Carthage. He was the first Christian scholar to produce an extensive corpus of Latin Christian work. One of his works is *De Monogamia* (*On Monogamy*).]

15 [Basil of Caesarea, or Saint Basil the Great (c. 330 - 379), Bishop of Cappadocia. He was a theologian, defended the Nicene Creed and opposed heresies such as Arianism. His main theological writings are *On the Holy Spirit* and *Refutation of the Apology of the Impious Eunomius*. Approximately twenty four of his homilies have been preserved, including the *Homily on Psalm 14, Against Usury*, and *Homily VIII, On Famine and Drought* (*In Famem et Siccitatem*). These homilies are valuable for the insights they afford into the history of morals.]

usury, hunger and drunkenness; St. Gregory[16], brother of St. Basil, of usury and of love of the poor: he wrote precious commentaries on the Beatitudes. St. John Chrysostom[17] left entire sermons on these same subjects and a treatise on education. Perhaps the most meritorious work in relation to our subject is *The City of God*, by St. Augustine[18] (fourth century), in which he portrayed the Christian conception of history and politics, the role of religion in civic life, the conditions of true peace, etc.

Christian doctrine in this early period was not pure theory; it transformed ways of life. The first Christian communities in Jerusalem organized a life together in the endeavor to make a great family of Jesus' disciples, in which there was neither rich nor poor. The difficulties engendered by this practice soon made it disappear, and prevented it from spreading. The spirit that animated it, however, remained the same: sermons insisted on rigorous equality among Christians (before faith, there are neither free men nor slaves). This principle made the most fervent Christians free their slaves, and even confer on them the means to survive once freed; those who did not liberate their slaves softened their conditions and respected their fundamental freedoms. Once the social influence of Christianity was felt, after the conversion of Constantine, these principles strongly influenced laws that attenuated social rigor.

2.2. THE MIDDLE AGES

The ruin of the Roman Empire and the barbarian invasions impeded intellectual activity and required immediate action, to be undertaken in light of the deeply rooted thought of the Gospel. The Church at this time dedicated herself to the new barbarian peoples, trying to soften their customs, to organize them juridically and to establish peace. Bishops appeared as the organizers of civic life, the «defenders of the nation». In this universal anarchy, they were the only ones who managed to lead, through their culture, their spiritual prestige and their magnanimity, which led them even to sacrifice Church treasures to rescue

16 [Gregory of Nyssa (c. 335 - c. 395), Bishop of Nyssa, was the younger brother Basil of Caesarea. They were, together with their friend Gregory of Nazianzus, called the Cappadocian Fathers. Gregory is the author of several homilies, such as one condemning usury and several on the Lord's Prayer and the Beatitudes.]

17 [John Chrysostom (c. 347-407), Archbishop of Constantinople, was the author of *On Vainglory* and *The Right Way for Parents to Bring up their Children.*]

18 [*De Civitate Dei Contra Paganos*, Augustine of Hippo (354-430) was a North African theologian, philosopher and saint. He is viewed as one of the most important Church Fathers in Western Christianity.]

captives. The mission of the bishops was supported by the monks, who were the founders of new villages and extended settled land into the marshes. The monks also preserved ancient culture and transmitted it to those generations of barbarians who, under monastic influence, were educated, civilized and pacified. By their example, the monks taught the value of manual work, which had been despised by warriors who preferred hunting and banquets.

During the Carolingian era, bishops and monks, as imperial envoys, travelled among the communes, founded schools and recommended fair practices. The feudal regime was softened by leagues of peace fostered by the Church, and the communal regime was Christianized by the action of Franciscans and Dominicans who harmonized troubled relationships between humble people and the powerful. The new sovereigns were admonished as to their duties to administer justice to all and to impose peace. The model was St. Louis, who was accessible to all subjects and who knew how to impose justice with as much force as humility. He also had the honor of codifying the customs that served as laws in his time.

In the Middle Ages, guilds flourished under the protection of the Church, and thus, each rejoiced in being under the patronage of a saint. In these medieval associations, workers were harmoniously organized in a spirit that served as an inspiration for Pius XI to propose modern associations as a form of organized profession that would soften the social conflicts of his era. A young man entered the association as an apprentice, and after learning his occupation he continued there as a worker, under the master's direction. That worker, when qualified enough, might become a master in that association or in a different one. Thus, production served consumption and was regulated by it; sterile competition was avoided, because associations were conveniently grouped and coordinated; and even international trade was influenced, if not controlled, by these associations. Unfortunately, by the end of the Middle Ages, guilds had declined.

In the twelfth and thirteenth centuries, there was a remarkable intellectual flourishing, crystallized mainly in the *Summas* and the *Sentences*[19]. Aristotle became known in the West through St. Thomas, and the teaching of the Fathers

19 [Saint Thomas Aquinas (1225-1274), Domenican theologian, Doctor of the Catholic Church, author of several works, including *Summa Contra Gentiles* (1259-1265) and *Summa Theologica* (1265-1274). Peter Lombard (1096-1160), theologian and Bishop of Paris, author of *Libri Quattuor Sententiarum* (*Four Books of the Sentences*, written around 1150).]

of the Church was systematized by the Scholastics. They, especially St. Thomas, taught principles of social morality and applied them to the problems of their time; principles which continue to illuminate our times.

Saint Thomas Aquinas, in the *Summa Theologica* (especially at II-II, explaining the moral virtues), in his studies of law and of conscience, in his commentaries on Aristotle, and in the *De Regimine Principum*, which is unfinished, set forth very interesting social conclusions. St. Thomas's work contains a wonderful exhibition of Christian principles and a very fine analysis of the social conditions of his time, as well as eternal norms in which men of all times will seek inspiration. St Thomas attracts attention because of his extraordinary openness of spirit, always attentive to reality and charity.

The Schism, the Hundred Years War, and the Black Death exerted painful influences on intellectual endeavors, which seemed to cease.

2.3. THE MODERN ERA

Starting in the sixteenth century, the world was transformed. The Renaissance and the Reformation debilitated the Christian spirit. Capitalism was born; the bourgeoisie came to power by establishing a wall between religious life, which was identified as part of the private domain, and public life, which was thought to be absolutely secular. The discovery of the New World brought enormous wealth to Europe, and the printing press contributed to the dissemination of knowledge. New institutions such as banks, and commercial instruments such as bills of exchange, created economic and also moral problems. Circumstances not previously considered raised questions as to the charging of interest on loans, colonization and war.

Morality appeared as an independent discipline, separate from dogmatic theology, and adopted a more casuistic character. The treatises *De Justitia et Jure*[20] reviewed all the problems of economics and social morality of that time; among those treatises are the ones written by the priests Molina, S.J.[21], and Les-

20 [Starting in the sixteenth century, several authors wrote treatises entitled *De Justitia et Jure*. They were important contributions to moral, legal and economic studies. Domingo de Soto O.P. and three Jesuits: Leonardus Lessius, S.J., Luis de Molina, S.J., Juan de Lugo, S.J. —were among the most prominent authors of such treatises.]

21 [Luis de Molina (1535-1600), Spanish theologian and Jesuit priest. His work *De Justitia et Jure* appeared in installments in 1593, 1593 and 1600; in it Molina developed a legal theory concerning contemporary economic and political concerns. He also wrote a commentary upon the first part of Saint Thomas Aquinas' *Summa Theologica* (*Commentaria in Primum Partem D. Thomæ*, 1592) and made an important contribution to the science of theology with his work *Concordia* (1588), which addresses the problem of reconciling grace and free will.]

sius, S.J.[22] Multiple Church interventions condemned usury. In 1745, Benedict XIV published his remarkable encyclical *Vix Pervenit*[23]. The priests Vitoria, O.P.[24], and Suárez, S.J.[25], laid the foundations of international law, and in social matters they taught respect for indigenous peoples, and established limiting conditions for wars of colonization, a key topic then in America.

In Latin America, bishops and missionaries undertook the defense of the natives: of their personal liberty, their lands and their right to receive instruction. Without them, the Native American would have disappeared in Latin America, as they almost did in the United States.

In Paraguay, the Jesuits founded their celebrated reductions[26] (an experiment in community life inspired by religion) whose remaining structures cause admiration even today. Across immense regions people worked together, under the paternal direction of the missionaries, while they prepared for an autonomous life.

In Chile, the missionaries preached, with heroic courage, respect for the property and lives of indigenous peoples. Missionaries even instructed soldiers that they could not conscientiously obey commands to violate such rights. Friar Gil de San Nicolas, O.P., Fr. Antonio de San Miguel, O.F.M., (the first Bishop of the Diocese of Imperial), Msgr. Rodrigo González de Marmolejo (organizer of the Diocese of Santiago) and Friar Diego González de Medellín stand out, and, to-

22 [Leonardus Lessius (1554-1623), Flemish moral theologian and Jesuit priest. Lessius' work *De Justitia et Jure* (1605) dealt extensively with economic questions such as those relating to the charging of interest.]

23 [Benedict XIV, Encyclical on Usury and other Dishonest Profits *Vix Pervenit* (1 November 1745), at The Holy See, http://www.papalencyclicals.net/ben14/b14vixpe.htm (hereinafter referred to as *Vix Pervenit*).]

24 [Francisco de Vitoria (1483-1546) Spanish philosopher, theologian and jurist. He was the founder of what is called the School of Salamanca and is noted especially for his contributions to the just war theory and international law. He is considered by some scholars as one of the fathers of international law.]

25 [Francisco Suárez (1548-1617) Spanish Jesuit priest, philosopher and theologian. He was one of the leading figures of the School of Salamanca, and is generally regarded as among the greatest scholastics after St. Thomas Aquinas. He drew an important distinction between natural law and international law in his treatise *Tractatus de Legibus ac Deo Legislatore: in Decem Libros Distributus* (*Treatise on the Laws and God the Lawgiver*) (1612).]

26 [Guaraní settlements, known as *reducciones* (reductions) were established during the period from 1609-1780. They were located in the Spanish La Plata territory that encompassed the present-day republics of Paraguay, Argentina and the south of Brazil. Jesuit missionary organizations founded more than 30 settlements; in them the Guaranis people were organized into Catholic communities, and were protected from Brazilian slave traders.]

gether with them, many others whose names we encounter in the history of the worker's movement in Chile[27].

The Jesuits, in particular Fathers Luis de Valdivia[28] and Diego Rosales[29], struggled to change offensive wars into defensive ones and to free indigenous people from personal service[30], arguing these matters before the Spanish Court and even to the Pope. In a document from 1608, the Provincial Father of the Jesuits in Chile, Fr. Torres Bollo[31], gave freedom to all the indigenous people who were in personal service to priests. He also established rules (models of a social spirit) under which indigenous people would be able to work on the priests' properties: their salaries were required to be sufficient for their families, so that workers' wages would allow them to sustain their entire families and save for old age. Furthermore, Fr. Torres established disability and retirement insurance plans for the workers, and stipulated the kind of instruction that would be given to apprentices. In Mr. Domingo Amunátegui's[32] opinion, this remarkable document, which is quoted in full in the above-mentioned book[33], could be taken as a treatise on social science and reflects the degree of maturity reached by Christian social morality in the seventeenth century.

27 See Alberto Hurtado Cruchaga, *Sindicalismo: Historia, Teoría y Práctica.* [(*Syndicalism: History, Theory and Practice*) (1950, reprinted ed. 2016), pp. 194-201 (hereinafter referred to as *Syndicalism*).]

28 [Luis de Valdivia, S.J., (1560-1642), Spanish missionary who defended the rights of the natives of Chile and pleaded for a diminution in the hostilities with the Mapuches in the Arauco War (a conflict which began between the Spaniards and the Mapuches in the 1530's and continued to rage between independent Chile and the Mapuches in the 1880's.]

29 [Diego de Rosales, S.J., (1601-1677) Spanish chronicler, author of *Historia General del Reyno de Chile: Flandes Indiano* (*General History of the Kingdom of Chile: Indian Flanders*) (1674).

30 [The author is referring to an «*encomienda*»: a grant by the Spanish Crown to a colonist in America conferring the right to demand tribute and exact forced labor from the Indian inhabitants of an area.]

31 [Diego de Torres Bollo, S.J., (1551-1638), was the first provincial of the Jesuit Province of Paraguay, which included Paraguay, Perú, Bolivia, Brasil, Argentina and Chile. He was a leading promoter of the Paraguayan reductions and of missions in the southern part of Chile. In Rome, Fr. Torres published *Breve Relación de la Compañía de Jesús en el Perú (Brief Account of the Society of Jesus in Peru)* (1603), which included accounts of missionaries in the present territories of Perú, Bolivia and Argentina. In Spain, he presented, in 1603, a detailed report to the *Consejo de Indias* on the plight of the Indians and the ways in which it might be remedied.]

32 [Domingo Amunátegui Solar (1860-1946), Chilean historian. He was also a government minister, Rector of Universidad de Chile and leader of the Liberal political party.]

33 [*Syndicalism*, pp. 204-206.]

2.4. FROM THE FRENCH REVOLUTION TO THE PRESENT

The French Revolution brought profound social consequences. Public law was grounded on the concept of popular sovereignty and accepted the absolute freedom of the citizens as a principle. In religious matters, a process of laicization has been operating ever since, and in the social sphere, one of individualism has proceeded; guilds were suppressed.

In the economic field, the process of industrialization was intensified, with all the consequent social conflicts we will describe later. Against the dominant liberal school of thought, socialists organized themselves: from Saint Simon, Fourier and Proudhon, to Marx and Engels.

In France, Catholics may be divided into different schools of thought: some, such as those of De Maistre[34] and Bonald[35], were undemocratic; others had a tendency that was openly social. Lamennais, who after a beautiful beginning had a sad end[36], was one of the initiators of this social reform movement. Along the same lines were Lacordaire[37] and Ozanam[38], whose speeches, writings, and

34 [Joseph-Marie, Comte de Maistre (1753-1821), French philosopher, writer, lawyer and diplomat who advocated monarchy as a divinely sanctioned institution and the only stable form of government. De Maistre, together with Edmund Burke, was regarded as the founder of European conservatism.]

35 [Louis de Bonald (1754-1840), French counter-revolutionary philosopher and politician. He also advocated monarchy and developed a set of social theories, such as one related to the divine origin of language.]

36 [Hugues-Félicité Robert de Lamennais (1782-1854), French Catholic priest, philosopher and political theorist. He and his brother Jean sketched a program of reform of the Catholic Church in *Réflexions sur l'État de l'Église* (*Reflections on the State of the Church*)(1808) and they also defended Ultramontanism, a movement supporting papal authority and centralization of the Church, in contrast to Gallicanism, which advocated the restriction of papal power. He was one of the founders of the journal *L'Avenir* (1830), which attempted to combine Catholicism and political liberalism, advocating the separation of Church and State and freedom of worship, conscience, education and the press. Its liberal views were condemned by Pope Gregory XVI in the encyclical on Liberalism and Religious Indifferentism *Mirari Vos* (15 August 1832), at the Holy See, http://www.papalencyclicals.net/greg16/g16mirar.htm. Lamennais then attacked the papacy and the European monarchs in *Paroles d'un Croyant* («*The Words of a Believer*»)(1834), and this famous apocalyptic poem provoked the papal encyclical *Singulari Nos* (Gregory XVI, on the Errors of Lammenais *Singulari Nos* (25 June 1834), at the Holy See, http://www.papalencyclicals.net/greg16/g16singu.htm), which led to Lamennais' severance from the Church. Refusing to be reconciled to the Church, he wrote *Le Livre du peuple* (*The People's Own Book*)(1838), and he served in the Constituent Assembly after the Revolution of 1848.]

37 [Jean-Baptiste Henri-Dominique Lacordaire (1802 -1861), French priest, preacher, political thinker, journalist and political activist. He assisted in the re-establishment of the Dominican Order and was a co-founder of the journal *L'Avenir*. Lacordaire has been described as one of the greatest pulpit orators of the nineteenth century.]

38 [Antoine-Frédéric Ozanam (1813-1853), French social justice advocate, scholar, lawyer and journalist. He founded, with six other friends, the Conference of Charity, later known as the Society of Saint Vincent de Paul. Since Hurtado's day, Ozanam has been beatified.]

actions strongly inspired a group of brave men who held up the social flag of the Church in times of deep selfishness and corruption.

Montalembert[39], as a politician, fought for the abolition of child labor, and Veuillot[40] for Sunday rest. Ozanam and his classmates were dedicated to alleviating an immense misery that required immediate relief, which they did by the admirable work of founding the Conferences of St. Vincent de Paul. Among the Catholic social thinkers of that time, we cannot omit to mention Charles de Coux[41], Villeneuve-Bargemont[42], Buchez[43] and those who worked with the newspaper *L'Avenir*[44].

Slightly later, Le Play[45] founded the social sciences school *L'Ecole de Paix Sociale*, which significantly contributed to the development of the method of field

39 [Charles Forbes René de Montalembert (1810-1870), French parliamentarian, historian, journalist and publicist. He was a leading exponent of liberal Catholicism, and headed the magazine *Le Correspondant.* He coined the slogan «The Free Church in the Free State».]

40 [Louis Veuillot (1813-1883), French author and journalist. He was the editor of the newspaper *L'Univers* (1843), which popularized ultramontanism (a body of belief which emphasized pontifical authority).]

41 [Count Charles de Coux (1787-1864), French economist. He participated in the liberal movement of social Christianity, and founded, with Lacordaire and Montalembert, a free school in Paris, despite the State monopoly of teaching. He was Professor of Political Economy at the Catholic University of Mechelen, directed the Catholic newspaper *L'Univers,* and co-founded *L'Avenir.*]

42 [Jean-Paul-Alban Villeneuve-Bargemont (1784-1850)(in some places also referred as Villeneuve-Barcement), French viscount, economist and politician; member of the *Academia des Sciences Morales.* Strongly affected by a visit to Lille, where he discovered a vast amount of poverty, he supported social laws, such as one limiting child labor. He advocated a «vital and family salary», sufficient to sustain both the workman and his family, and he held that the employer ought to receive a profit only after the payment of this salary. The chief writings in which his ideas are set forth are the *Economie Politique Chrétienne, ou Recherches sur la Nature et les Causes du Paupérisme en France et en Europe, et sur les Moyens de la Soulager et de la Prévenir* (*Christian Political Economy, or Research into the Nature and Causes of Pauperism in France and in Europe, and into the Means of Alleviating and Preventing it*)(1834); *Histoire de L'économie Politique, ou Etudes Historiques, Philosophiques et Religieuses sur L'économie Politique des Peuples Anciens et Modernes* (*History of Political Economy, or Historical, Philosophical and Religious Studies of the Political Economy of Ancient and Modern Peoples* (1841) and *Le Livre des Affligés* (*The Book of the Afflicted*)(1841).]

43 [Philippe-Joseph-Benjamin Buchez (1796-1865), French historian, sociologist and politician. He was the founder of the newspaper *L'Atelier,* and served briefly, in 1848, as the president of the Constituent National Assembly. In his *Essai d'un Traité Complet de Philosophie au Point de Vue du Catholicisme et du Progrès* (*Towards a Complete Treatise of Philosophy from the Point of View of Catholicism and Progress*)(1839-1840), he sought to integrate, in a single system, the religious, moral, political and natural worlds.]

44 [From this point in the text through the end of this section, much of the text of this translation is conjectural, because the manuscript is mostly hand-written and incomplete.]

45 [Pierre Guillaume Frédéric Le Play (1806 -1882), French sociologist and economist, is considered to be one of the founders of modern French sociology. His book *Les Ouvriers Européens* (*European Workers*)(1855) was based on the observation, not only of individuals, but of families. A

research[46] and opened the way to more scientific studies. The school's great collaborators were the Abbé de Tourville[47], creator of a method of social classification, and Edmond Demolins[48], a precursor of the field of human geography. This school formed sociologists such as Joseph Wilbois[49] and Paul Bureau[50], whose work *L'indiscipline de les Moeurs*[51] is of great value. Their tendency was to reaffirm social authority, and they had a paternalistic attitude —one of patronage— towards the more modest social classes. La Tour du Pin[52] and Albert de Mun[53] had a remarkable influence. The latter founded the Society of Catholic Worker Circles[54] which, although it failed because its members were not sufficiently prepared for action, was the seedbed of new initiatives. Albert de Mun also founded the Catholic Association of French Youth[55], which never failed to

great defender of the values of the family, the social order and the maintenance of the ruling elites, Le Play was very influential in Catholic circles. He was one of the theorists of corporatism and the social economy.]

46 Read Guillemin, *Histoire des Catholiques Français au XIX Siècle*, Genève, Edits. Lumière du Monde.

47 [Henri de Tourville (1842-1903), French priest and sociologist. He led a school centered around the journal *Science Sociale*, developing new classifications for observations about social groups and family structures.]

48 [Edmond Demolins (1852-1907), French teacher, disciple of Le Play. He edited the journal *Réforme Sociale*. After the death of Le Play, Demolins and de Tourville split off from most of the other members of the Le Play school and founded a new journal, *Science Sociale*.]

49 [Joseph Wilbois (1874-1952), French sociologist who wrote at length on the organization of the corporation. His most original contribution was his advocacy of an alliance among sociology, metaphysics and the study of command and management techniques. He was the author of several works, including *Devoir et durée: Essai de Morale Sociale* (*Duty and Duration: Essay of Social Morality*) (1912), *Le Chef d'Enterprise, sa Fonction et sa Personne* (*The Head of the Enterprise, his Function and his Person*) (1926), *La Nouvelle Organisation du Travail: Réflexions sur ce qui se Passe en France Depuis Juin* 1936 (*The New Organization of Labor: Reflections on What is Happening in France since June 1936*) (1937) and *Comment Fonctionne une Entreprise* (*How a Business Works*) (1946).]

50 [Paul Bureau (1865-1923), French moral thinker, sociologist and lawyer. He was a disciple of Le Play, and for a time adhered to the school of the *Science Sociale* led by de Tourville. Bureau wished to avoid sociological determinism and emphasized the role of individual initiative in social development.]

51 [*L'Indiscipline Des Moeurs; Étude de Science Social* (*The Indiscipline of Morals; Social Science Study*) (1921).]

52 [Charles Humbert René La Tour du Pin (1834 -1934), French Catholic thinker, influenced by the ideas of Le Play. La Tour du Pin played an important role in the studies undertaken by the Union of Fribourg that prepared the way for *Rerum Novarum*. He greatly influenced Albert de Mun's legislative projects and strongly encouraged León Harmel in the transformation of his company and in his appeal to Christian employers.]

53 [Adrien Albert Marie, Comte de Mun (1841-1914), French political figure and social reformer. In 1872, with La Tour du Pin and Eugene Meigen, he founded *L'Oeuvre des Cercles Catholiques D'Ouvriers* (Catholic Worker Circles).]

54 [*L'Oeuvre des Cercles Catholiques d' Ouvriers*.]

55 [*Association Catholique de la Jeunesse Française*.]

reflect the social spirit of its founder. De Mun, as a member of the National Assembly, defended or improved all kinds of social bills that were submitted to the Assembly.

The movement *Le Sillon* had magnificent beginnings and a beautiful spirit, but unfortunately confused politics and religion[56]. Pius X warned the *Sillonists* of their errors, warnings that they received with great respect[57]. Great leaders of the cooperative and social movement and politicians of Christian inspiration emerged from this movement.

Les Semaines Sociales[58], presided over by Duthoit[59], Gonin[60], and now by Flory[61], have been real itinerant universities that popularize a solid and coherent body of doctrine. The doctrines of *Les Semaines Sociales* have been implemented by Social Secretariats, and also the C.F.T.C.[62] in the trade union field, the J.O.C.[63] and the A.C.O.[64] in the field of Catholic workers' action and the M.P.F.[65], in broader territories, in collaboration with non-Catholic elements.

56 [*Le Sillon* («The Furrow», or «The Path») was a French political and religious movement founded by Marc Sangnier (1873-1950) which existed from 1894 to 1910. It aimed to promote republican and socialist ideals within the Church, and so to provide an alternative to hostile labor movements.]

57 [*Le Sillon* was condemned by Pius X's Apostolic Letter *Notre Charge Apostolique* (*Our Apostolic Mandate*) (15 August 1910), at The Holy See, http://www.papalencyclicals.net/pius10/p10notre.htm. As a result, the organization dissolved itself.]

58 [Social Weeks or *Semaines Sociales de France* was founded in 1904 by two lay Catholics, Marius Gonin and Adéodat Boissard, to promote dialogue between Christians and society, to address contemporary problems, and to improve the conditions of the working class, denounced as inhuman in *Rerum Novarum.* The Social Weeks of France still exist today, and its annual congresses are attended by several thousand people. The organization's websites may be viewed at http://www.ssf-fr.org/56_p_11337/qui-sommes-nous.html (in French) and http://www.ssf-fr.org/56_p_13248/the-origins-of-the-semaines-sociales.html (in English).]

59 [Eugène Duthoit (1869-1944) was a law professor in Lille.]

60 [Marius Gonin (1873-1937), French journalist and Catholic social activist.]

61 [Charles Flory (1890-1981), French professor of economics.]

62 [«C.F.T.C». refers to the *Confédération Française des Travailleurs Chrétiens* (French Confederation of Christian Workers).]

63 [«J.O.C». refers to the *Jeunesse Ouvrière Chrétienne* (*Young Christian Workers*).]

64 [«A.C.O». refers *Acción Católica Obrera* (*Workers Catholic Action, W.C.A.*).]

65 «M.P.F». refers to *Mouvement Populaire des Familles* (*Popular Movement for Families.*)

L'Action Populaire[66], founded by priests of the Society of Jesus and under the direction of Desbusquois, S.J.[67], and Jean Villain, S.J.[68], has been a laboratory of thought and social action for almost 50 years. *Economie et Humanisme*[69], managed by Fr. Louis-Joseph Lebret, O.P.[70], prepared the bases of a human economy with precise studies of the global and national situation.

L'Action Populaire and *Economie et Humanisme* have published numerous books and magazines, among which we will point out *Revue de L'Action Populaire, Cahiers d'Action Religieuse et Sociale, Dossiers de L'Action Populaire, Economie et Humanisme* and *Diagnostic.* There were also other magazines representing other sectors, such as *Efficacité, Etudes, La Vie Intellectuelle, Masses Ouvrieres* and *Chronique Sociale de France*, which contained abundant works of economic, social and philosophical research.

66 [*L'Action Populaire* (Popular Action), a Jesuit organization dedicated to social action, was founded in 1903 by Abbé Henry-Joseph Leroy, S.J., and Gustave Debusquois, S.J., French priests who were engaged in work among the poor. They created Popular Action as an information bureau, library and publishing agency for French Catholics who were interested in social questions. It was one of the most significant and influential organizations in the Catholic social movement.]

67 [Fr. Gustave Desbusquois, S.J., (1869-1959), co-founder of *L'Action Populaire* and director of that organization from 1905 to 1946.]

68 [Jean Villain, S.J., (1892-1982), French priest. In 1946, Villain became director of *Action Populaire.* He was the author of the book *L'enseignement Social de L'Eglise* (*The Social Teachings of the Church*) (1954) and one of the founders of Catholic Action.]

69 [In the manuscript, the name *L'Action Populaire* (Popular Action) was written in Spanish, and *Economie et Humanisme* (*Economy and Humanism*), was first in French and then, later on the same paragraph, in Spanish. For the sake of consistency, this translation uses only the French.]

70 [Louis-Joseph Lebret (1897-1966), French Dominican social scientist and philosopher, pioneer of development ethics. In 1941, he founded the movement *Economie et Humanisme* (*Economy and Humanism*). Later, after Hurtado's death, Lebret joined a high-level group within the United Nations and worked to establish international action to combat inequalities and promote a new development ethic. Lebret played a leading role in bringing increased attention within the Catholic Church to the problems of international development. He took an important part in the preparation of the documents of the Second Vatican Council and of *Populorium Progresso* (Paul VI, Encyclical on the Development of Peoples *Populorium Progresso* (26 March 1967), at the Holy See, http://w2.vatican.va/content/paul-vi/en/encyclicals/documents/hf_p-vi_enc_26031967_populorum.html.)]

Two Catholic schools of social thought were opposed at the end of the nineteenth century: Angers, with a rather conservative and anti-interventionist tendency (Freppel[71], Périn[72] and C. Jannet[73] worked there); and Liège, which was interventionist (Msgr. Doutreloux[74] and Abbé Pottier[75] operated there). During this period, Msgr. Mermillod founded the Fribourg Union[76], in Switzerland, in which Catholic sociologists from other countries also participated, such as Decurtins[77] and Léon Harmel[78], a manufacturer from the North of France whose factory at Val-des-Bois was placed at the service of the Catholic social movement. His example led many people to social action. The Union of Fribourg paved the way for the encyclical *Rerum Novarum*. Discussing with Msgr.

71 [Charles-Émile Freppel (1827-1891), French priest, economist, theologian and deputy of the National Assembly. Freppel was a consultant at the First Vatican Council and was appointed Bishop of Angers, where he helped to found a Catholic university in 1875. He was a defender of social Catholicism and had a great influence on the drafting of *Rerum Novarum.*]

72 [Charles Périn (1815-1905), Belgian lawyer and economist. His major work, *De la Richesse dans les Sociétés Chrétiennes* (*Wealth in Christian Societies*) (1861), gained for him an international reputation. His main principle was Christian renunciation, which he considered to be a requirement for all moral and material progress.]

73 [Claudio Jannet (1844-1994), French professor of political economy, disciple of Le Play. He wrote several books, including *Les États-Unis Contemporains, ou les Mœurs, les Institutions et les Idées depuis la Guerre de la Sécession* (*The Contemporary United States, or Customs, Institutions and Ideas since the War of Secession* (1876) and *Le Socialisme d'État et la Réforme Sociale* (*State Socialism and Social Reform*) (1890).]

74 [Victor-Joseph Doutreloux (1837-1901), Belgian priest and Bishop of Liège. In 1886, 1887 and 1890, he convened three large social congresses at Saint-Servais College which studied questions concerning labor. These meetings led to the development of a center of reflection, thought and Christian social action called the School of Liège.]

75 [Antoine Pottier (1849-1923), Belgian priest, Professor of Moral Theology and politician. He set up Catholic consumers' and producers' cooperatives, founded a Christian Democratic newspaper, *Le Bien du Peuple*, defended fair wages and workers' ownership and helped to organize unions. Pottier is regarded as a leader of social Catholicism and Christian Democracy in Belgium.]

76 [Gaspard Mermillod (1824-1892), Bishop and later Cardinal of Lausanne and Geneva. He founded *L'Union Sociale D'études Catholique et Économiques* (*Social Union of Catholic and Economic Studies*), also known as the Union of Fribourg, which included some of the leading figures in Social Catholicism of the time, including René de La Tour du Pin and Albert de Mun. The Union of Fribourg was a think tank of lay intellectuals who met from 1884 to 1891 in Fribourg (Switzerland) to discuss the social problems which had emerged during the era of industrialization. The work of the Union of Fribourg is considered to have been one of the main sources of inspiration of Pope Leo XIII in his writing of *Rerum Novarum.*]

77 [Gaspard Decurtins (1855-1916), Swiss political figure and Professor of Sociology at the University of Fribourg. He was one of the leading figures in the Union of Fribourg and contributed to the preparation of *Rerum Novarum.* In 1887, Decurtins initiated an important initiative leading to the creation of the International Labor Organization (I.L.O.).]

78 [Léon Harmel (1829-1915), French industrialist and private chamberlain of Pope Leo XIII. Harmel experimented with applications of the social doctrine of the Church in his spinning mill at the Val-des-Bois, paying the workers a family wage (above the market level), installing a factory council to promote the workers' autonomy and helping to create Catholic trade unions.]

Mermillod, Leo XIII said: «They say of you that you are socialist; wait a little then you will see my thought». This was *Rerum Novarum.*

Social Catholics had to endure bitter criticism and contradiction, even from some Catholics who were not reconciled to the social teachings of the Church: some of them even came to oppose the Roman Pontiff himself, as Pius XI regrets in *Quadragesimo Anno* when referring to the work of Leo XIII[79].

In Spain, at the beginnings of the same period (1810-1848), Jaime Balmes[80], one of the greatest minds of his century, in his work *Protestantism*[81], comparing it to Catholicism, gave an important place to the social problem. Orti y Lara[82], Cepeda[83], Vicent[84] and Llovera[85] wrote and extended Catholic social thought.

From the end of the last century[86] and until today, Severino Aznar[87] has been a teacher and a tireless advocate of workers' action. In our times, the bishops of Málaga, León, Granada and the Canaries, Msgr. Herrera Oria, Almanh, Menendez Raigada and Pildain led a vigorous social movement. The Bishop of Málaga opened the way to the scientific and social formation of the clergy; the

79 [*Quadragesimo Anno,* §14.]

80 [Jaime Luciano Balmes y Urpiá (1810 -1848), Spanish priest, sociologist and philosopher. He wrote *Filosofía Fundamental* (*Basic Philosophy*) (1852) and the important work on Protestantism which is cited just *infra.*]

81 [*El Protestantismo comparado con el Catolicismo en sus relaciones con la Civilización Europea* (*Protestantism and Catholicity Compared in their Effects on the Civilization of Europe*) (1850). This book is often cited as disputing the thesis that Protestant thought was central to the development of modern society.]

82 [Juan Manuel Orti y Lara (1826 -1904), Spanish neothomist and conservative philosopher, lawyer and journalist. He was the editor of several journals and magazines, such as *El Siglo Futuro* (*The Future Century*), *El Universo* (*The Universe*) *La Ciudad de Dios* (*The City of God*) and *Ciencia Cristiana* (*Christian Science*), and wrote several books, such as *Ética o Filosofía Moral* (*Ethics or Moral Philosophy*) (1878), *Metafísica y Ontología* (*Metaphysics and Ontology*) (1887), *Curso Abreviado de Metafísica y Filosofía Natural* (*Short Course of Metaphysics and Natural Philosophy* (1891) and *La Última Etapa del Liberalismo Católico (The Last Stage of Catholic Liberalism)* (1893).

83 [Rafael Rodríguez de Cepeda y Marqués (1850-1918), Professor of Natural Law at the University of Valencia, known for his defense of Catholic social thought on labor issues. He was the author of several books and articles, including *Las Clases Conservadoras y la Cuestión Social* (*The Conservative Classes and the Social Question* (1891).]

84 [Antonio Vicent, S.J., (1837-1912), Spanish priest, one of the fathers of the Spanish social Catholicism. Vicent was the first to confront the social problem in both theory and practice, organizing Workers' Circles modeled on those organized by Albert de Mun. His major work was *Socialismo y Anarquismo* (*Socialism and Anarchy*) (1893).]

85 [Josep Maria Llovera i Tomàs (1874 -1949), Spanish priest, sociologist and writer. His best known work is *Tratado de Sociología Cristiana* (*Treatise of Christian Sociology)* (1909).]

86 [The nineteenth century.]

87 [Severino Aznar Embid (1870-1959), Spanish sociologist, academic and journalist. He was the founder of the magazine *Paz Social* (*Social Peace*) and a member of the Royal Academy of Moral and Political Sciences. He is recognized as one of the fathers of Spanish social Catholicism.]

Bishop of León encouraged the cooperative movement; the Bishop of Granada conducted learned studies on property that renewed the Thomist tradition; and the Bishop of the Canaries provided brave pastoral instructions on communism, the black market, etc. The magazine *Revista de Fomento Social*, an initiative of priests of the Society of Jesus led by Fr. Joaquín Azpiazu[88], is carrying out a major program social formation in Spain and Latin America. Fr. Azpiazu is one of the most learned and balanced men to deal with the social morality problems of our times, and at the same time, he is a meticulous expert in the economic reality of our days. Priests Florentino del Valle, S.J.[89], and Brugarola, S.J.[90], lead people towards social understanding. The «*International Catholic Conversations of St. Sebastian*» fulfills the same mission[91].

In Italy, Fr. Taparelli d'Azeglio, S.J.[92], published *Theoretical Treatise on Natural Law Based on Fact*[93], which is universally recognized as a reference work. In more modern times, Toniolo's[94] thought appears to inspire many encyclicals.

88 [Joaquín Azpiazu Zulaica, S.J., (1887-1953), Spanish priest and lawyer, member of the Royal Academy of Moral and Political Sciences. He wrote several books such as *Moral Profesional Económica* (*Economic Professional Morality*) (1940), *La Moral del Hombre de Negocios* (Businessman's Ethics *Man Ethics*) (1944), and *El Estado Corporativo* (*The Corporative State*) (1951).]

89 [Florentino del Valle, S.J., (1907-2009), Professor of Sociology and director of *Revista de Fomento Social*. Del Valle was the author of *Las Reformas Sociales en España* (*Social Reforms in Spain*) (1946), *El Padre Antonio Vicent y la Acción Católica Española* (*Father Antonio Vicent and the Spanish Catholic Social Action*) (1947) and *Diccionario de Moral Profesional según los Documentos Pontificios (Dictionary of Professional Morality according to the Papal Documents)* (1962).]

90 [Fr. Martín Brugarola i Mas (1908-1988), Co-founder of *Revista de Fomento Social*.]

91 [The International Catholic Conversations of San Sebastian (*Las Conversaciones Católicas Internacionales de San Sebastián*) was a series of intellectual meetings convened during the summers of 1947 to 1959; they aimed to promote dialogue and discussion between Spanish Catholics and those of other European countries. They served as a meeting point for some of the most important persons in Catholic and cultural life during that period.]

92 [Luigi Taparelli d'Azeglio (1793-1862), Italian scholar of the Society of Jesus who, some believe, coined the term «Social Justice». He co-founded the journal *Civiltà Cattolica* in 1850 and wrote for it for many years; its social teachings influenced *Rerum Novarum*. Taparelli was a proponent of reviving Thomism and applying natural law theories to the social and political questions of the nineteenth century.]

93 [Luigi Taparelli d'Azeglio, *Saggio Teoretico di Dritto Naturalle Appoggiato sul Fratto* (*Theoretical Treatise on Natural Law Based on Fact*) (1840-1843).]

94 [Blessed Giuseppe Toniolo (1845-1918), Italian Catholic economist and sociologist. Toniolo led the Catholic Social Action movement in Italy and advocated worker protection. In 1889, Toniolo founded a union to fight for workers' rights and also worked to limit the work week and protect women and children. Toniolo believed in institutions which could mediate between individuals and the state, notably the family, unions and professional associations. His ideas especially influenced Popes Leo XIII and Pius X.]

The magazine *Rivista Internazionale di Scienze Sociali* spread social thought[95]. Nowadays, Mr. Luigi Sturzo[96], despite his old age, continues to direct the social thought of the Christian Democrats in Italy. Sturzo was the founder of this political party, before the advent of fascism, with the name of *Partito Popolare Italiano*; dissolved during the period of Mussolini, it is now the ruling party of Italian politics, and its leader, De Gasperi[97], by his own initiative or that of his collaborators, La Pira[98], Fanfani[99], Igino Giordani[100], etc., is carrying out social reforms, in particular an agrarian reform.

95 [*Rivista Internazionale di Scienze Sociali*, a journal of economics and sociology, originally at *Università Cattolica del Sacro Cuore* (Catholic University of the Sacred Heart). The journal was founded in 1893 and was first edited by Giuseppe Toniolo. The recurrent theme of this journal and of its collaborators, who included the future Pope Pius XI, has been the reconstruction of society based on the primacy of Christianity. The journal contested the doctrines of Marxism, and was in harmony with the teachings of *Rerum Novarum*. The journal continues to be published today, now under the aegis of the Catholic University of Milan.]

96 [Luigi Sturzo (1871-1959), Italian priest, philosopher and important politician. In 1919, Sturzo founded, with others, *Partito Popolare Italiano* (Italian Popular Party), with the permission of Pope Benedict XV, and was forced into exile in 1924 with the rise of fascism. In philosophy, Sturzo elaborated a dialectic based primarily on the thought of St. Augustine. According to Sturzo, man is at once individual and social, free and conditioned; he is in process rather than entirely fixed by nature.]

97 [Alcide Amedeo Francesco De Gasperi (1881-1954), Italian statesman and politician. He succeded Luigi Sturzo as a leader of the Italian Popular Party when Sturzo was exiled, and he later founded *Democrazia Christiana* (Christian Democratic Party). From 1945 to 1953 he was the Prime Minister in eight successive governments. Ministers in those governments promoted reforms in the areas of housing, rents, pensions and unemployment insurance. De Gasperi is considered to be one of the founders of the European Union; he met with Konrad Adenauer and Robert Schuman to organize the Council of Europe and supported the Schuman Declaration, which in 1951 led to the foundation of the European Coal and Steel Community, an antecedent of European integration.]

98 [Giorgio La Pira (1904-1977), Italian politician and professor of Roman Law who belonged to the third order of Saint Dominic. He openly opposed the fascist government. He was elected as a Christian Democrat deputy to the Constituent Assembly and was reelected to the Chamber of Deputies. Later, he was elected Mayor of Florence and served as undersecretary at the Ministry of Employment and Social Insurance. He has been proclaimed a Servant of God; a cause for his canonization has been opened.]

99 [Amintore Fanfani (1908-1999), Italian politician and Prime Minister of Italy for five terms. He was a prominent member of the left wing of the Christian Democrats. Under De Gasperi, Fanfani was Minister of Labor, in which capacity he put 200,000 of Italy's many unemployed to work on a reforestation program and instituted the «Fanfani House» program for building housing for workers. Fanfani also served as Minister of Agriculture and instituted land reform initiatives.]

100 Igino Giordani (1894-1980), Dominican tertiary and Italian politician, writer and journalist. In 1920 he joined the Italian Popular Party; in 1924 he became the editor of *Il Popolo Nuovo* (*The New People*), a weekly newspaper of the Italian People's Party. Giordano was a member of the Focolare Movement.

In Germany, Bishop Ketteler[101] was a man of effective action. There was no social reform between 1850 and 1877 that he did not defend: reduction of working hours, legal holidays and prohibition of child and youth labor. He organized workers' production societies, which he entrusted to the workers themselves. The V*olksverein* popularized Catholic social doctrines[102]. Fathers Cathrein[103] and Lehmkuhl[104] [authored][105] some treatises on ethics and morals. In Austria «the Christian Barons» Liechtenstein and Vogelsang[106]. In the Netherlands, Msgr. Nolens[107], Secretary of Labor, promoted social reforms. The trade union movement K.A.B.[108] has 275,000 members and a wonderful network of services, social schools and print media.

In Belgium, Msgr. Pottier[109], and later, down to the present day, Fr. Rutten, O.P.,[110] worked hard through the academy, as well as through action and in the

101 [Fr. Wilhelm Emmanuel von Ketteler (1811-1877), Bishop of Mainz and German theologian and politician. His social teachings became influential during the papacy of Leo XIII and had an impact on *Rerum Novarum.*]

102 [*Volksverein für das Katholische Deutschland* (*People's Association for Catholic Germany*) was a political party founded in 1890 by Franz Hitze, a Catholic theologian and member of the Reichstag, and Franz Brandt, a manufacturer. Their aim was to counter the Social Democratic Party by addressing social problems from a Catholic point of view.]

103 [Victor Cathrein, S.J., (1845-1931), Swiss moral and legal philosopher. Fr. Cathrein was the author of several books, including *Philosophia Moralis: in usum scholarum* (*Moral philosophy*) (21st edition 1959).]

104 [Augustin Lehmkuhl, S. J., (1834-1918), German theologian. His research focused on probabilism, labor issues, strikes and alcohol consumption. Lehmkuhl was also active as a social politician. He is the author of *Theologia Moralis* (*Moral Theology*) (1883).]

105 [This word has been added by the editors of this book.]

106 [The author did not finish the sentence, as the manuscript shows. The «Christian Barons» he is referring to are:

- Prince Louis of Liechtenstein (1846-1920), Austrian politician and social reformer nicknamed as «the Red Prince» (*der rote Prinz*). He opposed liberalism, serving in the Reichsrat from 1878-1889 as a Catholic-Conservative member of parliament. He joined the *Christlichsozialen Partei* (Christian Social Party) when it was founded in 1891.
- Karl Freiherr von Vogelsang (1818 -1890), journalist, politician and Catholic social reformer. He was one of the leaders of the Christian social movement in Austria-Hungary, establishing the Christian Social Party in 1891, and struggled to help the poor and to establish new social laws.]

107 [Msgr. Wilhelmus Hubertus Nolens (1860-1931), Dutch politician and priest. In 1904, Nolens and other Catholic politicians founded the General League of Roman Catholic Caucuses, later renamed the Roman Catholic State Party. He strove to ameliorate the conditions of workers and favored improved social security measures.]

108 [The *Katholische Arbeitnehmer-Bewegung* (K.A.B. or *Catholic Workers Movement*) is a social organization in Germany, Austria and Switzerland which has its roots in the Christian labor movement of the nineteenth century. It originated in Germany through the support of the Bishop of Mainz, Wilhelm Emmanuel von Ketteler. The K.A.B. is part of the *World Movement of Christian Workers* (W.M.C.W.) (*Mouvement Mondial des Travailleurs Chrétiens*).]

109 [See footnote 75.]

110 [Martin-Hubert Rutten (1841-1927), Belgian priest and Bishop of Liège.]

senate of the kingdom, on social matters. Belgium, rather than a land of writers, is a land of accomplishments, and thus it can be held up to the world as the field of the most fertile social experiences.

Today, the Young Christian Workers, founded by Cardijn[111], comprises several million young workers who are willing to unite their Christian destiny with their working lives, not only in their homelands but also in the world. Christian syndicalism now has in Belgium more than half a million members who have managed to improve their standards of living and to introduce, through industrial legislation, a most interesting ongoing experiment in business reform. In the rural areas, the *Boerenbond*[112] connects more than one hundred thousand families, gives them family and agricultural education about farming their small properties and, through a network of cooperatives and services, assists small landowners and the national economy.

In England, Cardinal Manning[113] mediated numerous social conflicts[114].

In Chile, we cannot fail to mention the names of Francisco de Borja Echeverría[115], Blas Cañas[116], Abdón Cifuentes[117], Miguel Cruchaga Montt[118], Domingo Fernández Concha[119], Juan Enrique Concha Subercaseaux[120], Bishops

111 [Joseph Leo Cardijn (1882-1967), Belgian cardinal. In 1919 he founded *La Jeunesse Syndicaliste* (*Young Trade Unionists*) an organization that met resistance from some Catholics, but which received a blessing from Pope Pius XI in 1925. In 1924 the organization changed its name to *Jeunesse Ouvrière Chrétienne* (J.O.C. or *Young Christian Workers*). J.O.C. grew rapidly throughout the world and its members were often known as «Jocists».]

112 [The *Boerenbond* (literally, «*Farmers' League*»), was a Belgian association of farmers, founded in 1890. It was closely connected to the Catholic Church.]

113 [Henry Edward Manning (1808-1892), English Cardinal of the Roman Catholic Church and second Archbishop of Westminster. He was an Anglican cleric who converted to Catholicism in 1851, and was very influential in setting the direction of the modern Catholic Church. He promoted a modern Roman Catholic view of social justice. These views are reflected in *Rerum Novarum.*]

114 [In the manuscript, there next appears a sentence fragment: «In the United States: Ireland, Gibbons, Spalding (see Pattee)». Probably Hurtado is referring to Richard F. Pattee's book *El Catolicismo en los Estados Unidos* (*Catholicism in the United States*, 1945).]

115 [Francisco José de Borja Echeverría (1848-1904), Chilean Conservative Party deputy and diplomat.]

116 [Blas Cañas (1827-1886), Chilean priest. He founded *Casa de María* (*Mary's House*), dedicated to women, and *Patrocinio San José* (*Patronage of Saint Joseph*), for children.]

117 [Abdón Cifuentes Espinoza (1835-1928), prominent nineteenth century Chilean Catholic politician. He was a founder the *Unión Católica de Chile* (*Catholic Union of Chile*) and member of Congress.]

118 [Miguel Cruchaga Montt (1840-1887), Chilean lawyer and Conservative Party deputy.]

119 [Domingo Fernández Concha (1838-1910), Chilean businessman, Conservative Party Deputy and Senator.]

120 [Juan Enrique Concha Subercaseaux (1876-1931), Chilean lawyer and Conservative Party Senator, Deputy and Mayor of Santiago. He was a forerunner of the Christian social movement in Chile and fought to spread and apply the social teachings of the Catholic Church in the Conservative Party.]

Miguel Claro[121] and Rafael Edwards[122], Martin Rucker[123] and Father Fernando Vives Solar[124], among the deceased; they, with their writings, lectures and personal action kept alive the social thought of the Church. Among present prelates and priests, and in the young generation of laymen, there are numerous people who have devoted their lives to social work with immense abnegation.

2.5. THE ACTION OF THE SOVEREIGN PONTIFFS[125]

Among all those who have contributed to form modern Catholic social science, Roman Pontiffs are the ones that have made the most precious contribution.

During his long pontificate, Leo XIII aspired to teach in a direct and positive way about matters that concerned modern society, and also to promote the work of social reconstruction. His main documents on social matters are the following: *Inescrutabili Dei Consilio* (1878) on the evils of human society and their remedies; *Quod Apostolici Muneris* (1878) on socialism, communism and nihilism; *Arcanum* (1880) on Christian marriage; *Diuturnum Illud* (1881) on authority in the State; *Nobilissima Gallorum Gens* (1884) on Christian governance of domestic and civil society; *Inmortale Dei* (1885) on Christian constitution of states; *In Plurimis* (1888) to the bishops of Brazil on the abolition of slavery; *Libertas* (1888) on human freedom; *Sapientiae Christianae*[126] on the main duties of Christian citizens; *Rerum Novarum* (May 15, 1891), which has been called the Magna Carta of Christian workers and is the starting point of an intense social movement in all countries; and *Graves de Communi Re* (1901) on Christian democracy, which was motivated by fiery discussions in France and Belgium.

121 [Miguel Claro Vásquez (1861 -1921), medical doctor, priest and Auxiliary Bishop of Santiago. He was one of the first to translate *Rerum Novarum* into Spanish, making this new teaching known, especially among priests, workers and university students in Chile.]

122 [Rafael Edwards Salas (1878-1938), Chilean priest, teacher and bishop in the Archdiocese of Santiago. He founded *Juventud Católica Femenina* (*Feminine Catholic Youth*) and *Cruzada Eucarística para los Niños* (*Eucharistic Crusade for Children*) and he was a General Counsel of *Acción Católica* (*Catholic Action.*) He was an active defender of the rights of the Rapanui people.]

123 [Martín Rucker Sotomayor (1867-1935), Chilean priest, Bishop of Chillán and Rector of the Pontifical Catholic University of Chile from 1914 to 1921.]

124 [Fernando Vives Solar (1871-1935), Chilean priest. He was one of the creators of the Christian social movement which emerged in Chile at the beginning of the twentieth century. His writings and actions greatly assisted in the popularization of the social doctrine of the Church. He was Alberto Hurtado's spiritual director. He had a great influence on the generation of young people who formed the National Falange (1935-1957), a Christian political party that split from the Conservative Party and which was the basis of the Christian Democratic Party.]

125 [Almost all of the papal documents referred to in this section are available at Vatican.va and therefore they are not for the most part cited in the editors' footnotes.]

126 [1890.]

The Pope prescinded from all political implications and assimilated Christian democracy to popular Christian action. He returns to these subjects in the documents *Nessuno Ignora* (1902) and *E Noto a Tutti* (1903).

The documents of Leo XIII opened the way for modern social thought, facing the problems of the time with a courage that scandalized some people, but oriented and gave encouragement to social apostles.

Pius X left us a *Motu Proprio* (1903) on Christian popular action. This social teaching was completed for Italy by several documents: *Notre Charge Apostolique* (1910), which is a condemnation of *Le Sillon*[127]; *Singulari Quadam* (1912) to Cardinal Kopp[128], to settle disputes over the participation of Catholics in mixed labor associations[129].

Benedict XV (1914-1922) governed the Church at the very difficult time of the war and the immediate postwar period, and for that reason he devoted his main activity to the promotion and maintenance of peace, deserving to be called the Pontiff of Peace. On social matters, the following documents stand out: *Dès le début de Notre Pontificat,* (1917) on the bases of peace; *Soliti Nos* (1920) to the Bishop of Bergamo[130] on social action; *Intelleximus*[131] (1920) to the bishops of Venice, on the same subject.

127 [See footnotes 56 and 57.]

128 [Georg von Kopp (1837-1914), German priest. He sought to achieve a closer understanding between the German government and the papal curia. He was a member of the Parliament, where he assisted in mitigating some anti-Catholic legal provisions. In 1887 the Pope appointed him Prince-Bishop of Breslau, and in 1893 he was made a cardinal.]

129 [Pius X, Encyclical on Labor Organizations *Singulari Quadam* (24 September 1912), at The Holy See, http://w2.vatican.va/content/pius-x/en/encyclicals/documents/hf_p-x_enc_24091912_singulari-quadam.html (hereinafter referred to as *Singulari Quadam.*) This encyclical was addressed to Cardinal George Kopp and to the other archbishops and bishops of Germany. Paragraph four states:
«... [W]hen there is a question about associations which directly or indirectly touch upon the sphere of religion and morality, it would not be permitted to foster and spread mixed organizations, that is, associations composed of Catholics and non-Catholics, in the areas just mentioned. Over and above other matters, in such organizations there are or certainly can be for our people serious dangers to the integrity of their faith and the due obedience to the commandments and precepts of the Catholic Church».]

130 [Benedict XV, Letter on the Need to Distrust Socialist Propaganda *Soliti Nos* (11 March 1920), at The Holy See, http://w2.vatican.va/content/benedict-xv/it/letters/1920/documents/hf_ben-xv_let_19200311_soliti-nos.html. In that letter, Benedict XV warned Msgr. Marelli, Bishop of Bergamo, against the adoption by the diocese's Catholic trade union organization *Ufficio di Lavoro,* of socialist methods of class struggle.]

131 Benedict XV, Letter on Social Conflicts that Disturb Population *Intelleximus ex Lis* (14 June 1920), at The Holy See, https://w2.vatican.va/content/benedict-xv/it/letters/1920/documents/hf_ben-xv_let_19200614_intelleximus.html.]

Pius XI strongly insisted on the social duties of Christians and laid the foundations of social reconstruction: *Ubi Arcano* (1922) on the peace of Christ in the kingdom of Christ, affirming the law of nations in opposition to exaggerated nationalism and social modernism; *Divini I llius Magistri* (1929) on Christian education. This same year the Sacred Congregation of the Council, on behalf of His Holiness, sent the Bishop of Lille a letter which aimed to end the conflict between employers and workers, which has been called «the Letter of Syndicalism». *Quadragesimo Anno* (May 15, 1931), perhaps the most important social document emanating from his pontificate, commemorated the fortieth anniversary of the publication of *Rerum Novarum,* updating Leo XIII's teachings. *Nova Impendet* (1931) on the difficult global economic situation and the growth of weapons; *Non Abbiamo Bisogno* (1931) on the difficult situation in Italy and Catholic Action; *Mit Brennender Sorge* (1937) on the situation of the Church in Germany; *Divini Redemptoris* (1937), a document of extraordinary importance about atheistic communism and the attitude of Catholics towards social reconstruction; *Nos es Muy Conocida* (1937) to the bishops of Mexico on the religious and social situation of their homeland; *Letter to the Philippine Episcopate,* January 18th, 1939.

Pius XII began his pontificate with the encyclical *Summi Pontificatus* (October 20th, 1939), on the spiritual, social and political necessities of that time. The encyclical on the mystical body re-emphasized the bases of the social bond[132]. The doctrine of the present Pontiff is especially evident in his Christmas messages, in his consistorial speeches and in his speeches addressed to specific groups of pilgrims: employers, workers, Jocists[133], members of associations of social studies, bankers, etc. His speech on women's political and social duties (November 15, 1935) has had special importance[134]. *Sertum Laetitiae* [was] a message to the Catholics of the United States[135]; [he also authored] a commemora-

132 [The author is probably referring to the Encyclical *Mystici Corporis Christi* (29 June 1943) http://w2.vatican.va/content/pius-xii/en/encyclicals/documents/hf_p-xii_enc_29061943_mystici-corporis-christi.html.]

133 [Jocists are members of the J.O.C, (*Jeunesse Ouvrière Chrétienne* or *Young Christian Workers*).]

134 [The author is probably referring to Pius XII, Address to Members of Various Catholic Women's Associations on Women's Duties in Social and Political Life: *Questa Grande Vostra Adunata* (21 October 1945), http://catholictradition.org/Encyclicals/questa1.htm. It is unlikely to be a speech delivered on November 15, 1935, because Pius XII was not inaugurated until 1939.]

135 [Pius XII, Encyclical on the Hundred and Fiftieth Anniversary of the Establishment of the Hierarchy in The United States *Sertum Laetitiae* (1 November 1939), at The Holy See, http://w2.vatican.va/content/pius-xii/en/encyclicals/documents/hf_p-xii_enc_01111939_sertum-laetitiae.html.]

tive speech on the fifty years of *Rerum Novarum* (1941)[136] and a message on priestly sanctity, in which he mainly emphasized priestly duties[137]. Various acts of Pius XII have been collected in volumes, each of which contains the addresses and messages of the year. Spanish Catholic Action has printed them organized by subject matter[138].

2.6. CATHOLIC EPISCOPAL ACTION

Along with the social magisterium of the Roman Pontiff, the bishops' magisterium scattered around the world should also be noted. Each one in his dioceses explains, applies and commends the social documents of His Holiness, and supplements them with new teachings that respond to the problems of his particular jurisdiction. A collection of these episcopal social documents would fill many thick volumes. The most recent have been gathered in a second volume, which follows a volume of the pontifical documents on social matters, with the title *El Orden Social Cristiano en los Documentos de la Jerarquía Católica*, by Alberto Hurtado Cruchaga, S.J., Club de Lectores, Santiago de Chile, 1947[139].

There are joint pastoral letters from the episcopacies of almost every nation and letters from bishops addressing their dioceses on every contested social issue that was discussed. The assembly of these documents in a compilation will reveal to us the true sense of the Church as to social matters. Reading them will be, at the same time, a strong encouragement and stimulus for those who wish to put these principles into practice.

136 [Pius XII, Radio Message for Pentecost on the 50th Anniversary of Rerum Novarum *La Solennità* (1 June 1941), at The Holy See, http://w2.vatican.va/content/pius-xii/es/speeches/1941/documents/hf_p-xii_spe_19410601_radiomessage-pentecost.html (hereinafter referred to as *La Solennità*).]

137 Pius XII, Apostolic Exhortation to the Clergy of the Entire World on the Development of Holiness in Priestly Life *Menti Nostrae* (23 September 1950), at The Holy See, http://w2.vatican.va/content/pius-xii/es/apost_exhortations/documents/hf_p-xii_exh_19500923_menti-nostrae.html.]

138 [The author is referring to a collection published in several volumes by *Acción Católica Española* (Spanish Catholic Action), *Colección de Encíclicas y Documentos Pontificios* (*Collection of Encyclicals and Papal Documents*). This is an extensive collection of papal documents from Gregory XVI's encyclical *Mirari Vos* (15 August 1932) to John XXIII's Vatican II documents (25 October 1962).]

139 [*The Christian Social Order in the Documents of the Catholic Hierarchy.*]

The documents of the Catholic hierarchy allow us to distinguish between Catholic Action, which is the work of lay people acting under the hierarchy of the Church to Christianize people and institutions, and temporary social action, which is the work of lay people who, conscious of their faith and in full harmony with it, act on their own responsibility, running all the risks and dangers of such an enterprise. This is the field of work of unions, cooperatives and political parties. The action of Catholics will thus be complete: some will strive to baptize this world, and others to build it up in a healthy way, worthy of baptism. The two lines of endeavor, spiritual and temporal, contribute to the creation of a world that is faithful to the principles of the Gospel.

Chapter 2

Social Life and Natural Societies

1

Man's Tendency to Live in Society

Man is an eminently social animal. He cannot subsist, nor develop, alone. That is why man tends spontaneously to live in the company of others, and to associate with them in a way more or less stable, depending on the different types of societies. This happens because man is man: it is something that comes from his nature, something that is «natural».

In *Rerum Novarum*, Leo XIII says:

«The consciousness of his own weakness urges man to call in aid from without. We read in the pages of holy Writ: "It is better that two should be together than one; for they have the advantage of their society. If one falls the other shall support him. Woe to him that is alone, for when he falleth he hath none to lift him up"[140]. And further: "A brother that is helped by his brother is like a strong city"[141]. It is this natural impulse which binds men together in civil society; and it is likewise this which leads them to join together in associations which are, it is true, lesser and not independent societies, but, nevertheless, real societies»[142].

«For it cannot be doubted but that, by the will of God, men are united in civil society; whether its component parts be considered; or its form, which implies authority; or the object of its existence; or the abundance of the vast services which it renders to man. God it is who has made man for society, and has placed him in the company of others like himself, so that what was wanting to his nature, and beyond his attainment if left to his own resources, he might obtain by association with others»[143].

140 [The encyclical here has a footnote as follows: Ecclesiasates 4:9-10.]
141 [The encyclical here has a footnote as follows: Proverbs 18:19.]
142 [*Rerum Novarum*, § 50.]
143 [Leo XIII, Encyclical on the Nature of Human Liberty *Libertas* (20 June 1891) § 21, at The Holy See, http://w2.vatican.va/content/leo-xiii/en/encyclicals/documents/hf_l-xiii_enc_15051891_rerum-novarum.html (hereinafter referred to as *Libertas*).]

This statement is repeated many times in the Encyclicals (*Immortale Dei* § 3[144], *Diuturnum* § 11[145], *Quadragessimo Anno* § 118.) We need only look superficially at man to realize that, to be born, he needs the union of two rational beings; for his education, he needs other people, who received knowledge from their elders, to teach him language. For his development, man needs a room that others have built for him, factories that many people, united in a common effort, have been able to assemble and perfect. Nothing is clearer than the need for society. The Code of Social Principles of Mechlin synthesizes this doctrine: «[i]t is not true that the individual is sufficient unto himself. No one, however gifted, can maintain his existence or perfect his mind and heart save in that society in which he is called to live»[146].

2
Concept of Society

Society is defined as a group of people united morally and permanently in search of a common good, under a permanent authority.

Hence, every society is required:

1) to have a plurality of people.

144 [Leo XIII, Encyclical on the Christian Constitution of the States *Immortale Dei* (1st November 1885), at The Holy See, http://w2.vatican.va/content/leo-xiii/en/encyclicals/documents/hf_l-xiii_enc_01111885_immortale-dei.html (hereinafter referred to as *Immortale Dei.*)]

145 [Leo XIII, Encyclical on the Origin of Civil Power *Diuturnum* (29 June 1881), at The Holy See, http://w2.vatican.va/content/leo-xiii/en/encyclicals/documents/hf_l-xiii_enc_29061881_diuturnum.html.]

146 [The author here quotes *Union Internationale des Études Sociales* (*International Union of Social Studies*), *Code Social* (*A Code of Social Principles*) § 2 (second French edition,1930). An English translation of this book, prepared by the International Union of Social Studies, was published in 1937 (hereinafter referred to as *A Code of Social Principles*).]

This *Union Internationale* was founded at Mechlin, Belgium, in 1920 (the city is called Mechlin in English, Mechelen in Dutch, Malines in French). The object of the International Union was to study social problems in the light of Catholic ethics, to consider and approve principles applicable to such problems, to publicize these determinations, especially among social workers and to establish a center of information on social matters. (The Union had some points of similarity with the Union of Fribourg (see footnote 76), which worked for similar ends between 1884 until 1891.) Prominent representatives from France, Belgium and, later, Spain, the Netherlands, the United States, Switzerland and Italy took part. The summary of the work done by the Union's annual sessions, which were held between 1920 and 1924, resulted in a sort of catechism containing a social synthesis from the Christian and Catholic standpoint, setting forth doctrines on many of the social questions that were discussed at that time, including ones which were far from entirely economic.]

2) to desire to unite for a long—or even a very long— period of time. Because there is no willingness to join together, there is no society among the passengers traveling together on a train; because of the absence of the latter, there is no society among those attending a meeting, although everyone aims at the same end.
3) to pursue a common good appropriate to that society. We understand by «common good» the set of goods, those of matter or the spirit, that men can procure for themselves in an organized society. Every society has its own common good. This tendency of the associates all to procure the same common good is the internal bond that unites them in substance.
4) to be governed by an authority, which is its external social bond. The authority has the power to give orders or laws that rationally oblige its subjects in relation to their own common good.

3 *The Origin of Human Society*

Three main explanations are offered:

1) *Social Contract*: The philosopher of Geneva, Jean-Jacques Rousseau, has been its main supporter. Men were born good and called to live independently, but they resolved to live together and made a contract to form society, and gave the commission of social leadership to a representative elected by them.

There is no historical trace of such a covenant. To the contrary, one cannot imagine a moment in which man has not lived in society.

Rousseau wanted to build a theory that would rule out the idea of original sin: everything in man is good. This thesis was used by the physiocrats and the liberal school, whose tendency was to trust nature, in which everything is good. Evil comes only through the pressure of human intervention.

The great doctrinal importance of Rousseau comes from his purely naturalistic explanation of the origin of authority.

2) *Evolution*: There are numerous authors who, disregarding any philosophical explanation of the ultimate origin of society, are satisfied by simply pointing

out the different forms of society during different periods of time. Some pretend to give a scientific explanation based entirely on evolution from inorganic matter, which in the final stage results in man, the true inventor of society.

> This hypothesis, insofar as it conceives only of a materialistic evolution in which man is nothing more than evolved matter, is absolutely false. That man has adopted new social forms during his history is absolutely true, and it is proper for sociology to consider such evolutions, but they do not exclude the true ultimate origin of the society, which is supplied to us by [the social nature of man.][147]

3) *The Social Nature of Man*: God, in creating man, gave him a nature that could only be developed and perfected in society. God is, in this sense, the remote cause of all society. Each society, in particular, has found its origin in the precise will of those who formed it: this will of man is the immediate cause. The first society that existed on earth was the first family, and then came groups of families, a clan, a tribe, patriarchal groups, until they formed nations and, in our day, the society of nations, which is recognition of the multiple links that bind us to each other.

> «Civil society exists for the common good, and hence is concerned with the interests of all in general, albeit with individual interests also in their due place and degree. It is therefore called a public society, because by its agency, as St. Thomas of Aquinas says, "[m]en establish relations in common with one another in the setting up of a commonwealth"»[148].

4
Social Groups that Form Human Society

Positivist sociologists have made innumerable classifications of human social groups, each taking a different starting point. Faithful to the principle that it is man's social nature that leads him to found societies, we will divide them into natural and free.

147 [The manuscript did not finished the sentence. It says: «[…] which is supplied to us by». The logical meaning would conclude with the phrase «social nature of man», that was added by the editors, and which the explanation that follows.]

148 [*Rerum Novarum*, § 51.]

Natural societies are so intimately linked with the nature of man that they are universal and spontaneous. These are the family and civil society.

There is debate as to whether social classes, professions and international society are part of this category. Certainly, man lives in those societies spontaneously, but they lack specification of their own common good and the recognition of a governing authority. The social nature of man is not something static but dynamic that develops along with his growth and perfection and can lead to the transformation of that which today is a «means» or style of life.

In addition to these necessary natural societies, there are the *private* or *free societies* that man conducts in order to satisfy cultural, economic, sporting and other needs. Examples of these are unions, federations, schools and soccer teams.

The State or public authority does not have the power to prohibit the existence of these private societies, says Leo XIII: «[f]or, to enter into a "society" of this kind is the natural right of man; and the State has for its office to protect natural rights, not to destroy them; and, if it forbid its citizens to form associations, it contradicts the very principle of its own existence, for both they and it exist in virtue of the like principle, namely, the natural tendency of man to dwell in society»[149]. «There are occasions, doubtless, when it is fitting that the law should intervene to prevent certain associations, as when men join together for purposes which are evidently bad, unlawful, or dangerous to the State. In such cases, public authority may justly forbid the formation of such associations, and may dissolve them if they already exist. But every precaution should be taken not to violate the rights of individuals and not to impose unreasonable regulations under pretense of public benefit. For laws only bind when they are in accordance with right reason, and, hence, with the eternal law of God. ("Human law is law only by virtue of its accordance with right reason; and thus it is manifest that it flows from the eternal law. And in so far as it deviates from right reason it is called an unjust law; in such case it is no law at all, but rather a species of violence". Thomas Aquinas, *Summa Theologiae*, Ia-Ilae, q. xciii, art. 3, ad 2m.)»[150]

This teaching of Leo XIII is of eternal relevance. In different countries, especially in totalitarian states, it is continuously seen that the State strives to suppress free associations that man, in his own right, has formed. Sometimes states

149 [*Id.*]

150 [*Id.* § 52. In the official version in English of this paragraph at Vatican.va, the quote of *Summa Theologiae* appears as a footnote rather than as part of the text; Alberto Hurtado, however, placed it in the text in his manuscript.]

try to suppress religious congregations; other times, confessional schools or labor unions of workers or employees. Sometimes they deny the right to federate or to confederate, and in all of these cases, not for reasons of common good, but owing to ideological or economic interests. Thus, for example, the prohibition of peasant workers to be members of a union, or making this right derisory by preventing them from improving their conditions, is a flagrant violation of the natural rights of these workers.

5
Supernatural Society

The societies that we have analyzed are on the plane of natural law. In the *supernatural order*, there is another society: the Church. «Now there are three necessary societies, distinct from one another and yet harmoniously combined by God, into which man is born: two, namely the family and civil society, belong to the natural order; the third, the Church, to the supernatural order»[151].

The supreme goal of all human life is the possession of its supernatural end, which is to personally possess God, to know Him and to love Him for eternity. For man, everything else is only a means and has a secondary importance in the face of this end. «But seek first the kingdom [of God] and his righteousness, and all these things will be given you besides». (Mt 6:33)[152]. The Church is the society instituted by Jesus Christ, the true Son of God, to help man to fulfill his mission. That is why the Church is placed above every other society, not in the sense that she can replace them in their own domain, but because she pursues a nobler end, the means she employs are superior, her foundation was made directly by Jesus Christ in person, and she is permanently assisted by the Holy Spirit.

151 [Pius XI, Encyclical on Christian Education *Divini Illius Magistri* (31 December 1929) § 11, at The Holy See, http://w2.vatican.va/content/pius-xi/en/encyclicals/documents/hf_p-xi_enc_31121929_divini-illius-magistri.html (hereinafter referred to as *Divini Illius Magistri*).]

152 [All Scripture quotations, other than those within passages from encyclicals or within other quoted passages, are taken from The Catholic Study Bible (third edition, Oxford University Press, 2016), which are taken from the New American Bible Revised Edition, 2010, unless otherwise noted. Thus, none are translated from Hurtado's Spanish.]

6

Harmony of the Social Structure

The Christian social conception that we have just studied offers us a perfectly harmonious picture. Man is oriented by God to form societies, and he finds different forms suitable to satisfy each of his fundamental needs: the *family*, which brings him into being and gives him food and education; *civil society*, which cares for his temporal common good; the *Church*, which guides him to the attainment of his supernatural destiny. Man's life also moves within natural social forms, such as the *social classes*, in which man finds a cultural and economic environment and a means of perfection; and the *occupations* that, duly organized, must take responsibility for their own technical, economic, cultural and social improvement. *Free associations* are added to these societies, and they are as numerous as the aspirations of mankind. As man becomes aware of the universal fraternity of mankind, he will become more and more aware that he is part of the *universal society* whose good he must contribute to form his own good.

Man enters civil society not immediately as an individual, but through the family of which he is a part; he is part of international society through his nation. The comparison that St. Paul gave for the Church is valid for natural societies: they are formed like a great body, made up of members. Each cell adheres to the body, through the member of which it is part.

Both liberalism and totalitarianism, opposed in so many ways, have a different outlook which is consistent in its disregard for the rights of persons, of natural societies that are not the State and of the Church. Society consists of isolated individuals who must look to the State as their ultimate goal. This supposed liberation of the individual is the best way to effect his stagnation, his oppression and the practical denial of his personality.

Modern man has to fight for his right of association to be respected by modern oppressive super-states, and also for the various societies to keep each to its own place in harmony and respect for the rights of the others. Among them there can be no conflicts, since each of them has its own field of responsibility. If conflict, impossible in law, is produced in practice by wrongful intervention by those who preside over those societies, the right of the society of the higher order would clearly prevail over that of the lower order.

Chapter 3

The Family: Mission and Constitution of the Family. The Education of Children

1

The Mission of Family

Aristotle defined the family as the community imposed by nature for everyday life[153]. Taking into account the natural and supernatural orders, family could be defined as the society whose purpose is the permanent propagation of the human race, according to the conditions demanded by our nature and by our natural and supernatural destiny. The family is the basic cell of social organization. The Social Code of Mechlin says: «[t]he family being the source which gives us life, the school where first we learn to think, and the first temple where we learn to pray, we must fight against everything that tends to destroy or shake it, while praising and encouraging all that favours its unity, stability and fecundity»[154].

God did not want to create men simultaneously, as he created the angels, but with their free collaboration, through a power of procreation under the control of his reason and his will.

The end of the family shows us that children are the reason why family exists, and they are the ones that will determine its constitution. Children should be able to find in the family everything they need to be born and to develop physically, intellectually and morally. They will be able, in turn, once reaching maturity, to form new families that transmit life and education. When a family has trained its children to create new homes, it can be said that its mission has been fulfilled. Other societies may be constituted for purposes of short duration, but the family requires long years before completing its task: to form human beings in the complete sense of the term.

No other institution can fulfill the mission of the family. The family can look for the intervention of auxiliaries that are still necessary in our complicated civilization, such as the Church, the State and the school. But the family is the one that must put the child in contact with those institutions, and the one that must coordinate their influence, at least while the child is incapable of doing it for himself. All attempts to replace parents have failed: no one has their affection, nor their conditions, nor their responsibility.

153 [Aristotle states in the *Politics* that «[t]he family is the association established by nature for the supply of men's everyday wants». 12526b 13 -14. B. Jowett. Jonathan Barnes Ed., The Complete Works of Aristotle, Volume II, 1984, p. 1986, 1987.]

154 [*A Code of Social Principles* §10.]

2

The Constitution of the Family

«The family, which is an institution proceeding directly from nature, has marriage as its principle and foundation; marriage monogamous and indissoluble, raised by Jesus Christ to the dignity of a sacrament.

The family includes conjugal society which joins the parents and paternal society which, if the marriage has been fertile, unites the parents with the children born of the marriage. The family also includes, by analogy, adoptive children and personal servants»[155].

The law of instinct and the law of love lead man to marriage. Instinct leads men and women to use their faculties of perpetuating themselves, but in them, unlike in irrational beings, instinct is subject to the control of reason and will. It is strong, pleasant, but not irresistible. Above instinct, and giving all their greatness to human beings, is love, which is an inclination at the same time physical and sentimental. Love responds to the complexity of human beings, with their appetites, emotions and feelings, both sensitive and spiritual. Instinct alone leads irrational animals to reproduce the species; in man and woman the success of their stable union requires, above all, the deep fusion of souls.

The primary purpose of marriage is the procreation of the children under conditions that further their ends. There are also secondary purposes, which are the orderly satisfaction of the sexual instinct, the enjoyment of conjugal love, the mutual support of the spouses in the difficulties of life and the common realization of works of good, all of which bring joy to home life.

Marital society has, by natural right, two essential properties: *unity* and *indissolubility*. Correcting the deviations that paganism and even the Jews had introduced into marriage, Jesus Christ solemnly proclaimed that marriage could only be between a man and a woman, so *polygamy* and *divorce* contradict the will of the Creator. Jesus Christ wanted to expressly establish that marriage, one and indissoluble, responds to the divine plan; it is also the only association that responds to the rights of the child and ensures an appropriate education until the moment of his independent life.

155 [*Id.* §§ 11 and 12.]

Cohabitation, even if it is undertaken in a spirit of idealism, is nothing but an uncontrolled satisfaction of instinct—a denial of the common good—and brings untold evils to the individual and to society. Soviet communism has gone further in this idealization of free love, since it has given rise to family alienation. Nevertheless, learning from the experience of its tremendous failures, Soviet communism has tempered its original policy on this matter[156]. Undoubtedly, the stability of the conjugal union brings, in particular cases, inconveniences and sacrifices that a Christian conscience knows how to unite with the redemptive passion of Christ. The slightest exception in the matter of the indissolubility of marriage would entail more disastrous consequences for the common good than all the particular pains of indissolubility.

The Church does not have the power to dissolve a regularly celebrated marriage, except in three particular cases: instances covered by the Pauline privilege[157]; a solemn profession made by one of the spouses in a religious institute before the consummation of the marriage; and, in the case of those faithful who have not yet consummated the marriage, if the Holy See believes that there are reasons of great importance to intervene[158]. When the Holy See pronounces a judgment of annulment, it does not declare a divorce, but simply proclaims that, because there was a serious impediment or there had been a fundamental violation of the form in which marriage was celebrated, there was never a marriage. Such impediments are exhaustively enumerated in Canon Law, and include lack of minimum age (16 years in men and 14 years in women), lack of marital consent that can be reliably proven, kinship in a very close degree without previous dispensation, prior valid marriage and some similar circumstances.

Chilean law does not allow divorce with dissolution of the bond, but does provide for the divorce that maintains the conjugal union and only authorizes an external separation[159]. Fraudulent practices have brought about civil annul-

156 «(1) Put data». [The intention of the author was probably to support this statement with a footnote containing evidence, but there is no other information.]

157 [Pauline privilege: «A marriage entered into by two non-baptized persons is dissolved by means of the Pauline Privilege in favor of the faith of the party who has received baptism by the very fact that a new marriage is contracted by the same party, provided that the non-baptized party departs». Code of Canon Law, canon 1143 number 1 (1983), http://www.vatican.va/archive/ENG1104/_P44.HTM.]

158 [«For a just cause, the Roman Pontiff can dissolve a non-consummated marriage between baptized persons or between a baptized party and a non-baptized party at the request of both parties or of one of them, even if the other party is unwilling». Code of Canon Law, canon 1142 (1983), http://www.vatican.va/archive/ENG1104/_P44.HTM.]

159 [The Chilean Law of Civil Marriage of 1884, in effect at the time this book was written, stated: «Art. 19. Divorce does not dissolve the marriage, but suspends the common life of the spouses».]

ment by lying. Such a practice has unfortunately arisen through the complicity of numerous lawyers interested in money, and even of judges acting other than under the guidance of conscience. The Church punishes with excommunication the person who, being validly married before the Church and the law, annuls his marriage by fraudulent means. This punishment also applies to the party that does not oppose such an annulment, the attorney who brings the case and the false witnesses.

To the properties of unity and indissolubility, must be added reciprocal *fidelity* and *harmony*. Fidelity obliges both spouses in the same way. Christian morality has rejected pagan morality, which favors the husband. The Church insists that the husband's failure is as serious as the wife's. Spouses no longer belong to themselves: they have given themselves to each other so as to achieve the ends of marriage. *Harmony* introduces hierarchy and makes the father the natural head of the household. The mother is associated with this authority and is called upon to exercise it, without sharing it with anyone, in default of the father. Whoever has the authority, also has it for the common good of the family partnership: it is not the right to command despotically, but its mission is to protect the weakest. For the husband, the wife is «a help similar to him, that God has prepared»[160]. It is natural that, following the healthy evolution of custom, the rights of women should be more carefully considered.

The person who has authority in the family, as the manager of its common good, «has *duties and rights* before and above all human law. These duties and rights flow from the end assigned by nature to family society, *i.e.*, to unite the married pair, and thereafter to transmit, preserve and develop life to the point of moral perfection, and to perpetuate the human species»[161].

Before concluding this point, it should be remembered that:

> «The public authority, being obliged to adopt and hold sacred, as alone and lawful, the law of transmission of life through the family, must also repress everything that may endanger this law, such as immoral propaganda, disorganization of labor, bad distribution of profits or public burdens.

160 [This probably is derived from Gen. 2:18: «The Lord God said, «It is not good for the man to be alone; I will make a helper suited to him».]

161 [*A Code of Social Principles* §13.]

The family has a right to be protected against many plagues that threaten it with dissolution, e.g., the licence of the streets, of the theatre, and of a section of the press; drunkenness; tuberculosis; slum dwellings; and birth prevention»[162].

3
The Right of the Child

Many are those who talk only about the rights of parents and systematically silence the rights of the child. Children, however, have very clear rights. The child is a *person*, with all of a person's rights and duties. Among the first is the child's right of autonomy and independence with respect to all other beings, except God. The child is not at the service of anyone: no person, not even the family, can consider him as a means, nor can the family prefer its good to the good of the child. The family is for the child and not the child for the family.

While the child is small, he needs intimacy with those who prepare him to exercise his rights and to fulfill his duties.

The child has the right to be able to reach the fullness of his physical development. He has, therefore, the right to be protected against disease and to receive the necessary care as to his food, hygiene, dress and accommodation.

«The child has the right to physical, intellectual, moral and religious development»[163]. A child has a right to education, at least to the minimum necessary to earn a living, and to meet the child's future professional and civic obligations. This implies a certain understanding of *general knowledge* —a primary education— to enable the child to act some day as a learned man among educated men, and it also implies *technical knowledge*, appropriate to the child's expected profession, so as to enable him to earn a living honestly and honorably and to establish a new home. The child has a right to *education*, which will draw from him (as is suggested by the term *e-ducere*: to draw from) and will develop his own qualities. Education will habituate him to fight against his defects and to cultivate his qualities, will give him a hatred of evil and a love of good, and will teach him to coexist as a man of education and character. We cannot count on a formation that is pure instruction and not education. The child needs moral norms to act in life just as much as purely intellectual ideas.

162 [*Id.* §§ 16 and 17.]
163 [*Id.* §19.]

This formation must be completed by spiritual formation that prepares the child to reach his ultimate end. The word of the Gospel holds an eternal value: «What profit is there for one to gain the whole world and forfeit his life?» (Mk 8:36). The practical lesson has been satisfactorily learned, after very sad experiences, that a moral education is impossible if it is separated from a religious education. Morality disconnected from religion is totally devoid of its *raison d'être.* How worthy is a law if there is no legislator or the legislator is unknown? It becomes a pure human imperative, which can be broken when the slightest difficulty arises.

4
Who is Responsible for the Protection of the Rights of the Child

The family, the Church, the State and the occupations[164] are called upon to ensure the rights of the child, especially in matters of education.

4.1. FAMILY AND EDUCATION

The family is primarily —most directly interested— in the education of the child. The right of the family is imprescriptible and prior to all other rights and cannot yield except to the right of the Church, the spiritual family of Christians, within its own field. With respect to other societies or individuals, the family has the strict right to enforce its mission as an educator and to enjoy the freedom and means necessary to fulfill it. No other institution or person has the necessary affection for the child, as has the family, to fulfill this difficult educational mission. For a long time, the child is unable to discern what is best for him, and his parents must guide him: hence they have a tremendous responsibility from which they must give an account before God at every moment, and before the child when he is able to discern.

The Code of Social Principles of Mechlin thus summarizes the rights and duties of the family:

164 [The Spanish word used by Hurtado here is «*profesiones*», which has a broader meaning than the English word «professions». The dictionary of the Spanish Royal Academy defines «profesión» as «employment, faculty or office that someone exercises and for which he receives compensation».]

«The child has the right to physical, intellectual, moral and religious development. The obligation of providing for this development rests on the parents, who must be protected in their efforts to fulfill this duty. They are at fault when they omit or neglect to fulfill their educative task. They injure the rights of the child—rights which are the more sacred because the subject is not able to give effect to them for himself. Laws must indeed protect the rights of the child against incapable, negligent or criminal parents, and also against such third parties as may endanger effective action on the part of the parents.

In the majority of cases parents cannot undertake in full detail the absorbing task of completing the education and instruction of their child.

The purpose of the school is to complete the educative work of the parents, and to supplement their teaching as far as may be needful. The schoolmaster is thus, by his very office, the delegate of the parents.

Associations of teachers, however lawful in themselves, cannot claim supposed rights in educational matters which would run counter to the rights of the parents.

The rights of parents and of the teachers who take their place are, nevertheless, not absolute, but in accordance with the rights of the Church and of the State»[165].

4.2. THE CHURCH AND EDUCATION

In the spiritual world, the Church has the same mission as has the family in the natural order. She has the characteristic that, before her and in the spiritual order, all of us always remain her children in need until the last moment of her help, so we can attain our supernatural destiny. Fathers and children are here on the same level, and receive from the Church spiritual instruction and the means of grace to live and achieve it. Parents, in relation to the supernatural order, have no direct power over the soul of the child.

The normal relationship between the Church and the parents is that of close collaboration. The Church entrusts the religious and moral formation of the child to the parents and commits to them an immense responsibility, since the spiritual life of the child, the most important aspect of his life, will depend on them. Therefore, the error of parents is clear, and even perhaps criminal, when giving priority to secondary aspects of formation such as the study of a language, the practice of a sport or certain social contacts, they send their children to neutral or non-Catholic schools, with very serious damage to their religious

165 [*A Code of Social Principles* §§ 19, 20 and 21.]

formation. If, because of economic impossibility or other serious reasons, parents are sometimes forced to send their children to secular schools, they have a serious obligation to compensate for the lack of religious education.

«In regard to teaching, the Church has rights which come to it from its Divine Founder, who said: "Going therefore, teach ye all nations ... teaching them to observe all things whatsoever I have commanded you". (Mt 28:19-20).

The Church then has the exclusive right to teach all the truths of religion, and a real right to teach also philosophic, historical and social matters related to dogma or morals.

As regard the other branches of knowledge, the Church enjoys the same rights that all persons—whether individual or associations—have to communicate to others what is true, and to that end to found schools of all kinds, elementary, secondary and university.

The Church has for this a special title to the right to found and maintain schools of all grades, in consequence of the necessary and close relations which exist between profane teaching and religious teaching, between instruction strictly so called and moral and religious education. This right must be recognized and sanctioned by all legislation, and the faithful must contribute to its fulfillment by their generosity and by their willingness to promote attendance at Catholic schools and especially at Catholic universities.

Furthermore, the Church has the right to ensure that in those schools which are attended by her children, the teaching of matters relating to dogma and morals, and even of ordinary subjects, when given by teachers not of her own choice, should not in any way distort the religious truths of which she is the custodian»[166].

4.3. THE STATE AND EDUCATION

The State is the supreme authority in charge of administering civil society, which consists of an aggregation of families joined together politically. The State is, therefore, in the service of society and not the end of society. The State is for society and not society for the State. The State is responsible for supplying the deficiencies of individuals in educational matters. Therefore, it should respect the rights of the family and the Church, each of which is sovereign in its own field, and support them in fulfilling their missions. The State may inspect the work of

166 [*Id.* § 22.]

individuals and complete it, when it is ineffective or insufficient, even through schools and institutions that depend on the State. But the State's main effort should be to support private initiative, so that parents everywhere have schools at their disposal.

> «The State may demand and take measures to ensure that all citizens have a knowledge of their civic and national duties, and possess a minimum of intellectual, moral and physical culture, which in view of present-day conditions is really necessary for the common welfare.
>
> It exceeds its rights, however, and its monopoly of education and teaching is unjust and illegal, when it uses physical or moral compulsion to force families to send their children to state schools, contrary to the obligations of Christian conscience or even to legitimate preferences»[167].

Totalitarian ideas are not dead, for now they are the dominant philosophy in that immense sector of the world dominated by communism. For totalitarianism, the State is the absolute master that controls the bodies and souls of the citizens, and education is the means to form men who are entirely subject to it. In the educational field, totalitarian movements frequently aimed at an educational State; the State is the only one qualified to teach and the only one with the mission to do so. Ultimately, the fanatical aspiration to end Christian education is hidden under such a name; it is the old slogan of masonry that tries to take refuge in the field of education in Latin America. It is astonishing to hear the champions of the educational State brag of being Democrats and Libertarians while showing evidence of anti-democratic and anti-libertarian actions in the educational field.

The State is interested in seeing that the professions, and other organizations necessary for the common good, are well represented. Also, the State is interested in the physical, intellectual and moral flourishing of culture throughout the country, but it is indifferent as to who will provide this culture and preparation, so long as it is well provided. The State certainly has a *right of inspection* and control, but not the right to curtail the freedom of education of the family and the Church. If their actions are deficient, the State may push and stimulate their activities, but never suppress them. On the other hand, the State as an educator

167 [*Id.* § 24.]

is less capable than private entities, and would be even less so if it did not have the incentive of healthy competition.

The formula that best reflects equity is that of *proportional distribution* of the national school budget among schools that meet the required conditions. Therefore, families that send their children to the school of their choice should not be forced to pay twice for their education: once to the State, through educational taxes, and again to the school, through the school fee.

School neutrality is far from ideal. Education must be comprehensive and must always be given in accordance with a philosophy and a religion: concepts must be completed so as to form an organic whole; otherwise skepticism is introduced into the mind of the child. *Religious neutrality*, which ignores God and his laws, is essentially bad and antisocial. *Confessional neutrality*, which accepts natural religion and prescinds from any specific religion, though it is problematic in principle, may be *tolerated* in situations of religious plurality, provided that instead of opposing supernatural religion, it prepares the student to receive instruction from a minister of the student's religion. But this tolerance is accepted only as a lesser evil: the ideal is education that integrates religion into life and life into religion. The Code of Social Principles of Mechlin teaches:

> «In communities where there is no longer unity of belief, the State should see to it that, in the teaching establishments established and maintained by itself, each school shall, as far as is possible, group together only children of the same faith. These will there receive religious teaching in accordance with schemes arranged by mutual agreement between the educational and ecclesiastical authorities.
>
> If circumstances oblige children of different faiths to be grouped together in the same school, religious instruction should at least be given separately to each category of children by qualified teachers»[168].

On the intervention of the State in education, nothing is more complete than the teaching of Pius XI in his encyclical *Divini Illius Magistri* and *Mit Brennender Sorge*[169].

168 [*Id.* § 28.]

169 [Pius XI, Encyclical on the Church and the German Reich *Mit Brennender Sorge* (14 March 1937), at The Holy See, http://w2.vatican.va/content/pius-xi/en/encyclicals/documents/hf_p-xi_enc_14031937_mit-brennender-sorge.html (hereinafter referred to as *Mit Brennender Sorge*.)]

4.4. THE CRAFTS

«The crafts, too, being concerned with the formation of their future members, have their due part to play by providing suitable teaching for technical and vocational training, in co-operation with associations devoted to the Christian education of youth»[170].

Harmony among all who contribute to education:

«The alliance of educative authorities—the family, the school, the Church, the State, or the craft—is a first necessity of the social order.

This alliance presupposes that in every school, whether set up by the family, the Church, the State or the craft, all lawful authorities can fulfill their duties and exercise their rights»[171].

5
The Patrimonial Rights of the Family

5.1. THE ECONOMIC PROBLEM

The family needs abundant resources to provide for its many necessities: among others, the care of its children—all those that God wishes to give to it. Christian morality absolutely rejects the artificial limitation of births, which is growing more and more frequent owing to the propagation of contraceptive methods. It is a grave duty of the State to prevent such propagation.

His Holiness Pius XI in *Casti Connubii,* in the most solemn form that has been used in the encyclicals, states that the Catholic Church «raises her voice in token of her divine ambassadorship and through Our mouth proclaims anew: any use whatsoever of matrimony exercised in such a way that the act is deliberately frustrated in its natural power to generate life is an offense against the law of God and of nature, and those who indulge in such are branded with the guilt of a grave sin»[172].

170 [*A Code of Social Principles* § 25.]
171 [*Id.* §§ 26 and 27.]
172 [Pius XI, Encyclical on Christian Marriage *Casti Connubii* (31 December 1930) § 56, at The Holy See, https://w2.vatican.va/content/pius-xi/en/encyclicals/documents/hf_p-xi_enc_19301231_casti-connubii.html (hereinafter referred to as *Casti Connubii.*)]

The Church has not ceased to repeat in many documents the condemnation of the artificial limitation of births. This does not mean that she does not allow spouses to prudentially use their right to cohabitation so, by honest continence, they can space births in the way they deem compatible with their family situation. This is not forbidden in any way, since spouses do not violate the laws of nature, but by adhering to them, they restrict the use of them. In addition, spouses can use the method of rhythm, without breaking the moral law, provided weighty reasons and not pure selfishness lead them to such decision.

The duty of parents to use marriage correctly brings with it a right of the family to be provided with the necessary resources for meaningful work and for the education and maintenance of their children in a decent manner, worthy of human beings. Talking only about the parents' duty in marriage and not addressing the social consequences of their decisions is not to take the matter seriously. A problem of personal and social morality must have a personal and social solution. Unfortunately, there has not been much insistence on finding a solution to the double aspect of the problem.

5.2. THE FAMILY WAGE

The primary source of funds for parents to meet their expenses is the salary. We will deal more fully with this subject later, but of course it is essential to state that the Christian doctrine is that «every effort must be made to bring about that which Our predecessor Leo XIII, of happy memory, has already insisted upon[173], "namely, that in the State such economic and social methods should be adopted as will enable every head of a family to earn as much as, according to his station in life, is necessary for himself, his wife, and for the rearing of his children, for "the laborer is worthy of his hire"[174]. To deny this, or to make light of what is equitable, is a grave injustice and is placed among the greatest sins by Holy Writ[175]; nor is it lawful to fix such a scanty wage as will be insufficient for the upkeep of the family in the circumstances in which it is placed»[176].

In *Quadragesimo Anno*, the Pontiff himself stated, «[i]n the first place, the worker must be paid a wage sufficient to support him and his family[177]. That

173 [The encyclical here has a footnote as follows: «Encycl. *Rerum novarum*, 15 May 1891».]
174 [The encyclical here has a footnote as follows: «Luke, X, 7».]
175 [The encyclical here has a footnote as follows: «*Deut.* XXIV, 14, 15».]
176 [*Casti Connubii* § 117.]
177 [The encyclical here has a footnote as follows: «Cf. Encyclical, *Casti Connubii*, Dec. 31, 1930».]

the rest of the family should also contribute to the common support, according to the capacity of each, is certainly right, as can be observed especially in the families of farmers, but also in the families of many craftsmen and small shopkeepers. But to abuse the years of childhood and the limited strength of women is grossly wrong. Mothers, concentrating on household duties, should work primarily in the home or in its immediate vicinity. It is an intolerable abuse, and to be abolished at all cost, for mothers on account of the father's low wage to be forced to engage in gainful occupations outside the home to the neglect of their proper cares and duties, especially the training of children. Every effort must therefore be made that fathers of families receive a wage large enough to meet ordinary family needs adequately. But if this cannot always be done under existing circumstances, social justice demands that changes be introduced as soon as possible whereby such a wage will be assured to every adult workingman»[178]. Pius XII has repeated this doctrine many times.

Pius XI praises those who have tried «various ways of adjusting the pay for work to family burdens in such a way that, as these increase, the former may be raised and indeed, if the contingency arises, there may be enough to meet extraordinary needs»[179]. Fortunately, the idea of a family wage has entered into many statutes in a more or less complete way, and is implemented through compensation funds. In Chile, each year a living wage is fixed and an amount which corresponds to each employee's family burdens. Unfortunately, there is no legislation guaranteeing such rights to all workers, some of whom are not paid the living wage and not given the family allowance. Some factories voluntarily pay workers family allowances, or unions have obtained those benefits. Unfortunately, almost all workers are very far from covering the expenses imposed by their family burdens.

Achieving a just family wage and making it really sufficient are urgent objectives for the safeguarding of family life.

5.3. PENSIONS. SAVINGS. SOCIAL INSURANCE. DOMESTIC EDUCATION

The bitterest problem that a family of scarce resources has to face is lack of security. When His Holiness Pius XII depicted the contemporary world (Septem-

178 [*Quadragesimo Anno* § 71.]
179 [*Id.*]

ber 1st, 1944)[180], he stated «we see the countless number of those who, deprived of any direct or indirect assurance about their lives, are no longer interested in the real and higher values of the spirit, abandon their aspiration for genuine freedom, and throw themselves at the feet of any political party, slaves to anyone who promises them bread and security in any way»[181].

Direct security is given by the ownership of assets; the indirect support by social security. Referring to this: there is a part of social security that is given by the state directly or through quasi-public institutions or private institutions. Such is the case in Chile for public, quasi-public and private employees' pensions, as well as the reduced workers' welfare guaranteed by Law 4054, which is fortunately in the process of reform[182].

As for private savings, accumulated by interested parties on their own, we must recommend them with utmost praise. His Holiness Pius XI, after discussing the need for family wages, continues: «[c]are, however, must be taken that the parties themselves, for a considerable time before entering upon married life, should strive to dispose of, or at least to diminish, the material obstacles in their way. The manner in which this may be done effectively and honestly must be pointed out by those who are experienced»[183].

Direct savings and unemployment, old age and occupational-injury insurance must be recommended at all times. Unfortunately, there are several factors which inhibit saving: low wages, people's lack of foresight and wasteful habits and inflation that reduces to nothing savings gained with a lot of effort. That is why it is necessary to try, at all costs, to direct savings towards the possession of real estate.

180 [Pius XII, *Radiomessaggio di Sua Santità Pio XII Nel V Anniversario Dall'Inizio della Guerra Mondiale* (*Radio Message Oggi al Compiersi on the Fifth Anniversary of the Beginning of the War*) (1 September, 1944), at The Holy See, https://w2.vatican.va/content/pius-xii/es/speeches/1944/documents/hf_p-xii_spe_19440901_al-compiersi.html, (hereinafter referred to as *Radio Message Oggi al Compiersi on the Fifth Anniversary of the Beginning of the War.*)]

181 [Alberto Hurtado Cruchaga, *El Orden Social Cristiano* (*Social Christian Order*) item 8 (1947) (hereinafter referred to as *Social Christian Order*). This book is a collection made by Hurtado of pieces of different encyclicals, addresses and other Papal documents from Leo XII to Pius XII, organized according to the subject matter. In item 8, Hurtado paraphrased part of what appears in § 27 of the Spanish official version of the document cited in the previous footnote. The translation was made by the editors of this book.]

182 [Hurtado added here in parenthesis: «Put in a footnote, the benefits provided by these pensions». He did not complete this reference.]

183 [*Casti Connubii*, § 118.]

Domestic education is indispensable in order to reduce household expenses. Countless low-income families do not know how to cook, nor the nutritional value of food, nor how to make their own clothes, so they must buy them. All this makes a deficient budget become even more deficient. Furthermore, domestic education would contribute to the wife's being able to present a pleasant and attractive home and to know how to educate her children.

The organization of cooperatives for credit, pensions, consumption and construction is a precious assistance to families whose resources are scarce; in many cases this may be the only way to help them to meet their various needs. Cooperatives are also a great means of worker education in social and political life, and afford the opportunity to discover people with qualities to lead and organize.

5.4. THE FAMILY DWELLING

The most urgent need of a family is that of adequate housing. This need is even more imperative than clothing. There are primitive people who lack clothes, but no one is known who lacks housing. Man needs a private place where he can be free and independent, where he can rest from his work, where he keeps his personal goods, where he can read and think peacefully, where he can love his people. Arriving home! That is the ideal of every man; it means as much as for the ship to reach port after the storm.

The housing of the low-income worker classes is the most serious social problem in almost all Latin America.

Housing of workers in our cities is, first of all, insufficient. Architects have been repeating for several years that Chile lacks 400,000 houses: maybe this number is debatable, but one cannot deny the shortage of many thousands of houses. A slow growth of the population, by about 120,000 people per year, would require at least 20,000 new houses every year only to satisfy the need created by this increase. In recent years, only 6,000 houses have been built in Chile, which indicates that this deficit has not been covered and is increasing every day. The condition of Chilean slums[184], or that of the *favelas* of Brazil, is a shame for a civilized country: overcrowded, improvised hovels with dirt floors, roofs made of discarded tin or corrugated cardboard, walls of wood, cane and even paper: these cannot be called houses. Each of those slums is a tremendous «I accuse» directed at society.

184 [Hurtado used the Chilean words of «*poblaciones callampas*», which means, literally «mushroom settlements».]

Most of our people live in this type of house, in tenement housing or in subleased rooms: there the entire family is crowded. The result of a sanitary inspection of 891 tenements was the following: 541 in terrible conditions, and 232 in a regular state. Twelve percent of those tenements had eight people per room, none of which was bigger than nine square meters. The ordinary room of a worker usually has no other ventilation than the door. People eat, sleep, work and sometimes cook there, as shown by the walls blackened by smoke. The courtyard serves as a dump. Many houses have no toilet facilities, not even a latrine. A population of almost 7,000 souls in Santiago has one faucet for the entire slum: people have to queue from one and two in the morning to fill their jars. Most of these slum houses have dirt floors; they have no electricity and they must use candles for lighting.

In rural areas, the worker's home is at least a house. In some areas there are nice little houses that welcome family life. But in other areas there are shacks with reed roofs and dirt floors. The neglect of the worker's farming plot, which could provide for the whole family, if they knew how to cultivate it, demonstrates a total lack of family education.

But those who lack a house have a more serious problem than those who have poor housing. In the countryside, outsiders stay with a family, often leaving behind an unsolvable moral problem. In the city, there are thousands of vagabonds who sleep in the streets or in some emergency hostelry that does not offer any home environment. Can we imagine the immense bitterness of someone who does not have a modest space that he can call his room, a bed that he can call his bed?

Low-income housing is *deficient* in quantity, *unhygienic, anti-familial, immoral* and therefore, *anti-Christian.* It is also horribly expensive: it consumes 25 to 30% of the worker's budget, which is excessive. If we speak of construction, a worker today cannot have a basic house of two bedrooms, a dining room, kitchen, bathroom and small patio for less than 180,000 pesos, an astronomical figure compared to the salaries that the vast majority of workers earn.

Thus, a campaign for low-income housing, as energetic as if the country were at war, is necessary: otherwise, the problem will not be solved. While this problem persists, a state of domestic warfare is latent, as it is impossible for people who lack the most basic necessities to live in peace. As long as housing miseries are not addressed, the repression of seditious movements with oppressive laws is futile.

A solution is possible. Legislators, government leaders and even technical experts, must make this their principle: a solution is possible if the country attacks the problem with the same seriousness as if it were repelling an invasion of its territory. All other construction should be postponed until low-income housing is built: such was the postwar British policy as to reconstruction. In Chile, fortunately, all that is required for construction is inside the country: what is needed is that it be channelled into low-income housing and that the pace of production be intensified. The central government and the municipalities must provide all kinds of facilities to carry out such construction: the delivery of unused lands, the easing of regulatory requirements, the provision by agencies of surveys and plot plans, the formation of construction cooperatives, exemption from all kinds of taxes for new low-income housing and the provision of legal advantages to credit companies which charge a minimum of interest for construction projects.

5.5. HOME OWNERSHIP

Only providing a house cannot solve the problem of family housing. It is necessary to go further: the family should own the house.

The deepest desire of every man and every woman who wants to form a family is to have their own home. How many sacrifices are made to achieve this, sometimes taking out a piece of bread from the mouth to pay the monthly installment!

The right to possess goods necessary for subsistence is natural to man. Among these goods, housing is the most urgent, the most pressing: this is the reason why society must assist the worker in realizing this fundamental aspiration[185].

185 [In the original, the following paragraph remains unfinished: «Engineer Francisco Valsecchi has a beautiful page on individual and family advantages of home ownership: the own house "constitutes II, 119-128."» Francisco Emilio Valsecchi (1907-1992) was an Argentinian professor and the author of many books, who was inspired by the ideas of the Christian philosopher Jacques Maritain. Some of Valsecchi's books are *Bases Morales y Sociales de la Economía de Acuerdo con las Encíclicas Rerum Novarum y Quadragesimo Anno* (*Moral and Social Bases of the Economy According to the Encyclicals Rerum Novarum and Quadragesimo Anno*) (1941) and *Silabario Social* (*Social Primer*) (1939-1943). This last work comprises three volumes; for many years it was required reading for Catholics concerned about social problems in Argentina. Hurtado probably intended to cite this book. *Silabario Social* analyses legal regulations in labor and social matters and proposes numerous initiatives.]

In our days the convenience of building large collective housing projects for the people has been emphasized: housing where all services are centralized and in which workers can have advantages that would not be achieved in a small personal house. Even in big cities the construction of such collective housing has already begun. Catholic morality is uniformly supportive of the individual family home, and this is for several reasons. The first is that the conditions of private property in an apartment are more difficult and less valued than in a house, particularly in popular thinking. Furthermore, collectives necessarily bring with them the crowding together of many families who must be in close contact at all times, and the worker desires nothing more than to be able to come back to a separate place where he will be tranquil and alone with his own people, and where neighbors do not impose upon the intimacies of his home. Moreover, a detached house with adjoining land furnishes a most precious means of leisure, a solace after work, a constant incentive to be economical and an opportunity to expand one's building as the family increases and resources allow. Collective housing is not an ideal, not even for wealthy families: in those «luxurious tenements of the rich» a child is superflous: there is no place for a new arrival in this world, and those who have already arrived disturb everyone with their hustle and bustle. Therefore, it is necessary for them to stay in the streets and at the cinema for as long as possible.

Pontifical teaching is insistent in commending family home ownership: His Holiness Pius XII in the Christmas Message of 1942 states:

> «He who would have the Star of Peace shine out and stand over society ... should give to the family — that unique cell of the people — space, light and air so that it may attend to its mission of perpetuating new life, and of educating children in a spirit corresponding to its own true religious convictions, and that it may preserve, fortify and reconstitute, according to its powers, its proper economic, spiritual, moral and juridical unity ... he should strive to secure for every family a dwelling where a materially and morally healthy family life may be seen in all its vigor and worth; he should take care that the place of work be not so separated from the home as to make the head of the family and educator of the children a virtual stranger to his own household»[186].

186 [*Christmas Message of 1942.* The English version does not contain section numbers; the quoted passages appears under the heading «Five Points for Ordering Society» under number 2.]

In recognition of the fiftieth anniversary of *Rerum Novarum*, His Holiness Pope Pius XII wrote insistently on the same theme:

«Should not private property secure for the father of a family the healthy liberty he needs in order to fulfill the duties assigned him by the Creator, regarding the physical, spiritual and religious welfare of the family? . . . If private property is conducive to the good of the family, all public standards and especially those of the State which regulate its possession must not only make possible and preserve such a function —a function in the natural order under certain aspects superior to all others— but must also perfect it ever more»[187].

«Of all the goods that can be the object of private property none is more conformable to nature, according to the teaching of *Rerum Novarum*, than the land, the holding in which the family lives, and from the products of which it draws all or part of its subsistence. And it is in the spirit of *Rerum Novarum* to state that as a rule only that stability which is rooted in one's own holding makes of the family the most vital and most perfect and fecund cell of society, joining up in a brilliant manner in its progressive cohesion the present and future generations. If today the concept of the creation of vital spaces is at the center of social and political aims, should we, above all, think on the family's vital space and free it of the conditions which ties the family and does not even allow them to imagine a home ownership?

Our planet, with all its extent of oceans and seas and lakes, with mountains and plains covered with eternal snows and ice, with great deserts and tractless lands, is not all the same, without habitable regions and vital spaces now abandoned to wild natural vegetation and well suited to be cultivated by man to satisfy his needs and civil activities; and more than once it is inevitable that some families, migrating from one spot to another, should go elsewhere in search of a new homeland. Then, according to the teaching of *Rerum Novarum*, the right of the family to a vital space is recognized. When this happens, emigration attains its natural scope as experience often shows; we mean the more favorable distribution of men on the earth's surface suitable to colonies of agricultural workers; that surface which God created and prepared for the use of all. If the two parties, those who agree to leave their native land and those who agree to admit the newcomers, remain anxious to eliminate as far as possible all ob-

187 [*La Solennità*. This radio message is translated by the editors; in the Vatican website it is only in Italian, Spanish and Portuguese and does not have sections, only paragraphs.]

stacles to the birth and growth of real confidence between the country of emigration and that of immigration all those affected by such a transference of people and places will profit by the transaction: the families will receive a plot of ground which will be a homeland for them in the true sense of the word; dense lands will be relieved and their people will acquire new friends in foreign countries and the States which receive emigrants will acquire industrious citizens. In this way the nations which give and those which receive will both contribute to the increased welfare of man and the progress of human culture»[188].

5.6. THE TWO PILLARS OF HOME OWNERSHIP[189]

5.7. THE FEMINIST PROBLEM

It can be said that the feminist movement is very recent. In Europe it was born after the war of 1870 between France and Germany, and had a revolutionary nature. A Catholic-inspired feminist movement appears only after *Rerum Novarum.*

Many causes have influenced feminism. Woman, in the modern times, has seen the enormous role that she can play in all fields, especially in charitable projects. On the other hand, a good number of women have been condemned to remain single because the number of men was greater than that of women[190]. Women have had to think seriously about their economic futures, about being admitted to professional careers, to public and private employment and to factories. They soon became aware of the inadequate preparation they received and of the need to reform the laws to give them equal treatment with the men they worked with. To this end, they organized newspapers, leagues, great movements: revolutionary in appearance, but basically appropriate for the situation in our century, which needed reconsideration.

«The same false teachers who try to dim the luster of conjugal faith and purity do not scruple to do away with the honorable and trusting obedience which the woman owes to the man. Many of them even go further and assert that such a subjection of one party to the other is unworthy of human dignity, that the rights of husband and wife are equal; wherefore, they boldly proclaim the emancipation of women has been

188 [*Id.*]

189 [This subsection contains only the following: «Engineer Valsecchi, whom we shortly mentioned previously, is the champion of single-family affordable housing, correctly suggests, "It is not enough to provide ... copy II, 122-123"». See footnote 185.]

190 [Hurtado probably meant the opposite.]

or ought to be effected. This emancipation in their ideas must be threefold, in the ruling of the domestic society, in the administration of family affairs and in the rearing of the children. It must be social, economic, physiological: —physiological, that is to say, the woman is to be freed at her own good pleasure from the burdensome duties properly belonging to a wife as companion and mother (We have already said that this is not an emancipation but a crime); social, inasmuch as the wife being freed from the cares of children and family, should, to the neglect of these, be able to follow her own bent and devote herself to business and even public affairs; finally economic, whereby the woman even without the knowledge and against the wish of her husband may be at liberty to conduct and administer her own affairs, giving her attention chiefly to these rather than to children, husband and family»[191].

5.7.1. *ENHANCING THE DIGNITY OF WOMEN*

Contrary to pagan beliefs that woman was made for motherhood, for pleasure or for domestic work only, and that she was inferior to man, the Catholic Church has taught that a woman, as much as a man, is a person, who has the same essential rights and the same supernatural end. This is not an obstacle to man's and woman's psychologies being different nor to each sex being more suitable for certain functions.

Assuming this equality of nature between man and woman, the Church has placed two restrictions on women: the first, their exclusion from sacred orders, reserved for man; the second, her subordination to the husband in the family society, which must have a head. «The order of love», as St. Augustine called it, must flourish in domestic society. This order includes both the primacy of the husband with regard to the wife and children, the ready subjection of the wife and her willing obedience, which the Apostle commends in these words: «Wives should be subordinate to their husbands as to the Lord. For the husband is the head of his wife just as Christ is head of the church, he himself the savior of the body» (Eph. 5,22-23).

«This subjection, however, does not deny or take away the liberty which fully belongs to the woman both in view of her dignity as a human person, and in view of her most noble office as wife and mother and companion; nor does it bid her obey her husband's every request if not in harmony with right reason or with the dignity due to

191 [*Casti Connubii*, § 74.]

wife; nor, in fine, does it imply that the wife should be put on a level with those persons who in law are called minors, to whom it is not customary to allow free exercise of their rights on account of their lack of mature judgment, or of their ignorance of human affairs. But it forbids that exaggerated liberty which cares not for the good of the family; it forbids that in this body which is the family, the heart be separated from the head to the great detriment of the whole body and the proximate danger of ruin. For if the man is the head, the woman is the heart, and as he occupies the chief place in ruling, so she may and ought to claim for herself the chief place in love.

Again, this subjection of wife to husband in its degree and manner may vary according to the different conditions of persons, place and time. In fact, if the husband neglects his duty, it falls to the wife to take his place in directing the family. But the structure of the family and its fundamental law, established and confirmed by God, must always and everywhere be maintained intact.

With great wisdom Our predecessor Leo XIII, of happy memory, in the Encyclical on Christian marriage which We have already mentioned, speaking of this order to be maintained between man and wife, teaches: "The man is the ruler of the family, and the head of the woman; but because she is flesh of his flesh and bone of his bone, let her be subject and obedient to the man, not as a servant but as a companion, so that nothing be lacking of honor or of dignity in the obedience which she pays. Let divine charity be the constant guide of their mutual relations, both in him who rules and in her who obeys, since each bears the image, the one of Christ, the other of the Church"[192].

These, then, are the elements which compose the blessing of conjugal faith: unity, chastity, charity, honorable noble obedience, which are at the same time an enumeration of the benefits which are bestowed on husband and wife in their married state, benefits by which the peace, the dignity and the happiness of matrimony are securely preserved and fostered. Wherefore it is not surprising that this conjugal faith has always been counted amongst the most priceless and special blessings of matrimony»[193].

Except for the two matters pointed out, the Church has constantly fought to equalize man and woman: the sin of man and woman are the same, and there are not two different moral systems. In intimate marital relations, both woman and man have the same rights with respect to one other. The Church esteems as her saints and elevates both men and women to the altars; and above all the

192 [The following footnote appears in the Encyclical at this point: «Encycl. *Arcanum divinae sapientiae*, 10 Febr. 1880».]

193 [*Casti Connubii*, §§ 27-30.]

saints and angels there is a woman, the Virgin Mary. It is impossible to measure the influence of all these elements of judgment on the daily experience of the Church. They have added substance to the Christian principle that St. Paul articulated in his letter to the Galatians: «There is neither Jew nor Greek, there is neither slave nor free person, there is not male and female, for you are all one in Christ Jesus». (Gal. 3:28).

Furthermore, the simple observation of daily life among Catholics will show us the place that women occupy in it. She not only acts, in the life of the home, as wife and mother, but also directs many charitable works: in education and in the social apostolate—and even at the parliament and on the throne. She is admired and respected everywhere for her self-denial, her intelligence and her courage. Comparing the esteem of women in the Catholic Church with her esteem in the separated churches, among the Jews and among pagan peoples, we see that only in the first instance does the woman occupy the place of worthy companion to the man to whom God joined her.

5.7.2. *THE SOCIAL ACTION OF WOMEN*

In November 1945 His Holiness Pius XII delivered a valuable address to the women of the world, in which he emphasized the dignity of women and their activities in modern times[194]. From this document, we will identify concepts that are related to women's activities.

The identical dignity of man and woman cannot be preserved unless each one respects and cultivates the special qualities that God gave to the other. Physical and spiritual attributes cannot be eliminated, and they cannot be transformed without nature's restoring its balance. The two sexes are mutually complementary, as is shown in every phase of human life.

The feminine way of life, its innate disposition, is motherhood. Every woman is born to be a mother: a mother in the physical sense of the word, mother in the most spiritual and exalted (but not less real) sense. The woman who is truly a woman always contemplates the problems of life in the light of the family. Her

194 [Pius XII, Address to Members of Various Catholic Women's Associations on Women's Duties in Social and Political Life *Questa Grande Vostra Adunata* (21 October 1945), http://catholictradition.org/Encyclicals/questa1.htm (hereinafter referred to as *Women's Duties in Social and Political Life*).

At this point Hurtado includes a parenthetical citing items 380-390 of his book *Social Christian Order.*]

exquisite sensitivity warns her of any danger that threatens to frustrate her mission as a mother or which hovers over the good of the family.

5.7.3. *THREATS TO WOMEN POSED BY TOTALITARIANISM AND CAPITALISM*

Unfortunately, the destiny of women is threatened in the present political and social situation.

«It is to woman that various political movements are now turning in the hope of gaining her support. A certain totalitarian regime tempts her with marvelous promises: equality of rights with men; assistance during the period of gestation and labor; communal kitchens and other public services relieving her of domestic burdens; public creches[195] and other institutions, maintained and administered by the State and local authority and exempting her from her maternal obligations towards her children; education without fees, public assistance in the case of illness...»[196]

The Pontiff continues:

«We have in fact Ourself insisted that, for the same work and the same service rendered, women have a right to equal pay with men ... In the concessions that are being made to woman it is easy to see, not so much the respect which is due to her dignity and her vocation, as rather a desire to build up the economic and military power of the totalitarian State, to which everything must be inexorably subordinated...

And what of a regime in which capitalism is dominant? Does it offer a prospect of real welfare for woman? We have no need here to describe the economic and social consequences of this system. You know its characteristic signs and you yourselves labor under the burden it imposes: the excessive crowding of the population into the cities; the ever-growing and all-invading power of big business; the difficult and precarious condition of other industries, especially the crafts and even more especially agriculture; the disquieting spread of unemployment.

Restore woman as soon as possible to her place of honor in the home as housewife and mother! This is the universal cry today. It is as though the world had suddenly

195 [«Creches» refers, in British English, to «a nursery where babies and young children are cared for during the working day». https://en.oxforddictionaries.com/definition/creche.]

196 [*Women's Duties in Social and Political Life.*]

awakened in alarm and horror to see the results of a material and technical progress of which it had hitherto been so proud»[197].

5.7.4. PERNICIOUS CONSEQUENCES OF THE ABSENCE OF WOMAN FROM THE HOME

«Here is the wife who, to augment her husband's income, also goes out to work in a factory, leaving the home neglected during her absence. Already squalid and confined enough, perhaps, the house becomes even more desolate for lack of care. And here are the members of the family, working separately at different hours in different parts of the city and hardly ever meeting one another, not even for the principal meal or for the rest at the end of the day's work, much less for family prayers. What remains of family life? And what attractions has it to offer the children?

In addition to these unhappy consequences, the mother's absence from the home has another and more lamentable result: it affects the children's education, especially the girl's training and preparation for real life. Accustomed to her mother being always absent from home and to seeing the home itself so dismal in its neglected condition, she will not be able to find anything attractive in it; nor will she feel the slightest inclination for the austerities of housework, any appreciation of its dignity and beauty, any desire to devote herself to it one day as wife and mother.

The same is true of every class of society and of every condition of life, The worldly woman's daughter, seeing the management of the home left entirely in the hands of strangers while the mother busies herself with frivolous occupations and futile amusements, will follow her example; she will want her own freedom as soon as possible, she will want —according to that unfortunate expression— "to live her own life". How, in such circumstances, can she possibly conceive the desire of becoming one day a true "domina", mistress of a home in a family which is happy, prosperous and worthy of the name?

As for the working classes, obliged to earn their daily bread, careful reflection would perhaps convince the housewife that in many cases the additional wages, which she earns by working away from home, are soon swallowed up by other expenses and even by ruinous waste in housekeeping. The daughter, who also goes out to work in factory, shop or office, finds herself deafened by the turmoil in the midst of which she lives; dazzled by the glamor of a tawdry luxury; hungry for equivocal pleas-

197 [*Id.*]

ures which distract without giving satisfaction or repose; frequenting the music halls and dancing palaces which, often for purposes of party propaganda, are springing up everywhere to corrupt the morals of the young. She is a "lady of fashion" now, and has no use for the moral standards of two centuries ago. How can she fail to find her modest home uninviting and even more grim than it is in reality! To take any pleasure in her home, and to want to make one for herself in the future, she would have to be able to counterbalance a natural impression by a serious intellectual and moral outlook, by the strength of mind that springs from a religious education and a supernatural ideal. But what sort of religious education, in conditions such as these, can she have received?

And this is not all. Her mother with the passing of the years has become old before her time; she is worn out and broken by sorrows, anxieties and work that has overtaxed her strength. When she sees her daughter return home very late at night, far from finding in her a prop and a support, she must herself arise and discharge all the duties of a domestic servant for one who is unaccustomed and unequal to the work of a woman and housewife. The father will be no better off when advancing years, illness, infirmity, unemployment have forced him to depend for his meager support on the good or ill will of his children. How is the august and sacred authority of father and mother dethroned from the seat of its majesty!»[198]

All these evils are deeply deplorable. But it would be useless to preach the return of woman to home while those conditions that compel her to stay away from it still remain, since she has ordinarily been obliged to leave it owing to her permanent anxiety about the daily bread.

5.7.5. *THE ACTION OF WOMEN IN PUBLIC LIFE*

In the current disorder of the world, the destiny of woman, the family and human relations is at stake. Then, every woman

«without exception is under an obligation — a strict obligation of conscience, mind you! — not to remain aloof; every woman must go into action, each in her own way, and join in stemming the tides which threaten to engulf the home, in fighting the doctrines which undermine its foundations, in preparing, organizing and completing its restoration.

198 [*Women's Duties in Social and Political Life.*]

This is one motive, calling the Catholic woman to enter on the new path now opening to her activity. But there is another: her dignity as a woman. It is for her to work with man for the welfare of the civitas in which she enjoys a dignity equal with his, and here each sex has its part to play according to its nature, its distinctive qualities, its physical, intellectual and moral capabilities. Both sexes have the right and the duty to work together for the good of society, for the good of the nation. But it is clear that while man is by temperament more suited to deal with external affairs and public business, generally speaking the woman has a deeper insight for understanding the delicate problems of domestic and family life, and a surer touch in solving them —which, of course, is not to deny that some women can show great ability in every sphere of public life. [...]

And where should we find these women if not especially [We do not, of course, say exclusively][199] among those to whom We have been alluding: those upon whom the force of circumstances has imposed a mysterious vocation; those whom events have destined to a life of solitude which was not in their thoughts or aspirations, and which threatened to be nothing more than a selfishly useless and purposeless existence? [...] Thus a wide field is opened to woman's activity an activity primarily intellectual or primarily practical, according to the capabilities and qualities of each individual. [...]

This direct action, this effective co-operation in social and political life, in no way alters the distinctive character of woman's activity. Associated with the work of man in the sphere of civil institutions, she will apply herself especially to matters calling for tact, delicacy, the maternal instinct, rather than administrative rigidity. In such questions as those of woman's dignity, a girl's honor and integrity, the protection and education of the child, who better than a woman can understand what is needed? And what a number of problems there are of this kind which require the attention of government and legislature! In the suppression of licentious behavior, for example, only a woman has the gift which can temper firmness with kindness without sacrifice of efficiency; in dealing with morally abandoned children, only a woman will know how to save them from humiliation and have them trained to a decent life and to the practice of the religious and civic virtues; only she can be truly successful in administering orphanages, in welfare work for released prisoners, and rescue work for fallen girls; she alone can give true expression to the lament of a mother's heart when she sees a totalitarian State—call it by what name you will—trying to rob her of the right to educate her children»[200].

199 [This phrase is included, with the brackets, in the Papal document.]
200 [*Id.*]

The social and political activity of women greatly influences the legislation of the State and the administration of local bodies.

«Consequently the vote is for the Catholic woman an important means of fulfilling her strict obligations of conscience, especially at the present time. For it is the proper duty of the State and of politics to assure for families of every class in the community the conditions in which they can develop as economic, juridical and moral units. Then will the family be really the vital nucleus of a society in which human beings honorably earn their temporal and eternal welfare. This every woman understands, if she is truly a woman, what she does not and cannot understand is that politics should mean the dominance of one class over the others, an ambitious striving for an ever greater economic and national ascendancy, on whatever pretext it is sought. For she knows that this sort of politics leads to civil strife, open or disguised, to a constant accumulation of armaments, and so to a perpetual danger of war; she knows by experience that this sort of politics is in any case detrimental to the family, which has to pay dear for it with its property and its blood. Therefore no wise woman favors a policy of class-war or belligerency. Her path to the voting booth is the path of peace; and to that path she will keep, in the interests of the family and its welfare, refusing her support to any tendency, from whatever quarter it may come, which would subordinate the internal or external peace of the nation to any selfish desires for domination»[201].

«Let all, then, join together, if need be even at the cost of serious loss, so that they may save themselves and all human society. In this union of minds and of forces, those who glory in the Christian name ought surely to take the foremost place, remembering the illustrious examples of the Apostolic age, when "the multitude of believers had but one heart and one soul" (Acts iv. 32), but besides these, all whoever sincerely acknowledge God and honor Him from their heart should lend their aid in order that mankind may be saved from the great peril impending over all. For since all human authority must needs rest on the recognition of God, as on the firm foundation of any civil order, those who would not have all things overturned and all laws abrogated, must strive strenuously to prevent the enemies of religion from giving effect to the plans which they have so openly and so vehemently proclaimed»[202].

201 [*Id.*]

202 [Pius XI, Encyclical on The Sacred Heart *Caritate Christi Compulsi* (3 May 1932) § 12, at The Holy See, http://w2.vatican.va/content/pius-xi/en/encyclicals/documents/hf_p-xi_enc_03051932_caritate-christi-compulsi.html (hereinafter referred to as *Caritate Christi Compulsi*).]

Chapter 4

Civil Society. The State

1

Elements of the State

«The State is made up of three elements: a community, a territory, and an authority.

As a *community*, the State is differentiated from other human groupings in the temporal order by its extent, and by its higher aim. It comprises, and within certain limits, it governs families, townships, and a diversity of institutions arising, for instance, from the following of a particular calling, from the need for co-operative help, or from the pursuit in common of some science or art.

The State is sovereign within its *territory*, in the sense that in the temporal order it does not depend in any way upon a super-State. Yet it has with other States relations of interdependence which need to be regulated by supra-national juridical bodies.

The *authority* of the State has as its function to direct the common good of the members that compose it»[203].

2

The Nature of the State

Fr. Antoine defines civil society as: «a complete society, made up of a multitude of families joining forces in the pursuit of the temporal common good»[204]. Let us analyze the terms of the definition:

- *Complete* society: is a society independent of any other, as regards its own sphere of action. It is provided with all the resources necessary for its development and activity.

- A society *composed of a multitude of families*: civil society is not made up of a multitude of individuals, but it is the normal development of the family. Society takes care of the needs and aspirations that families cannot meet on their own.

203 [*Id.* §§ 34-37.]

204 [Hurtado is referring to Charles Antoine, S.J., (1847-1921), Professor of Moral Theology and author of *Cours d'Économie Sociale* (*Course of Social Economics*) (1896). The definition of civil society quoted here appears in that book, page 50 of the 1921 edition, which the editors have, here, translated from the French.]

- The pursuit of *temporal common good*: society's own end is all that concerns human activity in the terrestrial field. This excludes only what concerns the supernatural order, which belongs to the Church. The temporal common good includes not only material interests, but also intellectual and moral matters; in a word, everything that constitutes civilization.

The concept of common good indicates that the State is concerned only with the common interests of the members of civil society, not with the interests of each one of them: their particular goods. Thus, for example, the State is not directly responsible for giving housing or work to each citizen: these each must procure for himself. On the other hand, the State is responsible for securing conditions of security, protection, education, communication facilities, pensions and welfare, which a person can use, through his activities, to acquire the goods he needs. Thus, individual happiness will largely depend on general well-being as directed by the State.

3
The State's Personality

«The State is perpetual by nature. It follows from this that the treaties it makes, and the financial and other obligations it assumes, are binding, whatever may be the changes that occur in the living persons who are its embodiment, or in the political forms in which it is clothed.

The State possesses moral personality. It is indeed composed of substantially distinct individuals, but these form a body unified by the convergence of their rational activities towards the end for which they are constituted a body politic.

Hence the State, being a unified body of substantially distinct individuals, has and can have no more than human rights and duties, but on a larger and wider scale than any individual. It is therefore subject to the same moral law and the same rule of justice as individuals, and in the sphere of its relations with bodies like itself —that is, with other States— it cannot evade the obligation of respecting that law and these rules.

It is indispensable for the attainment of the social end that the State should be legally subject to laws in the same way as individuals, though in a more extended sphere and with suitable modifications.

This personality does not proceed from positive law, but from nature itself»[205].

205 [*A Code of Social Principles* §§ 43-44.]

4
Origin of the State

It has been debated, for a very long time, whether civil society is the outright invention of man or whether it has a foundation in natural law, prior to the will of man, which of course gives a civil society its specific existence.

If civil society is a human invention, man can shape it the way he wants, as an artist can make whatever he wants of his artwork. If it is a matter of natural right, men should accommodate themselves to the natural order that is disclosed by reason, which is nothing other than the Creator's will. This would indicate that society must, in its organization, recognize an authority whose right to command would ultimately come from God, and that its laws cannot be shaped by caprice, but by the common good.

Rousseau, in his *Discours sur l'inégalité parmi les hommes*[206], and, above all, in his *Contrat Social*[207], has been the champion of the purely human origin of civil society resting only on the arbitrary will of the contractors. According to Rousseau, the primitive state of man, the one which made him truly happy, was that of total independence. The only natural society is family, and that only while the child needs his parents. But, unfortunately, the stronger try to reduce others to slavery, hence a convention to establish peace was imposed. The whole problem of the Social Contract is to find a form of association that could defend the person and property of each associate, in such a way that each one, while uniting with the others, would obey only himself, and could be as free as he was before. By this association a moral and collective body is produced that is composed of as many members as can vote in the assembly. The law is the expression of this general will and, therefore, is always just and imposes absolute obedience on all. The majority creates justice and law. It is easy to see the abuses this theory may produce and which abuses it has, in fact, given rise to in the course of history.

In opposition to the School of the Social Contract, Catholic morality affirms that civil society is a natural fact willed by God, as a complement to and

206 [Jean-Jacques Rousseau, *Discours sur l'origine et les Fondements de l'inégalité parmi les Hommes* (*Discourse on the Origin and Foundation of Inequality Among Men*) (1754).]

207 [Jean-Jacques Rousseau, *Du Contrat Social; ou Principes du Droit Politique* (*On the Social Contract, or Principles of Political Law*) (1762).]

expansion of the family destined to allow man to acquire new resources to obtain the fulfillment of his temporal common good.

What makes man unite with his fellow men is not a covenant, of which there is no memory or clue in history, but the *social instinct,* that leads him to complete himself through his fellow men. Hence, since the beginning of history, we see man socially united to others and never living a solitary life. This association allows its members *protection* against the abuses of force, quiet possession of their well-being and *expansion* of their activities. Men cannot deploy all their energies within the restricted field of family life. Man needs deeper and differentiated knowledge of his fellow men in order to enrich his life. Great works will be carried out, going far beyond the possibilities of the family: ports, roads, channels, electricity, nuclear power … all of these require a union of forces under a common authority. This makes us realize that the union that men have always engaged in is not the product of an arbitrary desire of man —something he merely invented— but the fulfillment of the deepest inclinations placed in his soul by God: that is, the realization of a natural tendency.

As a natural fact, society has laws that cannot be ignored without negating it: such as, for example, the necessity of an authority dedicated to the service of man and family, whose needs society is called upon to provide for and not to replace or undermine.

In the encyclical *Mit Brennender Sorge,* His Holiness Pius XI defends the concept of natural law against the racist totalitarianism that identified as a right whatever is useful to the nation:

> «To overlook this truth is to forget that the real common good ultimately takes its measure from man's nature, which balances personal rights and social obligations, and from the purpose of society, established for the benefit of human nature. Society, was intended by the Creator for the full development of individual possibilities, and for the social benefits, which by a give and take process, every one can claim for his own sake and that of others. Higher and more general values, which collectivity alone can provide, also derive from the Creator for the good of man, and for the full development, natural and supernatural, and the realization of his perfection. To neglect this order is to shake the pillars on which society rests, and to compromise social tranquility, security and existence»[208].

208 [*Mit Brennender Sorge* § 30.]

5
Authority in Society

a) There is no society without authority.

Philosophers have pondered over many problems that relate to authority in society. We will leave aside the purely speculative matters, stopping only on those that have a practical effect.

Catholic morality's first affirmation in this respect, is that *no society can subsist without authority*, whose mission is to imprint effectively upon each member the same drive towards the common good. Authority, as well as society, comes from nature and, therefore, from God himself. «An immediate consequence of this principle is that resistance to authority is resistance to the order established by God. "He that resisteth the power, resisteth the ordinance of God"[209]. Another consequence concerns the authority itself; he who bears it is appointed by God to serve the people. Public service is the sole reason for his power, and defines its limits»[210].

b) The divine origin of authority.

«Though authority comes from God, it does not takes the form of a gift to this individual or to that family. God does not point out the one who is to hold power. He has only done so exceptionally in the history of the Jews, on account of the special calling of that people.

Nor does God determine the title of the supreme authority, nor the forms of the constitution. These contingent matters come from human activities ...»[211] For example, they could come from people's ancient traditions, from a constitution legitimately approved or even from people's approval of rulers who came to power arbitrarily.

Taking into consideration what was already said, it is clear why it is affirmed that power has a divine origin. All rulers are of divine right, in the sense that from God and God alone they receive the power to command, but they are not

209 [The Code of Social Principle here cites: «(Rom. Xii, 2)».]
210 [*A Code of Social Principles* § 38.]
211 [*Id.* §§ 39 -40.]

of divine right in the sense that the form of government that each of them represents has been preferred and willed by God. The Creator leaves to each nation the care of choosing its form of government and determining its rulers, but once the choice is made it is God who confers the necessary authority to exercise this power in conformity to the constitution of each state.

c) Different forms of government.

The legitimacy of power is, as a result, not tied to any form of government: there is no monarchy, no aristocracy and no democracy of divine right. The Catholic Church, in its official relations with the states, does not take into account the forms that differentiate them. As a consequence, there is in fact a perfect coexistence of Catholics in a monarchical society like the British, in a democratic republic like the United States, under the Hindu regime or under the command of the Emperor of Japan. In all these regimes we find strong Catholics collaborating, even under pagan authorities, with the temporal common good of their nations. In some countries, France mainly, it was difficult for many Catholics to give up the idea that Catholicism was tied to the monarchy, but the Roman Pontiffs, especially Leo XIII, have firmly insisted on the doctrine just set forth.

> «This, then, is the teaching of the Catholic Church concerning the constitution and government of the State. By the words and decrees just cited, if judged dispassionately, no one of the several forms of government is in itself condemned, inasmuch as none of them contains anything contrary to Catholic doctrine, and all of them are capable, if wisely and justly managed, to insure the welfare of the State. Neither is it blameworthy in itself, in any manner, for the people to have a share greater or less, in the government: for at certain times, and under certain laws, such participation may not only be of benefit to the citizens, but may even be of obligation»[212].
>
> «In the speculative order, therefore, Catholics, like other citizens, have full liberty to prefer one form of government to another, precisely in virtue of the fact that none of these special forms is in itself contrary to the rule of right reason, or to the maxims of Christian doctrine»[213].

212 [*Immortale Dei* § 36.]

213 [*A Code of Social Principles* § 41.]

6
Position with Respect to Established Power

In matters of authority, the citizen is frequently dedicated to practical realities. «[E]ach one ought to accept the established government, and to attempt none other than legal means to overturn it, or change its form. To acknowledge for individuals the liberty of opposing by violence, either the form of government, or the person at its head, would be equivalent to setting up a permanent condition of disorder and revolt in the body politic. Only an insupportable tyranny, or a flagrant violation of the most obvious essential rights of citizens, can give, after other means of redress have failed, the right of revolt»[214].

Therefore, when a government is installed in power by a triumphant revolution or in any other way, and directs its activities towards the common good, it is the duty of all citizens to obey it. That government has the right to command: otherwise society could not exist with the tranquility that is needed to pursue the common good. Catholics cannot use their religion to support the overthrow of the government, except in the above-mentioned instances of unbearable tyranny or flagrant violation of human rights essential to the person. Thus, the practice of minor injustices or abuses, no matter how painful they may be, does not authorize the immense damage of a revolution. By peaceful means within their reach, they can bring their fellow citizens to pressure the government to respect the law, but they cannot plunge the nation into chaos.

7
Theories as to the Inmediate Origin of Power in Society

Having discarded Rousseau's and Hobbes's doctrine of the purely human origin of society, Catholic writers try to explain where the power to command originates. Does the ruler receive his power directly from God, or through society, for whose good God has constituted authority?

214 [*Id.*]

7.1. THEORY OF HISTORICAL-LEGAL EVENTS

There is a theory that is often called one of the «historical-legal events»[215]. It excludes any idea of a convention or pact between the nation and the person who exercises the power. It is enough that at a given moment an event occurs that makes it necessary for this individual to exercise power or that a specific form of government is established, such that the ruler receives directly from God the necessary authority for the governance of the country and others consequently, owe obedience to him. If at any given moment a person appears who, given his personal qualities, appears as the only one capable of securing order, he must assume the power that God confers directly on him for the common good of society.

This system erects realities into law, without a principle's appearing that justifies it. While circumstances may show that a particular person or form of government should be chosen, it does not follow that the specific person acquires by himself the right to become an authority that others must obey.

7.2. THEORY OF THE SOCIAL PACT

Cardinal Bellarmine[216] and Father Suarez[217] developed this theory. Both were Jesuits: the former from the sixteenth century and the latter from the seventeenth century.

This theory demands, for the legitimate transmission of power, the nation's assent by an explicit or implicit act. Initially, so to speak, God grants power to society in an indeterminate manner, so society may designate an authority to govern it and the rules to which it must adhere. This is stated in the oral or written constitution of the country. Then, society detaches itself from its power and transmits it to the chosen authority, which will have the right to command in the name of God; others will have to obey it. When a new form of government is established by usurpation or an act of violence, it will not be legitimate until the country has confirmed its authority at least by tacit acceptance. This doctrine,

215 [The manuscript says: «Teoría del hecho jurídico-histórico».]

216 [Roberto Bellarmino, S.J., (1542-1621) Italian Cardinal, Professor of Theology, Rector of the Roman College and Doctor of the Church. Bellarmino was one of the most important figures of the Counter-Reformation. He wrote *Dottrina Cristiana* (*Christian Doctrine*) (1597), which was very influential during the sixteenth and seventeenth centuries and has been translated into fifty languages.]

217 [Francisco Suárez, S.J., (see footnote 25) in his *Tractatus de Legibus ac Deo Legislatore: in Decem Libros Distributus* (*Treatise of the Laws and God the Lawgiver*) (1612), developed the theory that all legislative and paternal power derives from God's eternal law.]

unlike the previous one, requires the consent of the nation for the legitimate exercise of authority. Sometimes this consent will be given much against subjects' wishes, only to preserve the common good. Some have introduced a different modality into this theory, proposing the doctrine of *designation*: society does no more than designate authority, but power comes to it directly from God, without passing through the people.

This theory has nothing in common with Rousseau's, for whom power does not come in any form from God, but is the pure expression of the general will, the sum of individual wills, revocable at will. The rulers would not have their own authority, but would be the temporary delegates of the nation, in whose hands power remains in an inalienable form.

This doctrine is not to be confused with that condemned in the letter on *Le Sillon*[218]. What was condemned there was the doctrine that the people, as a nation, is the primary source of power, independent of God; and that the people, as a special class, have the inalienable possession of this power and therefore are the only ones who can confer it. In the doctrine of Bellarmine and Suarez, power comes from God, who grants it not to the people as opposed to other classes, for example to the aristocracy, but to the people as a nation comprising all classes.

Saying that God gives authority does not indicate that God approves all the acts of the ruler, who must give account of his acts to God. But the power to oblige people with regard to the common good comes from God, from whom also comes the social inclination of man: this gives nobility to obedience.

8
The Mission of Authority

The Code of Social Principles of Mechlin synthesizes this point with extraordinary clarity:

> «Authority being the director of the common good, must in the first place protect and guarantee the rights of the individuals and groups which it envisages; for the violation of such rights has profound and evil reaction upon the common good of which the State is guardian, while, on the contrary, respect for the rights of everyone helps

218 [See footnotes 56 and 57.]

increase the well-being of all. There must, therefore, be a power able to prevent abuses, to restrain the unruly and to punish offenders.

The authority of the State should also set itself to encourage the growth of material, intellectual, and moral good in the whole body of members of the community.

It does not follow from this that the State ought to make provision for everything in every branch of human activity.

Firstly, it is not concerned with leading men to eternal happiness. The Church has the care of this matter, though the State can and should give its aid, without taking the place of the Church.

Again, in the temporal order, the State, in its capacity as guardian of the common good, encounters private initiative, both individual and collective, and this also has a certain power of attaining good, either shared by many, or even common to the whole social body.

When private initiative is effectual, the State should do nothing that may embarrass or stifle the spontaneous action of individuals or of groups. But when it is inadequate the State should stimulate, aid, and co-ordinate it, and if necessary, supplement and complete it.

This way of caring for the common good of temporal communities is but an imitation of God's action in the general government of the world. He enlists every force, including that of the free human will, to assist the designs of His saving will.

In the same manner the State will bring the central power to co-operate with all national activities, according to a general plan whose main outlines it ought to fix, and which it will leave as far as possible to be carried out by individuals.

Human personality has rights antecedent to, and above, all positive law. These rights—individual or collective—have their origin in human nature, which is rational and free.

The law ought to protect the liberty of the person, not only against attacks from without, but also against the misuse of liberty itself. For every use of liberty can degenerate into licence, so that it is the task of the law to define the limits and control of the exercise of rights.

Modern political constitutions are particularly inclined to emphasize and proclaim the colloraries both of personal liberty and of equality in nature which are common to all men. In this they have often been influenced by philosophical systems which exaggerate the autonomy of the human person.

In enunciating and regulating by law the corollaries of personal liberty, legislators should never lose sight of the fact that human liberty is liable to go wrong, and that in consequence it is important not to confuse the use and the abuse of powers which it implies.

For this reason the use of rights of ownership, of publishing one's view in the press or by teaching, and of associating with one's fellows, is in principle only lawful within the limits of well-being.

It is the business of authority to define the frontiers beyond which the use of a supposed right becomes licence. It is only in order to avoid a greater evil, or to obtain or preserve a greater good, that the public authority may "use tolerance in regard to certain things contrary to truth and justice". (Encyclical *Libertas* of Leo XIII.)

In enunciating and legally settling the corollaries of equality in nature, such as equality before the law, before justice, in taxation, and in public administration, the legislator must take account not only of equality in nature, but also of the accidental inequalities that make individuals more or less fitted to exercise this or that faculty. For instance, it should not, under a pretext of equality, allow everyone, whether learned or ignorant, to practice medicine»[219].

This exposition allows us to see how the State is not an end in itself, but that it is at the service of the nation, namely, of the community. The State must, therefore, respect individual freedoms and rights that are compatible with the demands of the common good. The State would be wrong if it acted as the dispenser of personal freedoms: these are prior to the State and remain as something sacred before it. Therefore, the State cannot restrict them, except insofar as indispensable for the good of society. If in extraordinary circumstances a restriction of these rights is imposed, a situation cannot be considered normal, and the State must pursue normality as soon as possible. When truly legitimate civil liberties are threatened, political freedoms may be temporarily suspended, for example in the case of an attempted coup that tended to subvert public order. The State can never put itself at the service of a class or a party, it must govern for the good of all and it must leave to the citizens the largest amount of freedom compatible with the public order and the general good of the country. The dignity of man demands that the adult be treated as an adult and that he be called to participate in an important way in public affairs, at least in the election of his representatives.

219 [*A Code of Social Principles* §§ 45-52.]

Assuring tranquility, the State must achieve public prosperity, collaborate in the work of civilization and stimulate and coordinate private initiatives. Progress depends, first and foremost, on the genius and efforts of the people. The State cannot create progress but can remove obstacles and create a climate appropriate for development. This supposes that the State's leaders have a clear vision, a spirit of initiative and a permanent vigilance not to be transformed into a formal and sterile bureaucracy.

The danger of State absorption is very real. The State tends to substitute itself for individuals, whom it must stimulate but never absorb or replace. Ordinarily, private initiatives work in a more economical and efficient way than the State, as long as they are not obstructed. On the other hand, there are general works, such as those of meteorological stations, agricultural experimentation, studies on irrigation, etc., which involve vast resources and which by their very general nature belong more to the State than to individuals. The same is true of the proper functioning of consular services, customs and public roads, in which the action of the State is irreplaceable and indispensable for the common good.

In problems that relate to intellectual and moral life, the State must respect and encourage private initiative, since the most directly personal values of man are at stake. In such matters, the intervention of an anonymous collectivity like the State can be misguided and even tyrannical. In educational matters, the State has the right to intervene because the common good is at stake and therefore, may set a minimum level of compulsory instruction, but this cannot in any way justify an educational monopoly. The State may collaborate with the family, oblige the family to perform its duty, subsidize schools and open others to supply the deficiencies of private education: this principle is valid for all levels of instruction, even higher education.

As for the moral life, the State must combat dissipation in the streets, publications and films. It must protect the child and the woman and encourage the work of the Church, since a moral life is largely a reflection of elevated convictions.

The State cannot fulfill its mission in the same way everywhere. The more civilized a country is, the more it must encourage private initiative and utilize its resources; the younger and more primitive a nation is, as in colonial countries, the greater must be the intervention of the State to advance civilization and put the people in a position to enjoy general progress.

9
Legislative, Executive and Judicial Powers

Supreme power is exercised in three ways: promulgating general norms as to what must be done and avoided: *legislative power*; securing compliance with the laws and enforcing them: *executive power*; and effectively suppressing the abuses that disturb the established order: *judicial power*.

If any of these powers were lacking, state action would be insufficient or ineffective. In modern states, governmental action requires a multitude of virtuous and competent officials: their lack of competence or honesty would lead to significant damage.

From the point of view of social morality, two matters seem to be of special importance: the right to punish and the value of laws.

9.1. PENALTIES. THE DEATH PENALTY

Several partial theories try to explain the authority's right to impose penalties. Some say that penalties restore the violated order through the punishment of the guilty party, others indicate that penalties defend society by preventing the commission of new crimes owing to fear of punishment, and others say that penalties rehabilitate the guilty person by purging his crime and by instilling a desire for a better life and an appropriate education. None of these aspects is complete: but taken together they are the bases of the right to impose punishments.

As for the death penalty, one wishes that it were unnecessary. Laws that have suppressed the death penalty cannot be criticized, but neither can it be said that the imposition of the death penalty contradicts the natural law when there is no other effective way of defending society against incorrigible aggressors. Nonetheless, it must be imposed with extreme moderation and equity, because the evils it entails are irremediable. It is to be hoped that mankind will progress so much that it will become convinced that we can survive without such an atrocious sanction. Much has been said about the legality of *torture* to obtain the confession of a guilty party. Aristotle maintained that it was licit. Cicero, Seneca and Saint Augustine denied this. In theory, today the death penalty is abolished, but unfortunately the police apply it illegally and in concentration camps it has been used and continues to be used in the same way as in the darkest periods of history.

The right to impose punishments must be accompanied by a system of prisons that are schools for the rehabilitation of prisoners rather than schools for crime, as unfortunately they too often are. The rulers bear a tremendous responsibility for the growing corruption of those who should regenerate themselves in prison; prisoners are now degenerating and conceiving hatred of society.

9.2. LEGISLATIVE POWER. THE FORCE OF THE LAW

There is no similarity between the atheistic concept of law as an imposition of the will of a majority, and the Christian concept of law, which is respectful of authority, but also of the inviolable right of conscience.

The ultimate basis of the obligatory character of law lies in God's will that imperatively promulgates the order that He wishes to see rule the world. This providential plan, in which every creature receives its law according to its nature, is in God, and is what we call *the eternal law*, source of all obligation and of all right.

For man, this plan of God is promulgated in our consciences by the *natural law* in the form of general indications of what we must do and avoid, and in each particular case shows us the moral character of our acts. The human conscience apprehends such moral principles, imposed by a higher will that aims at an objective order. If he acts on those principles or violates them, the person experiences satisfaction or remorse of conscience.

Every social group needs more detailed prescriptions than these general norms: these prescriptions are the *positive laws*, which oblige in conscience because they emanate from a legitimate power willed by God to ensure order in the world. The law, following St. Thomas, is an ordinance of reason for the common good by one who has legitimate authority[220]. From the moment that the commands of the authority cease to be ordinances of reason, they lose their true nature and cease to obligate. The law promulgated by the legitimate authority is presumed to be in accordance with reason. Therefore, it will be necessary to prove that the law contradicts reason in order to authorized its non-compliance. In our times this problem is more real than previously, because of the continuous abuses and violations of natural and positive law committed by all totalitarianisms.

220 [*Summa Theologica*, I-II, Q. 90.]

«The authority of the State is far from being unlimited. It can ordain all that contributes to the common good of its members and to society, and such things only.

Material force is doubtless a means so indispensable to authority, that, if deprived of the use of that force, a government would be incapable of exercising its function.

But the use of force is subordinate to the end of society, which is itself derived from reason»[221].

The reconciliation of authority and freedom is a very difficult problem: the first ensures a strong government; the second guarantees the independence of the individual. A combination of these two elements is indispensable, although the requirements of the common good are difficult to determine in specific situations.

9.3. THE OBLIGATION OF UNJUST LAWS

To what extent does an unjust law oblige, if it offends the conscience, violates the superior rights of God or the norms of justice? Such a law does not oblige, because it is not a law. In certain cases the subject may submit to an unjust law to avoid a greater evil, provided it is not in opposition to a superior law and only violates private interests. Nonetheless, if the precept is intrinsically evil, we must remember the whole Christian tradition: «we must obey God rather than men» (Acts 5:29), as the Apostles, who knew how to die in defense of the integrity of their consciences, demonstrated[222].

His Holiness Leo XIII in *Sapientiae Christianae* summarizes the doctrine of Church:

«It is a high crime indeed to withdraw allegiance from God in order to please men, an act of consummate wickedness to break the laws of Jesus Christ, in order to yield obedience to earthly rulers, or, under pretext of keeping the civil law, to ignore the rights of the Church; "we ought to obey God rather than men"[223]. This answer, which of old Peter and the other Apostles were used to give the civil authorities who enjoined un-

221 [*A Code of Social Principles* § 42.]

222 [In the manuscript at this point Hurtado includes: «(Textos. Cfr. Lallement)» He is referring to Abbé Daniel-Louis Lallement (1892-1977), French theologian, sociologist and philosopher, who taught extensively on Saint Thomas of Aquinas at the *Insitut Catholique de Paris.* At the request of the Assembly of Cardinals and Archbishops of France, he wrote a book which was a synthesis of Catholic social doctrine at that time, called *Principes Catholiques d'Action Civique* (*Catholic Principles of Civic Action*) (1935).]

223 [The following footnote appears in the Encyclical: «Acts 5:29».]

righteous things, we must, in like circumstances, give always and without hesitation. No better citizen is there, whether in time of peace or war, than the Christian who is mindful of his duty; but such a one should be ready to suffer all things, even death itself, rather than abandon the cause of God or of the Church.

Hence, they who blame, and call by the name of sedition, this steadfastness of attitude in the choice of duty have not rightly apprehended the force and nature of true law. We are speaking of matters widely known, and which We have before now more than once fully explained. Law is of its very essence a mandate of right reason, proclaimed by a properly constituted authority, for the common good. But true and legitimate authority is void of sanction, unless it proceeds from God, the supreme Ruler and Lord of all. The Almighty alone can commit power to a man over his fellow men[224]; nor may that be accounted as right reason which is in disaccord with truth and with divine reason; nor that held to be true good which is repugnant to the supreme and unchangeable good, or that wrests aside and draws away the wills of men from the charity of God. Hallowed, therefore, in the minds of Christians is the very idea of public authority, in which they recognize some likeness and symbol as it were of the Divine Majesty, even when it is exercised by one unworthy. A just and due reverence to the laws abides in them, not from force and threats, but from a consciousness of duty; "for God hath not given us the spirit of fear"[225]. But, if the laws of the State are manifestly at variance with the divine law, containing enactments hurtful to the Church, or conveying injunctions adverse to the duties imposed by religion, or if they violate in the person of the Supreme Pontiff the authority of Jesus Christ, then, truly, to resist becomes a positive duty, to obey, a crime; a crime, moreover, combined with misdemeanor against the State itself, inasmuch as every offense leveled against religion is also a sin against the State»[226].

9.4. CRIMINAL LAWS

Many moralists say that penal laws are those that the legislator imposes, not with the intention of obliging in conscience, but only in order to penalize those who transgress. Those who have developed the concept of the «purely criminal

224 [The following footnote appears in the Encyclical: «Note the extreme importance of this principle; it justifies the doctrine according to which the only conceivable foundation of political authority must be divine in origin».]

225 [The following footnote appears in the Encyclical: «2 Tim. 1:7».]

226 [Leo XIII, Encyclical on Christians as Citizens *Sapientiae Christianae* (10 January 1890) §§ 7, 8 and 9, at The Holy See, http://w2.vatican.va/content/leo-xiii/en/encyclicals/documents/hf_l-xiii_enc_10011890_sapientiae-christianae.html (hereinafter referred to as *Sapientiae Christianae*).]

laws», find it very difficult to distinguish those laws from others. Most of the criteria suggested by them are problematic; but above all, the very idea of purely criminal law is even more controvertible and there is a strong current in our times against the acceptance of such a category. Because, how can a law oblige a person in conscience to accept and comply with a penalty, which is secondary, when the primary part of the law does not oblige? Furthermore, could there be a legislator who enacted a law without the intention of obliging? What could be thought of a legislator who only valued the sanctions sections of a statute? The concept, then, of purely criminal law must be dismissed and replaced by the doctrine that all kinds of laws —civil, customs, tax, etc.— oblige in conscience, provided that such laws are just.

Is it therefore a serious offense to commit an important violation of the laws that some call criminal, such as customs laws or tax laws? And if the matter is trivial, is the offense minor? Fr. Azpiazu, S.J., in his book *Professional Economic Morality*, solves the problem:

«To be rigorous in this matter would be to make life impossible; to be lax would be like throwing away all the laws.

The solution of these questions must be developed in light of the common good which is the primary aim of the law.

The law must be appraised in each particular instance according to the common good.

There are instances in which the common good orders things in a clear way. Moralists say that the common good clearly requires and establishes rules: for example, certain laws of property, such as acquisition of title by prescription, eviction, good faith possession, etc., in order to avoid the problems that would multiply in an amazing way in the absence of clear and specific legal norms to define property. That is why the obligation to comply with them is clear.

But there are other cases in which the common good is also the aim of the law, but an aim that is obscured or diminished. Such a situation is presented by the tax laws, which include a multitude of instances that under *epikeia* can be classified as exceptions.

The common good is the aim of the law, but the common good cannot be opposed to the particular good of any large group and in circumstances not foreseen by the law. Although the common good is superior to a particular good, it is in truly serious circumstances and supposing that all cooperate to bear the burdens of the same common good that is not to be supported only by the shoulders of sincere Catholics[227]. See these ideas in St. Thomas (II-II, q 120, a.1).

Let's briefly discuss the justice of the civil law.

Saint Thomas, in enumerating the various headings under which the justice of the law is to be appraised, states that "laws are said to be just, both from the end, when, to wit, they are ordained to the common good —and from their author, that is to say, when the law that is made does not exceed the power of the lawgiver— and from their form, when, to wit, burdens are laid on the subjects, according to an equality of proportion and with a view to the common good"[228]. (I, 2, q 96, a.4).

In fact, positive law is, by its very nature, addressed to millions of men in cases and circumstances that are very diverse and unstudiable by the legislator. Positive law is necessarily rigid and impossible to adapt to particular cases, so its observance may even be, in particular cases, an obstacle to the greater good. In such a case, one is not oblige to observe the law when to do so would be excessively inconvenient, even if the transgression of the law was an external legal fault that could be punished by law.

Therefore, it is indisputably necessary to resort to *epikeia* or to equity in civil law. And although there is undoubtedly a strong danger of delusion when one judges one's own case, the danger is no greater than that of a bad formation of conscience: a danger that must be avoided by the advice of wise men or the like. In sum: human law does not oblige one to bear a grave discomfort disproportionate to the nature of the law, if the reasonable presumption that had the legislator known of the case it would have covered it by the law. For this, an honest presumption seems sufficient.

This does not indicate a loosening of the obligation imposed by the law; on the contrary, it rather signifies a requirement as to what should be demanded of human law.

This weakness in human law is much larger in every law in the economic order, whether related to taxation or currency or the like, because the cases covered by these laws and those which the legislature cannot know about, are so different and almost infinite in number that it is impossible to cover them in one mandatory law.

Thus, according to Saint Thomas, it is necessary that the burdens of the law be justly proportioned; if they were not, the law would lack distributive fairness and would cease to be just.

227 [This sentence make no sense in Spanish either.]

228 [This internal quote was not taken from the Azpiazu text because it was unclear there, but from Saint Thomas of Aquinas's *Summa Theologica* I, II.]

And what about the case in which such proportionality is lacking (accidentally, but lacking), so that people of lax or evil conscience avoid the burdens associated with their fortunes and impose those burdens on other persons who have more sensitive consciences and who therefore must carry their own burdens and also the burdens of others who did not want to bear them? This is the case with many taxes necessarily imposed in the economy of the State, which are avoided by people with less demanding consciences and fall more heavily on the best citizens. May not these people also avoid themselves, as if excused from unjust abuse deliberately imposed by a State?

Alongside this problem there may be other similar ones, which are not within our competence.

The extent to which these laws oblige depends on the degree to which they have been adjusted to circumstances and accord to more or less extreme exigencies that human law cannot or does not know in advance, and on the various events that lead the individual to the formation of conscience in the light of the circumstances of each case.

Thus, without falling into the exaggerations of those, such as Fr. Alfonso de Castro, who maintained that the criminal law imposes an inexcusable obligation and those who believed every law is criminal, a person can have a clear conscience owing to *epikeia* and even disregard the existence of mere criminal laws while admitting their enforceability.

Nonetheless, whether criminal laws exist or not, the problem of conscience is resolved»[229].

10
State Intervention in Social Problems

10.1. RIGHT OF THE STATE TO INTERVENE

The Christian conception of the State's mission in social life avoids the liberal extreme, which absolutely rejects intervention, and the socialist extreme, which exaggerates that mission to the extent of becoming a Totalitarian State in which everything is the responsibility of the State[230].

229 [Joaquín Azpiazu, S.J., *Moral Profesional Económica* (*Economic Professional Morality*) pp. 38-41 (1942) (hereinafter referred to as *Economic Professional Morality*).]

230 In this chapter we follow closely that which J. Folliet explained in his *Morale Sociale*, Chap. IX, *La Corporation et l'Etat*. [Joseph Folliet (1903-1972) was a French priest, sociologist and writer. He was the co-founder of *Compagnons de Saint François* (*Companions of St. Francis*), a movement

Christian doctrine does not forget that the State is in charge of the common good, which includes economic prosperity and social justice. To ensure them, the intervention of authority is justified, especially because there is no opposition between the political and the economic, but subordination. Economic and social activities aim at the common good of society and they are directed to it as means to end.

«The duty of intervention does not mean statism. Frankly, this word is rather vague and the liberals use it to discredit the initiatives they dislike. It has to be specified by some designations. There is a statism of a socialist tendency, which is not necessarily totalitarian, and a totalitarian statism, like fascism, and even more, Bolshevik communism. Statism of a socialist tendency is manifested in an increasing intrusion of the State into economic life, and by a tendency to withdraw economic activity from the hands of the family, business and occupation and to entrust it to the direct management of the State: this statism increases nationalizations, state monopolies and administrative regulations. This tendency is dangerous because it leads the State to deal with affairs in which it is not competent and to take on a very heavy burden, which in the end falls on the taxpayers. On the other hand, statism transforms an increasing number of citizens into state officials, reduces personal initiative, removes influence from intermediary groups from which a person derives his freedom, and is oriented to a totalitarian statism. This is not a trend, but a theory: the fullness of existence is only possessed by the State. The individual exists only in the State and by the State: intermediate bodies must either be radically suppressed or sponsored by the State and absorbed into the State, from which they derive a participatory existance, revocable on command. [...]

Christian morality totally rejects these totalitarian arrangements. Though the State is in charge of the common good, it has no special responsibility for the particular good, which must be managed freely by legitimate owners, subject only to the restrictions and controls required by the general interest and if considerations of the common good require the recognition of additional, stronger, rights of other persons and intermediary bodies, it does not abolish the rights of any of them; on the contrary, the defense and vindication of just particular goods enter into the very notion of the common good.

The State, then, in Christian morality is neither liberalism's super-gendarme, nor statism's omniscient and omnipotent providence. The mission of the State is to assure private liberties the best conditions of exercise and to make them converge towards the common good. [...] This is what confers on the State the power to intervene in the field of private activity»[231].

Among French and Belgian Catholics in the last century and at the beginnings of the present one, there were two tendencies: the interventionist and the anti-interventionist. The so-called School of Angers was anti-interventionist, while the Liege school promoted State intervention. Today no conscientious Catholic denies the right of State intervention in the social problem: only the extent of this intervention is discussed.

10.2. THE FIELD OF STATE INTERVENTION

Leo XIII's *Rerum Novarum*, as Pius XI recognized forty years later, «boldly breaking through the confines imposed by Liberalism, fearlessly taught that government must not be thought a mere guardian of law and of good order, but rather must put forth every effort so that "through the entire scheme of laws and institutions ... both public and individual well-being may develop spontaneously out of the very structure and administration of the State"»[232].

Leo XIII recognizes, first of all, the State's right of direct and immediate intervention when the general interest or the good of a person or a community is violated or seriously threatened, in order to restore justice or prevent injustice. «Rulers should, nevertheless, anxiously safeguard the community and all its members; the community, because the conservation thereof is so emphatically the business of the supreme power, that the safety of the commonwealth is not only the first law, but it is a government's whole reason of existence; and the members, because both philosophy and the Gospel concur in laying down that the object of the government of the State should be, not the advantage of the ruler, but the benefit of those over whom he is placed ... Whenever the general interest or any particular class suffers, or is threatened with harm, which can in no other way be met or prevented, the public authority must step in to deal with it»[233].

of young workers for the peace and friendship of peoples, the editor of *Temps Présent* (*Present Times*), Director of *Semaines Sociales de France* after Marius Gonin and founder of *La Vie Catholique Illustrée* (*Illustrated Catholic Life*). He wrote more than sixty books; one of them is *Morale Sociale* (*Social Morality*) (1937).]

231 [Joseph Folliet, *Morale Sociale* (*Social Morality*) (1937), Volume II, Chapter XI, pp. 144-146. This passage was translated by the editors from the French edition.]

232 [*Quadragesimo Anno* § 25. At the end of the quoted passage there is a footnote that states in the Encyclical: «Encyclical, *On the Condition of Workers*, 48».]

233 [*Rerum Novarum* §§ 35-36.]

The Pope cites a few examples: if in workshops there were dangers to morals or if employers laid burdens upon their workmen which were unjust or imposed upon them conditions repugnant to their dignity as human beings, or if health were endangered by excessive labor or by work unsuited to sex or age. «[I]n such cases, there can be no question but that, within certain limits, it would be right to invoke the aid and authority of the law ... the law must not undertake more, nor proceed further, than is required for the remedy of the evil or the removal of the mischief»[234].

The action of the State just described could be said to be negative, but it must, in certain cases, exercise positive and indirect action. «The foremost duty, therefore, of the rulers of the State should be to make sure that the laws and institutions, the general character and administration of the commonwealth, shall be such as of themselves to realize public well-being and private prosperity. This is the proper scope of wise statesmanship and is the work of the rulers. Now a State chiefly prospers and thrives through moral rule, well-regulated family life, respect for religion and justice, the moderation and fair imposing of public taxes, the progress of the arts and of trade, the abundant yield of the land—through everything, in fact, which makes the citizens better and happier»[235].

Is there a direct and positive intervention of the State in economic life? Is a *directed economy* advisable? If by this we mean a detailed organization of the economic activities of private individuals by conforming them absolutely to the points of view of the government, directed economy is statism with all its dangers. If by «directed economy» we understand that the State, with the accord of occupational organizations, guides the general economy of the country and the movement of national and international exchange rates, and stimulates production when it is deficient, such direction is within the limits of justice, and rather than a directed economy, it deserves to be called an *organized economy*.

The direct and positive intervention of the State should be restricted to those services that individuals cannot perform or to those which are dedicated to the common good, such as national defense, postal service, certain airlines, ports, etc[236].

234 [*Rerum Novarum* § 36.]

235 [*Rerum Novarum* § 32.]

236 [Hurtado states at this point: «Cfr. H.H. Pius XII speech on enterprise?» and in the margin «Copy CSM 150-159». The editors could not identify the first document he cites. Up to this point, all the materials under this heading «The Field of State Intervention» are nearly identical to passages in Folliet's book *Morale Sociale* (*Social Morality*), under the heading *Les Interventions de l'Etat* (*State Interventions*), pp. 146-48. (1937).]

«The State, the guardian of justice and of the common good, should take positive action in economic life.

Nevertheless to withdraw from lesser authorities duties which they can fulfill themselves in order to hand them over to the State would be both an injustice and an injury to social order.

It is wise to entrust the direction of less important business to groups of lesser importance, because the State will be in a position to fulfill more perfectly the functions which belong to it alone: to direct, watch, stimulate or restrain according as circumstances permit or necessity may demand.

This action relates in the first place to protection of human life. With this higher purpose is connected protective legislation for labour, limiting the length of the working day, forbidding night work, providing Sunday rest, hygiene, and security of employment.

The State can also rightly take the means which are in its power to ensure justice and good faith in business. It has the full right to combat unjust speculation and every kind of usury by both preventive and repressive means. It should not fail to protect consumers, especially against fraud in connection with essential commodities.

That form of company in which partners limit their risk and may relinquish their share is not of its nature illicit.

Still under cover of anonymity very serious evils are perpetrated to the harm of both shareholders and public.

It is important then that the public authority should keep strict control over these companies and eventually revise their legal status[237].

The State, while in principle leaving to individuals the ownership and management of enterprises, lawfully interferes either to protect these enterprises against foreign competition (by customs duties of a compensatory but not prohibitive kind), or to help it to enter foreign markets (through consular services and commercial agents).

It belongs to the State to give a general direction to the national economy, and for that purpose to set up a national economic council, representative of the corporative organization, which will enable the public authorities to keep in close touch with qualified and competent representatives of every branch of production.

Special reasons may urge the State to take over the entire management as a State monopoly, of certain industrial, commercial or agricultural undertakings. But in general it should avoid absorbing the country's economic life in this way. If the nature

237 [The Spanish translation used by Hurtado states here «régimen jurídico» which can be translated as «legal order».]

of the service requires that the undertaking shall not be wholly in private hands, the State should endeavour, preferably to conducting it as a State concern, to retain a partial interest through some form of leasing out or granting concessions. In such cases private initiative may take a suitable share with the public authority, and under its supervision, in the management of services or undertakings of public interest, such, for instance, as railways.

It is particularly desirable that the bank which has the responsibility of issuing fiduciary money should be distinguishable from the State, though acting under State control and with its assistance.

In any case, the central authority should not act as though it were itself alone the State, for the State is the organized nation with all the living forces that compose it. A co-ordination of all these forces is particularly necessary in great undertakings of public importance which tend to develop the national resources, such as the control of rivers, canals, harbours, oil-wells, mines and forests.

The different States are mutually dependent in the economic order, and so should pool their experience and efforts by means of suitable institutions, in order to bring about, along with occupational and inter-occupational organization, international economic coordination»[238].

10.3. THE STATE AND WEAK AND INDIGENT PEOPLE

The State, as responsible for distributive justice, must take care of all social classes, without exception, and not allow any injustice to them. But the State must surround the weakest with special protection, a principle that for many goes unnoticed: «Still, when there is question of defending the rights of individuals, the poor and badly off have a claim to especial consideration. The richer class have many ways of shielding themselves, and stand less in need of help from the State; whereas the mass of the poor have no resources of their own to fall back upon, and must chiefly depend upon the assistance of the State»[239]. Shortly before, in the same encyclical, Leo XIII recognized in the proletarians «a better right» to be assisted and he states that no one can accuse them of being meddlers when asserting this right[240].

238 [*A Code of Social Principles* §§ 150-159.]
239 [*Rerum Novarum* § 37.]
240 [At this point Hurtado cites *Rerum Novarum* § 33.]

«Justice, therefore, demands that the interests of the working classes should be carefully watched over by the administration, so that they who contribute so largely to the advantage of the community may themselves share in the benefits which they create —that being housed, clothed and bodily fit, they may find their life less hard and more endurable. It follows that whatever shall appear to prove conducive to the well-being of those who work should obtain favorable consideration. There is no fear that solicitude of this kind will be harmful to any interest; on the contrary, it will be to the advantage of all, for it cannot but be good for the commonwealth to shield from misery those on whom it so largely depends for the things that it needs»[241].

«It must likewise be the special care of the State to create those material conditions of life without which an orderly society cannot exist. The State must take every measure necessary to supply employment, particularly for the heads of families and for the young. To achieve this end demanded by the pressing needs of the common welfare, the wealthy classes must be induced to assume those burdens without which human society cannot be saved nor they themselves remain secure. However, measures taken by the State with this end in view ought to be of such a nature that they will really affect those who actually possess more than their share of capital resources, and who continue to accumulate them to the grievous detriment of others»[242].

The State must also protect the freedom of labor and trade union freedoms. The State will not tolerate corporatism[243] to unjustly damage businesses, or employers to deny the workers unionization rights.

10.4. THE STATE AND PRIVATE PROPERTY

A mission of the State is to protect private ownership from any unjust violation. Through appropriate regulations, the State may defend family property against the possible imprudence of a parent, declaring it immune from seizure and from divisions so excessive as to destroy it.

241 [*Rerum Novarum* § 34.]

242 [Pius XI, Encyclical on Atheistic Communism *Divini Redemptoris* (19 March 1937) § 75, at The Holy See http://w2.vatican.va/content/pius-xi/en/encyclicals/documents/hf_p-xi_enc_19370319_divini-redemptoris.html (hereinafter referred to as *Divini Redemptoris*).]

243 [Hurtado here used the world «*gremio*» whose exact translation is «guilds». The word «*gremio*» was used also to mean corporativism or corporatism, which was defined in 1884 by the Union of Fribourg as «a system of social organization that has at its base the grouping of men according to the community of their natural interests and social functions, and as true and proper organs of the State they direct and coordinate labor and capital in matters of common interest». Howard J. Wiarda, *Corporatism and Comparative Politics: The Other Great Ism*, p. 35 (1996).]

The State also has a duty to control the management of particular goods so that they serve the common good. In certain cases the State may expropriate particular goods, with compensation, and may also nationalize those companies whose nature or extent creates special dangers, or where nationalization is necessary for the common good.

The State may legislate to prevent sterile accumulation of property and may impose special taxes on superfluous goods to favor the most dispossessed elements. In setting tax rates, the State must take into account that, beyond a certain point, taxes are unfair and destroy income as a source of revenue. When taxes are fair taxpayers are obliged in conscience to pay them: they are a contribution to the common good, which benefits everyone.

Inheritance taxes are in themselves legitimate, but they cannot be allowed, especially in cases of direct-line inheritance, to amount to confiscation, as happens in countries under socialist influence. The progressivity of this tax must be established according to the importance of the estate, so that small and even medium size fortunes can be exempted.

> «It follows from what We have termed the individual and at the same time social character of ownership, that men must consider in this matter not only their own advantage but also the common good. To define these duties in detail when necessity requires and the natural law has not done so, is the function of those in charge of the State. Therefore, public authority, under the guiding light always of the natural and divine law, can determine more accurately upon consideration of the true requirements of the common good, what is permitted and what is not permitted to owners in the use of their property. Moreover, Leo XIII wisely taught "that God has left the limits of private possessions to be fixed by the industry of men and institutions of peoples"[244]. That history proves ownership, like other elements of social life, to be not absolutely unchanging, We once declared as follows: "What divers forms has property had, from that primitive form among rude and savage peoples, which may be observed in some places even in our time, to the form of possession in the patriarchal age; and so further to the various forms under tyranny (We are using the word tyranny in its classical sense); and then through the feudal and monarchial forms down to the various types which are to be found in more recent times"[245]. That the State is not

244 [The following footnote here appears in the Encyclical: «Encyclical, *On the Condition of Workers*, 14».]
245 [The following footnote here appears in the Encyclical: «Allocation [sic] to the Convention of Italian Catholic Action, May 16, 1926».]

permitted to discharge its duty arbitrarily is, however, clear. The natural right itself both of owning goods privately and of passing them on by inheritance ought always to remain intact and inviolate, since this indeed is a right that the State cannot take away: "For man is older than the State"[246], and also "domestic living together is prior both in thought and in fact to uniting into a polity"[247]. Wherefore the wise Pontiff declared that it is grossly unjust for a State to exhaust private wealth through the weight of imposts and taxes. "For since the right of possessing goods privately has been conferred not by man's law, but by nature, public authority cannot abolish it, but can only control its exercise and bring it into conformity with the common weal"»[248].

10.5. THE STATE AND COMMERCE

With regard to trade and commerce, the first duty of the State is protection: energetic repression of acts that violate commutative justice, speculative manipulation and hoarding; price vigilance so that real prices do not deviate from the fair prices; prohibition or control of products that can be specially harmful, such as narcotics and alcoholic beverages.

«As for foreign commerce, the State will beware of two contrary and harmful excesses: *autarchy*, that is, the retreat of a people into itself, which, taken into its limits, may suppress all commercial relations among nations and prevent commerce from playing the compensatory and unifying role assigned to it by Providence; and *imperialism* that seeks, by trick or violence, raw materials and commercial outlets. The State will maintain a fair balance between a free exchange opposed to the immediate interests of its residents and protectionism contrary to the interests of the human species. It will see in customs a fiscal procedure and a defense against excessively dangerous competition, not a means of war. You cannot warn people too much of the tendency of the State to retain a monopoly of foreign trade. This practice could be imposed as a momentary expedient, a lesser evil than anarchy, but it cannot be considered as a normal and stable organization of international commercial relations»[249].

246 [The following footnote here appears in the Encyclical: «Encyclical, *On the Condition of Workers*, 12».]
247 [The following footnote here appears in the Encyclical: «Encyclical, *On the Condition of Workers*, 20».]
248 [*Quadragesimo Anno* § 49. The following footnote here appears at the end of quoted part of the Encyclical: «Encyclical, *On the Condition of Workers*, 67».]
249 [Joseph Folliet, *Morale Sociale* (*Social Morality*) pp. 152-53 (1937).]

10.6. THE STATE AND SOCIAL EVILS

What should be the position of the State as regards physical and moral ills, such as alcoholism, prostitution, shameful diseases, infant mortality, tuberculosis, malnutrition, etc. that threaten the future of society?

No one denies the right of the State to suppress the public manifestation of those ills, to prevent their propagation, for example, by punishing drunks, limiting liquor stores, prohibiting immoral shows, etc. But this action must be accompanied by preventative and curative efforts through health and moral education, medical examinations, the care of women and children and social security laws.

The State would go beyond its powers if it established measures that infringed personal rights, for example by so-called «eugenics» that deprived not-well-constituted people of the right to life and by the sterilization of those who are expected to have retarded offspring; or by artificial insemination to reproduce the best physically endowed; or by euthanasia to shorten the lives of the «useless». As for the way of carrying out its actions, the State would be wrong if it ignored private initiative in this area, which has ordinarily been the leader of the fight against social evils. The State must respect such efforts, materially and morally encourage them, and supply their deficiencies.

10.7. THE STATE: AN EXAMPLE OF PRUDENT AND SOBER ADMINISTRATION

«The State itself, mindful of its responsibility before God and society, should be a model of prudence and sobriety in the administration of the commonwealth. Today more than ever the acute world crisis demands that those who dispose of immense funds, built up on the sweat and toil of millions, keep constantly and singly in mind the common good. State functionaries and all employees are obliged in conscience to perform their duties faithfully and unselfishly, imitating the brilliant example of distinguished men of the past and of our own day, who with unremitting labor sacrificed their all for the good of their country. In international trade-relations let all means be sedulously employed for the removal of those artificial barriers to economic life, which are the effects of distrust and hatred. All must remember that the peoples of the earth form but one family in God»[250].

250 [*Divini Redemptoris* § 76.]

10.8. THE DUTY TO RESPECT AND SUPPORT SPIRITUAL VALUES

«At the same time the State must allow the Church full liberty to fulfill her divine and spiritual mission, and this in itself will be an effectual contribution to the rescue of nations from the dread torment of the present hour. Everywhere today there is an anxious appeal to moral and spiritual forces; and rightly so, for the evil we must combat is at its origin primarily an evil of the spiritual order. From this polluted source the monstrous emanations of the communistic system flow with satanic logic. Now, the Catholic Church is undoubtedly preeminent among the moral and religious forces of today. Therefore the very good of humanity demands that her work be allowed to proceed unhindered»[251].

10.9. FRUITS OF CATHOLIC DOCTRINE ON STATE INTERVENTION

«With regard to civil authority, Leo XIII, boldly breaking through the confines imposed by Liberalism, fearlessly taught that government must not be thought a mere guardian of law and of good order, but rather must put forth every effort so that "through the entire scheme of laws and institutions ... both public and individual well-being may develop spontaneously out of the very structure and administration of the State"[252]. Just freedom of action must, of course, be left both to individual citizens and to families, yet only on condition that the common good be preserved and wrong to any individual be abolished. The function of the rulers of the State, moreover, is to watch over the community and its parts; but in protecting private individuals in their rights, chief consideration ought to be given to the weak and the poor. "For the nation, as it were, of the rich is guarded by its own defenses and is in less need of governmental protection, whereas the suffering multitude, without the means to protect itself relies especially on the protection of the State. Wherefore, since wage workers are numbered among the great mass of the needy, the State must include them under its special care and foresight"[253].

We, of course, do not deny that even before the Encyclical of Leo, some rulers of peoples have provided for certain of the more urgent needs of the workers and curbed more flagrant acts of injustice inflicted upon them. But after the Apostolic voice had sounded from the Chair of Peter throughout the world, rulers of nations, more fully

251 [*Divini Redemptoris* § 77.]
252 [The following footnote appears in the Encyclical: «Encyclical, *On the Condition of Workers*, 48».]
253 [The following footnote appears in the Encyclical: «Encyclical, *On the Condition of Workers*, 54».]

alive at last to their duty, devoted their minds and attention to the task of promoting a more comprehensive and fruitful social policy.

And while the principles of Liberalism were tottering, which had long prevented effective action by those governing the State, the Encyclical *On the Condition of Workers* in truth impelled peoples themselves to promote a social policy on truer grounds and with greater intensity, and so strongly encouraged good Catholics to furnish valuable help to heads of States in this field that they often stood forth as illustrious champions of this new policy even in legislatures. Sacred ministers of the Church, thoroughly imbued with Leo's teaching, have, in fact, often proposed to the votes of the peoples' representatives the very social legislation that has been enacted in recent years and have resolutely demanded and promoted its enforcement.

A new branch of law, wholly unknown to the earlier time, has arisen from this continuous and unwearied labor to protect vigorously the sacred rights of the workers that flow from their dignity as men and as Christians. These laws undertake the protection of life, health, strength, family, homes, workshops, wages and labor hazards, in fine, everything that pertains to the condition of wage workers, with special concern for women and children. Even though these laws do not conform exactly everywhere and in all respects to Leo's recommendations, still it is undeniable that much in them savors of the Encyclical, *On the Condition of Workers*, to which great credit must be given for whatever improvement has been achieved in the workers' condition»[254].

«And while the State in the Nineteenth Century, through excessive exaltation of liberty, considered as its exclusive scope the safeguarding of liberty by law, Leo XIII admonished it that it had also the duty to interest itself in social welfare, taking care of the entire people and of all its members, especially the weak and the dispossessed, through a generous social program and the creation of a labor code.His call evoked a powerful response; and it is a clear duty of justice to recognize the progress which has been achieved in the lot of workers through the pains taken by civil authorities in many lands. Hence was it well said that *Rerum novarum* became the *Magna Charta* of Christian social endeavor»[255].

254 [*Quadragesimo Anno* §§ 25-28.]
255 [*La Solennità*.]

11

Civic Duties

11.1. PATRIOTISM

The citizen must consider his country as his homeland, the extension of the family, and he must feel for it something similar to what he feels for his parents.

The country appears as a moral person, an incarnation of feelings of veneration, affection and dedication. The country evokes a whole family history of glorious and sad events in which our elders participated; a feeling of solidarity that unites compatriots with quasi-family ties much more intimate than those with citizens of other countries; a sense of obligation to it, of working for it, of making it greater, so that all the goods that the country potentially or actually comprises bring happiness to its citizens. Patriotism, rather than an emotional feeling, should awaken in citizens the awareness of gratitude for goods received and a sense of duty and honor to the motherland.

Patriotism must not be bellicose towards other countries. The nation is defined, rather than by its borders, by its *mission.* Wishing the country to grow does not necessarily mean to expand its borders, but to fulfil its mission. What is the mission of my country? How can it fulfill that mission? How can I assist it? This requires of all of us a deep social sense, one most lacking in our days.

National problems so charged with passion ought to be solved peacefully. This would be possible if people who have many privileges gave up some of them, so that those who had none could have some. Professionals and students should approach working-class people to learn their problems, to organize educational and cultural crusades, to study how to make life cheaper, how to create new wealth, how to serve more efficiently and at less cost, bearing in mind that a profession, rather than a means for profit, is a service.

The concept of homeland and a good understanding of the family, require sacrifices by all the members of the national family so that they may have, if not equality —that is impossible— at least lives worthy of men. Otherwise, what can the homeland signify for those pariahs who have received nothing from it? How can they love and respect it, when they see that fundamental human rights are neglected and trampled upon? So many revolutionary movements have found their roots and then their breeding grounds in misery and in the lack of respect for the human dignity.

«In the face of the dangers of the social and political anarchy so widespread in our days, a desire for a policy of force may easily arise. Respect for institutions may seem out of place. An attitude of violence may seem more effective than the education of consciences; instead of the charity that transforms souls, the sword that cuts off discussions; in place of the humble apostolate, strength and punishment. And some may aspire to replace democracy with totalitarianism.

Authority is absolutely necessary. There is an immense lack of respect for the established power that must be supported. Effective sanctions are indispensable and need to be truly effective in the face of the great as well as the small, and especially regarding the great, because their responsibility is greater. But when judging anarchy, let us judge its causes; let us consider them in a profound spirit of justice and charity, and before we ask for cannons we should be sure that we are not harboring injustices.

Revolutions are combated not with rifles but with just renewal. Communism is not contemplated in a country of happy people. The best way to end strikes is to end the misery and prejudices that maintain a climate of social unrest. Ending misery is impossible, but fighting it is a sacred duty. Let the country see that its politicians do not pursue their personal interests but those of the nation, and that they devote all their energies to enhancing the well-being not of a group but of the mass of their fellow citizens; that if the people do not receive all they want, it is because of the poverty of the nation and because the lack of human and technical means does not allow further progress. That convinces. More effective than victory by violence is victory by reasonable persuasion. That is why, in our national emblem, reason comes first and force comes after»[256].

11.2. PARTICIPATION IN PUBLIC LIFE

The citizen cannot disregard civic duties. Politics is designed to create institutions of social justice that look to the common good. Education, welfare, freedom, respect for conscience, organization of economic life, defense of the homeland, depend on the laws. It is not licit for anyone to ignore a cause in which such important interests are at stake.

When speaking of politics it is necessary to distinguish great politics, or the politics of the common good, and the politics of political parties, which are groups of men with their leaders, their programs and their methods of action,

256 [Alberto Hurtado Cruchaga, *Humanismo Social* (*Social Humanism*) pp. 164-65 (1947)(hereinafter referred to as *Social Humanism*).]

into which citizens are divided in trying to achieve, in a concrete way, the temporal common good.

Participation in this great politics «is a duty of Christian justice and charity» and it is a duty of honest people to cooperate with the public good, either in the administration or in the government of the State. For a Catholic, «his very character as a Catholic demands that he make the best use of his rights and duties as a citizen for the good of Religion, which is inseparable from the good of the homeland»[257]. «The field of politics, which looks at the interests of the entire society and is the field of the broadest charity —of political charity it can be said that politics has no superior other than that of Religion»[258]. From this it follows that the apolitical school contradicts Catholic sentiment. «There can be no doubt that absolute abstentionism must be rejected because participation in politics constitutes for the faithful, for the reason already mentioned, a true and proper duty founded on legal justice and charity»[259].

Citizens have a grave obligation to enroll in the electoral registers and to cast their votes in conscience. «They would seriously neglect their duties if, to the best of their ability, they did not contribute to directing the policies of their cities, provinces or nations, for if they remained idle the reins of government would fall into the hands of those who offered but weak hopes of salvation»[260].

11.3. POLITICAL PARTIES

It is legitimate to have political parties in the country, but not irreconcilable groups, which indicate the rupture of the great national family. Politicians must understand that before serving a party they must serve the country, and that is why, when the good of the country demands it, they must know how to suppress their partisan prejudices and unite around the common good. Politicians, in their electoral struggles, should not resort to fraud, violence, false promises or

257 [Pius XI, Apostolic Letter to Bishops, clergy and people of Mexico on the conditions of Mexico *Paterna Sane Sollicitudo*, at The Holy See, (2 February 1926), https://w2.vatican.va/content/pius-xi/la/apost_letters/documents/hf_p-xi_apl_19260202_paterna-sane-sollicitudo.html. At vatican.va this document is only in Latin, so the editors translated it from Hurtado's text.]

258 [Pius XI, Speech to the Italian Catholic University Federation (18 December 1927). The editors translated this from Hurtado's Spanish text.]

259 [Letter of the Honorable Cardinal Eugenio Pacelli to the Chilean Episcopate (1934). The editors translated this from Hurtado's Spanish text. Cardinal Pacelli was later to become the future Pope Pius XII.]

260 [Pius XI, Apostolic Letter to the Bishop of Lithuania *Peculiari Quadam* (24 June 1928). The editors translated this from Hurtado's Spanish text.]

bribery, vices that should be excluded. Christian charity applies even to adversaries. Anything that can be done to purify electoral procedures and make them truly reflect the nation's sentiment should be viewed with sympathy, without fear of damaging the cause that ones sustains, for a just cause cannot be defended by unjust means. «You will know the truth, and the truth will set you free» (John 8:32), said Christ, and that should be a slogan not only for private life, but also for politics.

«Faithful to this concept, "*Catholic Action* (C.A.), without practicing politics itself, in the strict sense of the word, prepares its members for good politics, that is to say, a kind of politics which is completely inspired by the principles of Christianity, the only ones which can bring prosperity and peace. This will eliminate the fact that, despite being monstrous, it is not uncommon for men who profess Catholicism to have one conscience in their private life and another in their public life"[261].

Regarding great politics, the politics of parties must be placed in context; that is to say, the tendencies towards the common good as conceived by different groups of citizens who intend to solve economic, political and social questions according to their own schools and ideologies which, although not departing from Catholic doctrine, can reach different conclusions[262]. "It is natural that Catholic Action, as well as the Church, be above and beyond all political parties, since, as has been established, it should not defend the particular interests of any group, but seek the true good of souls, extending as far as possible the Kingdom of Our Lord Jesus Christ to individuals, families and society, and bringing forth, under their peaceful standards, a perfect and disciplined concord of all the faithful who desire to contribute to an apostolic work so holy and so broad"[263].

We will never insist enough that C.A. "should not be a slave to political quarrels, nor should she be confined to the narrow frontiers of a political party, whatever it may be"[264]. In other words, a political party, even if it aims to be inspired by the doctrine of the Church and defend its rights, cannot claim to represent all the faithful,

261 [The quoted document here cites: «Letter to the Cardinal Patriarch of Lisbon».]

262 [The quoted document here cites: «Letter of the Honorable Cardinal Pacelli to the Chilean Episcopate». (1934).]

263 [The quoted document here cites: «Pius XI, speech to the Italian Catholic University Federation». (18 December 1927).]

264 [The quoted document here cites: «Letter *Quae Nobis*». The author is probably referring to Pius XI, Letter to Cardinal Adolfo Bertram, Bishop of Breslau, on the Principles and General Foundations of Catholic Action *Quae Nobis* (13 November 1928).]

since its entire program can never have an absolute value for all, and its practical actions are subject to error. It is evident that the Church could not be linked to the activity of a political party without compromising its supernatural character and the universality of its mission[265].

"Only in times of grave danger do the bishops have the right and the duty to intervene when necessary, that is to say, to call for the "union" of all Catholics so that they, putting aside all political divergence, stand up in defense of the threatened rights of the Church. But it is evident that in such a case they would not engage in party politics"[266].

With regard to political parties, the Holy See inculcates in their *bishops and priests the idea that they should refrain from advocacy for a particular political party.* The Church hopes that the very serious obligation of working always and everywhere in public affairs is instilled in citizens, according to the dictates of conscience, before God and for the greater good of Religion and of the Homeland. However, this should be achieved in such a way that, pursuing to a declaration of this general obligation, the priest does not appear to defend one party more than another, unless one of them is openly opposed to religion.

"The faithful should be left to their freedom as citizens, to constitute particular political groups and to register in them, provided that they give sufficient guarantees of respect for the rights of the Church and of souls.

It is nevertheless the obligation of all the faithful, even if they participate in different parties, not always to treat everybody, and especially their brethren in the faith, with that special charity that distinguishes Christians, but also always to put the supreme interests of religion before those of the party, and always to be ready to obey their shepherds when they, under special circumstances, call the faithful to unite for the defense of the superior principles"[267].

Everything that has been said about the disctinction between the Church and politics is applied to C.A.: "*C.A. is outside and above political parties.* It neither practices politics nor is a political party"[268]. This same principle is clearly stated by our Holy Father Pius XII in his letter when he was a Secretary of State to the Chilean Episcopate: "Being a part of the Church's apostolate and directly depending on the ecclesiastical hierarchy, C.A. should remain absolutely oblivious to the struggles of the politi-

265 [The quoted document here cites: Letter of the Honorable Cardinal Pacelli to the Chilean Episcopate (1934).]

266 [*Id.*]

267 [Alberto Hurtado, *Puntos de Educación* (*Points on Education*) p. 244-246, (1942).] The quoted document cites here: Letter of the Honorable Cardinal Pacelli to the Chilean Episcopate (1934).]

268 [The quoted document cites here: «Pius XI, speech to the Federation of Men of the Italian C.A».]

cal parties even of those who are made up of Catholics. Consequently, the associations of young Catholics should neither be political parties nor affiliated with political parties. It would also be appropriate for the leaders of such associations not to be at the same time leaders of political parties or assemblies, so they do not intermingle, against due order, very different things"[269].

In order to safeguard to the end this separation of the C.A. with politics of a particular party, which the Holy See wishes to make clear, she ordains that "if it seems opportune to provide the youth with a special and higher instruction in political matters, different from the general formation of the citizen's conscience, it must be given, not in the headquarters or meetings of the members of the C.A. but in another place, and by men distinguished by the probity of their customs and by their integral and firm profession of doctrine. The principle must be clear: it is not appropriate for the Church's hierarchy to form and instruct young people's political associations, and above all, she should not direct young Catholics to such a degree that she inclines them to one political party more than others. She must give sufficient guarantees for the proper defense of the cause and rights of the Church"[270].

Once this principle of the independence of C.A. has been clearly laid down with regard to the policy of a particular party and after having established, not by virtue of a dogmatic principle but a prudential principle, that political leaders may not be at the same time leaders of C.A., the Church tries to avoid another obstacle. The Church tries to separate political parties from Catholic Action so that it would seem incompatible to be a leader and even a simple member of a political party and, at the same time, a member of the C.A.

This principle is clearly stated by Cardinal Pacelli's letter to the Chilean Episcopate when he says that "young people registered in associations of the C.A. can, as private citizens, adhere to political parties that give sufficient guarantees for the safeguarding of religious interests. Try, however, to always fulfill your duties as Catholics, and do not put the conveniences of the party before the superior interests and holy commandments of God and the Church"[271].

This same doctrine has been extensively explained in an signed letter from His Excellency Archbishop of Santiago, November 4th, 1941, which contains the rules for the Archdiocesan Council of the Catholic Youth in Santiago:

269 [The quoted document here cites: «Letter of the Honorable Cardinal Pacelli to the Chilean Episcopate». (1934).]
270 [*Id.*]
271 [*Id.*]

"Young people must be taught that there is no opposition between being a member of the C.A. and being a registered member and even a leader of a political party which, according to the norms given by the Holy See, Catholics may belong. It has only been stated that, in general, it is not appropriate for the leaders of the C.A. to be at the same time the leaders of political parties. And if they are affiliated with a political party, they can act in C.A. and Catholic Youth assemblies and even speak in them, provided it is not about party politics. Such actions in no way means that Catholic Action is united or confused with party politics, just as a leader of a commercial corporation can speak as a member of the youth or as Catholic Action militant without indicating that the corporation is the same as Catholic Action: it would only mean solidarity with the political opinions and the antipathies of parties in the spirit of those who are determined to find what does not exist. Catholic Action must be the common house, like the Catholic Church itself, of all Catholics, whatever opinions they may have on contentious or contingent matters. Doors that the Holy Church has not closed are not to be closed by the C.A. In C.A. is the place we should always encounter not only the superior ideal that should unite all hearts, but also a sincere charity that will overcome all difficulties"»[272].

11.4. YOUNG PEOPLE AND POLITICS

«A final problem arises in the relations of Catholic Action and politics: it concerns the participation of young people and especially of high school students in active politics.

The right of young people to participate in active politics is widely recognized in the letter of the Honorable Cardinal Pacelli, and also in other similar papal documents. However, we must remember that it is advisable for young people to delay their entry into active politics until they have a fully formed judgment. Politics easily excites spirits, fascinates and divides, and to meet its challenges the youth needs to possess a deep range of spiritual formation, supernatural life, Christian charity, prudence, which are not easy to find at that age. That is why we estimate that at least as long as a young person has not arrived at the age in which the law confers on him the right to vote, it would be more convenient, as a general rule, that he be dedicated to the activities of Catholic Action, without mixing them with partisan struggles.

272 [Alberto Hurtado, *Puntos de Educación* (*Points on Education*) p. 247-249, (1942).]

This principle, as will be well understood, applies especially to high school students, who, unfortunately, are drawn very early to party politics, spending in this activity most of the energies they should devote to their supernatural, intellectual, social and civic formation»[273].

11.5. TAXES. MILITARY SERVICE

Taxes are the ordinary means available to the government to procure the resources it needs for the common good. Individuals who take advantage of the benefits of managing the common good cannot escape tax burdens. This principle determines the *raison d'être* of taxes and at the same time indicates the limits of their obligations. The State cannot act arbitrarily: it can only ask for what it needs and it must avoid waste in public administration and avoid the destruction of the private fortunes that are a source of national wealth.

When a tax is just it is not lawful to evade it, because to do so would be to resist a just exercise of authority. The doctrine that proposes that tax contributions fall in the field of purely criminal law has been discussed in chapter on Criminal Laws.

«Taxation laws which are just, and justly applied, are binding in conscience. Catholic sociologists should endeavour to correct wrong opinions on this matter, and in the name of social justice to lead good people to participate loyally in the expenses of the State.

Taxation, *i.e.*, contributing to public funds without immediate gain to the contributor, is not a real, but personal obligation upon citizens, in the sense that it does not bear immediately upon property, but on its owner.

So far as the common good allows, distributive justice requires that taxes should not be directly proportionate to incomes, not levied on a scale increasing at a constant rate, but on a scale whose rate of increase gradually diminishes until at the upper limit it approximates to a proportional tax. Such tax may be called "progressive".

In theory, the ideal would be a single progressive income tax on income. But in practice a part of the public revenue must be obtained through indirect taxes, which are more willingly accepted and do not so easily become oppressive.

Direct taxation has, however, the advantage of asking from the citizens a conscious sacrifice which gives them an interest in public affairs.

In the choice of taxation the legislator should have regard to these three rules:

273 [*Id.* p. 253.]

(a) To avoid taxes which bring manifestly harmful results and those which admit of fraud; since the latter encourage habits of evasion.
(b) When imposing new taxes, to tap sources of revenue rather than funds which are economically sterile and otherwise reasonable. In any case, established forms of taxation are generally adjusted by their methods of application, or by reactions that bring about by degrees an equitable distribution of these public charges.
(c) Sumptuary taxes, on luxuries or undue extravagance, deserve to be encouraged. Even if their result is not great, the moral lesson they teach enlightens and strengthens the public conscience, and serves the common good at least to that extent.

Very high taxes on legacies, though justifiable in exceptional circumstances, undermine the principle of property. They scarcely differ from confiscation, and hinder the building up of national reserves»[274].

Another contribution that the citizen owes to the State is his personal service in the form of «service of labor», or of military service. It is very desirable and we must work to accelerate the moment when effective international justice makes permanent armies unnecessary, and only police intervention will be necessary. But until that time comes, the army represents a force at the service of law. A country incapable of defending itself will be a toy of other less scrupulous countries or domestic factions, and this makes the existence of an army necessary. Of course, it must not be more numerous or stronger than the circumstances demand. The military is not authorized to decide or to impose military political solutions; the government, on the other hand, cannot use the military to intimidate the weak in the exercise of their just rights. These unfortunately frequent mistakes have discredited the armed forces of many countries.

The duty of military service and the acceptance of the draft in case of war make the problem of conscientious objection a very interesting subject in these troubled days.

11.6. CONSCIENTIOUS OBJECTION[275]

11.7. THE RIGHT OF REBELLION[276]

274 [*A Code of Social Principles* §§ 143-149.]
275 [This paragraph was left unwritten. The manuscript states «see pages, Lyon».]
276 [This paragraph was left unwritten. The manuscript states «see Lallement, and letter to Mexicans. Cfr. Cavallera p. 348».]

Chapter 5

Social Classes

1
Characteristics of Social Classes

In addition to family and civil society that are organic natural societies in which every individual develops, there are two inorganic groups, which, more than societies could be called social environments: they are the social classes and the occupations. Both are called to exert an immense influence on the evolution of the person.

It is useless to ignore the existence of social classes. At first glance one can perceive the reality of groups or categories of people who have the same way of life, very similar cultures, very similar occupations, very similar psychological reactions.

In the constitution of each social class we see first an *economic element*: its means of living. Second, there is a *social element*: the work, activities and functions that each particular group performs in society. Third, there is a *cultural element*: the similarity of training received in the school, in the work environment, through reading, in the organizations which pertain to the group. And finally, there is an *emotional element*: similar reactions within each group to the same problems; reactions that are very different, sometimes opposed, from group to group.

A social class consists of all these elements. The mere presence of one or two of them is not enough to place a person in a certain social category. For example, a rich man who has become poorer and because of this participates in the working class will not feel solidarity for that class while culturally and emotionally he is not at the same level. Likewise, the son of a worker, educated at the university, will not immediately consider himself part of the ruling classes until he has united his culture with his psychological reactions and a certain economic independence.

A person is part of the class with which he feels solidarity, with which he feels united by class consciousness. Such a more or less explicit consciousness exists today in all social classes, and this promotes the formation of class associations: such as are trade unions, professional and artistic unions, societies for the promotion or protection of agricultural or mining production; societies of merchants and of employees. Underlying each of these groups there is ordinarily a class and a consciousness of class.

How many social classes exist? It is impossible to indicate a precise number. In a country of advanced culture and industry, it could be said that the number tends to infinity. Yet, we can speak of certain more differentiated groups:

The ruling class, improperly called superior as if it possessed some superior human qualities. This class includes people that have acquired culture by family cultivation, like the aristocracy, or through education, like distinguished professionals and artists; also banking and industry people and in general wealthy people. Finally, this group comprises high ecclesiastical, civil and military officials.

The middle class, formed by simple professionals, employees and small stockholders, landlords and landowners.

The working or lower class is formed, as its name indicates, by urban and rural workers.

2
The Harmony of Classes

Ruling classes are not superior classes, as they are called. Strictly speaking, no class is superior, as in the human body no part is superior to any other. In a well ordered society there must be different members and different roles, and each role is as important to the common good as the others, as long as they are not artificially created. Therefore, no social class has the right to be preferred over any other, nor has it a right to despise others or consider them inferior. St. Paul admirably describes this situation, speaking to the Christians of Corinth about the diversity of gifts received by them:

> «There are different kinds of spiritual gifts but the same Spirit; there are different forms of service but the same Lord; there are different workings but the same God who produces all of them in everyone. To each individual the manifestation of the Spirit is given for some benefit. To one is given through the Spirit the expression of wisdom; to another the expression of knowledge according to the same Spirit; to another faith by the same Spirit; to another gifts of healing by the one Spirit; to another mighty deeds; to another prophecy; to another discernment of spirits; to another varieties of tongues; to another interpretation of tongues. But one and the same Spirit produces all of these, distributing them individually to each person as he wishes.

As a body is one though it has many parts, and all the parts of the body, though many, are one body, so also Christ. For in one Spirit we were all baptized into one body, whether Jews or Greeks, slaves or free persons, and we were all given to drink of one Spirit.

Now the body is not a single part, but many. If a foot should say, «Because I am not a hand I do not belong to the body», it does not for this reason belong any less to the body. Or if an ear should say, «Because I am not an eye I do not belong to the body», it does not for this reason belong any less to the body. If the whole body were an eye, where would the hearing be? If the whole body were hearing, where would the sense of smell be? But as it is, God placed the parts, each one of them, in the body as he intended. If they were all one part, where would the body be? But as it is, there are many parts, yet one body. The eye cannot say to the hand, «I do not need you», nor again the head to the feet, «I do not need you». Indeed, the parts of the body that seem to be weaker are all the more necessary, and those parts of the body that we consider less honorable we surround with greater honor, and our less presentable parts are treated with greater propriety, whereas our more presentable parts do not need this. But God has so constructed the body as to give greater honor to a part that is without it, so that there may be no division in the body, but that the parts may have the same concern for one another. If [one] part suffers, all the parts suffer with it; if one part is honored, all the parts share its joy.

Now you are Christ's body, and individually parts of it. Some people God has designated in the church to be, first, apostles; second, prophets; third, teachers; then, mighty deeds; then, gifts of healing, assistance, administration, and varieties of tongues» (1 Cor. 12: 4-28).

The same idea is repeated in the Epistle to the Romans:

«For as in one body we have many parts, and all the parts do not have the same function, so we, though many, in Christ we, though many, are one body in Christ and individually parts of one another». (Rom. 12: 4-5).

This doctrine, profusely repeated throughout the New Testament, is fundamental in Christian morality: in the Body of Christ, which is the Church, there are no adults or minors, but members who exercise different functions. All of them are equally respectable, and in any of those functions a man can be noble, as long as he has the only true nobility: the nobility of spirit. To every work, to every category of man who performs it, is owed honor and respect, and also the means to be able to perform that work in a manner worthy of a man. Unfortunately, this principle is fulfilled to a very unsatisfactory extent, which is the reason why class struggles occur[277].

3
Occupations

Social classes are the spontaneous result of similar economic, social, cultural and emotional conditions in which certain categories of people live. Occupations are the result of the *function* or of the *work* that certain people perform. Those who exercise the same group of activities in order to provide society with the same goods or services are part of the same occupation. An occupation will provide its members with the wherewithal to supply their means of living.

In fact, every occupation, whether of manual work or a professional career, creates, by the very nature of things, a community of interests among those who exercise it. The natural thing is, therefore, that people of the same occupation form an organized occupational body.

> «Moreover, just as inhabitants of a town are wont to found associations with the widest diversity of purposes, which each is quite free to join or not, so those engaged in the same industry or profession will combine with one another into associations equally free for purposes connected in some manner with the pursuit of the calling itself»[278].

His Holiness Pius XI in *Quadragesimo Anno* makes the organized occupation one of the basic elements of social reform:[279]

277 [At this point Hurtado added a heading as follows: «The Class Struggle» which has only one short undeveloped paragraph. The same subject is explained later in Hurtado's manuscript in more detail, so the editors have decided to omit this paragraph. Hurtado also added at the end of this paragraph: «See *Sindicalismo* p. 41…» He refers to his book *Syndicalism.*]

278 [*Quadragesimo Anno* § 87.]

279 [(This point remained unfinished. The author pointed out some ideas with the intention of developing them later: «(plan: reform and the individual. exaggerated [sic] and provoked the reaction of the totalitarian state. Principle stated by the Pope: that no superior entity should absorb what the lower can do. OSC 263-Form the orders or professions, continue with OSC 264 … end with CSM 58-68».) The material in the text above is the editors' attempt to comply with these cryptic instructions.

«What We have thus far stated regarding an equitable distribution of property and regarding just wages concerns individual persons and only indirectly touches social order, to the restoration of which according to the principles of sound philosophy and to its perfection according to the sublime precepts of the law of the Gospel, Our Predecessor, Leo XIII, devoted all his thought and care.

Still, in order that what he so happily initiated may be solidly established, that what remains to be done may be accomplished, and that even more copious and richer benefits may accrue to the family of mankind, two things are especially necessary: reform of institutions and correction of morals.

When we speak of the reform of institutions, the State comes chiefly to mind, not as if universal well-being were to be expected from its activity, but because things have come to such a pass through the evil of what we have termed "individualism" that, following upon the overthrow and near extinction of that rich social life which was once highly developed through associations of various kinds, there remain virtually only individuals and the State. This is to the great harm of the State itself; for, with a structure of social governance lost, and with the taking over of all the burdens which the wrecked associations once bore, the State has been overwhelmed and crushed by almost infinite tasks and duties.

As history abundantly proves, it is true that on account of changed conditions many things which were done by small associations in former times cannot be done now save by large associations. Still, that most weighty principle, which cannot be set aside or changed, remains fixed and unshaken in social philosophy: Just as it is gravely wrong to take from individuals what they can accomplish by their own initiative and industry and give it to the community, so also it is an injustice and at the same time a grave evil and disturbance of right order to assign to a greater and higher association what lesser and subordinate organizations can do. For every social activity ought of its very nature to furnish help to the members of the body social, and never destroy and absorb them.

The supreme authority of the State ought, therefore, to let subordinate groups handle matters and concerns of lesser importance, which would otherwise dissipate its efforts greatly. Thereby the State will more freely, powerfully, and effectively do all those things that belong to it alone because it alone can do them: directing, watching, urging, restraining, as occasion requires and necessity demands. Therefore, those in power should be sure that the more perfectly a graduated order is kept among the various associations, in observance of the principle of "subsidiary function", the stronger social authority and effectiveness will be the happier and more prosperous the condition of the State.

First and foremost, the State and every good citizen ought to look to and strive toward this end: that the conflict between the hostile classes be abolished and harmonious cooperation of the Industries and Professions be encouraged and promoted.

The social policy of the State, therefore, must devote itself to the re-establishment of the Industries and Professions. In actual fact, human society now, for the reason that it is founded on classes with divergent aims and hence opposed to one another and therefore inclined to enmity and strife, continues to be in a violent condition and is unstable and uncertain.

Labor, as Our Predecessor explained well in his Encyclical[280], is not a mere commodity. On the contrary, the worker's human dignity in it must be recognized. It therefore cannot be bought and sold like a commodity. Nevertheless, as the situation now stands, hiring and offering for hire in the so-called labor market separate men into two divisions, as into battle lines, and the contest between these divisions turns the labor market itself almost into a battlefield where, face to face, the opposing lines struggle bitterly. Everyone understands that this grave evil which is plunging all human society to destruction must be remedied as soon as possible. But complete cure will not come until this opposition has been abolished and well-ordered members of the social body—Industries and Professions— are constituted in which men may have their place, not according to the position each has in the labor market but according to the respective social functions which each performs. For under nature's guidance it comes to pass that just as those who are joined together by nearness of habitation establish towns, so those who follow the same industry or profession —whether in the economic or other field— form guilds or associations, so that many are wont to consider these self-governing organizations, if not essential, at least natural to civil society.

Because order, as St. Thomas well explains[281], is unity arising from the harmonious arrangement of many objects, a true, genuine social order demands that the various members of a society be united together by some strong bond. This unifying force is present not only in the producing of goods or the rendering of services —in which the employers and employees of an identical Industry or Profession collaborate jointly— but also in that common good, to achieve which all Industries and Professions together ought, each to the best of its ability, to cooperate amicably. And this

280 [The following footnote appears in the Encyclical: «Cf. Encyclical, *On the Condition of Workers*, 31. Art. 2».]

281 [The following footnote appears in the Encyclical: «St. Thomas, *Contra Gentiles*, III, 71; cf. *Summa Theologica*».]

unity will be the stronger and more effective, the more faithfully individuals and the Industries and Professions themselves strive to do their work and excel in it»[282].

[Finally, we can end by citing the Code of Social Principles of Mechlin, which states:]

«When based upon vocational associations, human society is in a condition conformable to its natural structure. If built up on hostile classes it is in a condition of violence and instability. In the light of Christian social philosophy, then, vocational associations may be considered as natural organs of civil society, if they are not essential organs of the same in so far as they are autonomous bodies enjoying true authority.

The principle of unity binding together the members of the same calling is to be found in the production of goods and the rendering of services resulting from their common activity.

The principle of unity for the totality of occupations lies in the common good to which all must tend, each in its own way, by coordinated effort.

Individual activity in industry cannot, without risk of anarchy, be left entirely to itself. The exercise of rights and the fulfilment of mutual duties in view of the common good of the profession and of society demand, in the vocational group itself, an authority whose chief function is to regulate internal disputes which might arise, to establish suitable regulations, to manage and to direct the activity of the profession.

If authority is necessary in the profession to regulate the activity of its members, it is still more necessary that there be a supreme authority over all industries, with power to regulate their mutual relations and to direct their activity towards the common good. Social justice therefore requires inter-professional organization on regional, national and even international lines.

Experience shows that such corporations are exposed to a grave danger: induced by a certain group selfishness they are prone to forget and to neglect their chief duty, which is to work as effectively as possible for the general welfare of the country. Hence a just relationship of dependence should be established and maintained between the State, guardian of this welfare, and the vocational groups. Vocational organization should relieve the State of many tasks which at present weigh heavily upon it, without however either absorbing or weakening it, but rather perfecting and strengthening it.

282 [*Quadragesimo Anno* §§ 76-84.]

Once the vocational bodies have been established, three tasks will remain to be accomplished: (i) the unity of kindred associations and the creation of at least two federations, one for the trades and the other for the liberal professions; (ii) the uniting of the corporations and federations under a supreme professional authority; (iii) the integration of this supreme authority into the political structure of the nation and by this the attainment of the highest point towards which corporative organization tends and in which it ought to find its full realization.

Corporative organization is not of its very nature bound up with any particual form of State or government. On the contrary, just as in the political order, different forms of government are legitimate, providing they make for the common good, so in the professional order, the forms of corporative organization are likewise left to the preferences of the parties concerned.

Chief among the various duties of the corporative groups must be placed the technical training of the future members of the profession. This belongs primarily to each corporative group and in this matter the State retains only a subsidiary function. It is likewise the function of the authority within the profession to maintain services for vocational direction and placing in employment.

It may happen that divergent interests arise among members of the same vocational body; notably as regards the special interests of employers and employed. Corporative organizations ought then to guarantee to either party the possibility of independent deliberation in order to safeguard its legitimate interests and prevent abuses which the other might cause by the advantage of its position.

For the perfect realization of the corporative order, institutions should draw their inspiration from the principles of social justice and be mindful that each group has but a subsidiary function in the social hierarchy, and should not crush the activity of those subordinate to it. It may then be hoped that economic activity, that very important function of social life, will recover rectitude and balance in order»[283].

283 [*A Code of Social Principles* §§ 58-68.]

Chapter 6

International Society

1
Existence of an International Society

«The interdependence of nations is shown by the following facts, the development of which is according to nature:

The existence of international trade.

The existence of unions for international good, such as the Postal Union and the Union for the protection of literary, industrial and artistic property.

The existence of international private companies and industrial associations.

International meetings and congresses.

And above all international treaties.

These facts show the existence of a natural society among nations, and consequently of an international law antecedent to, and higher than, all conventions»[284].

The latest wars have made more evident the interdependence among nations, founded on the identity of nature among men. This community is much greater among Christians, members of the same Mystical Body, the Church, animated by the same grace and called to the same supernatural vocation.

The interests of men are the same wherever they may be. As inventions advance, the world is becoming more and more one, and everyone can realize that their problems are not personal, not familial, not national, but human. Literature, art, the progress of civilization, commerce and the whole economy are developing today on an international scale.

Recognition of these new bonds must correspond to a truly international spirit. All attempts to promote international understanding by the creation of international law and institutions, must elicit from us encouragement and approval.

Hatred against other countries, systematic suspicion, «anti» preaching, racial prejudice, pride of national superiority, all these must be eliminated, as they oppose international fraternity. Love of the homeland, more than the widening of its borders, must be directed to the fulfillment of its mission.

International fraternity demands a criterion of justice that should prevail among the nations. Regarding the rights of others, instead of maintaining a complicit silence, people should protest violations, especially when an outrage is

284 [*Id.* § 171.]

committed by strong nations. Fortunately, the existence of an organization of nations allows all countries to make their voices heard in a forum which, although it is neither strong enough nor dispassionate, is at least a medium for making the voice of justice heard. Economic injustices and the vexations suffered by peoples in colonial or semi-colonial countries must be denounced.

Besides justice, there is an international charity that establishes, beyond the law, an atmosphere of cordial sympathy and it makes us see what benefits other countries. When such beneficial measures are effective, a Christian cannot refuse them.

There can never be any opposition between love of country and love of the human race. Catholic principles are frankly resistant to any deviation towards exaggerated nationalism or internationalism.

2
Towards a Society of Nations

Developments are now taking place among countries which are similar to those which transpired among regions that today form a single state. Many of them had customs, dialects and even different languages, but a central power has prevailed and has given them unity, assuring them all the benefit of uniform justice. This meant sacrifice, compensated by the fruits of union. Something similar is now commencing among nations.

Countries can be associated in two different ways: by the organization of a kind of supranational state, with power to impose its decisions on states whose sovereignty would be limited; or under a contractual arrangment, which leaves each state its full sovereignty, obliging it to comply with certain conventions.

Through the initiative of President Wilson, a provision was inserted in the Treaty of Versailles, 1920, creating the League of Nations. That provision endorsed the idea of creating an institution that would not be over the states but on their side, despite some later developments that displayed a certain authoritarian character[285].

285 [In the manuscript there appears at this point a note in parenthesis as follows: «If it is convenient to describe Soc. De los Nacs., Cavallera, 380-385. Find information on the new form of the UN, its interventions, and on other international organizations such as UNESCO, BIT, Bureau Int. de Education, FAO, Iro, Cepal, etc».]

3

The Problem of War[286]

No one disputes the tremendous seriousness of war, which has been greatly increased in recent years. Mercenary armies are no longer the ones that are fighting, but the whole nation is mobilized towards the defense of the country. Modern weapons, especially atomic ones, cause incalculable and unpredictable damage. Hatred among peoples, and economic, moral and religious damages remain as a sad heritage of war. It is to be hoped that the promotion of more humane habits and the strengthening of a truly international society will make war disappear from the earth, as has happened with slavery and with other barbaric institutions.

However, in the present state of affairs, unfortunately, there are circumstances in which war appears to be the only effective means of securing redress for a violated right or defense against an unjust aggressor. Such a war is *defensive,* even if the offended nation initates the war.

For a defensive war to be just, there must be: a real aggression; other means to secure reparation for the damage caused must be or appear to be insufficient; and the war must be one that would be effective in obtaining the restoration of the order which had been violated. The operations of war must be conducted with moderation.

The goal of war is, therefore, the reparation of the damage caused, the restitution of the right, and the securing of a condition in which the enemy is unable to damage the country again. This does not authorize, in any way, the use of war for the purpose of revenge, which is forbidden to nations as it is to individuals. War must be conducted without hatred for the guilty, but only for the purpose of restoring the violated order.

This understanding of war determines how it can be conducted. The combatant country has no right to destroy or to sack inhumanely, but only to the extent necessary to put the enemy out of action. It is never just to accelerate the end of the war by terror and indiscriminate destruction. International Law has been developing and introducing certain principles in conventions, such as respect for non-belligerents, for prisoners, who must not be used as cannon fod-

286 [In the manuscript appears at this point: «see Lallement».]

der in the front row in order to be killed first, and respect for civilian buildings, especially hospitals and Red Cross facilities. War does not authorize the use of perjury, fraud or instruments of mass destruction such as poisonous gases, or the shelling of open cities.

There are certain particularly dangerous means of warfare which have begun to be employed and which are feared to be even more grave in succeding wars: such as targeted bombing which destroys entire cities, and even more the atomic weapon. The evil of the latter does not proceed from its being atomic, because if it is directed strictly against a military objective, for example an aircraft carrier, it is a licit weapon like any other. However, atomic weapons should not be used against cities, because they make the survival of the inhabitants impossible, and also because of the subsequent radioactive effects. This leads us to think that their use is immoral and must be absolutely proscribed. On this matter there is no uniform criterion[287].

A treaty of peace must be according to justice, therefore its purpose is not the annihilation of the defeated country, but its punishment so far as the repair of the violated right and the security of posterity require. In determining reparations, Christians must take justice and charity into account. Benedict XV gave clear rules on this point in his address to heads of state of August 1, 1917, and in his letter on peace of May 23, 1920[288].

4
To Live in Peace

Peace, according to the beautiful thought of St. Augustine, is «the tranquility of order». It is indispensable for men to work and enjoy the benefits God has given them. Peace signifies an undisturbed possession of that which is one's own; that each one occupies his own place; that no attack or violence is feared; and that there are sincere and just relations among peoples and among individuals.

287 [At this point the author states in parenthesis: «Put the data: Reaction of the Vatican to the first atomic bombs, Archbishops of France, Address of Stockholm».]

288 [The author is referring to the following documents:

- Pope Benedict XV, Note to the Heads of the Belligerent Peoples (1 August 1917), http://www.pas.va/content/accademia/en/magisterium/benedictxv/1august1917.pdf.
- Pope Benedict XV, Encyclical on Peace and Christian Reconciliation *Pacem, Dei Munus Pulcherrimum* (23 May 1920), at the Holy See, http://w2.vatican.va/content/benedict-xv/en/encyclicals/documents/hf_ben-xv_enc_23051920_pacem-dei-munus-pulcherrimum.html.]

«Every legal organization for international relations has as its aim international common weal, and consequently peace. The bases of a just and durable peace are:
a) "Simultaneous and reciprocal reduction in armaments according to rules and guarantees to be laid down, to the extent necessary to maintain public order in each state".
b) "The settling up of arbitration according to rules to be agreed, and penalties to be determined against the State that would refuse either to submit international questions to arbitration or to accept the decisions" (Benedict XV, note of 1st August 1917.)»[289]

The covenant of the League of Nations explicitly recognizes the solidarity of nations. Each of the states that signed it has the right to address the Assembly or the Council on anything that may affect peace in international relations. The same covenant establishes a procedure for cases of such complaints. In addition to the Council and recognized by the League of Nations, the International Court of Justice operates at the Hague, and is responsible for giving its judgment on the interpretation of treaties and other points concerning international law.

In August of 1928, the Kellogg-Briand pact was signed in Paris condemning war as a means of resolving difficulties between nations, and proposing conciliation and arbitration. These efforts demonstrate that a more respectful attitude towards law is slowly but surely penetrating consciences[290].

289 [*A Code of Social Principles* § 174.]
290 [At this point the author states in parenthesis: «See institutions born from the last war, alluding to the current state of disruption, causes, remedies given by Pius XII in his international messages».]

Chapter 7

The Social Disorder. The Social Question

1

Meaning of the Social Question

The term «social question» is modern, but it is a reality as old as man, although it did not appear as a separate problem until sufficient light had been shed on the social order. Plato in *The Republic* and Thomas More in *Utopia* elaborated on their ideal social orders, but the conceptions contained in these works were very much in diapers. The denunciation of social evils is old, and we find it in the prophets of the people of Israel and repeated in every period of history.

The current approach to the social problem dates back to the last century, which called upon the social order then prevailing, capitalism, to control the grave defects which weakened it. When the term «social question» began to be used, it was equivalent to «the workers problem», or «labor problems». This sense is accurate but not complete because the social question is not only about the evils of one social class, but all the disorders in the functioning of the contemporary social system. The social question consists in the fact that society fails to achieve its own end, which is the common good, so that a considerable portion of its members do not proportionally participate in the common endeavor.

2

Is a Perfect Social Order Possible?

Individualists and collectivists say yes. The former say that social order will be obtained through the liberty of social factors; the latter believe that social harmony will be the fruit of general planning with the help of science and technology. Christianity, which is realistic and an expert in the true nature of man, affirms that the best social order can only approximately be achieved. This implies that no social order will be free of the social question. The weaknesses consequent upon original sin affect the mind, which is not capable of full lucidity, and the will, that is feeble in its tendency to the good, and therefore in knowing and establishing adequate means for perfect social cooperation. Since the destruction of the state of grace in which God created our first Parents, the earth gives its fruits with labor and produces thorns and thistles.

As perfect society is impossible, each society will have its own social question, according to the characteristic features of that society. In a society, good and evil live together, and experience shows us that the forces that deviate from the good, unfortunately, act with greater force. The doctrine of original sin does not teach that the social order is fundamentally perverted, nor does it teach that man is incapable of achieving his own purpose and perfection, but that the social body has a tendency towards disease, and order a tendency to disorder. That is why an uninterrupted effort and vigilance is absolutely necessary in order to reduce these failures to a minimum. Christian doctrine thus rejects, on the one hand, naive optimism based on an erroneous conception of human nature and, on the other, defeatist pessimism. Christian doctrine is deeply realistic and urges us to an action whose fruits we are sure to obtain through the regenerating influences of the Redemption deposited with the Church, whose action is indispensable to solve the social problem at its root.

3
General Causes of the Social Question

The first cause, as we have just seen, is human weakness and the insufficiency of the means of production. Then, there are ideological influences. Marxist theory does not admit, as the ultimate *substratum* of any social problem, anything other than the power of material production and the economic relations that are the determinants of human consciousness. Marxism, by reducing the social problem to economic factors, arbitrarily reduces other influences that create it. Ideological factors have their own value, at sometimes slowing down and at others accelerating changes in ways of life, and for that reason, in order to achieve a social conquest it is necessary to begin, at least, by gaining the favorable opinion of a sector of the society. This is well known in techniques of modern propaganda: formidable instruments of social change. Next, ideologies influence through the doctrines with which they try to solve the social problem. In each social system there are many ideologies that compete to direct the community: Christian, liberal, capitalist, nationalist, communist, fascist. This fact is so certain that the last world war could be called a war of ideologies. Ultimately, ideologies influence by proposing values and thus, ends towards which to aspire. Thus, *homo-oeconomicus*, as a representative of the individualist-capitalist ideology, indicates a path dominated by the motive of interest; the idea of national sovereignty determines the scheme of international relations in the liberal period; the needs of the community are the slogans of totalitarian systems.

To the extent that the underlying ideological forces in each system tend towards ends that deviate from the true good of human nature, the social process will be opposed to the common good, and thus harm many members of the community. The ideological factor is selective of the ends that determine the social process, and therefore, is one of the primary causes of the social question.

In the third place[291], the *institutions ordered to serve society* in the political, educational, economic, technical, etc., influence the social question for various reasons. First, because of institutions' natural *process of decay and maladaptation* in the face of new needs that arise, so that institutions that are capable of social development in one period can become antisocial at a later time. Then, by the *misuse* of such institutions, which orient towards private good what was created for the public good, for example the system of banks and credit that dictatorially dominate life today and that «regulate the flow, so to speak, of the lifeblood whereby the entire economic system lives, and have so firmly in their grasp the soul, as it were, of economic life that no one can breathe against their will»[292].

Institutions, which were created to help man in his development, *absorb and enslave* man. Thus, for example, technology in modern society, rather than a service to the worker has become his sepulcher: he is part of a mechanism to which he must be sacrificed like the slave tied to the chain. The «technical age», of which so much was expected, has come to consume the best human energies and turn man into a piece of a machine. Institutions that were created for the service of man can become useless and even harmful owing to their great complexity, such as legal institutions, for example: inaccessible to the simple citizen except with the help of a lawyer —and the complicated procedures of public offices that discourage one who intends to use them and may even nullify the rights created by the laws because of the complexity of the offices' demands.

291 [Here the author introduces, in addition to the two causes of the «social question» which he has previously identified —human weakness and ideological influences— a third cause, institutional in nature.

At this point, the author handwrote the following in the margin: «Influences Born of Institutions».]

292 [*Quadragesimo Anno* § 106.]

The excessive power given by certain institutions to their managers is another factor of social disorder, and can put society under the control of managers. Institutions established for the common good end up serving the particular good, escape the control of the public power and end up imposing their laws on all citizens: laws of finance, methods and credit. J. Burnham[293] admirably explains this danger in *The Managerial Revolution*.

4
Aspects of the Social Question

Each social system operates within specific circumstances, different from those of other countries and times, according to its particular ideology, its economic capabilities and its institutions. The failure of the common good in each system will be different in each case and it will be vain to seek a program to respond to the social question which applies to every time and country. For example, in Rome, the particular feature of the social question towards the end of the Republic was the depopulation of the countryside, owing to the recruitment of armies, the tax system and the exploitation of small proprietors by the usurers from the cities, with the consequent formation of *latifundia*, the augmentation of the urban proletariat and the number of slaves and the increasing importance of their functions. The Middle Ages knew its particular social problem, and at the end of this period it was exacerbated by the extraordinary increase in the maritime commercial power of the Italians and English. When the powerful merchants of the cities protected themselves against the competition of the guilds, it was impossible for the workers and apprentices to become masters; they could not marry; up to 11% of them were unemployed[294], and they constituted the medieval proletariat that provoked violent insurrections, as history indicates.

293 [James Burnham (1905-1987), American philosopher and political theorist. His most important work was *The Managerial Revolution* (1941), in which he theorized about the future of capitalism and the formation, after the First World War, of a new ruling class he called «managers».]

294 [In the manuscript, Hurtado adds at this point: «2(2)». It is not possible to know the meaning of this.]

5
The Social Problem in Our Days

The modern world has ideologies, institutions and techniques that are uniquely its own, and, unlike previous periods, have spread to a large portion of humanity. It seems that the world has changed more in the last century than in all the previous thousands years. (An octogenarian French farmer in our day tells of the surprise he had in reading Hesiod, for he found in the descriptions of the peasant customs of that time the same customs and peasant traditions of his childhood.).

Fr. Lebret, O. P., in an interesting series of lectures summarized the characteristics of our social problem:

Man has made an immense effort to understand nature, but he has not come to dominate what he has discovered. In the face of very rapid scientific progress, technical activity disproportionate to human nature has arisen. Man today feels himself to be a prisoner of such activity, as Gheorghiu describes it in *The 25th Hour*[295]. He can communicate instantaneously with men who live thousands of miles away, but still feel he is a slave. The ideologies of our time push man towards greater knowledge and power, but he does not realize that because he is not given liberal compensation at the same time, he is being chained the more.

Technical progress can only be achieved by a gigantic effort of production driven by the profit interest. The worker aspires to the highest wage, the capitalist to the highest interest, to the greatest capital, to the most productive business. Modern ideology is not dominated by the words «service» or «interest of the community», but by interest, gain and profit.

States, for immediate prosperity, compromise their futures: large loans, new issues of money, inflation, which will weigh heavily on tomorrow's world.

5.1. MILITARY CONFLICTS

We can say that during all this century we have lived under the threat of wars, which are on the verge of exploding at every moment. And in the hours in which we live, we are all under the anxiety of [not] knowing when the third world war will erupt: the most cruel that humanity will have known. According to Swedish

295 [Constantin Virgil Gheorghiu (1916-1992), Romanian writer, author of the novel *The 25th Hour* (1949).]

economist Gunnar Silverstolpe[296] (cited by Lebret), the war of 1914-1918 cost 186,000,000,000 dollars; the one of 1939-1944, 666,000,000,000 dollars; and the destruction is estimated at 200,000,000,000 dollars. The total human losses reached 13 million in the war of 1914, and 25 million in the latter. The Swedish economist himself adds: «if a human life is estimated to represent a productive capital of 10,000 dollars, having lost 25,000,000 men, the world has lost 250,000,000,000 dollars in goods and services. It is probable that humanity will suffer for decades, perhaps for centuries, the repercussion of these deaths and destructions». And what the economist does not point out is that humanity is suffering the bankruptcy of charity and fraternal love, and a spirit of suspicion, distrust and even hatred that dominates the earth.

If we read the national budgets of different countries, we see that the great majority allocates the most important part of them to military expenses in order to be able to face the emergency of a new war. Before the American Congress, new projects are constantly requiring billions of dollars for direct or indirect military defense. If all this immense sum of money were spent in meeting the overriding needs of the people: housing, education, clothing, health —we would not have this horrendous contemporary social problem.

5.2. THE SPECTER OF ANOTHER WAR

Faced with scientific progress, wise men tremble. One of them tells us: in early 1939 Joliot-Curie[297] discovered an explosive reaction in series—in a chain in the nucleus of uranium. The projectiles of the nuclear bombardment (the famous neutrons) increase in geometric progression; the phenomenon propagates like a fire or an epidemic. One kilogram of disintegrated uranium is equivalent to 20,000 tons of TNT in its explosive power. A single uranium bomb has a destructive effect 2,000 times greater than a ten-ton bomb. The dropping of a single atomic bomb has the same effect as a bombing by 12,000 airplanes. This wise man was writing just when the war ended, and had not yet heard of hydrogen bombs, whose results are vastly more damaging than those of uranium or plutonium. Three months after the explosion of the first atomic bomb, Einstein

296 [Karl Gunnar Silverstolpe (1891-1975), Swedish economist and professor at the School of Economics at Gothenburg. His book *National Economics for All* (1922) was published more than ten times and translated into several languages.]

297 [Irène Joliot-Curie (1897-1956) French scientist and the daughter of Marie and Pierre Curie, and her husband, Frédéric Joliot-Curie (1900-1958), were jointly awarded the Nobel Prize in Chemistry in 1935 for their discovery of artificial radioactivity.]

declared in an American magazine that in the next conflict two-thirds of the human species would be annihilated.

In today's world, few masters rule vast masses, and in the service of these masters there are techniques of unspeakable power that give these masters an authority unprecedented in history.

A great American scholar, a Nobel laureate, said: «I write to frighten you. I am a frightened man myself. All the scientists that I know are frightened —frightened for their lives— and frightened for your life»[298] and there is another who said, «science has made us gods even before we are worthy of being men. We will learn to release intra-atomic energy, we will travel to the stars, we will prolong life, we will cure tuberculosis, but we will never find the secret of being governed by the less unworthy»[299].

Humanity, with evangelical spirit, cannot fail to applaud without reservation all kinds of scientific conquests. A single grain of uranium will be more effective than ten tons of coal; we will have the power to water the deserts, transform the seasons, change agriculture, escape the attraction of the earth ... but «science without conscience is but the ruin of the soul», and it is not a question of only one soul but of all humanity's conscience and its universal ruin. We must balance science and conscience. The scientific triumphs of the modern world demand a more and more vigorous conscience.

5.3. THE CLASS STRUGGLE

Within each people there is another struggle: the class struggle. Within each country there is dissatisfied proletariat and, suffering even more, a sub-proletariat, which is too widespread in Asia and in most countries of Latin America: unskilled people, without education or the opportunity to rise. Having moved to big cities, attracted by the hope of a better standard of living, of greater culture, better futures and more ample distractions, they are eventually torn to shreds. The «*favelas*» in Brazil, «*callampas settlements*»[300] in Chile, and with dif-

298 [Harold Urey (1893-1981), American physical chemist whose work on isotopes earned him the Nobel Prize in Chemistry in 1934 for the discovery of deuterium. On January 5, 1946, Urey issued an open letter to the American public, in which he included the quoted phrase.]

299 [Jean Rostand (1894-1977), French biologist, philosopher and science writer, very active against nuclear proliferation. The previous quote was probably taken from his book *Pensées d'un Biologiste* (*Thoughts of a Biologist*) (1939).]

300 [The term in Spanish is «*poblaciones callampas*» and that could be literally translated as «mushroom neighborhoods», referring to the very poor settlements that spring up in a place from one day to the next.]

ferent names the same situations in all our Latin American cities, constitute a painful scandal: the blackest misery, the tremendous insecurity about tomorrow: will we have work? For how long? In our old age, what will we do when we become disabled? How will we survive? These millions of beings do not have property or social security for their days of unemployment, old age or illness. This appalling misery contrasts with luxury and waste, making it more painful.

> «But when on the one hand We see thousands of the needy, victims of real misery for various reasons beyond their control, and on the other so many round about them who spend huge sums of money on useless things and frivolous amusement, We cannot fail to remark with sorrow not only that justice is poorly observed, but that the precept of charity also is not sufficiently appreciated, is not a vital thing in daily life»[301].

206 5.4. UNEMPLOYMENT AND STRIKES

Unemployment has become a chronic and cyclical phenomenon of our capitalist civilization. An extraordinary boom in production is followed by a downturn. In 1932 in Great Britain unemployment rates among workers reached 22 per cent; in 1935 Germany had 11.6 per cent; and Canada in 1938 reached 15.1%. In 1940, the United States had 7,298,000 people without a job.

The instability of the situation of the working class is the cause of continuous strikes. The strikes of 1946 in the United States, and of 1947 and 1948 in France, endangered national stability; in our countries, in addition to various attempts at a general strike, the continuous strikes of different sectors of workers are an index of general malaise. Sometimes they compromise the welfare of the entire nation.

The atmosphere of constant insecurity that afflicts the proletariat is translated into a permanent tension among the various social classes. Communist forces take advantage of this situation to stir up just demands in order to achieve revolutionary political ends and to accelerate world revolution.

«How can there be peace», said Pius XII in 1939, «when … hundreds of thousands and millions are without work? Who does not see this horrible crisis of unemployment, these immense multitudes humiliated by their lack of work, whose sad condition is aggravated by the bitter contrast offered by others living in pleasure and luxury, unconcerned about the needs of the poor?»[302].

301 [*Divini Redemptoris* § 47.]

302 [At this point, the author cites his book *Social Christian Order*, item 9, which attributed these words to Pius XII, dated April 9, 1939.]

Fr. Lebret, O.P., points out, among the serious symptoms of contemporary social conflict, the still unresolved problem of exchange among large categories of producers, particularly between industry and agriculture, as well as between extraction and transformation. Peasants must borrow money to be able to continue working their land; otherwise they must give up their properties and move to the big cities. The more industry produces, the more it must locate an outlet for its goods, but when peasants are impoverished they have no purchasing power. This conflict, still without a solution, is complicated by international trade conflict. Large-scale producing nations, such as the United States now and also England, Germany and Japan previously, do not find purchasing capacity in other countries in proportion to the volume of their production. If the other countries do not have dollars, what is going to happen to the American production? Will we have unemployment again? Through the structuring of international negotiations, some countries aim to control and even monopolize foreign trade in order to know how their scarce dollars are invested. A country's excessive accumulation of wealth is a danger for its people.

In an underfed world we are even witnessing an effort to restrict production in order to maintain prices. The spectacle could not be more dramatic. On one side, there are millions of men suffering from hunger; on the other side there is a systematic effort to produce less or to destroy products, preferring that to lowering prices. Alarmed producers form coalitions that assure them an adequate price. In the case of cotton, the major producers signed a contract to destroy plantations. Those who accounted for 73% of the area planted with cotton undertook to destroy 1/3 of their crops. They collected 13,000,000 bales instead of 17,000,000 the previous year; so the price that in 1932 was 6.53 cents then rose to 9.72 cents. Farmers also received a premium to compensate them for the destroyed plantations. The case of the pigs: in 1932 there were 46,500,000 heads of pig in the USA. The forecast for 1933 was 47,500,000, and even more for 1934. The solution: liquidate 8,500,000 heads: 443,000,000 pounds of pork were destroyed, and partially given to the unemployed. The price that in 1932-1933 was 3.36 dollars went to 6.82 dollars in 1934-1935.

In the case of wheat a non-production bonus has been paid. The money paid as this premium was calculated on the basis of the discount to the total price of the produce.

5.6. INFLATION OF STATE BUDGETS

Not only the smaller nations but also the big countries have horribly inflated budgets and a strong annual deficit. The English budget deficit in 1945 was £ 2,200,000,000.

In 1946, the French Ministry of Finance presented an account of the country's difficult situation and explained its causes: the increase of bureaucracy. In 1914, the French State had 469,000 civilian employees; 697,000 in 1936; and 1,070,000 in 1946.

With the suppression of autonomous organizations the State becomes responsible for the outcomes of the management of most productive and commercial activities. The State transports, produces energy, distributes fuels, builds ships and mechanical objects and is also an insurance company and banker. The State is responsible for eighty per cent of major projects.

This inflation is increased by excessive military expenses in preparation for a possible war; social expenditures, which are highly justified, weigh heavily on the national budget; economic subsidies to reduce living expenses burden the State with expenses that benefit the consumer. The State has surpassed its normal capacity and, if it continues in that way, it can yield to into the totalitarian temptation.

5.7. DISORDER AND PARASITISM IN DISTRIBUTION

There is already an excess of non-productive men in the national administration; there is also an excess of unproductive people in distribution chains, which greatly increases the cost of living.

In 1896 there were eight merchants for every hundred active people in France; in 1936 there were 20.2 per 100 producers. Retail trade immobilizes a very important part of the population. The food trade, not including hotels, cafés and restaurants, immobilized 500,000 people in France in 1900; 820,000 in 1937[303].

5.8. FREQUENT DECREASE IN THE PURCHASING POWER OF SALARY

It is indisputable that wages, taken numerically in pesos, increase frequently, but this increase does not always correspond to an increase in purchasing power or to a better standard of living[304].

303 [The meaning of these two last sentences is not clear. Maybe the author was trying to say «mobilize» and not «immobilize».]

304 [Hurtado intended to include statistics here. In the manuscript he states: «Copy Statistics, Lebret, 8 and 9».]

5.9. INTERVENTION WITH SOCIAL SECURITY MEASURES

The disproportion between wages and the cost of living, the unemployment that strikes daily different groups of workers, the lack of private property to support them during bad times, illness and accidents: all these require that social security measures permanently intervene in the life of the contemporary wage-earner, to supply him with what he cannot provide with his ordinary resources.

Social security measures cost the nation a considerable effort, but their results are deficient. As long as we do not find a better solution, we cannot think of abandoning these measures, which give the worker some indirect security. But, would not it be interesting to investigate whether current social structures might not be repaired in order to achieve a better solution? Pius XII said on June 13, 1943: «... it is the whole society, in its complex structure, which needs to be repaired and improved, because its very foundations are shaking»[305].

5.10. RURAL EXODUS AND CITY HAZARDS

Alongside these great matters of the social problem we should describe thousands of disorders of daily life. There has been a massive migration of peasants to the big cities, because of the economic and cultural impossibility of the countryside's retaining them. Large cities have a pernicious influence on the majority of the population: they sterilize populations, by decreasing birth rates and increasing mortality. In France, the replacement rate for women in large cities is 50%. In the big cities peasants find an increase in tuberculosis, alcoholism, cancer and syphilis, prostitution, vagabond and delinquent young people and promiscuous life within tenement housing and improvised settlements. The future of a country is threatened by each of these dangers that we have briefly mentioned, although they would require deep discussion in order to understand their gravity[306].

305 [Here Hurtado quotes his book *Social Christian Order,* item 7. The document cited here is Pius XII, *Speech To the Italian Workers* (13 June 1943), at The Holy See, https://w2.vatican.va/content/pius-xii/it/speeches/1943/documents/hf_p-xii_spe_19430613_lavoratori-italia.html, (hereinafter referred to as *Speech to the Italian Workers.*) The speech on the Vatican website is only in Italian, so the editors translated it from Hurtado's book.]

306 [The author intended to include statistics here. In the manuscript he states: «Set forth Data of vagrancy, mortality...».]

In order to judge this delicate point, let us turn to the texts in which the Roman Pontiffs analyze the distribution of the wealth in the modern world. Already in 1891 Leo XIII said: « ... working men have been surrendered, isolated and helpless, to the hardheartedness of employers and the greed of unchecked competition ... [T]he hiring of labor and the conduct of trade are concentrated in the hands of comparatively few; so that a small number of very rich men have been able to lay upon the teeming masses of the laboring poor a yoke little better than that of slavery itself»[307].

Forty years later, Pius XI repeated this thought in *Quadragesimo Anno*: « ... the immense multitude of the non-owning workers on the one hand and the enormous riches of certain very wealthy men on the other establish an unanswerable argument that the riches which are so abundantly produced in our age of "industrialism", as it is called, are not rightly distributed and equitably made available to the various classes of the people. Therefore, with all our strength and effort we must strive that at least in the future the abundant fruits of production will accrue equitably to those who are rich and will be distributed in ample sufficiency among the workers»[308].

In the same encyclical Pius XI did not hesitate to speak of the undeserved indigence of the proletarians and sought to relieve those «who could in no way convince themselves that so enormous and unjust an inequality in the distribution of this world's goods truly conforms to the designs of the all-wise Creator»[309].

In the same encyclical Pius XI points out the character of the current capitalist regime:

> «In the first place, it is obvious that not only is wealth concentrated in our times but an immense power and despotic economic dictatorship is consolidated in the hands of a few, who often are not owners but only the trustees and managing directors of invested funds which they administer according to their own arbitrary will and pleasure.

307 [*Rerum Novarum* § 3.]
308 [*Quadragesimo Anno* §§ 60-61.]
309 [*Quadragesimo Anno* §5.]

This dictatorship is being most forcibly exercised by those who, since they hold the money and completely control it, control credit also and rule the lending of money. Hence they regulate the flow, so to speak, of the life-blood whereby the entire economic system lives, and have so firmly in their grasp the soul, as it were, of economic life that no one can breathe against their will.

This concentration of power and might, the characteristic mark, as it were, of contemporary economic life, is the fruit that the unlimited freedom of struggle among competitors has of its own nature produced, and which lets only the strongest survive; and this is often the same as saying, those who fight the most violently, those who give least heed to their conscience.

This accumulation of might and of power generates in turn three kinds of conflict. First, there is the struggle for economic supremacy itself; then there is the bitter fight to gain supremacy over the State in order to use in economic struggles its resources and authority; finally there is conflict between States themselves, not only because countries employ their power and shape their policies to promote every economic advantage of their citizens, but also because they seek to decide political controversies that arise among nations through the use of their economic supremacy and strength»[310].

Who does not understand in these words of the Pope a multitude of facts about our contemporary economic organization; who does not see in them the intimate history of so many political tragedies that have ended in blood in our countries of America and in the whole world; who does not discover in his sad warnings the key to the latest international conflicts? Still without leaving *Quadragesimo Anno* we find in the encyclical a severe condemnation of the history of the capitalist regime presently prevailing in the world: «Property, that is, "capital",has undoubtedly long been able to appropriate too much to itself. Whatever was produced, whatever returns accrued, capital claimed for itself, hardly leaving to the worker enough to restore and renew his strength»[311].

On September 1, 1944, Pius XII sketches a picture of contemporary social disorder, and his words are as somber as those of Pius XI and even as those of Leo XIII fifty years ago: «On the one hand we see immense wealth that dominates economic life, public and private, and often even civil life; on the other, countless numbers of those who have no direct or indirect security in their lives, are no

310 [*Quadragesimo Anno* §§ 105-108.]
311 [*Quadragesimo Anno* § 54.]

longer interested in the real and higher values of the spirit, who abandon their aspiration for genuine freedom and throw themselves at the feet of any political party, slaves of anyone who promises them bread and security in some way»[312].

The situation of the proletariat in Latin America causes anguish to the Roman Pontiff. Thus Pius XI, speaking in *Quadragesimo Anno* of the beneficial effects of *Rerum Novarum* points out with distress, «not only in the countries called new, but also in the realms of the Far East that have been civilized from antiquity, the number of the non-owning working poor has increased enormously and their groans cry to God from the earth. Added to them is the huge army of rural wage workers, pushed to the lowest level of existence and deprived of all hope of ever acquiring "some property in land"[313], and, therefore, permanently bound to the status of non-owning worker unless suitable and effective remedies are applied»[314].

The words of Pius XI contain a bitter truth that invites reflection and may also invite consideration of the actual distribution of goods in our American countries. For lack of time we do not conduct this analysis, whose results are terrifying. A small number of people own the vast majority of the land. (In one of our countries, 1,400 proprietors own 60% of the agricultural land, while 129,000 small landowners —who own less than 20 hectares— own only 2.5% of those cultivable lands. Meanwhile, parcels of less than five hectares do not exceed 0.6% of the farmland in that same country). Referring to North America, Father Bigo[315] (*Travaux de L'Action Populaire*, October 1949, p. 567) cites the case of 326 American families with an annual income of more than $500,000, while 2,143,432 families had monthly incomes lower than U.S. $250. The overall incomes of these two groups of families, 326 on the one hand, 2,143,432 on the other, are the same. The difference between the income of the one group compared to that of the other is 2,000 to one. These considerations invite us to ana-

312 [Here Hurtado quotes his book *Social Christian Order*, item 8, which cites Pius XII, *Radio Message Oggi al Compiersi on the Fifth Anniversary of the Beginning of the War* (1 September 1944), at The Holy See, https://w2.vatican.va/content/pius-xii/es/speeches/1944/documents/hf_p-xii_spe_19440901_al-compiersi.html. The speech on the Vatican website is only in Italian and Spanish. The editors here translated this passage from Hurtado's book.]

313 [The encyclical here has a footnote as follows: «Encyclical, *On the Condition of Workers*, 66».]

314 [*Quadragesimo Anno*, § 59.]

315 [Pierre Bigo, S.J., (1906-1997), French priest and Doctorate of Law, President of *Action Populaire* (*French Catholic Action*) from 1952 to 1958, and founder of the Latin American Institute of Doctrine and Social Studies. In his doctoral thesis *Marxisme et Humanisme* (*Marxism and Humanism*) (1953) he showed his openness to learning from Marxist ideas.]

lyze the situation in our own country. What is that situation? What is the disproportion between the capitalist, the proletariat and that immense subproletariat, with totally subhuman living conditions that are a permanent reproach to our non-fulfillment of the precepts of the Gospel? This examination of conscience must be undertaken with seriousness, without fear of any consequences, as crushing as they may seem. With respect to Chile, the author of these lines has proposed this in a book —one that provoked very divergent reactions— the title of which, *Is Chile a Catholic Country?*[316], sufficiently indicates its content[317].

Withdrawal from Religion by the masses: this iniquitous distribution of goods has alienated from God «those immense multitudes of their brother-workmen who, because they were not understood or treated with the respect to which they were entitled, in bitterness have strayed far from God»[318]. Pius XI points out a remarkable reason in *Divini Redemptoris* for this estrangement from God: bitterness because the workers were not understood or treated with the dignity to which they were entitled.

The proportions of this religious conflict are appalling. In *Quadragesimo Anno*, Pius XI says: «[f]or We are now confronted, as more than once before in the history of the Church, with a world that in large part has almost fallen back into paganism»[319]. In *Divini Redemptoris* he affirms, «[f]or the first time in history we are witnessing a struggle, cold-blooded in purpose and mapped out to the least detail, between man and "all that is called God"»[320].

316 [Alberto Hurtado Cruchaga, *¿Es Chile un País Católico?* (*Is Chile a Catholic Country?*) (1941).]

317 [At this Point Hurtado added two paragraphs about the «abandonment of the home by the woman», which the editors decided to exclude. These theses here were developed in the section of this book headed *Pernicious Consequences of the Absence of Woman from the Home*. The language in both is much the same, but more extent and detail is provided in the first one.]

318 [*Divini Redemptoris* § 70.]

319 [*Quadragesimo Anno* § 14.]

320 [*Divini Redemptoris* § 22. The encyclical here has a footnote as follows: «Cf. *Thessalonians*, II, 4».]

5.12. SOCIAL DISORIENTATION

Having taken this quick look at the contemporary social problem, it is extremely striking to see so many men, even Catholics, who seem to ignore this horrendous tragedy. What is even worse is that once they come to know it they remain indifferent; they believe it to be an absolutely irreformable situation, and criticize, as utopian or even malicious, any denunciation of our evils and confound all movements of social reform with communism, thus bestowing unjust praise on Marxism and levelling the most atrocious accusation at Catholicism[321].

321 [Hurtado next wrote: «With great frankness (Copy ib.12, Decline of man, Translate Lebret 10, 11, 12)». To read more about Lebret, see footnote 70.]

Chapter 8

Systems for Resolving the Social Question

Among the great systems proposed for resolving the social problem we will analyze only liberalism, capitalism, socialism, communism and social Catholicism.

1

Liberalism

We must begin by distinguishing the different meanings of the word liberal. Liberality is one of the attributes of God and characterizes His inclination to communicate His goods to the beings He created.

In a general way, the word liberalism is used to designate any system that affirms that freedom is the supreme good for man. Liberalism establishes, as the central point of every program and of every religious, political, economic and social organization, the idea of working to secure the maximum use of freedom, which constitutes the end of such organizations. The purpose of the law is to promote the development of such freedoms.

Under this general concept of liberalism we will distinguish absolute liberalism, liberalism mitigated in its social range and economic liberalism. The first two are carefully studied in the encyclical *Libertas* of Leo XIII, and the second[322] one is mentioned in *Quadragesimo Anno* and *Divini Redemptoris* of Pius XI.

1.1. ABSOLUTE LIBERALISM

Absolute or radical liberalism affirms as its first principle:

> «…[T]he sovereignty of human reason, which, refusing due submission to the divine and eternal reason, proclaims its own independence, and constitutes itself the supreme principle and source and judge of truth. Hence, these followers of liberalism deny the existence of any divine authority to which obedience is due, and proclaim that every man is a law unto himself; from which arises that ethical system which they style *independent* morality, and which, under the guise of liberty, exonerates man from any obedience to the commands of God, and substitutes a boundless license. The end of all this it is not difficult to foresee, especially when society is in question. For, when once man is firmly persuaded that he is subject to no one, it follows that the efficient cause of the unity of civil society is not to be sought in any principle external to man,

322 [Hurtado wrote «second» but he was probably referring to the third kind of liberalism.]

or superior to him, but simply in the free will of individuals; that the authority in the State comes from the people only; and that, just as every man's individual reason is his only rule of life, so the collective reason of the community should be the supreme guide in the management of all public affairs. Hence the doctrine of the supremacy of the greater number, and that all right and all duty reside in the majority. But, from what has been said, it is clear that all this is in contradiction to reason. To refuse any bond of union between man and civil society, on the one hand, and God the Creator and consequently the supreme Law-giver, on the other, is plainly repugnant to the nature, not only of man, but of all created things; for, of necessity, all effects must in some proper way be connected with their cause; and it belongs to the perfection of every nature to contain itself within that sphere and grade which the order of nature has assigned to it, namely, that the lower should be subject and obedient to the higher.

Moreover, besides this, a doctrine of such character is most hurtful both to individuals and to the State. For, once ascribe to human reason the only authority to decide what is true and what is good, and the real distinction between good and evil is destroyed; honor and dishonor differ not in their nature, but in the opinion and judgment of each one; pleasure is the measure of what is lawful; and, given a code of morality which can have little or no power to restrain or quiet the unruly propensities of man, a way is naturally opened to universal corruption. With reference also to public affairs: authority is severed from the true and natural principle whence it derives all its efficacy for the common good; and the law determining what it is right to do and avoid doing is at the mercy of a majority. Now, this is simply a road leading straight to tyranny. The empire of God over man and civil society once repudiated, it follows that religion, as a public institution, can have no claim to exist, and that everything that belongs to religion will be treated with complete indifference. Furthermore, with ambitious designs on sovereignty, tumult and sedition will be common amongst the people; and when duty and conscience cease to appeal to them, there will be nothing to hold them back but force, which of itself alone is powerless to keep their covetousness in check. Of this we have almost daily evidence in the conflict with *socialists* and members of other seditious societies, who labor unceasingly to bring about revolution. It is for those, then, who are capable of forming a just estimate of things to decide whether such doctrines promote that true liberty which alone is worthy of man, or rather, pervert and destroy it»[323].

323 [*Libertas* §§ 15-16.]

Therefore, this absolute liberal system establishes, at the level of theory, complete freedom of conscience, and the duty of the State to oppose any attempt to restrict in any way this total freedom of conscience. As a result, the liberal State will be in principle, a non-religious State, practically an atheistic State, and also —a curious paradox for a system of freedom— a State which is a persecutor of the Catholic Church, because she does not admit the principle of absolute freedom of conscience. Every religion worthy of the name is a bond of conscience to God, to dogmas, to morals.

Hence, freedom of thought, of the press, of propaganda and of teaching are established, but not in the case of Catholic teaching, which is forbidden because it is contrary to this absolute freedom. Every doctrine must be able to express itself freely, for there is no absolute truth; today's error may be the truth of tomorrow. Naturally, this system is condemned by the Church.

This system began with Rousseau and his doctrine of social contract and was spread by the French encyclopedists, arrived in Latin America and took the form of what Alberto Edwards called «the liberal religion», so fashionable in the nineteenth century.

1.2. MITIGATED LIBERALISM

Its supporters, «compelled by the force of truth, do not hesitate to admit that such liberty is vicious, nay, is simple license ... and therefore they would have liberty ruled and directed by right reason, and consequently subject to the natural law and to the divine eternal law. But here they think they may stop, holding that man as a free being is bound by no law of God except such as He makes known to us through our natural reason»[324].

This restriction of obedience leads to self-contradictory behavior by refusing compliance with revelation. «[R]everence for the divine law will be apparent rather than real, and arbitrary judgment will prevail over the authority and providence of God»[325]. It is therefore necessary that the norm be compliance not only with natural law, but also with each and every one of the laws that God has given. «Laws of this kind have the same origin, the same author, as the eternal law, are absolutely in accordance with right reason, and perfect the natural law»[326].

324 [*Libertas* § 17.]
325 [*Id.*]
326 [*Id.*]

Leo XIII points to an even more moderate liberalism. «There are others, somewhat more moderate though not more consistent, who affirm that the morality of individuals is to be guided by the divine law, but not the morality of the State, for that in public affairs the commands of God may be passed over, and may be entirely disregarded in the framing of laws. Hence follows the fatal theory of the need of separation between Church and State»[327]. They forget that the State, like individuals, must conform to the laws of God and facilitate its observance and act in accordance with the Church, because although State and Church have two different immediate ends, their subjects are the same, and not infrequently they deal with the same matters, though in different ways. Therefore, «there must necessarily exist some order or mode of procedure to remove the occasions of difference and contention, and to secure harmony in all things»[328].

The affirmations of these absolute and mitigated liberal systems are opposed to the public good and to the truth itself. Experience shows us every day that, in view of the need for the defense of the superior goods of the family and of the State, those who have authority must impose certain restrictions required by the public good. In abnormal circumstances, such as in the case of war, these restrictions may often be considerable.

Even considering the nature of truth itself, it is clear that man is not morally free to embrace it or not. All truth once known requires our adherence; and if it is a religious truth, there is also the supreme motivation of God's will: we cannot therefore consider ourselves morally indifferent on the issue of whether or not to embrace it. A freedom of conscience understood in this sense does not exist. This does not mean that one is obliged to admit a truth that one does not know or not see to be true, nor does it mean that anyone is forced to deny his convictions or to be prevented from following them within the forum of his own conscience.

The press has no right to knowingly propagate error, and if the law restricts its freedom when it comes to the honor of a third party, for the same reason the law must prevent the propagation of errors that will damage the truth and the people who, for lack of preparation, are not able to defend themselves internally. If one accepts that there are truths, instruction in principle cannot ignore these truths, although some people deny them[329].

327 [*Id.* § 18.]

328 [*Id.*]

329 [In the manuscript appears the following: «Put in a note the most important paragraphs from 24 to 39 of *Libertas* pp 196-202». Because of the extent of the passages mentioned and because it is

1.3. THE TOLERANCE OF THE CHURCH

When speaking of tolerance of error, it is convenient to distinguish two species: dogmatic and civil tolerance.

We call dogmatic tolerance which is based on the principle that every idea, every cult has an equal right to be respected. In the end, this tolerance ignores the difference between truth and error and denies the exclusive rights of truth. This tolerance can never be accepted.

Civil or practical tolerance recognizes the rights of truth, but it tempers its application in practice according to the actual circumstances: the willingness of men to receive the truth; the invincible error in which many are found; and the struggles that would ensue upon urging certain behavior. Civil tolerance is lawful and its application is governed by the virtue of prudence.

In this regard, Pope Leo XIII says:

> «The Church most earnestly desires that the Christian teaching, of which We have given an outline, should penetrate every rank of society in reality and in practice; [...]
>
> Yet, with the discernment of a true mother, the Church weighs the great burden of human weakness, and well knows the course down which the minds and actions of men are in this our age being borne. For this reason, while not conceding any right to anything save what is true and honest, she does not forbid public authority to tolerate what is at variance with truth and justice, for the sake of avoiding some greater evil, or of obtaining or preserving some greater good. God Himself in His providence, though infinitely good and powerful, permits evil to exist in the world, partly that greater good may not be impeded, and partly that greater evil may not ensue. In the government of States it is not forbidden to imitate the Ruler of the world; and, as the authority of man is powerless to prevent every evil, it has (as St. Augustine says) to overlook and leave unpunished many things which are punished, and rightly, by Divine Providence[330]. But if, in such circumstances, for the sake of the common good (and this is the only legitimate reason), human law may or even should tolerate evil, it may not and should not approve or desire evil for its own sake; for evil of itself, being a privation of good, is opposed to the common welfare which every legislator is bound to desire and defend to the best of his ability. In this, human law must endeavor to imitate

not possible to determine what Hurtado calls «the most important paragraphs», the editors have chosen not to include them.]

330 [The encyclical here has a footnote as follows: «Augustine, *De libero arbitrio*, lib. 1, cap. 6, n. 14 (*PL* 32, 1228)».]

God, who, as St. Thomas teaches, in allowing evil to exist in the world, "neither wills evil to be done, nor wills it not to be done, but wills only to permit it to be done; and this is good"[331]. This saying of the Angelic Doctor contains briefly the whole doctrine of the permission of evil.

But, to judge aright, we must acknowledge that, the more a State is driven to tolerate evil, the further is it from perfection; and that the tolerance of evil which is dictated by political prudence should be strictly confined to the limits which its justifying cause, the public welfare, requires. Wherefore, if such tolerance would be injurious to the public welfare, and entail greater evils on the State, it would not be lawful; for in such case the motive of good is wanting. And although in the extraordinary condition of these times the Church usually acquiesces in certain modern liberties, not because she prefers them in themselves, but because she judges it expedient to permit them, she would in happier times exercise her own liberty; and, by persuasion, exhortation, and entreaty would endeavor, as she is bound, to fulfill the duty assigned to her by God of providing for the eternal salvation of mankind. One thing, however, remains always true—that the liberty which is claimed for all to do all things is not, as We have often said, of itself desirable, inasmuch as it is contrary to reason that error and truth should have equal.

And as to *tolerance*, it is surprising how far removed from the equity and prudence of the Church are those who profess what is called liberalism. For, in allowing that boundless license of which We have spoken, they exceed all limits, and end at last by making no apparent distinction between truth and error, honesty and dishonesty. And because the Church, the pillar and ground of truth, and the unerring teacher of morals, is forced utterly to reprobate and condemn tolerance of such an abandoned and criminal character, they calumniate her as being wanting in patience and gentleness, and thus fail to see that, in so doing, they impute to her as a fault what is in reality a matter for commendation. But, in spite of all this show of tolerance, it very often happens that, while they profess themselves ready to lavish liberty on all in the greatest profusion, they are utterly intolerant toward the Catholic Church, by refusing to allow her the liberty of being herself free»[332].

331 [The encyclical here has a footnote as follows: «*Summa Theologica*, la, q. XIX, a. 9, ad 3m».]
332 [*Libertas* §§ 32-35.]

1.4. ECONOMIC LIBERALISM[333]

This one does not have much in common with the Liberalism we have just discussed, except the name and a certain preference for freedom. Economic liberalism refers to the domain of production, distribution and transformation of wealth.

Economic liberalism fosters freedom and interest as the means of economic well-being. Its maxim is from economists of the School of Manchester of the nineteenth century: «*laissez faire, laissez passer*»[334]. It is necessary to place confidence in liberty because by its exercise liberty will cure the abuses that it creates; and therefore it is necessary to reduce to a minimum the intervention of the State and of the other associations that would disturb the exercise of liberty. Very soon, the producer and the consumer will come to realize that, instead of fighting, they must understand one another so that they spontaneously obtain social equilibrium. Its classic authors are Bastiat[335], Stuart Mill[336], Say[337], Rossi[338], Adam Smith[339], Ricardo[340] and Malthus[341]. The principles of economic liberalism, as we see, have nothing to do with those of the philosophical liberalism we have just

333 [In the manuscript there appears at this point: «See pamphlet P. Aldunate».]

334 [The author is referring to Manchester Liberalism: a set of political, social and economic movements initiated in Manchester, England, in the nineteenth century. The Manchester School, led by Richard Cobden and John Bright, took its ideas from the economic liberalism of David Hume, Adam Smith and Jean-Baptiste Say, and sought to apply them to public policy.]

335 [Claude-Frédéric Bastiat (1801-1850), French liberal economist, strong advocate of an unrestricted free market. Bastiat developed the concept of opportunity cost and the broken window fallacy (breaking a window can raise the GDP, but harm the economy.) He was a prolific writer, and in one of his most famous works, *La Loi* (*The Law*) (1850), he states that «each of us has a natural right—from God— to defend his person, his liberty, and his property».]

336 [John Stuart Mill (1806-1873), British philosopher and economist, one of the most influential thinkers of liberalism. In his book *On Liberty* (1859) he addressed the nature of power and its limits.]

337 [Jean-Baptiste Say (1767-1832), French liberal economist, known by the *Say's Law* or law of markets. His most important work was *Traité d'Économie Politique ou Simple Exposition de la Manière dont se Forment, se Distribuent et se Composent les Richesses* (*A Treatise on Political Economy or Mere Exposition of the Way in which Wealth is Formed, Distributed and Composed*) (1804).]

338 [Pellegrino Rossi (1787-1848), Italian economist, jurist and politician. He taught law and political economy in several prestigious Italian, French and Swiss universities, and is the author of *Cours d'Économie Politique* (*Course of Political Economy*) (1838-54).]

339 [Adam Smith (1723-1790), Scottish economist and philosopher, best know by his classic works, *The Theory of Moral Sentiments* (1759), and *An Inquiry into the Nature and Causes of the Wealth of Nations* (1776). Smith laid the foundation of classical free market economic theory.]

340 [David Ricardo (1772-1823), British political economist. Ricardo's most famous work was *Principles of Political Economy and Taxation* (1817). He developed a labor theory of value.]

341 [Thomas Robert Malthus (1776-1834), English political economist and cleric, known by his work, *An Essay on the Principle of Population* (1798). During the 1820s he engaged in an intellectual debate called the «Malthus-Ricardo debate», relating to economic rents.]

reviewed. The liberal economists are attentive only to laws that govern economic phenomena and in this field claim for themselves an exclusive competence. Political Economy is a science autonomous and independent from morality.

In so formulating their position, liberal economists have encountered the opposition of Catholic moralists, who laid upon them the responsibility for the great moral and material disorders which, along with great material advantages, characterized the new industrial world that was created under these doctrines. It is necessary that moral principles also govern the world of economics, that the State intervene to save the weak, and that workers be able to associate and defend their interests. A conflict between economics and morality has dominated the world of industry and commerce for the last century.

1.5. ECONOMIC NEOLIBERALISM

Since 1938 we speak about «neoliberalism». In that year, renowned economists and liberal sociologists celebrated in France what has been called the «Walter Lippmann Colloquium»[342], whose conclusions formulated in an «Agenda» contain the essential principles for the renewal of what has been called neoliberalism. This movement has developed. Other trends also point in the same direction. The essential ideas are as follows.

In the first place, neoliberals revise the liberal system and analyze the causes of its decadence. These causes would not be internal but external to the system: legal freedom has not been sufficient to maintain the state of free competition.

They say that the mistake of the classical liberals has been to believe that the spontaneous equilibrium that arises from the free interplay of economic laws would maintain itself. «*Laisser faire, laisser passer*» was interpreted not as a revolutionary slogan, but as a slogan commending the passivity of the State. This allowed the concentration of capital and the monopolies that have killed competition. In addition, the system of stock companies, which has allowed great achievements, facilitated the domination of the economy by finance. The dissociation of capital ownership from company management has allowed shareholders, bankers and financiers to seek profit at the expense of production, profit rather than satisfaction of needs. Trusts and monopolies have been formed be-

342 [The Walter Lippmann Colloquium, a conference organized in 1938 by the French philosopher Louis Rougier (1889-1982) to discuss the creation of a new form of liberalism. In that conference, Alexander Rustow (German sociologist and economist, 1885-1963) coined the term «neoliberalism» as name for a theory which rejected liberalism based on *laissez-faire*.]

cause the State allowed them, when it should have opposed their creation because they destroy competition. The passivity of the State has allowed the existence of the Manchester system[343], which is not true liberalism. Far from abstaining from action, public authority was required to ensure the maintenance of effective freedom through appropriate legislation. Liberalism declines because of the anti-liberal behavior of the State.

The essential positive doctrines of neoliberalism, leaving aside many nuances, are the following: seek an intermediate path between Manchesterian *laissez-faire* and totalitarian and communist collectivism. This would have four fundamental principles: rejection of the belief in a necessary evolution towards collectivist society; benefits of individualism; necessity of the inequality of human conditions with certain corrections; and the necessity of the intervention of the State to maintain the State's and free market's interplay.

Neoliberals do not accept that the capitalist machinery and technique are the things that have caused industrial concentration, but the passivity of the State. If men have accepted centralized planning regimes, that has been in order to find a certain security, which *laissez-faire* did not give them. There is, therefore, no necessary evolution towards collectivism, except insofar as the State does not intervene properly.

To obviate the depersonalization produced by collectivism, neoliberals want to focus the economy on the needs of the individual. The producer who seeks to satisfy his personal interest fairly will recover his place in production and will be a morally superior being.

Inequality of condition is the inescapable condition of an individualistic regime, but this inequality must be attenuated by a minimum of social security, an indispensable remedy for inequalities.

In the legal order, the intervention of the State is allowed so as to create laws that permit the operation of the free market. The State should, therefore, regulate property, contracts, banking systems, currency, etc.: all that constitutes the framework of the market; if this scheme is insufficient, it must be adapted again. So far as economic intervention is concerned, it should be limited to cushioning excessively violent disequilibrium in free competition. Direct intervention in pricing will be avoided, and only indirect intervention by means of regulations, for example through moderate customs tariffs, will be accepted. Free unions would be accepted, but not compulsory ones.

343 [See footnote 334.]

As can be seen, neoliberalism rejects the passivity of the State, monopolies, financial power and indifference to the social consequences of economic disequilibrium. Its adds interventionism, social justice and the idea that maximum utility is a social good, but not necessarily the only one to seek. But it retains all the fundamental characteristics of classical liberalism: the individualist foundation and the pursuit of greater monetary profit by the free market. Its spirit remains capitalist. This system is difficult to distinguish in practice from *dirigisme*. Moreover, in theory the distinction is clear, because in neoliberalism the purpose is individualistic, the intensity is moderate, the application is indirect; in *dirigisme* the intention is collectivist, the intensity is strong, the application to price levelling is direct.

These are the principles. Their application in contemporary society would go far beyond the purposes of this book. (The exposition of neoliberalism has been taken largely from Alain Barrère's course *The current aspects of Liberalism, Semaines Sociales de France*, 1947.)

Three reservations must be asserted about Neoliberalism's economic, social and moral order:

The neoliberalist attack on the State for not intervening opportunely seems to forget the terrible capitalist force that has dominated even States. In order for such a legal intervention by the State to be possible, a reform is necessary in the very structure of the State, accompanied by a profound moral reform. But the structural reforms accepted by neoliberals do not seem sufficient.

In its social aspect, neoliberalism has an orientation that continues to bear great resemblance to capitalism as it historically has developed; therefore it is difficult for it to accept the overcoming of the system of wages and the integration of the workers into economic life. If legislation is demanded as to private property, it is only to allow free market competition, not to facilitate a general access of individuals to private property. A reform of companies to allow the economic and social participation of workers is not in sight. Among the opposing classes: wage earners and employers do not allow space to occupational organizations that solve work problems.

In its moral aspect, the principal reservation about neoliberalism is its amorality. Pure economic science can be called amoral, but not when applied to man: economy, when it touches the human being, cannot be amoral. Reaction against a civilization of the masses is just, but it is not just to neglect the masses in order to rejoice in the emergence of some strong personalities that arise out of the struggle, only mitigating the struggle's pernicious effects. «Economic freedom is a precious good, but not the supreme one to which other goods should be sacrificed. Economic freedom is a good but its realization must be sought within an order that is the order of the person ... Economic freedom is subordinate to the more general freedom of the human person and inextricably linked to respect for his dignity, and to the exercise of the responsibilities that are necessary for his complete development»[344].

1.6. CONCLUSIONS OF THE POPES AS TO ECONOMIC LIBERALISM

The lastest Pontiffs have pronounced directly and indirectly about economic liberalism. Here are some statements.

Liberalism engendered this capitalist economy, which aspires to world domination:

> «This concentration of power and might, the characteristic mark, as it were, of contemporary economic life, is the fruit that the unlimited freedom of struggle among competitors has of its own nature produced, and which lets only the strongest survive; and this is often the same as saying, those who fight the most violently, those who give least heed to their conscience.
>
> This accumulation of might and of power generates in turn three kinds of conflict. First, there is the struggle for economic supremacy itself; then there is the bitter fight to gain supremacy over the State in order to use in economic struggles its resources and authority; finally there is conflict between States themselves, not only because countries employ their power and shape their policies to promote every economic advantage of their citizens, but also because they seek to decide political controversies that arise among nations through the use of their economic supremacy and strength.
>
> The ultimate consequences of the individualist spirit in economic life are those which you yourselves, Venerable Brethren and Beloved Children, see and deplore: Free competition has destroyed itself; economic dictatorship has supplanted the free market; unbridled ambition for power has likewise succeeded greed for gain; all economic life has become tragically hard, inexorable, and cruel. To these are to be added the grave evils that have resulted from an intermingling and shameful confusion of the func-

344 [At this point the author wrote: «Ib. 178». It is not clear to which book he is referring. It could refer to the course *The current aspects of Liberalism, Semaines Sociales de France*, written by Alain Barrère, mentioned in the previous page.]

tions and duties of public authority with those of the economic sphere—such as, one of the worst, the virtual degradation of the majesty of the State, which although it ought to sit on high like a queen and supreme arbitress, free from all partiality and intent upon the one common good and justice, has become a slave, surrendered and delivered to the passions and greed of men. And as to international relations, two different streams have issued from the one fountain-head: On the one hand, economic nationalism or even economic imperialism; on the other, a no less deadly and accursed internationalism of finance or international imperialism whose country is where profit is»[345].

Liberal principles here led to violations of justice and aroused great opposition.

«Property, that is, "capital", has undoubtedly long been able to appropriate too much to itself. Whatever was produced, whatever returns accrued, capital claimed for itself, hardly leaving to the worker enough to restore and renew his strength. For the doctrine was preached that all accumulation of capital falls by an absolutely insuperable economic law to the rich, and that by the same law the workers are given over and bound to perpetual want, to the scantiest of livelihoods. It is true, indeed, that things have not always and everywhere corresponded with this sort of teaching of the so-called Manchesterian Liberals; yet it cannot be denied that economic social institutions have moved steadily in that direction. That these false ideas, these erroneous suppositions, have been vigorously assailed, and not by those alone who through them were being deprived of their innate right to obtain better conditions, will surprise no one»[346].

The yearning for riches had no limits: it trampled down all scruples and went so far as to create an actual economic science far remove from the moral law. The faith and morals of the workers suffered horribly in factories dominated by the capitalist mentality.

«Since the instability of economic life, and especially of its structure, exacts of those engaged in it most intense and unceasing effort, some have become so hardened to the stings of conscience as to hold that they are allowed, in any manner whatsoever, to increase their profits and use means, fair or foul, to protect their hard-won wealth against sudden changes of fortune. The easy gains that a market unrestricted by any

345 [*Quadragesimo Anno* §§ 107,108 &109.]
346 [*Quadragesimo Anno* § 54.]

law opens to everybody attracts large numbers to buying and selling goods, and they, their one aim being to make quick profits with the least expenditure of work, raise or lower prices by their uncontrolled business dealings so rapidly according to their own caprice and greed that they nullify the wisest forecasts of producers. The laws passed to promote corporate business, while dividing and limiting the risk of business, have given occasion to the most sordid license. For We observe that consciences are little affected by this reduced obligation of accountability; that furthermore, by hiding under the shelter of a joint name, the worst of injustices and frauds are penetrated[347]; and that, too, directors of business companies, forgetful of their trust, betray the rights of those whose savings they have undertaken to administer. Lastly, We must not omit to mention those crafty men who, wholly unconcerned about any honest usefulness of their work, do not scruple to stimulate the baser human desires and, when they are aroused, use them for their own profit.

Strict and watchful moral restraint enforced vigorously by governmental authority could have banished these enormous evils and even forestalled them; this restraint, however, has too often been sadly lacking. For since the seeds of a new form of economy were bursting forth just when the principles of rationalism had been implanted and rooted in many minds, there quickly developed a body of economic teaching far removed from the true moral law, and, as a result, completely free rein was given to human passions»[348].

The liberal regime paved the way for communism:

«If we would explain the blind acceptance of Communism by so many thousands of workmen, we must remember that the way had been already prepared for it by the religious and moral destitution in which wage-earners had been left by liberal economics. Even on Sundays and holy days, labor-shifts were given no time to attend to their essential religious duties. No one thought of building churches within convenient distance of factories, nor of facilitating the work of the priest. On the contrary, laicism was actively and persistently promoted, with the result that we are now reaping the fruits of the errors so often denounced by Our Predecessors and by Ourselves. It can surprise no one that the Communistic fallacy should be spreading in a world already to a large extent de-Christianized»[349].

347 [The word used in the English official translation was «penetrated», but according to the Latin it should be «perpetrated».]

348 [*Quadragesimo Anno* §§ 132-133.]

349 [*Divini Redemptoris* § 16.]

Amoral liberalism has plunged the world into sad ruin:

> «In this same Encyclical of Ours We have shown that the means of saving the world of today from the lamentable ruin into which a moral liberalism has plunged us, are neither the class-struggle nor terror, nor yet the autocratic abuse of State power, but rather the infusion of social justice and the sentiment of Christian love into the social-economic order»[350].

2
Capitalism

We have analyzed the systems that seek to explain and guide economic life: liberalism, socialism, Marxism, Catholicism. Capitalism is not among them because it is not a theoretical system, but a practical regime. *Quadragesimo Anno* never talks about capitalism as a system, but always as a regime.

2.1. WHAT IS CAPITALISM?

Perroux says that capitalism is an explosive word; its very definition accumulates adversaries[351].

According to Pius XI in *Quadragesimo Anno* the capitalist regime is «that economic system, wherein, generally, some provide capital while others provide labor for a joint economic activity»[352]. Therefore, the first characteristic of this regime is the separation into two sides, capital and labor; other characteristics according to the Pontiff are the following:

- The enormous extension of the regime in the contemporary era, with the spread of industrialism;
- The growth, not only of wealth but of enormous power and economic arrogance, on the part of the very few, who often are not even owners, but only depositaries that govern capital at their own will and discretion;

350 [*Id.* § 32.]

351 [François Perroux, (1903-1987), French economist and college professor, founder of the *Institut de Sciences Economiques Appliquées* in 1944. Perroux was part of the Catholic social movement of Lyon and helped Fr. Lebret in the creation of the organization *Économie et Humanisme.* In his book *Le Capitalisme* (Capitalism) (1948), he wrote: «*Capitalisme est un mot de combat*». (Capitalism is a word of battle).]

352 [*Quadragesimo Anno* § 100.]

- The struggle to acquire economic strength followed by a fierce fight to gain dominance of the public power, and consequently, to abuse its forces and influences in economic conflicts. The final combat in the international field[353].

Looking at other aspects, we can also characterize the capitalist regime by the following elements:

- Immense predominance of capital over labor. Capital is the master, the owner of the enterprise; human labor is a rented service;
- The orientation of the regime is characterized by profit: to produce for gain, not for service;
- The dominant philosophy is liberal individualism;
- The main instrument of growth is credit;
- The typical organization —its creation— is the corporation; and next the concentration of corporations that centralize power in a few hands and limit as much as possible the power of others;
- Its strength: in industrial matters this is rationalization; in commercial matters this is rigorous accounting, in order to predict costs and control them.
- It exists in the private economic sector;
- It demands broad independence for businesses and free trade;
- In its conduct, capitalism is technological, scientific and revolutionary in its application.

2.2. A CAPITALIST CREATION: THE CORPORATION

A corporation is a limited liability company, with capital consisting of shares that reflect money or other assets contributed by shareholders.

The management of the corporation is carried out by a board of directors elected at a meeting of shareholders, each of whom has as many votes as shares. Those who get half plus one of the votes are elected.

353 [Hurtado's point here is apparently derived from §108 of *Quadragesimo Anno*, which is clearer: «This accumulation of might and of power generates in turn three kinds of conflict. First, there is the struggle for economic supremacy itself; then there is the bitter fight to gain supremacy over the State in order to use in economic struggles its resources and authority; finally there is conflict between States themselves, not only because countries employ their power and shape their policies to promote every economic advantage of their citizens, but also because they seek to decide political controversies that arise among nations through the use of their economic supremacy and strength».

At this point the manuscript also refers to § 38 of the Spanish version of *Quadragesimo Anno*, which correspond to § 54 in the English version. The editors are not copying that section here because it was already quoted some pages above.]

In the election of the directors resides one of the corporation's great dangers of abuse. Apparently the system is democratic, but minorities are basically powerless. Since many shareholders are not interested in attending meetings, those who control 40% of the shares actually control the whole corporation. There are registered and bearer shares. Very often, it is the case that representatives of commercial firms, of banks in particular, obtain by the election date an abundant portfolio of the bearer shares of the bank's clients, or hold them as security under the system called *réport* (as it is called in the instance of publicly traded stock) and manage to choose the directors they want, totally disregarding the interests of the minority. This new majority can give a new direction to the corporation and turn it towards the interests of a stronger corporation that comes to control it, and can even drive the corporation to liquidation.

232 2.2.1. *DANGERS OF THE CORPORATION*

In addition to the evils, described above, that affect shareholders, there are others that have an impact on society in general. The *raison d'être* of the corporation is its private interest, dominated by the concept of profit rather than the common good. The danger is all the greater because the activities of corporations have spread to all domains of national life.

The relations of the corporation with its workers are as impersonal as the corporation itself. The real owners, the shareholders, have nothing to do with them. The directors are mainly concerned with the business of the company and the distribution of good dividends. Employee benefits are assigned to a department by that name, to a social worker or sometimes not even to anyone, because many companies consider that benefits are a non-productive expense. As a consequence, frequent abuses as to wages, conditions of employment and dismissal, and a total ignorance of the problems of the individual are the rule.

Wage workers have no representation in the affairs of the corporation: they are mere workers who rent their services. At most, they have a representative in managment to make known their complaints regarding wages and benefits.

The administration of the corporation is in the hands of directors appointed by the majority of shareholders, often by a temporary majority interested in controlling the company. When the company is controlled by a responsible group, it appoints as directors persons who are also fully responsible. But it is not uncommon for directors representing banks or other entities that control a good part of the capital to be simultaneously directors of ten, fifteen or more corporations, and they cannot reasonably be interested in the good operation of each company, much less in the human problems of its subordinates. There should be a rule against being a director of more than four or five corporations.

The activity of the shareholders of the corporation are too restricted: attendance at meetings, approval or rejection of the financials, election of the new board. Their activities should be greater, because they are the owners; the ones responsible for the operations of the company.

2.2.2. *REMEDIES FOR THE CURRENT STRUCTURE OF THE CORPORATION*

A theory called «Institution» has been devised, defended mainly by Fr. Rénard, O.P.[354], by his disciple Hauriou[355] and Emilio Gaillard[356].

The theory of the institution aims to give the public company a more stable and permanent character than which is simply contracted for freely by the parties. The corporation is a moral person with norms that are independent of approval or rejection by a simple majority. It is a juridical, hierarchical corporate institution whose *raison d'être* is the realization of a certain aspect of the common good, which has been established in the charter and cannot be changed except by the will of its founders. The shareholders are linked to the corporation not only by the material possession of a block of shares, which they may hold owing to a simple deposit, but by a tie to the common good of the company that they should respect. Therefore there is a warrant to orient the company to the common good, which cannot be altered by a simple act of the majority except by closing the company down. Shareholders have an obligation to vote, and their votes depend on their relationship with the company —the number

354 [Georges Renard, O.P., (1876-1943), French jurist and professor. The philosophy of Renard is based on natural law. Renard wrote a book called *La Théorie de l'Institution* (Theory of the Institution)(1930) in which he developed a philosophical theory called «institutionalism», according to which institutions as well as rights are seen as instruments of synthesis between what is individual and what is social, allowing for the coordination of individual interests and the common good.]

355 [Maurice Hauriou (1856-1929), French sociologist and jurist, Administrative Law professor at the University of Toulouse. His textbooks *Précis de Droit Administratif et de Droit Public Général* (*Summary of Administrative Law and General Public Law*) (1892), *Précis Élémentaire de Droit Administratif* (*Elementary Summary of Administrative Law*)(1925), *Précis de Droit Constitutionnel* (*Summary of Constitutional Law*)(1923) and *Principes de Droit Public* (*Principles of Public Law*)(1910) were very influential and gave administrative law a new doctrinal basis. He also worked on the legal theory of institutionalism.]

356 [At this point Hurtado states: «Georges Renard, *Théorie de l'Institution, Essai d'Ontologie Juridique*, Recueil Sirey, 1930. *Philosophie de l'Institution*, Paris Recueil Sirey, 1930.- E. Gaillard, *Société anonyme de demain*. Sirey».]

of years they have been connected to it— because someone who founded the company or has held their shares for 40 years has much more affection for the company than someone who recently bought them for speculation. A vote may not even be cast by a shareholder or a director on a matter that concerns his own advantage and that might damage the company, in order to eliminate impropriety as to negotiations that might be proposed by directors representing another company. The various nuances that the authors of this theory have in mind are very extensive: all of them are aimed at avoiding arbitrariness, the influence of shifting majorities, the lack of continuity with the initial purpose and the play of corrupt interests on the company. The spirit that animates these reforms is very just. The problem is to translate it into legal institutions capable of frustrating the thousand stratagems devised by the spirit of profit.

234 2.3. CONCENTRATION OF POWER: FRUIT OF CAPITALISM[357]

The main characteristic of this phase of capitalism is not so much the concentration of capital, which exists, but the concentration of power in few hands. The shareholders of banks and other public corporations are in the millions, but managment is in very few hands, and uses at its discretion enormous amounts of capital that greatly influence economic, political, national and international life. Today, a board member, with little capital of his own, can do much more than the owner of valuable properties who lacks economic expertise.

The accumulation of power has been achieved by large accumulations of capital in the following forms:

- *Trusts*: *i.e.* combinations of similar companies into a new companies. For example, the match company created by the Swede Ivo Kreuger, who came to control almost all of the world's match production. In 1932 he committed suicide and the project ended.
- *Kartells*: *i.e.* agreements to monopolize certain products within a country or internationally. Such a central agreement contains clauses assigning markets, providing for the organization of the sale of products, etc. There are great international *kartells* of steel, oil, electric light bulbs, rubber, etc. Some of them control almost the entire world production.

357 [Hurtado quotes at this point *Quadragesimo Anno* §§ 105-106. The editors are not including those sections because they are quoted under the heading «Unjust Distribution of Wealth».]

- *Consortiums* and the *konzerne*: *i.e.* two very similar forms of union of many companies under a common administration, with common technical and economic services. Often in consortiums shares of one company amount to investments in the others of the consortium, and directors of one company also serve as directors of the others. A very old German statistic (1930) records the fact that of 12,000 corporations with 18,000,000,000 marks, there were 2,016 grouped in *Konzerne* which controlled 11,000,000,000 marks, which is 62% of the total. The *konzerne* of Standard Oil comprised around 500 companies in almost every country in the world.
- *Holdings*: *i.e.* companies that control one or several corporations and hold enough shares in their portfolios to have a majority at shareholders' meetings: half plus one of the shares represented at the meeting. Banks or other companies manage to obtain the proxies of shareholders or to acquire bearer shares, and thus come to control the corporation.
- Chains of companies: *i.e.* corporations that form and control the majority of the shares of other corporations; the others form and control the majority of yet others; and so on. One who controls the first company, controls all the subsidiaries.

Groups of complementary corporations: *i.e* companies like Ford Motor Company produce cars and also acquire, for example, iron, coal and transport companies; everything needed for production. In 1945 Ford had more than 300,000 workers.

Advantages and Disadvantages of These Large Concentrations:

The needs of modern technology have caused the enormous concentration of capital that is required to obtain costly machinery, to reduce general expenses, advertising and competition, and to produce cheaper products and promote their use, all purposes very worthy of pursuit. Thereby, production is more readily adapted to consumption; and commercial cooperation between similar industries, the search for new markets and the use of new discoveries are some of the many reasons that have led to the formation of large consortiums; that is why some countries even tend to make *kartells* obligatory under certain economic circumstances.

But alongside these advantages, such concentrations contain the great danger pointed out by the Pontiff Pius XI: an exaggerated increase of personal power in the economic field, which will try to extend into national and even international politics. Fierce struggles to seize political power and even international wars are too often caused by economic imperialism.

Regarding the interests of the workers, such concentrations, especially where workers are not well organized, leave them defenseless and constitute an extremely unequal force. Under these regimes, ruled by a the powerful few, workers are nothing but mere wage earners, with no hope of seeing their salary contracts softened by participation in the corporation. The distance that separates employers and employees grows greater every day as the corporation moves further away from the human scale. In these immense concentrations, management has totally lost sight of the needs of the workers, with whom any human contact is as impossible as with the inhabitants of another planet.

Regarding the idea of common good, in such concentrations created by the mere reason of profit, morality is subordinated to the interests and needs of production. What is most urgently needed is not produced; but only what generates more profit. Such concentrations even come to invent products and introduce them to the public on the basis of advertising, only in order to profit economically, even when they are harmful: beverages, cosmetics, luxury items.

Regarding other corporations, a strong corporation can control others through procedures that are often frankly immoral: in an acquisition of a corporation, the dominant party can easily arrange matters so as to harm the balance sheet after the acquisition, and thereby harm the shareholders who did not approve. A dominant corporation can buy the products it needs from the dominated corporation, causing losses to that corporation, and therefore, to the minority of shareholders. The board of directors can speculate with the reserves of the corporation and employ them, not to distribute the dividend that the needy shareholders expected, but to depress the shares' prices owing to the absence of dividends. As a result, the directors can repurchase those shares and then pay dividends at their discretion.

Regarding the avoidance of competition: if someone has a competitor as strong as himself, he will try to reach an understanding that is advantageous for both, by fixing prices or discounts, even if not convenient for the public. If he has a weaker competitor, he will try to sink it by all sorts of procedures: for example, by selling cheaper and even below cost. Having done so, he will be able to determine prices at will and generously recover the losses he incurred at the previous low price. On some ocassions, owing to the hoarding of products, a corporation may take the products out of the country, if it is convenient, to another country where prices are higher, failing to meet national needs. In the other country, by dumping, they can sink their competitors and become the controllers of prices.

By taking over others' corporations they can, once they control a sufficient number of shares, alter the value of the shares at will and even dissolve the corporation, imposing an immense loss on minority shareholders. A bank can lend money to a corporation, demand repayment at a difficult time, force the corporation into liquidation, and then, having purchased its means of production at a minimal cost, resume the same operations. All these methods, as one can see, are deeply immoral.

Great concentrations of capital and power will be moral if each of the acts they perform is moral. Their actions will be acceptable if they are justified by sufficient reasons, they serve the common good and are appropriate; they will be unacceptable if these norms are violated. It cannot be forgotten that the more power a concentration has, the greater the dangers involved, presenting a temptation to abuse. Real good has been brought about in the economic field, and along with it, untold moral evils.

2.4. ASSESSMENT OF CAPITALISM

Few topics have so passionately inspired contemporaries as capitalism. Books and more books have been written in praise and censorship of the system. Some argue that capitalism is condemned by the Church, others say it is not; some even consider capitalism to be the only Catholic system confronting Marxism.

These disputes arise, first, because there is no agreement as to the terms of the discussion. When they talk about it, debaters usually have before their eyes totally different definitions of capitalism. Then, passion and interest intervene, among those who attack and those who defend.

1) Capitalism is not per se condemned. As Pius XI defined it, capitalism is the separation of capital and labor in different hands and requires workers to rent their services under contracts. The Church has never condemned capitalism itself as to its fundamental elements. Pius XI says:

> «Important indeed have the changes been which both the economic system and Socialism have undergone since Leo XIII's time.
>
> That, in the first place, the whole aspect of economic life is vastly altered, is plain to all. You know, Venerable Brethren and Beloved Children, that the Encyclical of Our

Predecessor of happy memory had in view chiefly that economic system, wherein, generally, some provide capital while others provide labor for a joint economic activity. And in a happy phrase he described it thus: "Neither capital can do without labor, nor labor without capital"[358].

With all his energy Leo XIII sought to adjust this economic system according to the norms of right order; hence, it is evident that this system is not to be condemned in itself. And surely it is not of its own nature vicious. But it does violate right order when capital hires workers, that is, the non-owning working class, with a view to and under such terms that it directs business and even the whole economic system according to its own will and advantage, scorning the human dignity of the workers, the social character of economic activity and social justice itself, and the common good»[359].

2) Capitalism carries in itself a serious danger: because of its own indifference, it can become vicious and unjust. Power and wealth, as moralists and great saints have frequently warned, contain within themselves the tremendous danger of aspiring to indefinite growth. Not all capitalist businessmen and merchants have succumbed to this danger. Many of them have exercised their righteous private conscience in their business lives.

3) The actual conduct within the capitalist regime, as it has historically developed throughout the world, has deserved very grave moral reproaches from Popes, Bishops and private individuals, who have not ceased to criticize it. The principal reproaches addressed to it by the Pontiffs are the following[360].

The capitalist regime, as it has hitherto been realized, cannot be an acceptable solution for a Catholic. The judgments of Popes and Prelates constitute a true plebiscite that condemns it. Catholics, therefore, have to look for another regime that avoids those errors, or they have to purify the capitalist regime of its vices.

If capitalism seeks to survive, it must avoid a concentration of power and the dehumanizing consequences. It is vitally important that Capitalism cease to dominate labor, which is immensely noble: something human-divine in spite of its humble appearance. Respect, abundant livelihood and a greater participation in profits, in management and even in the control of the company[361].

358 [The encyclical here has a footnote as follows: «Encyclical, *On the Condition of Workers*, 28».]
359 [*Quadragesimo Anno* §§ 99-101.]
360 [At this point Hurtado added: «(Mensaje, 1) See Popes, Fernandez, 78 Bishops, 76».]
361 [At this point Hurtado handwrote: «Remedies for capitalism, O.S.C. (*Social Christian Order*) 378-379».]

3

Socialism[362]

3.1. DIVERSITY OF TRENDS

It is very difficult to define socialism because there are very different socialist doctrines. It would be more correct to speak of some socialism in particular: the one of Saint Simon, the one of Fourier, the one of Proudhon, etc. The essence of the socialist system is not easy to grasp, precisely because it is not a system but a set of confused desires and powerful feelings mixed with economic analysis and political opinions. Durkheim said that socialism is not a science or sociology, but a cry of pain and sometimes of anger uttered by those who feel our collective unrest[363]. According to Blum[364], socialism is a kind of morality and almost a religion as well as a doctrine. Socialism is the specific application to the present state of society of the general universal feelings upon which morality and religion have always been founded. Socialists agree that their doctrine is not only economic but political and philosophical. One of them affirms that, unlike democratic secularism, which fights mysticism in the name of reason, socialism fights one faith in the name of another faith.

Along with these declarations, which give socialism a marked philosophical and anti-religious character, other people like André Philip[365] declare: «[i]n the socialist party there is no difficulty in admitting Protestants or Catholics, no more than free thinkers. Socialism, in fact, is not a faith or a particular philosophical system but an institutional program. By the socialization of the main industries, socialism aims to direct the national economy, to carry out the ascension of workers to the management of businesses and effectively fullfil the democratic ideal»[366]. How much truth there is in these opposing statements?

362 [In this section Hurtado followed closely, and freely translated, Gerard Marcy, *Le Courants Socialistes* (*The Socialist Currents*) *at Le Catholicisme Social Face aux Grand Courant Contemporains* (*Social Catholicism Facing Contemporary Great Currents*), *Semaines Sociales de France*, Paris 1947, pp. 111-125.]

363 [«Socialism is not a science, a miniature sociology, it is a cry of pain and ocassionally of anger uttered by men who feel more acutely our collective malaise». Émile Durkheim, *Durkheim on Politics and the State* (1986), translated by W.D. Walls.]

364 [Léon Blum (1872-1950), French politician, three times Prime Minister of France and a moderate socialist. Blum led the negotiations for the *Matignon Accords* to end the strong waves of strikes in France by establishing labor reforms, such as the right to strike and collective bargaining.]

365 [André Philip (1902-1970), French politician, Free French Minister of Finance and of Interior during World War II.]

366 *Populaire*, December 5, 1944.

3.2. MAN, THE CENTER

In the beginning, there is the socialist faith in man, which for many people does not exclude faith in God. If socialism later became anti-religious and even atheist, this was owing—at least in France—to the influence of eighteenth-century philosophers. This attitude is not common to all socialists. Henri de Man[367] affirms that the socialist movement is at the same time the defender of the democracy abandoned by the bourgeoisie and the embodiment of the Christian ideal betrayed by the Church. It may be said, however, that although socialism appeared not to oppose religious faith, its internal tendency led it to deal exclusively with man as the central object of its preoccupations.

3.3. THE PRIMACY OF SOCIETY OVER THE INDIVIDUAL

In addition to this faith in man, socialism is perhaps an economic and social doctrine born of a reaction against liberalism. While liberals frequently call for personal initiative, socialists place their trust in the State. Therefore, socialism is a doctrine that affirms the primacy of society over the individual and the subordination of the latter to the former. In one sentence: it is a doctrine in which society is the end and the individual the means. Durkheim defined socialism as the doctrine that links all economic functions, or at least a good part of them, to the leading and conscious centers of society. When referring to society, most socialists do not think of the State. For this reason, they have abandoned what we might call «nationalization»: State's monopoly through expropriation. As to the action of the State, liberals say: «the good that the State does is wrongly done; and the evil that it does, is very well done».

Upon nationalization, industries are governed by autonomous cooperatives: a kind of semi-public organization that replaces corporations and their boards of directors.

The tripartite steering committees include consumers, trade unions, technicians and representatives of the government; those committees are a kind of arbiter and are in charge, in case of difficulty, of assuring that the general interest prevails. In the case of education, nationalization would mean monopoly, while expropriation would make even teaching a semi-public service that allowed

367 [Henri de Man (1885-1953), Belgian socialist politician, leader of the Belgian Labor Party. He wrote several books, including *Réflexions sur l'économie dirigée* (Reflections on the Directed Economy)(1932), *Le Socialisme Constructif* (*Constructive Socialism*) (1933), and *Corporatisme et Socialisme* (Corporatism and Socialism)(1935).]

a certain degree of freedom, and would replace consumers with parents on the steering committees. One can therefore say, in a general way, that a system is socialist when it links economic functions to society rather than leaving them diffuse. This link comes about for two reasons: first, a moral one—to favor the full development of the individual; and second, an economic one—the general interest is not born spontaneously from the sum of individual interests (as claimed by the liberals) but from a strongly organized common will. The periodic crises of capitalist society support this assertion. The economy must be channeled not to what is more profitable, but to what is most necessary.

There are three fundamental problems to which every socialist responds in the same way:

- The Property Problem: Every socialist rejects the capitalist conception of property. He thinks that private property as it exists now corresponds to one stage of private production —namely, to that of the craft industry. However, production has passed from the private to the collective form while the legal regime has not changed. Therefore, there is a contradiction between a mode of production that has now become collective and a mode of property that remains individual and private. Collective production must correspond to collective ownership. The socialists ask that the instruments of production become the property of all because they facilitate the work of all. Regarding the problem of property, any system that attacks, diminishes or restricts private property can be called socialist. Socialism recognizes only one source for private property: labor. Property without labor is robbery. A contemporary socialist states: where property and labor coincide, socialism has never advocated expropriation. Socialism is not the enemy of property that comes from labor, but of capitalist property. The socialist ideal is to nationalize the instruments of production and to leave to individuals and families only consumer goods.
- The Problem of Organization: A socialist system does not trust the interplay of selfish interests and thinks it necessary to impose a certain authoritarian organization. Socialism substitutes the directed economy for the free economy. Perrou points out the signs of socialization: first, the free management of productive assets is replaced by collective management according to a deliberate plan by the corresponding human group. Second, the purpose of the system is not greater monetary gain but the direct and complete satisfaction of the needs of all the individuals that constitute the human group.

Socialism ideally tends to a certain degree of international organization, but in reality it remains national.

Socialists understand that a political revolution that is not accompanied by an economic revolution is ineffective. They understand that it is impossible to change economic structures without transforming the State, as this would lead to giving more power to a nationalist State of an imperialist kind, and would strengthen the influence of the oligarchy over the direction of the country. When the high bourgeoisie lacks political power, it manifests its deprivation by aggravating social unrest until it achieves its objective by joining together political influence with economic power. If socialism aims to establish itself, it must therefore remove economic power from the bourgeoisie by means of the reform of major structures.

Many so-called nationalizations left in place the same influences that existed under the private capitalist economy. That is why modern socialists do not speak of nationalization but of «socialization», which involves the expropriation of the oligarchy and the delivery of expropriated property to the community of workers.

All these successive measures, however, fail to answer the following questions: Why would not a popular State be as imperialistic as a bourgeois State? Why would not a new bureaucratic oligarchy emerge in it, taking advantage of the social revolution for its personal interest?

- The Problem of Equality: Socialists look at their system as a general conception of the world that tends to make men equal. These egalitarian aspirations are in the socialist soul. That is why, not without pain, many of the most authentic socialists have observed that at the end of the war of 1945 the wage difference in Soviet Russia was one to ten, whereas in England it was only one to six. Socialism would prefer that life conditions and hierarchy of functions be a result less of birth and inherited wealth than of labor and individual capacity. Socialism wishes that, in the race of life, everyone starts at the same point. Hence, we can say that psychologically a socialist is deeply wounded by the social inequalities he sees around him. He wants a world in which more equal justice reigns and he looks for the technical and scientific means to realize it.

These are the traditional orientations of socialism which, as we indicated at the beginning, are quite vague because they are not part of a uniform system. After the war of 1939-1945, new aspirations appeared in certain sectors of socialism.

3.4. PRESENT DIRECTIONS OF SOCIALISM

3.4.1. *LABORISM*

Socialism recognizes the paramount importance of labor. The worker should not be excluded from the management of the company. The means to achieve this are not those of Marxism —the nationalization of production— but the organization of workers and the federation of their associations, which would run the «socialized» companies.

3.4.2. *HUMANISM*

Contemporary socialism expresses a double aspiration: to universalism and to the life of the spirit.

The aspiration is universal in the sense that it does not exclude any class and aims to surpass the strictly proletarian character of Marxism. It aims to offer all men the total development of their personalities, so that they may claim their rights to cultivate their bodies, their intelligence and their reason. Humanistic socialism aspires to educate men and cultivate all men. The promotion of labor cannot be fully accomplished until the working class can participate in a comprehensive culture.

The spiritual aspiration is shown by the acknowledgement of the moral value of culture, by the desire to surpass Marxist materialism by integrating its doctrine into a spiritual conception of man and the world. This is the tendency of Léon Blum in his work *A l'Échelle Humaine*[368]. Blum adheres to Marx's analysis of capitalist society, but not to his dialectical materialism. He admits that the spirit is not a mere reflection of matter and that human freedom is not subject to the physical needs that dominate the world. By preserving freedom Blum justifies democracy, without which socialism is powerless. Blum also departs from Marxism when he affirms that the end of social revolution is not only the liberation of man from economic exploitation and all its accompanying burdens, but also the assurance, within the collective society, of the fulfillment of his fundamental rights and of his vocation. According to Marxists, all problems could be solved by the rise of the proletariat and by the acceleration of technical progress. Blum further requires that revolution must be made for man, and he is not satisfied with the mere subjection of man, even momentarily, to the needs

368 [Léon Blum wrote *A l'Échelle Humaine* (*On the Human Scale*) (1945) during his imprisonment in Germany. In this book he developed a less ideological and more humanist kind of socialism.]

of the revolution. Blum himself states, «[n]othing that has been established by violence and maintained by force, nothing that degrades man and rests upon contempt for the human person, can be enduring»[369]. Finally, Blum corrects Marx by stating that the «class struggle» formula must be understood in the sense of «action of the classes;» that is, liberation of workers by workers.

3.4.3. *LIBERALISM*

Contemporary socialism aspires to be liberal in the sense that it affirms that there is no real development of the human person without a minimum of economic, political, spiritual and religious freedom. How to reconcile the demands of socialism and freedom? Modern socialists have not yet explained this.

The modern tendencies of humanistic socialism that we have set forth are in gestation: they still contain great gaps and their supporters are scattered and timid. Social Catholicism cannot but look sympathetically upon these efforts to reconcile social justice with the rights of the human person.

3.5. THE CHURCH'S CONCLUSION AS TO SOCIALISM

In 1878, in *Quod Apostolici Muneris*, Leo XIII designates under the name of socialists «that sect of men who, under various and almost barbarous names, are called socialists, communists, or nihilists, … strive to bring to a head what they have long been planning—the overthrow of all civil society whatsoever … [seditious people that are disloyal traitors, impatient of all restraint] have more than once within a short period raised their arms in impious attempt against the lives of their own sovereigns»[370]. In this encyclical, the Pontiff refers to the various attacks on the lives of monarchs, and specifies his charges against the socialist's doctrines as to civil authority, whose foundation in divine right they do not recognize. He also refers to domestic society, devoid of all religious character and true authority, and to private property and how socialists desire to replace it with collective property[371].

369 [There is no indication of the work from which this quote was taken.]

370 [Leo XIII, Encyclical on Socialism *Quod Apostolici Muneris* (28 December 1878) § 1, at The Holy See, http://w2.vatican.va/content/leo-xiii/en/encyclicals/documents/hf_l-xiii_enc_28121878_quod-apostolici-muneris.html (hereinafter referred to as *Quod Apostolici Muneris.*) The sentence in brackets is in the encyclical, but was not quoted by Hurtado.]

371 [At this point Hurtado states: «O.S.C (*Social Christian Order*) nn. 80-86». Those items in Hurtado's book contain long quotations from the encyclicals *Quod Apostolici Muneris* (§ 80-85) and *Rerum Novarum* (§ 86), which set forth the Church's teachings on socialism.]

Pius XI in *Quadragesimo Anno* points out:

> «Socialism, against which Our Predecessor, Leo XIII, had especially to inveigh, has since his time changed no less profoundly than the form of economic life. For Socialism, which could then be termed almost a single system and which maintained definite teachings reduced into one body of doctrine, has since then split chiefly into two sections, often opposing each other and even bitterly hostile, without either one however abandoning a position fundamentally contrary to Christian truth that was characteristic of Socialism.
>
> One section of Socialism has undergone almost the same change that the capitalistic economic system, as We have explained above, has undergone. It has sunk into Communism»[372].

1 This version of socialism deserves the same condemnation as communism, with which it differs almost exclusively in its less violent and more reformist methods of action, but not in its materialistic and atheist doctrines and its class hatred.

2 There is another moderate version of socialism, but one which remains socialist, and therefore incompatible with the dogmas of the Catholic Church, owing to its way of conceiving of society. The end of man and society is purely being well-off and «men are obliged, with respect to the producing of goods, to surrender and subject themselves entirely to society ... The possession of the greatest possible supply of things that serve the advantages of this life is considered of such great importance that the higher goods of man, liberty not excepted, must take a secondary place and even be sacrificed to the demands of the most efficient production of goods... Society, therefore, as Socialism conceives it, can on the one hand neither exist nor be thought of without an obviously excessive use of force; on the other hand, it fosters a liberty no less false, since there is no place in it for true social authority, which rests not on temporal and material advantages but descends from God alone, the Creator and last end of all things»[373].

«If Socialism, like all errors, contains some truth (which, moreover, the Supreme Pontiffs have never denied), it is based nevertheless on a theory of human society peculiar to itself and irreconcilable with true Christianity. Reli-

372 [*Quadragesimo Anno* §§ 111-112.]
373 [*Id.* § 119.]

gious socialism, Christian socialism, are contradictory terms; no one can be at the same time a good Catholic and a true socialist»[374].

3 Among those who call themselves socialists there is a moderate tendency, which should not be called socialist. Their postulates contain nothing contrary to Christian truth. There is a third section,

> «The other section, which has kept the name Socialism, is surely more moderate. It not only professes the rejection of violence but modifies and tempers to some degree, if it does not reject entirely, the class struggle and the abolition of private ownership. One might say that, terrified by its own principles and by the conclusions drawn therefrom by Communism, Socialism inclines toward and in a certain measure approaches the truths which Christian tradition has always held sacred; for it cannot be denied that its demands at times come very near those that Christian reformers of society justly insist upon.
>
> For if the class struggle abstains from enmities and mutual hatred, it gradually changes into an honest discussion of differences founded on a desire for justice, and if this is not that blessed social peace which we all seek, it can and ought to be the point of departure from which to move forward to the mutual cooperation of the Industries and Professions. So also the war declared on private ownership, more and more abated, is being so restricted that now, finally, not the possession itself of the means of production is attacked but rather a kind of sovereignty over society which ownership has, contrary to all right, seized and usurped. For such sovereignty belongs in reality not to owners but to the public authority. If the foregoing happens, it can come even to the point that imperceptibly these ideas of the more moderate socialism will no longer differ from the desires and demands of those who are striving to remold human society on the basis of Christian principles. For certain kinds of property, it is rightly contended, ought to be reserved to the State since they carry with them a dominating power so great that cannot without danger to the general welfare be entrusted to private individuals.
>
> Such just demands and desire have nothing in them now which is inconsistent with Christian truth, and much less are they special to Socialism. Those who work solely toward such ends have, therefore, no reason to become socialists»[375].

374 [*Id.* § 120.]
375 [*Id.* §§ 113 -115.]

4
Marxism

When speaking of Marxism, it is convenient from the beginning to distinguish certain terms which are used as synonyms, although they are not. Under the term «Marxism» we refer to the social philosophy, materialistic and dialectic, elaborated by Marx and Engels, which we will analyze later. The parties that have adhered to the Third International receive the name of communist parties. Lenininsm adds the doctrinal contribution of Lenin to the maturation of the philosophy of Marx and Engels, and in particular, his strategic plan for the realization of the proletarian revolution. Stalinism alludes to the doctrines of the current maximum leader of communism tending to consolidate the revolution in Russia and its subsequent extension to the other countries. The consolidation of communism in Russia and the support for his policy is, according to Stalin, the first duty of the world's communists.

4.1. MARX'S SYSTEM

The essential subjects of communism are mainly contained in the voluminous works of Marx and Engels, especially *Capital* (1867). The *Manifesto,* published in 1847, contains in summary the main Marxist theses. For the sake of clarity, we will distinguish Marxist philosophical, economic and political positions, and we will add the broad lines of the type of man that Marx intends to form[376].

4.1.1. *PHILOSOPHICAL POSITIONS*

There are historical and dialectical materialism.

a) Materialistic Aspect: In order to understand society at any given moment, we must start with the production of material goods and with the *economic infrastructure.* The economic infrastructure is determined by the productive forces: natural factors, machinery, channels of communication, etc. The set of productive forces existing in a given moment determines the *mode of production*: agri-

376 [At this point Hurtado added the following footnote: «We have used many reflections by Jean Lacroix: *The Marxist Man*, Sem. Social Fr., 1947 pp. 127-135». Jean Lacroix (1900 -1986), French philosopher and prolific writer, was the author of the article *L'Homme Marxiste.* Many of his ideas were later explained in Lacroix's book *Marxisme, Existentialisme, Personnalisme. Présence de l'Éternité dans le Temps* (Marxism, Existentialism, Personalism. Presence of Eternity in Time)(1949).]

cultural, artisanal, industrial, etc. The modes of production determine *social relations*, which are the fruit of economic relations. We have, then, an exploited and an exploitative class, which achieved its dominance through land during the feudal era, today through money. This exploiting class makes the other classes work to its advantage, directs the production and distributes the wealth.

Economic infrastructure, in turn, determines a dual social superstructure: legal and political, as the foreground; and religious, ideological, scientific, artistic, etc. as the background.

The political and legal superstructure is nothing more than a reflection of the economic and social infrastructure. Once ascending to power through its economically advantageous position, the ascendance of a class will take advantage of the political and legal system to consolidate and maintain its economic position: «[b]oth civil and political legislation do nothing but pronounce and verbalize the determinations of economic relations»[377]. «The State is, as a general rule, the State of the most powerful class: of those that have the economic dominance —which by its means becomes the politically dominant class and thus acquires new means of dominating and exploiting the oppressed class»[378].

The ideological, scientific and artistic superstructure is determined by the economic infrastructure and by the legal and political superstructure: «The ideas of the dominant classes are in all times the dominant ideas ... The dominant ideas are nothing more than the ideological expression of dominant material relations conceived in the form of ideas and therefore, the relations which make a class a dominant class, and consequently, the ideas of its domination»[379].

Morality and religion do not escape this determination, since they are only means used by the ruling class to assure its domination . The Catholic religion, in particular, is the form of religion that corresponds to the capitalist economy, since like capitalism, it is international and universal. Moreover, in preaching to workers resignation in this world so as to obtain happiness in a future life, she ameliorates class antagonisms, annihilates the revolutionary power of the proletariat, and acts as the «opium of the people». The destruction of religion is, therefore, an indispensable condition for the emancipation of the proletariat, which must increasingly become aware of the exploitation of which it is a vic-

377 Marx.
378 Engels.
379 Marx. [Marx and Engels' quotes here are translated from the Spanish from Hurtado's manuscript.]

tim. For Marx, the great foundations of religion, like the existence of God, of a spiritual and immortal soul, have no value.

The family is also a superstructure that must disappear along with the capitalist economy, to leave the way open to free love, Engels wrote in 1884[380].

b) Dialectical Aspect: Contemplative philosophy is of no interest to the Marxists, furthermore they reject it completely. Marxism has to overcome philosophy and solve through practice the theoretical problems it encounters. The Marxist is interested in following history along its great course towards human liberation. This historical timeline is not based on dogmas or theories: it is instead a method, an analysis of reality and a way of acting on it. As a consequence, Marxism is not interested in pure objectivity: knowledge is valuable to the extent that it serves to transform reality. If you analyze the present social state, it is to build the future. For Marx, criticism is no passion of the head, it is the head of passion[381].

To describe future society in a utiopian way is of no interest to Marxists. For them, it seems impossible that such a description could be made on the basis of the elements of the present world, which is destined to disappear. On the other hand, faithful to Marx, who analyzed the notion of capitalism and predicted its end, his disciples analyze the historical situation in which they live and strive to continue the liberation movement that is going to bring it to an end. «We call Communism», Marx says, «the effective movement that will suppress the present situation».

Contradiction is the engine of progress. Both society and institutions move forward by an internal or dialectical struggle, which Marx learned from Hegel, while varying his understanding. Hegel explained an idealist world this way; while Marx, a materialist world.

The nobility produced, during one period, the bourgeoisie which was in its service; thereafter, the bourgeoisie replaced the nobility. The capitalist bourgeoisie has produced the proletariat that will be its gravedigger. The lower class will very soon become the triumphant class; and then it will be supplanted as

380 [Friedrich Engels, *Der Ursprung der Familie, des Privateigenthums und des Staats* (*The Origin of the Family, Private Property and the State*) (1884). This treatise is in part based on notes by Karl Marx to Lewis Morgan's book *Ancient Society* (1877).]

381 [This phrase was taken from Karl Marx's *A Contribution to the Critique of Hegel's Philosophy of Right*, published in *Deutsch-Französische Jahrbücher* (February, 1844.) The complete sentence states: «In the struggle against that state of affairs, *criticism* is no *passion* of the head, it is the head of *passion* ... [Criticism] no longer assumes the quality of an *end-in-itself*, but only of a *means*. Its essential pathos is *indignation*, its essential work is *denunciation*». Marx is referring to the fight against the status quo in contemporary Germany.]

well. Marx, however, is confident that these successive catastrophes, which give rise to new types of societies, will nevertheless come to an end, because contradictions will become concentrated and more frequent. The mass of the exploited increases every day, confronting a smaller number of exploiters who are linked in a more abstract way with the institutions of which they are part. Marx predicts that, before the coming of the final stage, there will arise the dictatorship of the proletariat, which will destroy the vestiges of the capitalist system and build socialism. This proletarian State will be destroyed little by little as a state and as proletarian, and this will lead to a society without classes.

c) Marxist Values: What are the values that guide the communist in his action? In first place, he does not recognize any transcendent value that might judge man from the outside and from above. All reference to the eternal seems to him hypocrisy; a pretext for escaping from immediate struggle or a betrayal of the

proletarian class. For the Marxist, the important thing is to follow the course of history, which will culminate in the liberation of the proletariat. The class that rises and conquers represents the highest values of its time, while the other classes embody servitude and social perversion. The instruments of social ascent are science combined with technology and intransigent rationalism. Having achieved a dominant position using reason, classes after ascending to power abandon their rationalism and, invoking a transcendent justification, substitute faith for reason, according to Marx. In order to combat these ongoing ideologies, Marxism does not directly fight each system, but demonstrates that it is the product of a decadent era, which must be surpassed by the rise to power of the proletariat, which carries within itself the highest values. In fighting against capitalism, the Marxist believes he is fighting for man.

Morality and revolution are identical in the Marxist system. The most resolute deniers of God recognized an ideal that would replace Him, for example justice. Marxists, instead, have taken the denial of the transcendental to its final conclusions. The human act has nothing to do with God, it only arises from history, which is its only judge. A good act is one that goes the same direction as history; a bad act opposes it. The progress of mankind is, therefore, the supreme norm by which to judge the moral value of actions. The moral act is the most progressive. From this it follows that the end justifies the means, at least the means which are immanent to the end. Consistently with these principles, in international conflicts the Marxist will judge the most progressive State to be right, and in internal conflicts he will always be on the side of the proletariat.

4.1.2. *ECONOMIC POSITIONS*

In order to understand the capitalism of the nineteenth century, Marx starts from the labor theory of value and shows that the profit of the employer, the surplus value, is obtained at the worker's expense. The search for this surplus value on the part of the capitalists will precipitate them into the final catastrophe. Capitalism is founded on a contradiction that will grow worse: a contradiction between the world of the capitalists, who own the means of production and take most of the profits, and the world of the proletarians, who do the work and do not receive its gain. The search for surplus value leads every day to an increasing concentration of wealth, and therefore to a proletarization of the masses. Consequently, the class struggle cannot but intensify. Furthermore, concentration also leads to overproduction and crises that make the situation of the proletarians even worse; and this will lead them to dispossess the small minority which is rich. The dictatorship of the proletariat will precede a comprehensive communism.

4.1.3. POLITICAL POSITIONS

There is no break between the economic and political positions of Marxism. The proletariat is the class designated by history to overthrow capitalism and the bourgeois State, since progress can only be achieved by class struggle and revolution. The proletariat, guided by its ruling group the Communist Party, is in charge of intensifying the class struggle by all means, so as to accelerate the advent of the dictatorship of the proletariat.

The Manifesto of the Communist Party, consistently with this principle, states: communism is the consciousness of the proletariat. For Marx, to be communist means to know the proletarian condition in depth and to strive to destroy it by annihilating capitalism. The proletariat, the real crucified one of the modern world, is the only class capable of destroying the current social contradictions, the only one that can redeem man because it suffers the most. Proletarians are the worry of the world because they are its pain. The proletarian consciousness is a miserable consciousness; it is the restless consciousness; it is the «loss of man». Marx expects the proletariat to become aware of this loss and to rebel against it.

Lacroix[382], whom we are following in this commentary on Marxism, thinks that Marx's messianism reflects his consciousness of the necessary role of the

382 [See footnote 376.]

working class in the revolutionary endeavor. Unlike the bourgeois person, who is uninterested in everything around him, the deprived proletarian grasps the essential inhumanity of our society. The proletariat, rather than being a distinct class, is the result of the total decomposition of society, the product of its inherent contradictions. Therefore, its revolution will have a universal character, because it will fight against absolute error.

4.1.4. *MARXIST TACTICS*

Because the masses are the ones that suffer the most, a revolutionary movement spontaneously emerges in them. The bourgeoisie insists on attributing the movement to agitators, but Marx maintains that it is the spontaneous work of the masses. The communist is the one who believes in the spontaneity of the masses.

The spontaneous movement of the masses remains blind and ineffective. The mission of the communist is to become aware of the thoughts of the masses and to guide and direct them. In this sense, communism is the consciousness of the proletariat.

Just as communism is the consciousness of the mass, the leaders are the consciousness of communism. Its mission is to radicalize the masses. Its leaders should not instill their personal ideas in the proletarians, but should make them aware of what the leaders think and radicalize their thoughts. The mass without a leader will be anarchic and will be at the mercy of the exploiters. The leader who does not translate the thought of the mass, who is isolated in his own subjective concepts, becomes a rebel and a renegade. This was Marx's thinking, but contemporary communist practice clearly follows a different path. The leaders lead the masses wherever they want, without worrying about what the masses would spontaneously do. In this departure from Marxist intuition is perhaps one of the hidden causes of the internal decay of Communism.

4.1.5. *THE COMMUNIST MYSTIQUE*

The communist discovers much of the party's mystique in its being the only one capable of guiding the proletarian revolution. A Communist is not anyone who admires Marx, but someone who has understood where the historical dialectic is going, who participates in the movements of liberation of the proletariat, and who at every moment reviews the situation to see how it is oriented and what will permit human action to regenerate mankind. The path of liberation is hard, full of demands, and in it progress is made only one step at a time, along with the entirety of humanity. In this struggle the party is not one of many political parties: it is an authentic order, an absolute. According to him it is necessary to sacrifice everything to the party, not only life, but even honor and truth. The conflicts as to the truth exist only for non-Marxists, who have about it, as about honor, absolute beliefs without historical contexts. There is no truth outside the party. The party alone can lead to revolution, and revolution is necessary. How could we oppose individual opinion to it? The only freedom the communist knows is the freedom to join the party, in which he thinks that truth and history reside. The party is the only value. For Communists, the party is always in power: it exercises power in the name of the working class, and when the party reaches political authority it only gains a new field of revolutionary action. The communist does not favor individual inititives because they withdraw the perpetrator from the tutelage of the party. Before his party the militant makes a total renunciation that produces both admiration and horror. Marxism, rather than being an objective system of explaining the universe, is a fierce willingness to create a new world.

The Marxist experiences a total contempt for the degraded man of the bourgeois world: of this world that is nothing but the prehistory of humanity in which man has been fighting against man.

Faced with this situation, the Marxist lives in permanent combat: in a state of total war with present society. Dialectically, the proletariat is the negation of the bourgeoisie and this negation is not only theoretical, but actual. To deny the bourgeoisie is to exclude it; the fight is relentless.

No contact should be maintained between the proletariat and the capitalists in order not to weaken the fighting spirit. Maintaining man-to-man relations, and respecting the inherent rights of the human person —all this is alien to the communist conscience. Good intentions are of no use. What matters in politics are the results. This, of course, leads to profoundly inhuman consequences.

The reform of society cannot be achieved by reforming consciences but by reforming the conditions of life, since human consciousness is but a reflection of social relations. Internal and individual reform is ineffective. To seek a common human denominator between the bourgeoisie and the proletariat is to enervate the workers' consciousness and favor capitalism. Psychologically the communist is one who despairs: one who does not have any relationship with the capitalist world except one that motivates him to struggle to annihilate it.

This spirit of struggle envigorates the communist mystique as it gives the combatant the sense of fighting for the reconciliation of man, for an end to the alienation that enslaves him, for a cause for which one could well die.

The party does not neglect any opportunity to point out to its militants the decadence of the bourgeoisie: its despicable films, the superficiality of its customs, its alcoholism and morphine addiction, its debasing of the human conscience, its ideological poverty and its total lack of faith in man.

A mystique of the possession of nature, of the conquest of the world, of the resolution of great problems so as to bring humanity forward, encourages Marxist propaganda. Marxism is a double struggle: struggle of man with man, which is called class struggle; struggle of man with nature, which is called work. This struggle will end in a reconciliation of mankind in a society without classes that will constitute «the great evening»[383] of history and in a reconciliation of man and the world owing to his dominion over nature. Before arriving at this period of total liberation, we must pass through the dictatorship of the proletariat in which the formula «from each according to his ability» will be applied. In the final stage, «to each according to his need» will be enforced[384].

This last stage will coincide with the disappearance of the State and with the end of the classes that are its foundation. In the ideal Marxist regime there will not exist a duality between social and political issues, nor will there be a distinction between the private man and the citizen because the State will be absorbed by society.

4.2. CONTEMPORARY MARXISM

The ideas we have set out above appear to be at a purely idealistic stage, and in practice these coherent and logical propositions are replaced by blind obedience to the party, as Marxists clearly admit.

The economic theories of surplus value and the Marxist explanation of the crises are generally neglected.

383 [«The Great Evening» or «*le Grand Soir*» refers to the anarchist concept in which a revolutionary general strike would bring bourgeois society to an end: «Soon perhaps darkness lit by the flickering flames of the Great Evening will cover the earth. Then will come the dawn of joy and fraternity». From the newspaper *Le Cri du Peuple* (The Cry of the People) (1871), founded by Jules Vallès during the period of the Paris Commune of 1871.]

384 [«From each according to his ability, to each according to his needs» was a slogan that Karl Marx made popular in his letter *Critique of the Gotha Program* (1875), in which he explained his revolutionary strategy for transitioning from capitalism to communism, and discussed the dictatorship of the proletariat.]

Contemporary Marxism appears to be divided into many groups, some of which present themselves as leftist variations, such as the Trotskyist Socialism represented by the Fourth International and the International Communist Left. Each of these two tendencies claims to be authentic Marxism and to endorse all the doctrinal positions of Marx, Engels and Lenin. Their doctrinal disagreement with Stalin is related to the theory of the *permanent revolution.* They affirm the impossibility of establishing socialism in a single country which is surrounded by capitalist countries that will force it to curb its revolutionary aspirations. For this reason Lenin wanted to carry out the revolutionary struggle simultaneously in his country and in foreign countries. Stalin, on the contrary, thought it was possible to limit the revolutionary spirit in order to save the Soviet State. For this reason he negotiated with capitalist countries and assured repeatedly that the coexistence of communist and capitalist regimes was possible. Left-wing Marxists accuse Stalin of betraying the working class and the revolution.

Trotskyists and the communist left also agree on rejecting any collaboration with bourgeois parties at the political level. They want revolutionary struggle on both the national and international levels; they fight against all the churches; they fight against all forms of imperialism. The Trotskyists think that if Russia were attacked by the capitalist countries they should help it, because the Soviet State represents an undeniable advance beyond the capitalist states. To the contrary, the International Communist Left thinks that Stalinist imperialism is worth no more than bourgeois imperialism. According to the International Communist Left, the Trotskyists are also reactionaries.

4.3. CHURCH'S OPINION ON ATHEISTIC COMMUNISM

The position of the Church on «the bolshevistic and atheistic Communism, which aims at upsetting the social order and at undermining the very foundations of Christian civilization»[385] is very clear and decisive. In 1846, Pius IX condemned it and confirmed this statement in the *Syllabus*[386]; Leo XIII's *Quod Apostolici Muneris*; Pius XI's *Quadragesimo Anno, Miserentissimus Redemptor*[387],

385 [*Divini Redemptoris* § 3.]

386 [Pius IX's document *Syllabus Errorum* (8 December 1864) condemned a total of 80 errors or heresies. It was a document annexed to the encyclical *Quanta Cura.* http://www.papalencyclicals.net/piuso9/p9syll.htm.]

387 [Pius XI, Encyclical on Reparation to the Sacred Heart *Miserentissimus Redemptor* (8 May 1928), at The Holy See, http://www.newadvent.org/library/docs_pi11mr.htm.]

Caritate Christi[388], *Acerba Animi*[389], *Dilectissima Nobis*[390] and especially *Divini Redemptoris* were encyclicals devoted entirely to this subject[391].

The documents of the Episcopacy and those of Catholic theologians and philosophers are overwhelming in number and uniformity of doctrine. Let us summarize the official doctrine on this point.

How communism has managed to penetrate:

«A pseudo-ideal of justice, of equality and fraternity in labor impregnates all its doctrine and activity with a deceptive mysticism, which communicates a zealous and contagious enthusiasm to the multitudes entrapped by delusive promises. This is especially true in an age like ours, when unusual misery has resulted from the unequal distribution of the goods of this world. This pseudo-ideal is even boastfully advanced as if it were responsible for a certain economic progress. As a matter of fact, when such progress is at all real, its true causes are quite different, as for instance the intensification of industrialism in countries which were formerly almost without it, the exploitation of immense natural resources, and the use of the most brutal methods to insure the achievement of gigantic projects with a minimum of expense»[392].

«By pretending to desire only the betterment of the condition of the working classes, by urging the removal of the very real abuses chargeable to the liberalistic economic order, and by demanding a more equitable distribution of this world's goods (objectives entirely and undoubtedly legitimate), the Communist takes advantage of the present world-wide economic crisis to draw into the sphere of his influence even those sections of the populace which on principle reject all forms of materialism and terrorism. And as every error contains its element of truth, the partial truths to which We have referred are astutely presented according to the needs of time and place, to conceal, when convenient, the repulsive crudity and inhumanity of Communistic principles and tactics. Thus the Communist ideal wins over many of the better minded members of the community. These in turn become the apostles of the movement

388 [*Caritate Christi Compulsi.*]

389 [Pius XI, Encyclical on Persecution of the Church in Mexico *Acerba Animi* (29 September 1932), at The Holy See, http://w2.vatican.va/content/pius-xi/en/encyclicals/documents/hf_p-xi_enc_29091932_acerba-animi.html.]

390 [Pius XI, Encyclical on Oppression of the Church of Spain *Dilectissima Nobis* (3 June 1933), at The Holy See, http://w2.vatican.va/content/pius-xi/en/encyclicals/documents/hf_p-xi_enc_03061933_dilectissima-nobis.html.]

391 [At this point Hurtado left a sentence unfinished: «Pius XII has alluded to communism in hundreds of documents and declared excommunicated all those».]

392 [*Divini Redemptoris* § 8.]

among the younger intelligentsia who are still too immature to recognize the intrinsic errors of the system. The preachers of Communism are also proficient in exploiting racial antagonisms and political divisions and oppositions. They take advantage of the lack of orientation characteristic of modern agnostic science in order to burrow into the universities, where they bolster up the principles of their doctrine with pseudo-scientific arguments.

If we would explain the blind acceptance of Communism by so many thousands of workmen, we must remember that the way had been already prepared for it by the religious and moral destitution in which wage-earners had been left by liberal economics»[393].

«We cannot without deep sorrow contemplate the heedlessness of those who apparently make light of these impending dangers, and with sluggish inertia allow the widespread propagation of doctrine which seeks by violence and slaughter to destroy society altogether. All the more gravely to be condemned is the folly of those who neglect to remove or change the conditions that inflame the minds of peoples, and pave the way for the overthrow and destruction of society»[394].

4.4. MAIN COUNTERPOSITIONS TO CATHOLICISM

In its essence, they are dialectical and historical materialism.

«The doctrine of modern Communism, which is often concealed under the most seductive trappings, is in substance based on the principles of dialectical and historical materialism previously advocated by Marx, of which the theoreticians of bolshevism claim to possess the only genuine interpretation. According to this doctrine there is in the world only one reality, matter, the blind forces of which evolve into plant, animal and man. Even human society is nothing but a phenomenon and form of matter, evolving in the same way. By a law of inexorable necessity and through a perpetual conflict of forces, matter moves towards the final synthesis of a classless society. In such a doctrine, as is evident, there is no room for the idea of God; there is no difference between matter and spirit, between soul and body; there is neither survival of the soul after death nor any hope in a future life. Insisting on the dialectical aspect of their materialism, the Communists claim that the conflict which carries the world towards its final synthesis can be accelerated by man. Hence they endeavor to sharpen the antagonisms which arise between the various classes of society. Thus the class

393 [*Id.* §§ 15-16.]
394 [*Quadragesimo Anno* § 112.]

struggle with its consequent violent hate and destruction takes on the aspects of a crusade for the progress of humanity. On the other hand, all other forces whatever, as long as they resist such systematic violence, must be annihilated as hostile to the human race»[395].

Hence, there is a total negation of charity. It deprives man of the rights inherent in his personality.

«Communism, moreover, strips man of his liberty, robs human personality of all its dignity, and removes all the moral restraints that check the eruptions of blind impulse. There is no recognition of any right of the individual in his relations to the collectivity; no natural right is accorded to human personality, which is a mere cog-wheel in the Communist system. In man's relations with other individuals, besides, Communists hold the principle of absolute equality, rejecting all hierarchy and divinely-constituted authority, including the authority of parents. What men call authority and subordination is derived from the community as its first and only font. Nor is the individual granted any property rights over material goods or the means of production, for inasmuch as these are the source of further wealth, their possession would give one man power over another. Precisely on this score, all forms of private property must be eradicated, for they are at the origin of all economic enslavement.

Refusing to human life any sacred or spiritual character, such a doctrine logically makes of marriage and the family a purely artificial and civil institution, the outcome of a specific economic system. There exists no matrimonial bond of a juridico-moral nature that is not subject to the whim of the individual or of the collectivity. Naturally, therefore, the notion of an indissoluble marriage-tie is scouted. Communism is particularly characterized by the rejection of any link that binds woman to the family and the home, and her emancipation is proclaimed as a basic principle. She is withdrawn from the family and the care of her children, to be thrust instead into public life and collective production under the same conditions as man. The care of home and children then devolves upon the collectivity. Finally, the right of education is denied to parents, for it is conceived as the exclusive prerogative of the community, in whose name and by whose mandate alone parents may exercise this right»[396].

395 [*Divini Redemptoris* § 9.]
396 [*Id.* §§ 10-11.]

It suppresses God. It conceives of civilization as the fruit of blind evolution.

> «What would be the condition of a human society based on such materialistic tenets? It would be a collectivity with no other hierarchy than that of the economic system. It would have only one mission: the production of material things by means of collective labor, so that the goods of this world might be enjoyed in a paradise where each would "give according to his powers" and would "receive according to his needs". Communism recognizes in the collectivity the right, or rather, unlimited discretion, to draft individuals for the labor of the collectivity with no regard for their personal welfare; so that even violence could be legitimately exercised to dragoon the recalcitrant against their wills. In the Communistic commonwealth morality and law would be nothing but a derivation of the existing economic order, purely earthly in origin and unstable in character. In a word, the Communists claim to inaugurate a new era and a new civilization which is the result of blind evolutionary forces culminating in a humanity without God»[397].

4.5. ATTITUDE OF CATHOLICS VIS-A-VIS COMMUNISM

With great cunning, Communists «try perfidiously to worm their way even into professedly Catholic and religious organizations. Again, without receding an inch from their subversive principles, they invite Catholics to collaborate with them in the realm of so-called humanitarianism and charity; and at times even make proposals that are in perfect harmony with the Christian spirit and the doctrine of the Church. Elsewhere they carry their hypocrisy so far as to encourage the belief that Communism, in countries where faith and culture are more strongly entrenched, will assume another and much milder form. It will not interfere with the practice of religion. It will respect liberty of conscience. There are some even who refer to certain changes recently introduced into soviet legislation as a proof that Communism is about to abandon its program of war against God»[398].

Communism is inherently perverse and we cannot collaborate with it on any ground.

> «See to it, Venerable Brethren, that the Faithful do not allow themselves to be deceived! Communism is intrinsically wrong, and no one who would save Christian civilization

397 [*Id.* § 12.]
398 [*Id.* § 57.]

may collaborate with it in any undertaking whatsoever. Those who permit themselves to be deceived into lending their aid towards the triumph of Communism in their own country, will be the first to fall victims of their error. And the greater the antiquity and grandeur of the Christian civilization in the regions where Communism successfully penetrates, so much more devastating will be the hatred displayed by the godless»[399].

In condemning communism, the Holy Father has repeatedly stated that his condemnations are directed against the materialistic and atheist regime, but not for the Russian people, who personally suffer this sad experience.

4.6. JUDGMENT OF THE FACTS

The beautiful declarations of justice, of proletarian elevation, have inspired many generous spirits, but the outcomes have profoundly disillusioned those sincere men who have managed to learn the actual facts.

These facts are hardly well known because the Soviet rulers have devoted exquisite care to hiding their paradise behind iron curtains. Why? Why do they prevent their citizens from traveling abroad?

It is indisputable, in the first place, that the Soviet regime has made improvements in the lives of workers, who were in a state of extreme backwardness; it has completed large construction projects which it proclaims loudly in propaganda. To this end it has devoted the resources of an immense and rich country whose economy is completely controlled by the State. How far do these material conquests go? Russia is perhaps the only country in the world about which is difficult to form conclusions with confidence, because the foreigner cannot control Soviet information and there is plenty of history of unreliable sources of it.

Those who have managed to evade the Soviet regime, and many who have entered it as friends and have left as determined adversaries, speak of misery, poor construction, starvation wages, great ignorance and hatred of the regime[400].

Terrorism rules and, never in modern times and perhaps in the whole of history, has there been known a government more despotic, dictatorial and totalitarian, that concentrates all power in a Master and in its all-powerful secret po-

399 [*Id.* § 58.]

400 [In the manuscript there here appears, in handwriting, the following footnote: «Consult works such as that of forced labor in Russia, Kravchenko: *I Chose Liberty*, Koestler: *Le Zéro et l'Infini* (*Darkness at Noon*), Gide, Wright, Silone, Koestler... *The God that Failed*, *The Peasant: Life and Death in the U.S.S.R*».]

lice. In Russia one lives in uncertainty, in panic and in fear of systematic denunciation and betrayal.

The Soviet regime preaches peace and practices war. The oppression of states, which yesterday were independent and now are annexed to its imperialist orbit, is one of the major causes of the armaments race in which humanity is engaged. It has now forgotten all authentic proletarian demands, and deferred all that might dignify life so as to spend billions on arms.

What makes this situation even more miserable is the impossibility of contractual relations with Russia because of insecurity as to one's ability to trust its word. According to Communist principles, truth and morality are identified with the triumph of the Party: whatever conduces to this is moral and true. Before such a doctrine there can be no values, not even common concepts that make an agreement possible. This is why the world lives in constant anguish and distrust of Marxist promises.

Communism must lead Christians to examine, daily and with sincerity and realism, whether they live according to the doctrine of brotherly love characteristic of a disciple of Christ, and whether they are willing to make all the sacrifices necessary in order to bring about a world worthy of the children of God.

II

Chapter 9

Foundations of Catholic Social Morality

The various opposing systems of social morality that exist today are diversified and antagonistic, not so much owing to a different assesment of the use of economic means, but owing to a different philosophy about God, man and the world. The materialistic and spiritual views will have, from the beginning, totally opposed conceptions of man, of freedom and of wealth, and this will have repercussions as to social, economic and even technical matters.

His Holiness Pius XII, in the encyclical *Summi Pontificatus* says, «[f]or true though it is that the evils from which mankind suffers today come in part from economic instability and from the struggle of interests regarding a more equal distribution of the goods which God has given man as a means of sustenance and progress, it is not less true that their root is deeper and more intrinsic, belonging to the sphere of religious belief and moral convictions which have been perverted by the progressive alienation of the peoples from that unity of doctrine, faith, customs and morals which once was promoted by the tireless and beneficent work of the Church. If it is to have any effect, the reeducation of mankind must be, above all things, spiritual and religious. Hence, it must proceed from Christ as from its indispensable foundation; must be actuated by justice and crowned by charity»[401]. «Forces that are to renew the face of the earth should proceed from within, from the spirit»[402].

Social morality presupposes, therefore, some fundamental concepts that are the subject of other treatises, but we must summarize them because they are very important. Neither thought nor action must ignore these great principles.

1
God

In earlier times, men's philosophical and religious views were divided according to their different ideas of divinity, the different messages they thought they had received from God, and their different ways of worship, but all, morally speaking, believed in God. Our century has had the sad privilege of learning that millions of men call themselves atheists, and live enslaved by systems that are theo-

401 [Pius XII, Encyclical on the Unity of Human Society *Summi Pontificatus* (20 October 1939) § 83, at the Holy See, http://w2.vatican.va/content/pius-xii/en/encyclicals/documents/hf_p-xii_enc_20101939_summi-pontificatus.html (hereinafter referred to as *Summi Pontificatus*).]

402 [*Id.* § 81.]

retically or practically atheistic, while philosophers, economists and sociologists apply the implications of their atheism to their respective fields. All judgments of social morality are conditioned by an intimate attitude towards the problem of God. If this attitude is atheistic in theory or practice, Christian social morality will appear to be bereft of all foundation, strength and meaning. If a group of university students or trade unionists want to follow a course of social morality, they must clearly agree on this point of departure before moving on: if not, all their studies will have no foundation.

His Holiness Pius XI, in *Divini Redemptoris*, after exposing the errors of atheistic Communism, set forth the true notion of the «*Civitas Humana*» and stated that «[a]bove all other reality there exists one supreme Being: God, the omnipotent Creator of all things, the all-wise and just Judge of all men … not because men believe in God that He exists; rather because He exists do all men whose eyes are not deliberately closed to the truth believe in Him and pray to Him»[403].

God creates from nothing all material and spiritual beings, preserves them in being and life, and organizes and maintains the world that came forth from Him. Among these creatures are intelligent and free beings, to whom He gives a moral law that guides them in the exercise of their freedom, towards God himself. God is at once creator, legislator, owner of everything and supreme end of all that exists.

The world and all the things in the universe have been given to us by the Creator as instruments for the service of man. By the use of those things, each can realize his destiny. It is the plan of God that man will increasingly have dominion of the deep powers of the world. Genesis tells us that when God created our first Parents he blessed them, saying «[b]e fertile and multiply; fill the earth and subdue it. Have dominion over the fish of the sea, the birds of the air, and all the living things that crawl on the earth, God also said: «see, I give you every seed-bearing plant on all the earth and every tree that has seed-bearing fruit on it to be your food». (Gen. 1:28-29). When man makes a proper use of the world he achieves his ultimate end, which is the glory of God. St. Paul says to man: «[a]ll belong[s] to you; and you to Christ, and Christ to God». (1 Cor. 3:22-23).

403 [*Divini Redemptoris* § 26.]

2

Man

Man is the center of social morality. The dignity of the human person is the foundation of his rights: that is why it is necessary to understand dignity properly.

Man is an intermediary between pure spirit and purely material being. His sentient body is vivified by a spiritual soul, free and immortal, created in the image and likeness of God. Man is a person, a being with a destiny of his own that he must realize through the use of his freedom; he is the subject of sacred duties and rights, which are imposed and should be respected by all. Nothing and nobody, other than God, has direct dominion over man. Neither the family nor the State, or any other body is authorized, under any circumstances, to violate man's legitimate rights.

This greatness of man, seen only in the light of natural reason, is immensely increased by Christian revelation. God created man to make him His friend—His adoptive son to participate in His own nature— to give him eternal happiness, which is God Himself; to know Him as God knows Himself; to love Him as God loves Himself. This elevation of man to the supernatural level was terminated by the sin of our first Parents, who deprived us—through their fault— of God's free gift: His sanctifying grace. But upon the distruction of the first way to elevation to supernatural life, God's infinite love was not defeated by human weakness and chose a second and even more wonderful way to raise all men, of all eras, to participation in divine life. As soon as our Parents had sinned, the Lord announced to them that His Son would come to the earth and trample the head of the spirit of evil[404]. In the fullness of time, «the Word became flesh and made his dwelling among us» (John 1:14), so «we may be called the children of God. Yet so we are». (1 John 3:1). Those who from the dawn of creation have believed and hoped in Him, so far as this was possible to them according to the light received, have become true children of God. It is impossible to think of a gift of greater proportions[405].

404 [Cf. Gen. 3:15: «They will strike at your head, while you strike at their heel».]

405 It does not belong to the subject matter of this book to explain at length how those who were born before Christ or those who have not expressly known him could be saved. Theology deals with this: we only wish to indicate that to a man who does his utmost to follow the truth, as he knows it through his conscience, God does not deny His Grace. There is only one Truth and Christ said of Himself, «I am the way and the truth and the life». [(John 14:6).]

By Redemption, we can truly be genuine children of God, brothers of the Word, temples of the Holy Spirit: we can call God, with all certainty, our Father.

The Son of God, uniting Himself with human nature, elevated the whole human race. Christ is the firstborn of a multitude of brothers with whom he shares His own divine life. Christ is the head of a body, the Mystical Body, and we are called to be its members, without any limitation as to race, wealth or any other consideration. Being a man is the only requirement to be a member of the Mystical Body of Christ, which is to say to be Christ. Only the condemned are excluded from the possibility of this union.

He who accepts the Incarnation must accept it with all its consequences and extend its gifts not only to Jesus Christ but also to His Mystical Body. To forsake the least of our brethren is to forsake Christ; to relieve any of them is to relieve Christ in person. Touching one man is like touching Christ. This is why Jesus told us that whatever good or evil we do to the least of our brothers, we are doing to Him. The core of Jesus' revelation, «the good news», is the union of all men with Christ.

Christ has become our neighbor, imprisoned with inmates, and takes the form of the worker or the employer, the injured in a hospital or a beggar in the streets. If we do not see Christ in the man we meet everyday, it is because our faith is lukewarm and our love imperfect. For this reason, St. John tells us, «If anyone says, " I love God",but hates his brother whom he has seen cannot love God whom he has not seen». (1 Jn. 4: 20).

The communion of the saints, a basic dogma of our faith and one of the first realities, implies that all men are in solidarity. We all receive the Redemption of Christ and its wonderful fruits. The communion of the saints makes us understand that among those who belong to «the family of God» there are much more intimate bonds than those of camaraderie, friendship and social class. Faith teaches us that we are one in Christ: Americans and Russians, Japanese and Chinese, proletarians and businessmen —that we all share the goods of all and we all suffer the consequences— at least negatively —of one another's evils. We are assisted by invisible prayers, surrounded by graces that we have not deserved but others have acquired for us. How can we not love those who, in all truth, we can call our unseen benefactors?

Nothing is more opposed to Christianity than individualism. Each of us is part of a great whole: we are stones of the same building, branches of the same tree, members of the same body and heirs of the same destiny. The branch that breaks off becomes dry and serves only for the fire. A stone that falls from a building compromises the stability of the whole. Among all of us there is an exchange of services comparable to the circulation of blood in our body. St. Paul summarizes this wonderful doctrine when he teaches that just as each of us has one body with many members, and these members do not all have the same function, so in Christ we, though many, form one body, and each member belongs to all the others. If one member suffers, all suffer with it; if a member is glorified, they all rejoice with him[406].

Whoever understands this doctrine will understand the meaning of:

Social solidarity: that intimate bond that unites us with one another so as to help others obtain the benefits that society can give them;

Social sense: that spontaneous attitude that reacts fraternally to others and leads a person to put himself in the position of others as if it were his own; that does not tolerate abuse against of the defenseless; that is outraged when justice is violated;

Social responsibility: that which says very clearly that one cannot be content with not doing evil, but is obliged to do good and work for a better world.

3
Consequences of the Dignity of the Human Person.

3.1. THE PRIMACY OF MAN OVER MATTER

Wealth is at the service of man and not man at the service of wealth, said St. Antoninus of Florence[407]. Therefore, any social organization that subordinates man to matter, which makes him an instrument for the acquisition of wealth without considering his personhood, must be reformed. In this light we must consider the thinking of ancient philosophers: Aristotle said that the slave was «a living instrument»[408], and Cicero, «a plow that speaks»[409]. By this criterion we

406 Rom. 12:4,-5; 1 Cor. 12:4-6, 12-25; 1 Col. 18:24; Eph. 5:29-30.

407 [Antonio Perozzi, (1389-1459), Italian Dominican friar and saint, Archbishop of Florence. He was the author of *Summa Theologica Moralis* (1477) and *Summa Confessionalis, Curam Illius Habes* (1472). In his writings he showed his awareness of social and economic development.]

408 [«The slave is, therefore, to be considered a specific type of property —a living instrument or tool— but being unable to perform its task on command or by anticipating instructions, cannot relieve the master of the need for slaves». Aristotle, *Politics* 1253b33, 1253b38. Also, *Οἰκονομικά* (Economics), a work attributed to Aristotle or his succesor Theophrastus, described the relationship among different members of the household.]

409 [Varro, Cicero's contemporary, distinguished three types of agricultural equipment: instruments endowed with speech (slaves), inarticulate instruments (cattle) and speechless instruments (wagons and plows).]

have to judge the different types of industrial organization: capitalist and communist—in which men, women and children have been sacrificed to the intense pace of production, without any care for their material and moral needs.

3.2. PROPERTY AT THE SERVICE OF MAN

Goods have been given by the Creator for all his creatures, by the Father for all his children; and therefore so that all of them can live in a suitable way, appropriate to their human nature. In the same way, they can develop their physical potential, form a family and procreate children, develop their minds, and possess the minimum amount of goods necessary to practice the virtues that belong to a child of God. This is the primary purpose of the goods of the earth. In light of the equal rights of all men, there is no distinction of races, talents or secondary qualities. To positive law belongs the determination of the way in which the goods of the earth are to be divided so as to fulfill the providential plan. To the extent that laws oppose this plan, they violate the common good and infringe social justice.

The mission of private property rights is to guarantee the freedom that each man needs in order to ensure his independence and the possibility of dedicating himself to higher-order works, to give him tranquil rest in his old age and the possibility of educating and finding employment for his children.

In the possession of goods there will always be inequalities owing to differences in talent, effort, etc. Total egalitarianism is absurd. But, on the other hand, one cannot accept an accumulation of goods in a few hands that would make it impossible to obtain, with sufficient effort, the portion that the majority needs. Something that can never be allowed is that a quantity of goods indispensable to ensure the dignity of the human person should be sacrificed for the satisfaction of secondary needs or, for even stronger reasons, can never be devoted to the comfort and luxury of the most fortunate people.

This criterion for the distribution of goods applies not only to a particular country, but also to the inhabitants of the great country which is the world, the homeland of the children of God. Consequently, in the light of social justice, a juridical order that allows the consolidation of countries with a high standard of living at the expense of those less fortunate cannot be accepted. People from countries with a low standard of living must be prepared by culture and technical instruction so that they can obtain at least the minimum of goods that the dignity of the human person requires.

The concrete ways of implementing these principles must be discerned through the virtue of prudence, employing the means that circumstances permit; a universal social mentality must be the foundation for their complete achievement. Christian consciousness will be the leaven that will make the dough rise.

Christian charity will achieve what social justice will not be able to do: seeing in one's neighbors the Giver of all good.

3.3. RESPECT FOR THE AUTONOMY OF THE HUMAN PERSON AND HIS ULTIMATE ORIENTATION

Man is not a means, but an end in himself; not an ultimate end, but subordinated to God. Therefore, social organization must facilitate the intellectual cultivation of man and the fulfillment of his moral, religious, family, civic and professional duties. For this reason, the Christian can never accept the laicist principles of liberalism and Marxism, which ignore this supernatural purpose of man.

3.4. THE SUBSTANTIAL EQUALITY OF HUMAN NATURE AND THE NECESSARY INEQUALITY OF CONDITIONS

Men all have the same origin, the same nature, and therefore the same fundamental needs. They have the same supernatural destiny, and as a consequence are entitled to respect for their rights.

At the same time, in the world —as God has established it— there are inequalities of talents, conditions, strengths, ambition; and these will necessarily introduce a certain inequality in the possession of spiritual, intellectual and economic benefits. Total egalitarianism is unnatural. In addition, in every society there will be different functions: some must command and others obey, some perform intellectual work and others manual labor. These inequalities must not be accentuated, but on the contrary ameliorated but they can never cease to exist. If there is no authority, there is no society.

3.5. THE DUTY TO IMPROVE ONE'S CHARACTER

The awareness of our inner wealth and the precious instrument at our disposal: freedom —will move us to perfect and enrich our own persons, by observing the moral law. This involves fighting against our disordered appetites, of which each one of us is well aware; in that struggle we will encounter our nobility and our independence.

Christian morality, going beyond mere natural morality, counsels us to implement the advice of the Gospel: an affective and, if possible, effective detachment from the goods of this world; the acceptance of pain and of persecution for justice, and the practice of gentleness, purity and self-denial. While liberalism and socialism teach only about the pleasure and the possession of goods and reject as absolute evils poverty, disease and suffering, Christian morality teaches us to face these realities pursuing to a superior criterion. Before evil it does not preach resignation but struggle so long as possible, but at the same time it teaches one austerity, the acceptance of the inevitable as coming from God and its supernatural use for the growth of the Mystical Body of Christ.

3.6. PONTIFICAL TEACHING ON THE CONSEQUENCES OF THE DIGNITY OF THE HUMAN PERSON

272 Pius XI says of man that «he is a true "microcosm",as the ancients said, a world in miniature, with a value far surpassing that of the vast inanimate cosmos … In consequence he has been endowed by God with many and varied prerogatives: the right to life, to bodily integrity, to the necessary means of existence; the right to tend toward his ultimate goal in the path marked out for him by God; the right of association and the right to possess and use property»[410].

> «[I]t was Christianity that first affirmed the real and universal brotherhood of all men of whatever race and condition. This doctrine she proclaimed by a method, and with an amplitude and conviction, unknown to preceding centuries; and with it she potently contributed to the abolition of slavery. Not bloody revolution, but the inner force of her teaching made the proud Roman matron see in her slave a sister in Christ. It is Christianity that adores the Son of God, made Man for love of man, and become not only the "Son of a Carpenter' but Himself a "Carpenter". It was Christianity that raised manual labor to its true dignity, whereas it had hitherto been so despised …»[411]

Pius XI himself recognizes that «immense multitudes of their brother-workmen who, because they were not understood or treated with the respect to which they were entitled, in bitterness have strayed far from God»[412].

410 [*Divini Redemptoris* § 27.]
411 [*Id.* § 36.]
412 [*Id.* § 70.]

In his Christmas Message of 1942, Pius XII, discussing the conditions that would make peace possible said, «[h]e who would have the Star of Peace shine out and stand over society should cooperate, for his part, in giving back to the human person the dignity given to it by God from the very beginning; should oppose the excessive herding of men, as if they were a mass without a soul; their economic, social, political, intellectual and moral inconsistency; their dearth of solid principles and strong convictions, their surfeit of instinctive sensible excitement and their fickleness. He should favor, by every lawful means, in every sphere of life, social institutions in which a full personal responsibility is assured and guaranteed both in the early and the eternal order of things. He should uphold respect for and the practical realization of the following fundamental personal rights; the right to maintain and develop one's corporal, intellectual and moral life and especially the right to religious formation and education; the right to worship God in private and public and to carry on religious works of charity; the right to marry and to achieve the aim of married life; the right to conjugal and domestic society; the right to work, as the indispensable means towards the maintenance of family life; the right to free choice of state of life, and hence, too, of the priesthood or religious life; the right to the use of material goods; in keeping with his duties and social limitations»[413].

He went on to say, «[a]ll work has an inherent dignity and at the same time a close connection with the perfection of the person … the Church does not hesitate to draw the practical conclusions which are derived from the moral nobility of work, and to give them all the support of her authority. These exigencies include, besides a just wage which covers the needs of the worker and his family, the conservation and perfection of a social order which will make possible an assured, even if modest, private property for all classes of society, which will promote higher education for the children of the working class who are especially endowed with intelligence and good will, which promote the care and the practice of the social spirit in one's immediate neighborhood, in the district, the province, the people and the nation, a spirit which, by smoothing over friction arising from privileges or class interests, removes from the workers the sense of isolation through the assuring experience of a genuinely human, and fraternally Christian, solidarity»[414].

413 [*Christmas Message of 1942.*]
414 [*Id.*]

Chapter 10

Priciples of Catholic Social Morality

Social morality has three fundamental pillars: justice, charity and the common good. Justice and charity belong to the category of virtues.

In man there are natural and supernatural virtues. Natural virtues do not require in those who practice them the gift of sanctifying grace, but only the performance of a work in accordance with their natures: for example, paying a debt, helping a poor person and acts of filial piety. But when one who practices an act of natural virtue is in a state of sanctifying grace, that action has an immensely superior value because it proceeds from one who is penetrated by divine life and it constitutes an action meritorious as regards eternal life.

When speaking of justice, we speak of rights; when speaking of charity, we speak of love, which is obligatory but not enforceable by law.

1 *Justice*

Justice is the stable disposition of our will that leads us to respect the right of our neighbor. The right is a moral power to act or to possess: it is a manifestation of personality. Only a person is capable of having rights and obligations. When we talk about moral power, we point out its difference from physical ability. A right is not lost because it cannot be exercised.

Rights are reciprocal: if others must respect my rights, I must respect theirs. Justice, then, consists in this stable disposition to respect the rights of others in all their manifestations: bodily and spiritual goods: health, honor, wealth, freedom, association, etc. The rights of others creates in us corresponding obligations. One who has been injured in his rights can claim and demand —so long as it is possible given human imperfection— compensation corresponding to the damage caused.

Justice is a fundamental but unpopular virtue. It lacks refulgence because its demands are, at first sight, very modest, and for that reason it does not arouse enthusiasm, nor does its fulfillment confer glory. One may feel proud of one's alms, but not of not having killed someone: that is what one ought to do and nothing more. And yet it is a very difficult virtue and requires a great deal of rectitude. There are many who are willing to exercise charity, but do not commit themselves to act with justice; they are willing to give alms, but not to pay fair wages. Although it seems strange, it is easier to be charitable (of course, only in appearance) than just. This is only an apparent charity, because true charity begins where justice ends. Charity without justice will not bridge a social chasm, but will create deep resentment. Injustice causes far more evils than charity can repair.

The inversion of values in the practice of these two virtues is caused by a wrongful sentiment of vanity. One who feels superior likes to occupy a position of protection, placing himself above the protégé; instead, justice places all men on the same footing of absolute equality. But man, whatever his situation, does not desire benevolence but justice; no substitute can satisfy him.

«We are, happily, in a time that calls for justice. After long oppression, men do not want to be satisfied with anything less than justice and aspire to obtain it, even if in the attempt the social building should shattered.

Passion for justice explodes with devastating force. In many cases passion is blind and resorts to means that are destined to be disastrous. It is sad, as Pius XI deplores, that the clamor for bread, which is all about justice, is often accompanied by feelings of hatred that can never be justified.

Marxism and totalitarianism, amidst their exaggerations, have called on the masses to restore the justice ravaged by liberal economy. If Marxism and totalitarianism have found a profound echo, this has been not so much owing to the errors of liberal economy as to the soul of truth that they encompass and their clamor for justice. If so many workers have drifted away from faith in these days, this has often been because they have the mistaken idea that the Church is not unconditionally on the side of justice; the isolated actions of many Catholics who lack social sense have served as a pretext for this.

To this disorder we must oppose the order of justice, without fear of disturbances or catastrophes. Men will understand that they must wait for the gradual achievement of something that cannot be obtained at once, but they are not willing to continue to tolerate seeing justice denied and the bestowal of what they are rightfully entitled to only in the name of charity and out of an apparent mercy. We must be just before we are generous. Injustice causes more evils than can be remedied by charity»[415].

1.1. DIFFERENT KINDS OF JUSTICE

Justice can be particular or general. Particular justice can be commutative and distributive; general justice is also called legal or social.

415 [*Social Humanism*, p. 87.]

Commutative justice (from the Latin *commutare* = change) aims at the fulfillment of contractual relations, guided by the old Latin adage «*do ut des*». I bought a house, I must pay the price; I acquire a rail ticket, I must pay its value. Commutative justice is the most precise, the most definite because it is based on a certain equality, and can be discussed in courts. This is the only kind of justice understood by simplistic spirits, who despise other types of justice as imprecise and ethereal.

Distributive or *proportional justice* creates the right of each to be treated by the social authorities according to his abilities, his needs, his particular dignity, in distributing social burdens and benefits. For example, large families have a right to lower taxes or higher subsidies because they have more burdens. Distributive justice must be applied by the father in the family, taking into account each person's abilities when assigning work and his degree of responsibility when imposing punishment. Distributive justice must be applied within an occupation, because when establishing salary, besides the work itself, its quality, the training of the worker, his age, his obligations or family burdens, his seniority in the company and his initiative, must also be taken into account. The vice most opposed to distributive justice is what may be called «preference of persons», or favoritism, nepotism, class spirit or political partisanship, that is the distribution of burdens or benefits owing to considerations alien to the general good and which are born only of a specific good: relationship with the bestower, belonging to the same political party, etc.

Moralists argue as to whether a violation of distributive justice confers on the offended party a purely moral right and not a cause of legal action, or whether it confers a legal right. The latter opinion seems more probable and, by virtue of it, when distributive justice has been consciously violated there is a right to claim compensation. According to this doctrine, the restitution made to repair an injury to distributive justice is an act of commutative justice: «the distributive one imposes the restitution and the commutative executes it»[416]. This restitution, like all acts of distributive justice, is difficult to appraise. It is not an easy task to establish the dignity of each citizen, his merits, the part of the common good to which he has a right: all this will be done by approximation, as is often the case with commutative justice.

416 [At this point Hurtado states, «(Folliet, o.c., p. 30)». Hurtado is referring to Joseph Folliet, *Morale Sociale* (*Social Morality*) (1937), volume II, chapter VII, p. 30, which discusses distributive justice and restitution.]

In view of these difficulties, many seek to replace distributive justice with total *egalitarianism*: not to give to each according to his need, but to everyone equally: the same house, the same clothing, the same work ... This solution is absurd, because it would be, on the one hand, an impossible egalitarianism or, in the other hand, a depressing egalitarianism. Pretended egalitarianism has really led to unbridled favoritism, based only on whim. Thus, the notion of distributive justice retains all its value.

1.2. GENERAL, LEGAL OR SOCIAL JUSTICE

Commutative and distributive justice tend to generate good for a private physical person or a legal entity. General justice determines the good that is owed to a society as such.

Today, general justice is commonly called social justice, although this recent designation has had multiple interpretations that we here have omitted[417]. Here we will use the three words as synonymous: general, legal and social justice. General justice corresponds to the idea that all actions must be directed towards the common good of society; it overlaps with the acts of all virtues. Legal justice is exercised within the framework of laws that have as their object the common good and is imposed particularly on legislators, rulers and magistrates. According to St. Thomas, social justice has the function of promoting the common good[418].

Pius XI, in *Divini Redemptoris*, points out the field of social justice:

> «In reality, besides commutative justice, there is also social justice with its own set obligations, from which neither employers nor workingmen can escape. Now it is of the very essence of social justice to demand for each individual all that is necessary for the common good. But just as in the living organism it is impossible to provide for the good of the whole unless each single part and each individual member is given what it needs for the exercise of its proper functions, so it is impossible to care for the social organism and the good of society as a unit unless each single part and each individual member —that is to say, each individual man in the dignity of his human personality— is supplied with all that is necessary for the exercise of his social functions. If social

417 [Hurtado states here: «(see this point in Azpiazu *Economic Professional Morality* 17-29; Cavallera, 65-67.)» Hurtado is referring Cavallera's book *Précis de la Doctrine Sociale Catholique* (*Summary of Catholic Social Doctrine*)(1931).]

418 Cfr. II-II, q.58 a.6 [*Summa Theologica*.]

justice be satisfied, the result will be an intense activity in economic life as a whole, pursued in tranquility and order. This activity will be proof of the health of the social body, just as the health of the human body is recognized in the undisturbed regularity and perfect efficiency of the whole organism.

But social justice cannot be said to have been satisfied as long as workingmen are denied a salary that will enable them to secure proper sustenance for themselves and for their families; as long as they are denied the opportunity of acquiring a modest fortune and forestalling the plague of universal pauperism; as long as they cannot make suitable provision through public or private insurance for old age, for periods of illness and unemployment. In a word, to repeat what has been said in Our Encyclical *Quadragesimo Anno*: "Then only will the economic and social order be soundly established and attain its ends, when it offers, to all and to each, all those goods which the wealth and resources of nature, technical science and the corporate organization of social affairs can give. These goods should be sufficient to supply all necessities and reasonable comforts, and to uplift men to that higher standard of life which, provided it be used with prudence, is not only not a hindrance but is of singular help to virtue"[419].

It happens all too frequently, however, under the salary system, that individual employers are helpless to ensure justice unless, with a view to its practice, they organize institutions the object of which is to prevent competition incompatible with fair treatment for the workers. Where this is true, it is the duty of contractors and employers to support and promote such necessary organizations as normal instruments enabling them to fulfill their obligations of justice. But the laborers too must be mindful of their duty to love and deal fairly with their employers, and persuade themselves that there is no better means of safeguarding their own interests.

If, therefore, We consider the whole structure of economic life, as We have already pointed out in Our Encyclical *Quadragesimo Anno*, the reign of mutual collaboration between justice and charity in social-economic relations can only be achieved by a body of professional and inter-professional organizations, built on solidly Christian foundations, working together to effect, under forms adapted to different places and circumstances, what has been called the Corporation»[420].

The Pope then explains in detail the application of social justice to the subjects of wages, the extent of property holdings, social insurance, etc., and fin-

419 [The encyclical here has a footnote as follows: «Encycl. *Quadragesimo Anno*, May 15, 1931 (A.A.S., Vol. XXIII, 1931, p. 202».).]

420 [*Divini Redemptoris* §§ 51-54.]

ishes by proposing professional and inter-professional associations that would ensure compliance with social justice.

Fr. Isidro Gandía, S.J.[421], believes that social justice is that virtue by which society, by itself or through its members, satisfies the right of every man to what is due to him because of his dignity as a human person. It is this dignity of the person that underlies social justice.

Social justice contains two senses that are necessary in the modern world: the first, a social sense that will make us feel like servants of the common good, will make us understand the immense repercussions of our actions and omissions for the good or bad of many, will lead us to serve our homelands and what St. Thomas, centuries before the founding of the League of Nations, called the community of all under the commands of God. And the second, is a sense of responsibility that finds so much Gospel flavor in the parable of the talents, and consequently leads to a well-developed professional conscience, the faithful fulfillment of duty and, not as a matter of pure routine, the provision of goods of sound quality, the acceptance of true competition, loyalty in the service of clients, etc. Social justice demands that the rich not be prisoners of the selfish possession of their wealth, that the poor not let themselves be consumed by envy or hatred, that extreme poverty be suppressed, that property be affordable by all, etc.

Social justice is imposed on all subjects and rulers, but above all on those who have leadership roles in fields of thought, influence or government.

What does social justice oblige one to do? Fr. Azpiazu responds:

> «In general, it will oblige as a matter of grave or venial sin, according to the subject of the transgression; but maybe nothing more.
>
> The delicate question is: would it require restitution? Not by itself. As it cannot be said that in social justice generally there is equality between that which is owed as a matter of right and that which is breached by the violation of the right, one who violates only social justice cannot be required to make strict restitution.

421 [At this point Hurtado added: «*Razón y Fe*, 1938, p. 60». *Razón y Fe* (*Reason and Faith*) is a Jesuit monthly magazine that, since the beginning of the 20th century, has offered reflections on the social, cultural, political, economic and ecclesial situations in Spain and America. Isidro Gandía, S.J., published an article in that magazine in 1938.]

But it is worth noting that social justice's characteristic feature is its *unavoidable obligation*. So it follows that man, even in solitude, is required always to devote his life and goods usefully to society.

At the same time, the social function, which is the daughter of social justice, carries with it the obligation to repair damages caused by mismanagement of the capital received from God. So that, despite the imprecision and vagueness of social justice and the indeterminacy of the subject of the obligation and the extent of its duties, there nevertheless remains an obligation to repair, in some way, damages inflicted.

In some cases, it appears that social justice may also require restitution, perhaps not only in itself, but owing to the annexation to it of a contract or quasi-contract.

A contract in itself gives rise to an obligation of commutative justice in such a way that even where there has not been any actual injury the contract cannot, by will or discretion, be rescinded or breached.

In a similar way, a quasi-contract is born, which, for its part, originates from a service performed or an office assumed; such as, for example, the position of guardian with respect to his ward. And in such cases the obligation to make restitution is also imposed if the guardian voluntarily breaches his duty, damaging the ward.

That is to say, an act of social injustice can, at the same time, violate commutative justice if the act is tied to a contract or quasi-contract.

Notice an analogous case concerning distributive justice. The distribution of positions in ecclesiastical or civil society is a matter that relates to distributive justice, and yet one who distributes those positions is obliged by a quasi-contract with society not to confer them on unworthy persons. One who does wrong in this matter is compelled to repair the damages he could have foreseen, at least vaguely, and which are caused by those unworthy persons either to the community as such or perhaps to private individuals whose businesses have been made to suffer by such unworthy persons owing to their office.

Therefore, social justice, perhaps not by itself, but by virtue of the contracts or quasi-contracts to which it may be linked, will carry with it the obligation of restitution»[422].

422 [*Economic Professional Morality*, pp. 28-29.]

2
Charity

Those who do not understand the Christian spirit do not know the value of charity, and they reduce everything to the practice of justice. A Christian knows that justice without charity is insufficient because it «can never bring about union of minds and hearts»[423]. But charity will never be true charity if it does not take justice into account.

> «[A] "charity" which deprives the workingman of the salary to which he has a strict title in justice, is not charity at all, but only its empty name and hollow semblance. The wage-earner is not to receive as alms what is his due in justice. And let no one attempt with trifling charitable donations to exempt himself from the great duties imposed by justice. Both justice and charity often dictate obligations touching on the same subject-matter, but under different aspects; and the very dignity of the workingman makes him justly and acutely sensitive to the duties of others in this regard»[424].

Charity should not be confused with pure almsgiving or with mere philanthropy. It is something much bigger: it is the love of one's neighbor that emanates from the love of God. Charity is a direct effect of sanctifying grace. «Psychologically, charity is that effective love for our brothers and sisters, in which we see a clear sign of the love of God, whom we do not see. Socially, charity is the efficient cause of peace. Justice overcomes the obstacles to peace, the causes of struggle, like a demolisher who clears the site; effective charity builds peace, like the bricklayer who builds a cathedral. For if the need for justice brings men together and makes them accept social institutions, it is charity that brings them together and unites them. In it and for it they feel like brothers: children of the same human city and of the same city of God»[425].

Justice and charity complement each other. A charity that does not have the strength to move us to give our brothers what we owe them is not true charity. And justice not animated by charity is, in practice, a vain word. How can we expect fallen man to come out of himself and give his brother what he owes him if

423 [*Quadragesimo Anno* § 137.]
424 [*Divini Redemptoris* § 49.]
425 [Joseph Folliet, *Morale Sociale* (*Social Morality*) Volume II, chapter VII, p. 35 (1937).]

the fire of charity and the power of grace do not animate him? To fully do justice to others you must put yourself in their positions; understand their reasons and their needs. Namely, to understand the two evangelical maxims: «do to no one what you yourself hate;» «do to others as you would have them do to you»[426].

To appreciate in principle whether an obligation is one of justice or of charity is easy, but in practice it is difficult to see whether my obligations to a neighbor are based on a right or on love. As a norm of conduct, whenever we feel obligated we should ascend to the motive of love, and then we will act upon the highest of the virtues, which is charity.

It is charity that has made justice progress. Nowadays, everyone considers that justice requires us not to kill prisoners, not to reduce them to slavery, to give a pension to the elderly. Centuries ago, it would not have been thought so. Charity gradually brought these acts into the domain of equity and then to that of justice. Acts that are still considered charity today, tomorrow will be considered justice because charity will introduce us to a greater understanding of human nature and its demands. This does not mean that in time it may be thought that charity becomes useless. No matter how much progress is made in the institutions of justice, the site and the primacy of charity will remain unalterable.

3
Equity

For St. Thomas, social equity is a virtue that even in the absence of any written law, impels us to find and fulfill what the natural law ordains for the common good[427]. Equity is social justice tempered by social charity; it is the virtue that inclines us to use our rights in a humane way. Those who practice equity know how to understand their rights open mindedly and interpret their duties strictly; they will not go so far as they have a right to go; they will not appeal only to written law, but will take into account moral circumstances. Thus, the creditor will agree on easy terms with the debtor in distress; the employer will grant a share

426 [Tobit 4:15; Luke 6:31.]

427 II-II, q.120 in c. [Thomas Aquinas, *Summa Theologica.* In the corpus of the first article of Q. 120, states that in certain cases, «it is good to set aside the letter of the law and follow the dictates of justice and the common good». English Dominican translation.]

in employment benefits to his workers. It is a beautiful virtue that fills life with understanding and keeps alive in the world the memory of human fraternity[428].

4
The Common Good

Many times, the common good is mentioned when dealing with societal issues, since each society tends to it as its substantial bond. A society is founded on goods that must be loved and sought in common. St. Augustine said: «a people is an assemblage of rational beings bound together by a common agreement as to the objects of their love; therefore in order to discover the character of any people, we have only to observe what they love»[429]. A people is much better when it agrees to pursue higher goods.

A *good* is anything that is capable of satisfying a desire. There are goods that satisfy sensitive desires: water and wine, thirst; intimate union of man and woman, sexual appetite; a beautiful panorama, artistic desire. These sensible goods and all other kinds of good can only be called *moral goods* when they fill a desire that deserves to be called «human», worthy of man, according to God's plan for him and his supernatural end as the son of God. Goods that are not in conformity with the true nature of man on the moral level are false goods, or rather, moral evils.

Common good is what is desired in common by a group. Groups, like individuals, may desire false goods. The true common good of a human society is what must be desired in common by that society in order to fulfill its authentic purpose.

428 [At this point Hurtado handwrote: «Justice. Charity. Equity. The evil of the world, the violation of these virtues. *Social Christian Order* 15, 16, 29». Those portions of Hurtado's books refer to *Quadragesimo Anno* §§ 124-125 and *Divini Redemptoris* §§ 47 and 50, which discuss rights, justice and charity.]

429 [Augustine of Hippo, *De Civitate Dei Contra Paganos* (*The City of God*), book XIX, chapter 24. (In Hurtado's manuscript is not clear where the quote ends because the closing quotations marks are missing.).
Here is the passage and some of the surrounding text as translated by Henry Betenson:
«[I]f one should say, "a people is the association of a multitude of rational beings united by a common agreement on the objects of their love', then it follows that to observe the character of a particular people we must examine the objects of its love. And yet, whatever those objects, it is the association of a multitude not of animals but of rational beings, and is united by a common agreement about the objects of its love, then there is no absurdity in applying to it the title of a "people"». Page 890 of the 1972 edition.]

Every society has its own common good. That of the family comprises material possessions and moral goods: the harmony of the spouses, the good education of the children, etc. A labor union has as its own common goods: the intellectual and moral development of its members, the defense of their economic rights, the preparation of a social order that is more just.

In general, when we speak of the common good, we mean that of *civil society*. This is understood as the *set* of goods of a spiritual and material order that men can procure within society. The common good is defined by the *set* of goods that can be procured in society, and not by the *sum* of particular goods. Thus, there are goods that are not even quantifiable for example: the honesty of judges, the probity of customs, artistic taste, and equitable distribution within society. The common good of a state will therefore consist of that set of well-ordered social relations under a wise authority, maintained in justice, promoted in friendship and social charity, coordinated in the union of efforts towards a useful, virtuous, joyful and peaceful cooperation in the economic, intellectual and moral orders. If this good social life is obtained, even in a relative way, we will have public happiness.

The common good requires the presence of three categories of goods: the honest, the helpful and the delectable.

By *honest goods* we understand those that man can morally seek because they constitute an intermediate end of his life. Such are science, moral knowledge, the virtues, social peace, etc. *Useful goods* are not ends, but means to achieve other superior purposes: wealth, technical knowledge, forms of government and administrative systems that must be adapted to the end that is intended to be achieved by them. *Delectable goods* are the fine arts, monuments, artistic traditions of the country, etc.

4.1. THE COMMON GOOD AND INDIVIDUAL GOOD

The common good is superior to the good of individuals and private communities. The public interest is superior to the particular interest. In this matter Catholic morality is decidedly communitarian and not individualistic. If society asks the citizen for the partial or total sacrifice of his property and the request is not unjust, the citizen must submit. In moments of extreme gravity it can even ask him to risk his life, and the individual will sacrifice material things for the good of the community. Likewise, the international society of men can ask a particular society for sacrifices in order to obtain a superior good, and under the same logic, if the request is just it cannot be denied.

There is a sacrifice that neither the common good of society nor the international community of men can require, which is the sacrifice of the human person.

In Christian ethics, society is subordinated to the person. Man as a person is a free and reasonable being, constitutes an end in himself, worthier than all other intermediary ends. In society, man is part of a whole, but he is not a means to an end. Society is a means for man; but he is not a means for society. The good of society is on the temporal level, that of man on the eternal one.

Man, who is a person, is also an individual, meaning that he has a material, spatial element: in this sense, he is subordinated to the good of society, which can require sacrifices, even that of his temporal life. But as a person, man has a spiritual element, which cannot be sacrificed in any way to society. This, on the contrary, has been created to enable him to develop his whole being and to help him achieve his eternal destiny. If society demands of man an action that constitutes a sin, even a venial one, the society is dishonored and should not be obeyed. Order is inseparable from the person, and the person from order.

Christian morality attaches great value to institutions, it knows their influence on the development of the person, but —unlike the Marxists— it knows perfectly well that social reform will not be achieved merely by the reform of institution, unless accompanied by a reform of consciences. Neither one nor the other will be sufficient. They complement each other[430].

430 [At this point a new heading appeared, but not followed by any text. Hurtado's manuscript states: «Sins against the Common Good. See Lallement 101-102».]

Chapter 11

Work and Economic Life

1
The Meaning of Work

The first element of economic life is work. Pius XI admirably recognizes the value of labor when he says, in *Quadragesimo Anno*:

> «"The wealth of nations originates from no other source than from the labor of workers"[431]. For is it not plain that the enormous volume of goods that makes up human wealth is produced by and issues from the hands of the workers that either toil unaided or have their efficiency marvelously increased by being equipped with tools or machines? Every one knows, too, that no nation has ever risen out of want and poverty to a better and nobler condition save by the enormous and combined toil of all the people, both those who manage work and those who carry out directions»[432].

The word «work» suggests not only a means of earning a living, but a social collaboration. Work can be defined as: «the effort that is put at the service of humanity, personal in origin, fraternal in its aims, sanctifying in its effects»[433].

Work is a personal effort because for it man gives his best: his own activity, which is worth more than his money. No wonder the workers are offended by those who consider their work to be worthless: they despise the workers' efforts, yet take advantage of the results. The workers also sense how unfair it is that some seek to make them feel that they survive because society kindly offers them a job. It is more accurate to say that society survives because of the work of its citizens.

This personal effort is, moreover, beautiful. Work develops the body and the spirit, and distances man from the vices that derive from leisure. The thirst for energy that springs from a healthy body and mind will find its normal outlet in work which, although it is hard, is also happy and joyful.

Work is a fraternal effort; it is the best way to demonstrate love for our brothers, and responds to the demands of social justice and charity. An important part of education should be to discover the social meaning of each kind of work, since knowledge of the purpose of the effort will make the work itself more interesting.

431 [The encyclical here has a footnote as follows: «Encyclical, *On the Condition of Workers*, 51». This refers to *Rerum Novarum*.]

432 [*Quadragesimo Anno* § 53.]

433 [There is no indication of the source of this quote.]

Work is sanctifying in its results because through work, man collaborates with God's plan, humanizes, spiritualizes and divinizes the earth and penetrates it with thought and love. Through work man contributes to the temporal and spiritual common good of families, of nations and of the entirety of mankind. Through work a man discovers the bonds that bind him to all other men; he feels the joy of giving them something and receiving much in return. Work is sanctifying because it has a value of redemption, a value of purification and sacrifice, and is always at everyone's hand. Work is expiation and transforms all physical and moral sufferings into achievements of divine value, uniting them with the sufferings and merits of Christ.

For centuries labor was despised, especially manual labor, as something typical of slaves. Philosophers came to praise the work of the spirit, but not the physical work. Christianity gave the world the great lesson of the value of work: Christ, the Son of God, became a manual worker, and chose as collaborators simple fishermen. Paul is proud of not abandoning the work of his hands so as not to be burdensome to anybody; the monks have made of intellectual and even of manual work a *raison d'être* for their religious existence. All kinds of works, both intellectual and manual, can be seen to have been vindicated within Christianity. Intellectual and manual work are worth more or less not because of what they are, but because of the more or less pure intention with which each one performs his duty. Christianity «rejects the prejudice of white hands, and also that of black hands»[434]. «There is no virtue more eminent than simply doing what we have to do»[435].

2
The Mystique of Work

In recent last years a mystique of work has developed. The war did much to create it. The military leaders reinforced the idea that the work of the laborer is as necessary as the action of the generals; civil leaders must also teach that for peaceful human progress, work is as necessary now as it was during wartime. Since there are decorations for those who perform military feats and for diplo-

434 [Emmanuel Mounier (1905-1950), French theologian and philosopher, leader of the personalist movement and director of *Esprit* magazine.]

435 [José María Pemán (1897-1981), Spanish intellectual, novelist and poet.]

matic efforts, there should be decorations for the heroes of work, hidden heroes without whom one could not live. A humanism of work should replace the decadent humanism that glories almost exclusively in military feats and artistic values. This humanism of work finds its main greatness in the worker God.

3
The Personal Obligation of Work

Is man required to work? One must distinguish between moral obligation and legal obligation.

Morally, everyone is obliged to work, unless age or health impedes it. Work will be the means by which he will provide for his needs, otherwise he will become a parasite; it is also his means of fulfilling his obligations of charity, avoiding the dangers of laziness, developing his faculties, and bestowing charity on the neighbor he will help with his efforts, which always have a social purpose. This is why St. Paul says: «If anyone was unwilling to work, neither should that one eat». (2 Thess. 3:10).

This obligation to work also includes the rich, because the justifications for it are also applicable to him. Even if you do not have a lucrative profession, you should spend your time in a way which is useful for others in an important way.

The obligation to work is accompanied by the right of each to choose his work, or his profession, within the framework of the actual possibilities afforded by the environment in which he lives. Parents can advise but not impose a certain profession. Although they should assist the inexperienced child, they should always respect the child's dignity and personal vocation. This is especially true when it comes to a supernatural vocation to a life of Christian perfection.

Just as a man has a personal obligation to work, no other man—his equal—can ever legally bind him to work: if this right existed, we would have slavery again. The only legal obligation to work arises from a bilateral contract by which one undertakes to perform a particular agreement, under penalty of sanctions if not performed.

4
The State and Obligatory Labor

A public authority may sometimes impose forced labor, for example as a punishment for certain crimes, provided it is implemented in an environment that assists in the rehabilitation of the prisoners. The State may also repress social parasitism, punishing vagrancy and regulating begging, so long as one can honestly say that work is available to those who seek it.

A public authority may also require a period of civil work, as it imposes a period of military service, and for many this would be more useful; this might be imposed in the case of an extraordinary situation, as would be the case in a war, an epidemic or an earthquake, requiring everybody to work to provide for the needs of the common good; a public authority may also levy taxes in money or in services. But in no way may one acknowledge a right of the State to bind citizens permanently in its service: that would be a new form of slavery. When the State imposes temporary work it must compensate the workers, at least those who have no other source of livelihood.

5
Working Regimes

Work has been considered differently during diverse periods of history and in the various civilizations that have existed. We will make a tour through the principal legal regimes that have provided framework for the lives of workers.

Slavery is the oldest regime known, the most humiliating for the worker. The slave does not exist for himself but for his master, who uses him simply as an object or as a beast of burden. His master could sell him or lease him. Slaves lived near their masters, who had the privilege of not working: they were «free» men.

Christianity, after its appearance, acted as a leaven to alleviate slavery and mature consciousness until slavery disappeared. In fact, as soon as wealthy pagans converted to Christianity, they changed their attitude towards their slaves and, when a conversion was profound, freed them. At certain times some Catholic authors accepted a moderated form of slavery, in which the master, although he owned the slave, respected his fundamental human rights. Leo XIII gave us the encyclical *In Plurimis*[436], in which he condemned all forms of slavery.

Today, there are still twenty million slaves in the world in Asia and Africa. In some countries the system governing farm workers is such that in practice it amounts to the loss of freedom. In Asia is customary to sell daughters as maids: all these are vestiges of slavery that must necessarily disappear.

Servile labor was the next regime that prevailed for agricultural workers in the Middle Ages. The worker was not a slave: he was considered a person and had the right to form a family, but he was bound to the glebe, that is to the land that he worked, so that if the lord sold the land, he sold it with his serfs. The worker received protection, which was so necessary in that era of banditry, and also the necessary means to survive. When they were emancipated, these workers became tenants and later owners of the lands they worked.

Craftmanship was the prevailing regime in the cities during the Middle Ages. The craftsman was free, but he was linked to the other artisans of his own office in corporations or guilds. Usually the worker inherited his trade from his father, and occupied a position with him in the same guild, first as an apprentice, then as a worker; and the door was open for him to become a master. The worker found moral and professional education in the guild, and the economic means to enhance his life.

Encomienda was the prevailing regime in the rural sectors of the Spanish colonies[437]. The Crown distributed, as a sign of gratitude to the most distinguished military men, free Indian soldiers who were «entrusted» to them and had to pay them a personal tribute: that was how it was expected to secure resources and stabilize society. In Chile, by virtue of the circumstances, particularly the tenacious resistance of the aborigines, the tribute was replaced by work done by the Indians: this was called «personal service». The intention of the sovereigns was not to impose personal service, but the ambition of the *encomenderos*, the rudeness of character of the military men, coupled with the In-

436 [Encyclical on the Abolition of Slavery *In Plurimis* (5 May 1888), at the Holy See, http://w2.vatican.va/content/leo-xiii/en/encyclicals/documents/hf_l-xiii_enc_05051888_in-plurimis.html (hereinafter referred to as *In Plurimis*). Section 21 states: «It is, however, chiefly to be wished ... that slavery may be banished and blotted out without any injury to divine or human rights, with no political agitation, and so with the solid benefit of the slaves themselves ...»]

437 [See footnote 30.]

dians' laziness as to work and courage as to war, were the causes of this institution, against which the missionaries fought bravely during the Colonial period[438].

Inquilinaje[439] is a vestige of the *encomienda* regime and it still applies in the countryside today. The landlord[440], who needs to have «obligated» regular workers, gives his tenants housing and enclosures for vegetables, cattle pasturage, portion of food in some areas, pieces of land to farm, ordinarily under a sharecropping arrangement, and cash wages for the days they work, which constitute the smallest part of their remuneration. On the other hand, the peasant must personally perform the work of the estate, or else «put a peasant», that is, supply another worker in his place to serve on the estate. The situation of the tenants depends very much on the landlord; on some estates they have good housing and a set of «guarantees» owing to which the workers obtain good compensation, especially if they are educated and industrious; but in most cases cultural and economic conditions are deplorable and workers are deprived, because of their lack of education, culture and habits of savings, even of the power of conceiving the possibility of social ascent. Much responsibility for this state of affairs lies in the absolute lack of serious effort by landlords to train their tenants for an independent life.

This «paternalistic» regime has prevailed not only in the countryside but also, and especially, in domestic service and even in certain industries. Such forms of working organization are modeled on the family society, in which the authority of the father governs minor children; as they are incapable of governing themselves, he must watch over their interests. The «*patrón*» (from *pater*, father) sets the salary and the working regulations, proposes social works that will improve the condition of the workers and develops initiatives for their entertainment. The *patrón's* mission goes beyond the labor regime and follows the workers into their private and even their moral and religious lives. What is even more grave is that the *patrón* has come not only to advise as to his workers' political conduct, but also to direct their votes as if they were his own.

438 [At this point the author added: «(See historical antecedents of the labor problem in Chile, in *Sindicalismo*, pp. 190-209, by Alberto Hurtado, Santiago, 1950, Pacifico Publisher)». Hurtado is referring to his book *Syndicalism*.]

439 [This word, like the word *encomienda*, is not translated here, but is left in the original Spanish. *Inquilinaje* is a unique Spanish institution, which could be translated as «agrarian tenancy».]

440 [The word used in Spanish for landlord is «*patrón*», who was a kind of landowner with powers very similar to those held under a feudal regime. The world could also be translated «master».]

In general terms, this arrangement can only be allowed as for a transition regime, while the workers are incapable of caring for themselves: namely, when they are really minors. In such a case, they would not have the right to vote, because they would not able to do so, but in no event is the *patrón* justified in controlling his worker and ordering his will as if the worker was only a thing: this would violate the most sacred aspect of man's personality. If, during at a time of transition, such a regime is tolerable, it is the *patrón's* duty to prepare his workers rapidly for a regime for grown men, who have the right to speak on an equal basis with their *patrón*, face to face rather than with a servile attitude. A working organization should be regulated by civil society rather than according to family-society rules. A working organization is not a enlarged family but a small society. And the excuse that workers might misuse their freedom is not valid: God respects our liberty and gives us autonomy at an appropriate moment; and even at home there comes a time when the children have grown up. The great duty of parents is not to keep them at the youngest age possible, but to prepare them for their emancipation.

The authority and consequent responsibility of the *patrón* will be greater if he has authority over young apprentices, and also if he has people who eat and sleep under his roof; he will have less over outsiders who only come to work for a few hours. Domestic service tends to become more closely regulated in various countries. Washing and cleaning machines make the housewife's task easier.

The *patrón's* authority is determined by the employment contract and it ends at the company's door. The *patrón* and the director do not, in justice, have any authority over private lives or the civic lives of their workers. Charity may compel them to watch over their interests, but on the condition that the rights of both parties are secure.

Domestic Service[441]

A salary regime has largely dominated the world for these last two centuries, and includes the kinds of work that we have just discussed. The salary regime assumes that capital and labor are in different hands. Capitalists possess the

441 [Hurtado did not write any text under this heading. In the manuscript, after the title there appears only the phrase «see Piñera». Hurtado is probably referring to Bernardino Piñera Carvallo, born in 1915, a Chilean Bishop who met and worked with Hurtado. As of 2018, Piñera is still alive, aged 102; he was one of the main leaders of Hurtado's canonization. Piñera created the first Chilean association for domestic women workers in 1948 (ANECAP). The editors tried to identify the work Hurtado may have referred to but only found the name of an article called «*La Empleada de Casa Particular*» (*The Private House Domestic Worker*) (1950).]

means of production; the workers deliver their work in exchange for a certain salary. The invention of modern machines, the formation of large amounts of capital as a result of foreign trade, and the abolition of the old guilds brought about this regime.

A salary can be paid for years, for months, for days or for hours of work or upon the performance of a particular task: that which is usually called contract work or payment in installments. The salary regime itself is not unfair so long as the salary complies with the conditions set out below, but it is not the best regime and social Catholicism tends to recommend better ways. Under this system the worker is subordinated to capital: his technical ability is tied to the machine, of which he becomes something like an accessory. On the other hand, it will be difficult for him to regain his autonomy, since work in large industrial plants has reduced to a minimum small craft works: almost the only type within which a person can still be independent.

Under the salary system, labor becomes a simple commodity subject to the law of supply and demand, dominated by the desire for profit: the supreme aspiration of the contemporary economy. Under this system, interest rather than morality is dominant; rather than service, it is oriented to gain; rather than to producing what is necessary, it tends to produce whatever yields more profit, even if the consumer suffers.

The salary system, not by its intrinsic nature but by the way in which it has been run, has brought with it contempt for work: its classification as something that is bought or leased, and miserable living conditions. Leo XIII in *Rerum Novarum* said:

> «To this must be added that the hiring of labor and the conduct of trade are concentrated in the hands of comparatively few; so that a small number of very rich men have been able to lay upon the teeming masses of the laboring poor a yoke little better than that of slavery itself»[442].

Pius XI, forty years later writes:

> «And these commands have not lost their force and wisdom for our time because that "pauperism" which Leo XIII beheld in all its horror is less widespread. Certainly the

442 [*Rerum Novarum* § 3.]

condition of the workers has been improved and made more equitable especially in the more civilized and wealthy countries where the workers can no longer be considered universally overwhelmed with misery and lacking the necessities of life. But since manufacturing and industry have so rapidly pervaded and occupied countless regions, not only in the countries called new, but also in the realms of the Far East that have been civilized from antiquity, the number of the non-owning working poor has increased enormously and their groans cry to God from the earth. Added to them is the huge army of rural wage workers, pushed to the lowest level of existence and deprived of all hope of ever acquiring "some property in land"[443], and, therefore, permanently bound to the status of non-owning worker unless suitable and effective remedies are applied.

Yet while it is true that the status of non-owning worker is to be carefully distinguished from pauperism, nevertheless the immense multitude of the non-owning workers on the one hand and the enormous riches of certain very wealthy men on the other establish an unanswerable argument that the riches which are so abundantly produced in our age of "industrialism", as it is called, are not rightly distributed and equitably made available to the various classes of the people»[444].

In fact, we still see in many places and countries, and especially in Latin America, that the working conditions of the laborers, and especially of the unskilled ones, are often inhuman, especially in the mines, on farms and among female and domestic workers. The worker's housing is usually very poor, his salary low, the possibilities for culture and social ascension, difficult.

This is what has come to be called the «proletariat» (the name derives from *proles*: offspring), alluding to those men so poor that, in the Roman Empire, they could give nothing to the State except their children. In our day we call a worker proletarian if he enjoys abstract freedom, without the means effectively to claim it, so that the worker possesses only his work but has no property and no hope of ever possessing any. In theory, this man can become a millionaire and the President of the Republic, but a realistic calculation of probabilities would reduce his hopes to zero.

Every proletarian is a salaried worker, but not every salaried worker is a proletarian, because many people, especially skilled workers, avoid this condition. The real proletarian, on the other hand, cannot really escape his fate, and his

443 [The encyclical here has a footnote as follows: «Encyclical, *On the Condition of Workers*, 66».]
444 [*Quadragesimo Anno* §§ 59-60.]

children will also suffer what their parents have been suffering: an economic hell without hope. Insecurity is the other scourge of the proletarian. Will he have work tomorrow? In case of an accident, unemployment or old age, what would become of him and his family? In addition to this latter social stage there is the sub-proletariat, which now lives in a totally subhuman way and is unfortunately too frequent in our day: a true stigma on our pretended civilization and a mark of its lack of Christianity.

The proletariat has this paradoxical significance: it is the fruit of the theoretical liberation of man effected by philosophical liberalism, and of the practical slavery to capital brought by economic liberalism. Proletarianization does not cease to increase, for although many workers manage to escape from it by ascension, peasants are drawn to the city by the hope of easier labor, and in new countries the mass of the economically weak are drawn to factories, with the immense danger that they may become suddenly unemployed. Economic inflation has also plunged the middle classes and small rentiers into the category of proletarians.

The proletariat constitutes the greatest danger to the stability of a country: the most appropriate breeding ground for all revolutionary uprisings, and for the absorption of Marxist ideas. The spiritual life becomes impossible among the proletariat, as Pius XII recognizes:

> «On the one hand, we see the immense wealth that dominates public and private economic life, and often even civil life; on the other, the countless number of those who, deprived of any direct or indirect security in their lives, are no longer interested in the real and high values of the spirit and, abandoning their aspirations for genuine freedom, throw themselves at the feet of any political party, slaves of anyone who promises them bread and peace»[445].

The abolition of the proletariat is one of the first slogans of social morality, but this would require passing through several stages: the defense of the middle classes, of craftsmanship and small commerce; the fight against inflation and the rising cost of living so as to afford security to small rentiers; professional education for wage-earners and social-security systems that allow them access to

445 [Pius XII, *Radio Message Oggi al Compiersi on the Fifth Anniversary of the Beginning of the War*, § 27, at the Holy See, https://w2.vatican.va/content/pius-xii/es/speeches/1944/documents/hf_p-xii_spe_19440901_al-compiersi.html. This link is to the Spanish version, because the Vatican website contains only the Italian and Spanish versions; the translation here was made by the editors.]

small property holdings and support during their difficult days; and, at a deeper level, the transformation of the capitalist enterprise into a working community. These measures require an energetic will to de-proletarianise the masses, great legal intelligence, superior technical ability and the necessary time. This crusade calls for a determined willingness on the part of Christians to commit themselves completely to justice.

6
The Employment Contract

Entry into working society is made through the employment contract. The contract is *express* when two parties establish an agreement, which is ordinarily signed. This is ordinarily required by contemporary legislation. A contract is *implied* when the worker begins to do certain work, which is interpreted as an acceptance of the terms that apply there.

The employment contract may be a *lease of services*: certain services or hours of work in exchange for certain benefits; a contract between the employer and his work for the *distribution of benefits*; a contract for a *lump sum*, under which the employer assigns a job to someone who is in charge of doing it on his own and at his own risk, in exchange for a certain payment. There are many other varieties of labor contract: contracts for administrative work, contracts for work by crews, contracts which provide for the distribution of profits between the one who orders the work and those who perform it, etc. The terms must clearly specify the duration and the quantity of the work, rest periods, holidays, hygiene and safety guarantees, stability, promotions, and the social, civic, moral and religious conditions; payments and how they are to be made; and supplements by way of family allowances, participation in profits and social insurance.

The *collective bargaining agreement* between the employer and the union has ended up being adopted to great advantage, so that the weak individual who had to agree on his own might be protected.

Commutative justice governs the contract of employment. It implies an exchange of benefits, and in case one of the parties does not fulfill its commitment, it must compensate for the loss. The clauses of the contract must be known by both parties, under penalty of nullity. Fear diminishes freedom and causes the injured party to allow the rescission of the contract.

Distributive justice also governs the labor contract and thus there are norms of natural law that are higher than written law, which neither the employer nor the employee can disregard, and which void anything that is contrary to them. Thus, for example, a worker who, because of his miserable condition, accepts a job for which he is compensated inhumanely, is not required to complete his work.

7
Lease of Service or Partnership?

There has been a great deal of discussion among jurists and sociologists about the nature of the employment contract. Many have argued that by its nature it is merely a lease of services, while others make the worker a partner of the employer with all its consequences.

Supporters of the lease-of-services theory claim that the company is the property of the holder of the capital and, therefore, the worker does not have any stake in it; he does not risk anything in the company while the capitalist risks everything. Therefore the work is sufficiently compensated by the wage that the worker receives no matter what the situation of the company is. This is not quite accurate, because a bad situation for the company leads to the dismissal of the workers, who become unemployed, or else their salaries are reduced; thus their risks are as real as those of the employer.

If the conditions as to salary and others matters are fair, it cannot be said that the lease of services is immoral in itself, as Pius XI established:

> «First of all, those who declare that a contract of hiring and being hired is unjust of its own nature, and hence a partnership-contract must take its place, are certainly in error and gravely misrepresent Our Predecessor whose Encyclical not only accepts working for wages or salaries but deals at some length with it[s] regulation in accordance with the rules of justice.
>
> We consider it more advisable, however, in the present condition of human society that, so far as is possible, the work-contract be somewhat modified by a partnership-contract, as is already being done in various ways and with no small advantage to workers and owners. Workers and other employees thus become sharers in ownership or management or participate in some fashion in the profits received»[446].

446 [*Quadragesimo Anno* §§ 64-65.]

The arguments against the salary system that emerged from the Marxist theory of surplus value, according to which the employer steals the value the worker has created in the object with his work, are false. Under the current regime, capital is entitled to repayment and interest, and also technical workers are entitled to a greater salary because of the new value that they create in property with their labor, as has been recognized even by communist regimes that pay more to technical workers.

The salary system is not the final regime. Others have existed before it, and others will come later. It would be arrogant to stop the course of history with a regime which is far from perfect, even among those which have existed, and which has the formidable defect of alienating the worker from his instruments of work and fomenting class struggle.

What form of work contract is going to replace the salary system? This raises technical issues and not ones of social morality. The contract of partnership is undoubtedly more in conformity with the dignity of the worker and with the common good. Pius XI in the passage just quoted, and also Pius XII on numerous occasions, have recommended that the work contract be moderated by aspects of the partnership contract[447].

What the Pope really wants and asks for, as a matter of common sense, is that those proposed reforms for which it is lawful to fight, not impede the workers in achieving those things which improve their present situation. A better world, if it is to be true and durable, must be built upon the realities of today's world.

8
Projects to Reform the Company[448]

447 [At this point the author added: «(See Asp. and texts in Fern. Pr (Kath. Tag)». Hurtado is probably referring to works of Joaquín Azpiazu —see footnote 88— and Jorge Fernández Pradel, S.J., (1879-1961), Jesuit priest, author of books like *Acción Católica* (*Catholic Action*)(1934) and *Sindicalismo y Cooperativismo* (*Unionism and Cooperativism*)(1939).]

448 [Hurtado did not write any text under this heading. In the manuscript there appears, after the title: «Fernández Pradel 130-133, Pol. and Esp. April 51». Hurtado is probably referring to one of Jorge Fernández Pradel's books cited in the previous footnote. The second document cited is probably the Chilean magazine *Política y Espíritu* (*Politics and Spirit*), published from 1945 to 1975, which spread the ideas of corporatism and issued a critique of liberal democracy and capitalism.]

9
The Amount of Wages

Let us notice that, when speaking of wages, we make no distinction between what is commonly called a wage, applicable to the laborer; salary, applicable to the employee; and, so far as it is possible to extend this doctrine, also to the fees paid to the professional. Understood in this way, we would call «wage» any agreed remuneration that the worker receives from his employer for the work he has performed for him.

Before determining the amount of the wage it is necessary to distinguish the *nominal* wage, which is the sum of money received for the work, and the *real* wage, which corresponds to the goods and services that the worker can acquire with such money. The real wage determines the purchasing power of the worker.

As to the amount of wages there are several theories: the liberal Adam Smith and Ricardo hold that wages are a simple commodity subject to the law of supply and demand: when two employers compete for the services of a worker, wages increase; but when two workers compete for an employer, wages must decrease. Malthus, a liberal, also argues that the amount of wages depends on working capital and the number of workers who are going to be paid with it. To increase the salary you must increase working capital or decrease the number of workers. Lassalle[449], a socialist, believes he has discovered the so-called *iron law of wages*, according to which they are determined by the expenditure necessary to replenish the strength of the worker: this is the cost of labor. The law of supply and demand will establish it, but at a level not far removed from this cost. Karl Marx claims that all the value produced by the work is owed to the worker, since the value of goods is only established by the work that produces them. The difference between this higher value of the goods and the real wage is what the capitalist steals from the worker[450].

449 [Ferdinand Lassalle (1825-1864), German jurist and philosopher, known for his socialist political activism. Lassalle derived the idea from the economist David Ricardo that wage rates, in the long term, tend towards the minimum level necessary to sustain the life of the worker and to provide for his family. Lassalle coined a term for that idea: the *Iron Law of Wages*. For Lassalle, only producers' cooperatives established with the financial aid of the State would make the economic improvement of the workers' lives possible. As a consequence, he thought that political action by workers and trade unionism were extremely important.]

450 [At this point the author stated: «Copy Code of Mechelen p. 57-8 from "it would be an error..."». *A Code of Social Principles*. In §134 the Code deals with the wage system: «The wage system is

Leo XIII, based on the double aspect of work: *personal* (as it is the work of a man) and *necessary* (as it is the sole means of subsistence for the wage-earner) —concludes that because it is *personal*, human labor is not a mere commodity, but something inherent in the person and therefore cannot be subject to the law of supply and demand as if it were a material thing; and because it is *necessary*, it must serve to sustain life.

«The preservation of life is the bounden duty of one and all, and to be wanting therein is a crime. It necessarily follows that each one has a natural right to procure what is required in order to live, and the poor can procure that in no other way than by what they can earn through their work.

Let the working man and the employer make free agreements, and in particular let them agree freely as to the wages; nevertheless, there underlies a dictate of natural justice more imperious and ancient than any bargain between man and man, namely, that wages ought not to be insufficient to support a frugal and well-behaved wage-earner. If through necessity or fear of a worse evil the workman accepts harder conditions because an employer or contractor will afford him no better, he is made the victim of force and injustice»[451].

«To estimate justly the value of labour and to give it its exact remuneration, both the individual and social character of labour must be taken into account. A just wage then, is determined not by one but by many considerations»[452].

9.1. FIRST POINT TO CONSIDER RELATED TO WAGES: THE SUBSISTENCE OF THE WORKER AND HIS FAMILY

«The first point to consider is the sustenance of the worker and his family. A living wage, providing for the maintenance of the worker and his family, and insurance against risks of accident, illness, old age, and unemployment is the least wage due in justice from the employer»[453].

not unjust in itself, and it would be an error to wish to replace it entirely by an arrangement which would make capitalists and workers share losses and gains.

It is, however, more suited to existing social conditions that the wage contract should be modified as far as possible by some measure of contract of association». The following passages (§§134-142) deal with wages, family allowances and social insurance.]

451 [*Rerum Novarum* §§ 44-45.]

452 [*A Code of Social Principles* § 135.]

453 [*Id.* § 136.]

The notion of the living wage has evolved: at the outset it was only understood to be that which is necessary for the subsistence of a sober and honest worker, and all the authors agree that such an amount was owed to the worker as a matter of commutative justice, so that if the employer had not paid it, had incurred a debt he was obliged to pay. Today many authors and also the Social Code of Mechelen include in the concept of living wage that amount which is required to feed the family. All Catholic moralists argue that the family wage is absolutely owed to the worker. The reasons are several: firstly, because the worker has the primary natural right to set up a family and therefore the right to receive the means necessary to feed and maintain it in a humane way. The family wage is not based on the right of the family to be fed, but on the right of the worker as head of the family. It is fair that the other members of the family contribute according to their abilities to the maintenance of the home. The mother will usually attend to the household tasks, which themselves require a lot of work, and the children must receive adequate formation. It is a disgrace when the mother and the children must abandon their primary duties in order to seek a supplementary wage to remedy the deficiencies of the father's wage. When the children grow up they can do something else, until the time comes when they should think about forming their own homes. A second reason: the family wage is a common social good; society cannot subsist without a well-established family and family cannot subsist without a family wage. In addition, the same common good, viewed under an economic aspect, demands a family wage so that families can confidently have the number of children that industry will require, and can make them healthy and strong. The whole country will gain by having households that can ascend socially.

The family wage can be considered as *absolute* or *relative*. We would call «absolute family wage» one that is enough for the needs of an ordinary family of five or six people. «Relative family wage» is one that covers the real needs of all family members who actually exist. The family wage, both absolute and relative, is owed to the worker for the reasons indicated above, and must be such as to meet the ordinary and extraordinary needs of the family. We call «ordinary needs» the current expenses, fluctuating with the cost of living; and «extraordinary needs» those that caused by maternity, accident, sickness, old age and unemployment.

The absolute family wage is owed to every adult worker, both single and married. If he does not have a family yet, he has the right to form it, and prepare himself by saving money to establish a home before marriage. A lower wage than the absolute family wage cannot conscientously be paid. Moralists argue as to whether this obligation is a matter of social or commutative justice, but none of them, since the teachings of Pius XI in *Divini Redemptoris* and *Casti Connubii,* denies that the obligation is one of justice. The relative family wage is owed for reasons of social justice.

The method of payment of the family wage that is prevalent in many places is the following: the ordinary expenses of the worker are paid weekly or monthly by the employer; the extraordinary expenses for illness, old age, accidents, etc., are paid through social insurance; the expenses for each new member of the family are paid to the worker through compensation funds. These entities originally functioned within each company, which set aside an amount proportional to its number of workers; the total amount was distributed to the workers pro rata according to the number of his children. Nowadays this is usually done by means of employer payments to public agencies that are in charge of social insurance which pay a certain allowance for each dependent relative: the same for all kinds of insured persons, whatever their occupations. This latter system has the drawback that what the worker receives from the employer is usually only his personal living wage, inflicting an injustice on single workers, who would otherwise be entitled to receive an absolute living wage sufficient to enable them to prepare to form homes.

Unfortunately, family allowances and social insurance are non-existent for many categories of workers, or exist in a purely symbolic way, because the benefits they confer are ridiculous. For this reason, the Code of Social Principles urges that both systems be widely available:

> «Two consequences follow from the foregoing idea of living wage:
>
> (a) The family allowance system has in recent years shown a satisfactory development. It is fitting that the payment of such allowances should form a part of all agreements, whether individual or collective, between masters and men.
>
> (b) There is also a tendency for social insurance to become legalized. It must necessarily be made general, and is preferably carried on by industrial assurance societies, *i.e.*, societies supported and directed jointly by masters and men in each industry, under the control and with the support of the public authority.
>
> When the State requires membership in family allowance or social insurance societies, or when it subsidizes them, it ought at the same time to discriminate between families where the mother remains at home and those in which the mother works outside the home, and provide a more favourable scale for the former»[454].

454 [*Id.* § 137.]

9.2. SECOND POINT: THE SITUATION OF THE COMPANY

In the current capitalist type of company, wages are the normal way by which labor participates in the fruits obtained by the company, a good part of which is allocated to capital and the management of the company. Therefore, it is natural that wages bear a certain relation to the situation of the company. The living needs of the worker and his family constitute the minimum limit of a just salary. The abilities of the company constitute the maximum limit.

When the situation of the company is prosperous, wages must increase in proportion to the profits of the company. This increase, which amounts to profit sharing, should be established at the end of each year.

The participation can be given in the simple form of a percentage of the annual profits, or as shares that place the workers in the category of shareholders.

If the situation of the company is unfavorable, that is it does not obtain profits or suffers losses, wages will decrease to the limit of the family living wage, to avoid the ruin of the company.

It can even be conceived that the situation of the company is such that it cannot pay the family's living wage. If this situation is caused by the fault of the company, the workers will have the right to demand an end to this situation. At other times this may happen because of unforeseeable extraordinary circumstances.

If the company fails to pay the family's living wage, the workers have the right to demand that the capitalist businessman first sacrifice the interests of capital and the profits of the business. If this situation persists, it will be time to discuss the closure of the company.

9.3. THIRD POINT: THE COMMON GOOD AND ITS DEMANDS

«The third point to consider is the common good and its requirements. The common good requires that the worker can not only live on his wage but also save and build up a modest fortune.

On the other hand a wage level that is too low or excessively high gives rise to that lamentable evil—unemployment. Social justice demands a wage policy which offers employment to the largest possible number of workers and through it the means of providing for their maintenance.

It is important that by harmonious co-ordination of the various branches of economic activity—agriculture, industry, and the rest— a reasonable relationship be established between wages and the price of goods themselves»[455].

Catholic doctrine is essentially anti-individualistic: it considers men not as isolated individuals, but as beings living in society and, therefore, constituting a body in which a close bond of solidarity unites all its members in such a way that there is no human phenomenon that does not have its repercussion in society[456].

Hence, wages should not be considered as only the products of the employment contracts between employers and workers, but must be considered also as to their broader social consequences.

For society, the determination of an amount of wages is not a matter of indifference because it —as a social body devoted to seeking the common good of all its members— has rights that must be respected and that transcend the rights of the worker and the employer; consequently, society has an interest in assuring that wages are in accordance with social justice.

That is why Pius XI warns that «besides commutative justice, there is also social justice with its own set obligations, from which neither employers nor workingmen can escape. Now it is of the very essence of social justice to demand for each individual all that is necessary for the common good»[457].

It is clear that the amount of wages is not determined correctly if social justice is not respected; that is if the requirements of the common good are not taken into account.

But what are these requirements of the common good and what are their influences on fixing the amount of the fair wage? Catholic doctrine, articulated by Pius XI, affirms that these requirements are threefold:

- The common good requires that the workers gather, little by little, a modest personal estate, so they can acquire some small real property holding. Thus, social justice demands that wages be high enough to allow workers to save a part of their pay after the necessary expenses have been met.
- The common good requires that as many workers as possible find jobs, so that everybody may obtain the goods necessary to sustain their lives and those of their families: therefore, social justice requires that, out of a common

455 [*Id.* §§ 139-140.]
456 [At this point the author handwrote: «Valsecchi». See footnote 185.]
457 [*Divini Redemptoris* § 51.]

feeling and desire, wages be neither too low nor extraordinarily high, because in both cases the result would be the forcible cessation of work. On the other hand, wages should be regulated in such a way that a greater number of workers could use their productive capacities.

- The common good requires that there be certain equilibrium among the various occupations within society, so that all can unite and combine to form one body. In order to obtain this equilibrium, social justice requires that appropriate proportions be respected:
  - among the salaries of the various occupational categories (industry, agriculture, etc.);
  - among the prices of the products and services of the various productive branches;
  - among the wages and prices within the various economic activities.

310 These requirements of the common good call for a wise wage policy that takes into account the solidaristic character of society. It should not be forgotten that wages are one of the major channels by which wealth is distributed: therefore, in setting them, the rules of social justice must be respected, so that all members of society participate in the goods produced.

Pius XI admirably synthesizes this concept of economic solidarity:

> «For then only will the social economy be rightly established and attain its purposes when all and each are supplied with all the goods that the wealth and resources of nature, technical achievement, and the social organization of economic life can furnish. And these goods ought indeed to be enough both to meet the demands of necessity and decent comfort and to advance people to that happier and fuller condition of life which, when it is wisely cared for, is not only no hindrance to virtue but helps it greatly»[458].

Thus, in taking into account the requirements of the common good, a fair wage will be a social wage. In sum, the wage will be fair if it meets the following conditions:

- That it is sufficient for the needs of the worker and his family;
- That it responds to the technical value of the work;
- That it reflects the economic situation of the moment;
- That it is proportionate to the situation of the company;
- That it takes into account the requirements of the common good.

458 [*Quadragesimo Anno* § 75.]

Work's remuneration must have, as a minimum requirement, the needs of the worker and his family; as maximum requirement, the economic possibilities of the company; as a rule, remuneration must be guided by the requirements of the common good; alternative standards according to which remuneration might fluctuate include the technical preparation of the worker and the economic conditions of the moment.

How to determine fair wages in practice:
The principle by which the rules set out above should be applied is that of *common determination* by stakeholders, which in practice will be expressed by joint committees of employers and workers presided over by neutral persons. The results of such meetings will give at least prudent estimates for the moment, although they will not always fully satisfy the requirements of the above principles. If there were corporative organizations that represented occupational interests, such institutions would be the ones called upon to arrive at that common determination.

The State should not ordinarily intervene in fixing the amount of wages, which should be established by the interested parties, but it may in exceptional cases dictate a minimum wage in order to assure the worker and his family a fair wage as a point of departure. Leo XIII, referring to the determination of the amount of the wage, said that «in such cases the public authority should intervene, to see that each obtains his due, but not under any other circumstances»[459].

In the United States, Ford inspired a policy of high wages, which consisted in giving workers as much compensation as possible in order to increase their purchasing power and thereby stimulate national economic life. This method, where it is possible to apply it, is in itself beneficial to the workers and the businessmen themselves and maintains a high level of employment and production.

9.4. FOURTH POINT: CATEGORIES OF WORK

To these three points, presented by the Code of Social Principles of Mechelen as basic in setting salary, we can add two others. In the first place, we have to take into account the categories of the work in such a way that the worker who performs work at a higher level is, as a matter of strict justice, owed a higher salary. This higher salary is deserved because of previous learning, occupational train-

459 [*Rerum Novarum* § 43.]

ing, and the nature of the product produced. When speaking about categories of work, we also mean to include employment seniority, the greater fatigue caused by certain jobs, riskiness, the unhealthiness of the environment, and so on.

9.5. FIFTH POINT: MARKET CONDITIONS

The law of supply and demand cannot be the norm that determines wages, but within certain limits it indisputably influences them, and this influence is legitimate if the wage remains within the minimum and maximum limits of the fair wage. Pius XI alludes to this when he says: «free competition, when kept within certain limits, is justified and certainly useful»[460].

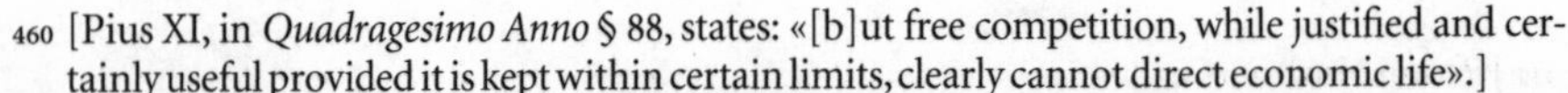

460 [Pius XI, in *Quadragesimo Anno* § 88, states: «[b]ut free competition, while justified and certainly useful provided it is kept within certain limits, clearly cannot direct economic life».]

Chapter 12

Rights and Duties of Workers

1

Duties of the Laborer

Leo XIII and Pius X specified the rights and duties of workers. In the *Motu Proprio* On Popular Action, Pius X summarized the just obligations of the laborer:

> «The obligations of justice, so far as the proletariat and the worker are concerned, are these: to fully and faithfully execute the work that he freely and equitably agreed upon; not to cause damage to the property, nor offense the employers; and in the defense of his own rights, to refrain from violent acts and not to turn those acts into revolts»[461].

We recently referred to the mystique of work that all occupations must awaken: the worker will be helped enormously if he remembers that he is serving the country, creating wealth, and raising the standard of living of his brothers. A worker has a very different spirit on the job when he thinks that he is only laying bricks than when he realizes that he is building a cathedral.

A sense of responsibility and an occupational consciousness will elevate the worker and make him worthy of greater respect. Occupational consciousness rules out negligent work, unjustifiable absence, false illness and accidents, slow work, excessive charges, fraud as to materials, etc. It also rules out bribes, unfair favoritism, pilferage even of minor assets of the company and turning a blind eye to injustices by people under one's supervision.

Respect for superiors demands not only not harming them but also obeying their reasonable orders, deferring to them, and even more, a brotherly love that must be greater the closer the worker and the superior are to one another. The Christian worker must remember that the supreme commandment of charity does not exclude anyone from its imperative of love. Along with courageously defending his rights, the worker should have an attitude of obedience to the reasonable orders of his supervisors, and of the deference and love appropriate for a Christian; he should contest slanderous accusations made about them, systematic distrust of their intentions, and anything else that may harm their interests: furthermore, supervisors must be able to count on their workers as collaborators in a common endeavor. The class struggle can never be a goal in the conduct of a Christian.

461 [*Social Christian Order*, item 176, VII.]

2
Duties of Employers

«The obligations of justice on the part of the capitalists and employers are these: to pay a just salary to the workers; not to damage their just savings either by violence or by fraud or by unfair express or implied charges; to give them the freedom to fulfill their religious duties; not to expose them to corrupting temptations or to the danger of scandal; not to alienate them from the family spirit or from the love of frugality; and not to impose excessive work on them or work that is not appropriate for their age or gender.

It is an obligation of charity on the part of the rich and those who have property to help the poor and destitute according to the teaching of the Gospel; a teaching which compels so strictly that, on the day of judgment, each one will be asked in a special way, as Christ Himself said (Mt. 25), whether it was fulfilled»[462].

3
Rights of Workers

Workers can require that they be allowed to perform their work in a physically and morally humane atmosphere. They may require the employer to ensure a healthy workplace: light, cleanliness, dining rooms, sanitary facilities and decent dressing rooms with adequate separation between men and women, protection against accidents and occupational diseases, chairs in which one may sit while working, and nurseries in which mothers may have their children cared for. In dangerous jobs or those which expose workers to occupational diseases such as cirrhosis, workers require protective measures to prevent the rapid destruction of their health. At the same time, unions must implement educational procedures to protect young workers from the dangers to which they are exposed, and of which they are ignorant.

In large industries far from population centers, especially in company towns in which everything is owned by particular companies —not only the factory, but the housing, the commercial establishments and even the recreation facilities— the workers have a full right to demand spacious housing to meet the

462 [*Id.* item 176, VIII and IX.]

normal demands of their families, with enough privacy to maintain family intimacy, and with hygienic facilities in each house. Warehouses or grocery stores, if the company owns them, must not exploit them with high prices. As for the practice of certain companies of reducing wages and making up for this by selling products at a very low price, it would be more appropriate for the price to be that currently charged for goods, and the same applies as to wages: this would be more educational for the worker, exposing him less to the danger of paternalism that maintains him in a childlike condition; and it would also protect him from such situations as endlessly waiting to obtain rationed items, making him believe that they are an extraordinary concession, when in fact they are paid for by him owing to difference of salary.

Workers need rest. It has come to be understood that machines cannot run uninterruptedly; still less can men. Unions must insist that in industries which require uninterrupted labor, there are enough workers to cover all three shifts, since for companies, it is more economical to reduce the number of workers and to ask those who remain to work for an extraordinary number of hours, a temptation to which the worker readily yields because of his interest in overtime pay, but to the undeniable detriment of his health. Normally speaking, the worker cannot take, for a prolonged time, more work than that ordinarily established in industry.

The holy days established by the Church, which in earlier times were much more numerous, were largely intended to provide the worker with needed rest. The social part of the Treaty of Versailles established that the weekly rest should coincide, so far as possible, with the Sunday rest[463]. This has been established by the Church so that every man can rest from his earthly obligations and cultivate his spiritual and family life. It is scandalous to see how easily the precept of the Lord as to resting and keeping the feast holy is breached.

Modern life has required certain jobs to be uninterrupted, such as transportation and entertainment services, etc., and such workers are not required to abandon these jobs owing to the lack of a Sunday break; but it is up to society to reduce

463 [The Versailles Treaty (June 28, 1919), Part XII entitled «Labour», established that «the League of Nations has for its object the establishment of universal peace, and such a peace can be established only if it is based upon social justice». In Article 427 it set forth nine general principles for the High Contracting Parties, «recognising that the well-being, physical, moral and intellectual, of industrial wage-earners is of supreme international importance». The fifth principle was «the adoption of a weekly rest of at least twenty-four hours, which should include Sunday wherever practicable».]

those jobs to a minimum, and up to employers to facilitate, so far, as possible the fulfillment of religious duties.

What today is called the «English week» —leaving Saturday afternoon free— was already the practice during the Middle Ages, so as effectively to facilitate Sunday rest, by doing the Sunday chores on Saturday afternoon.

Paid holidays for the workers, happily, have been instituted by many laws, which corresponds to real physical and spiritual needs, all the more so as urban life wears down the nerves.

A severance payment proportional to the number of years of service with a particular employer has begun, fortunately, to be introduced. This is fully justified by the fact that a worker, when leaving employment, needs a certain amount of money for security in his last years, or to work independently at a job more suitable to his age. Moreover, it is normal, unless the industry or the State provides an adequate old-age allowance, that the company in which a man has spent his life provide him, in proportion to the number of years of service, support for the worker in his old age. It is sad and humiliating for a parent to reach the end of his life and resign himself to being a burden on his children. Unfortunately, the amount of wages is usually such that because of the cost of living a hard-working man cannot accumulate subtantial savings for his later years.

The discovery of better and better machines, and at the same time a better appreciation of the health needs of the worker, has diminished the hours of daily work. From twelve, fourteen and up to sixteen hours of daily work at the beginning of the last century, we have now a 48-, 40-, and even 36-hour work week. Further decreases are to be expected. Some uneasy spirits protest these decreases. Such protests do not seem justified so long as production can be maintained at the necessary rate, and the workers are given education and opportunities to take honest advantage of the longer periods of rest. As to the necessities of production, it should be recalled that the number of idle hands is enormous in the machine era because of the chronic phenomenon of unemployment.

The moral health of workplaces must be jealously cared for by the workers themselves, who are most directly concerned. So long as they do not take this matter into their hands, nobody will be able to successfully do it for them. Women and adolescents should be especially cared for, as in both of their cases the future of the people is at stake.

4
Respect for the Dignity of Labor

Employers and laborers owe respect to each other, and this means, in the case of the laborers, that corporal punishments are not applied to them, even if they are trainees, that they are spoken to with deference, so that when giving them some order employers also give them the necessary explanations and, one hopes, the reason for what is being done. Some middle-management supervisors make themselves obnoxious to their subordinates, not because they are ill-willed or unjust, but because they wound without realizing it.

The laborer is also harmed by the intrusion of a stranger into his private life. If someone wants to exert a good influence, he can only do it by his example or by his personal authority: laborers in general distrust everything that may restrict them more.

A laborer's dignity demands that his own initiatives be taken into account, that an interest be taken in his work, that his suggestions be received: in some factories a mailbox is set up for suggestions and rewards are given for those that are valuable. Educational conferences, films of a technical nature, everything that makes the laborer understand the full meaning of his work must be encouraged. Likewise, as many laborers as possible should be persuaded to assist in the application of social laws, in the ordering of work, and in the presentation to the employer of the needs and deficiencies of the staff. In a word, one would have to try to remedy what Pius XI regrets so much: «[a]nd thus bodily labor, which Divine Providence decreed to be performed, even after original sin, for the good at once of man's body and soul, is being everywhere changed into an instrument of perversion; for dead matter comes forth from the factory ennobled, while men there are corrupted and degraded»[464].

The Code of Social Principles of Mechelen puts us on guard against certain excesses in rationalization of work:

> «However praiseworthy from some points of view may be that "scientific industrial management" which aims at increasing output in various ways, especially by introducing an ordered rhythm, it is needful to guard against any development of it that

464 [*Quadragesimo Anno* § 135.]

will make the workman an automaton and practically take away from him the exercise of his human faculties»[465].

Taylor[466] set out to study every gesture of the worker to reduce losses of time and effort to a minimum. His principle was: the maximum efficiency in the minimum time. As a work technique, Taylorism escapes morality, but its human repercussions do not escape it. Reducing useless fatigue is laudable, but while it is sometimes possible to reduce physical fatigue, nervous fatigue is easily increased. If this happens, the working day should be reduced. Wages would also have to be increased if a truly extraordinary return were obtained through this rationalization. In any case, we have to remember that efficiency is for the good of man, and not man for the good of efficiency.

5
The Work of Women

It cannot be stated as a principle that a woman cannot work as a laborer: a single woman or a widow can perfectly well do so, provided that due consideration is given to her. First, the job should not be dangerous to her physical or moral health. Some young women compromise their future motherhoods owing to the kind of work they are forced to do. As for respect for their moral lives, it would ordinarily be convenient for women to work with each other and under the direction of female personnel, because the authority exercised over them might often lead to immoral pressures. The wages owed to a woman for a job must be equal to that which would be paid to a man for the same task: «for equal work, equal wages». All principles established in determining the minimum wage are also valid for women, and laborers should be the first to protest against inhumane competition using women who are paid miserably.

We cannot, therefore, in our day simply repeat the slogan: the woman in the home. Many must work, and many desire to because they wish to meet their own needs or to help their families, or because of the activities in the social, apostolic

465 [*A Code of Social Principles* § 91.]

466 [Frederick Winslow Taylor (1856-1915), American mechanical engineer, one of the leaders of the Efficiency Movement. He was the author of *The Principles of Scientific Management* (1911).]

or civic spheres that they wish to conduct. Testimonies of women laborers demonstrate that they have found jobs that satisfy them.

The work of the married woman, especially if she is a mother, has many incoveniences: she jeopardizes her duties, neglects the home, wrongfully increases unemployment and creates strong moral dangers that often end in the ruin of the marriage. In addition, her health can hardly withstand the weight of her domestic and work obligations.

Despite these disadvantages, the married woman may be obliged to work owing to the insufficiency of the salary of her husband. The remedy lies in the reform of the present regime, starting with true family wages and allocations for children that are real and not merely nominal[467].

It would also be necessary to complement these measures with others of an educational nature to give the female a taste for home, to teach her how to be a homemaker and a good mother to her children. Many are going to the factory today in search of a change to make them forget the sadness of a miserable home.

6
The Work of Minors

At the beginning of the machine era the work of children was one of the most shameful abuses of the regime. Children even under the age of twelve were subjected to heavy work and prolonged hours that exhausted their health and permanently compromised their futures. The laws of many countries have regulated the work of minors to prevent these disadvantages[468]. However, because of their shortage of income, parents are obliged to make use of their children's labor, a situation that must be combatted by applying a remedy to the cause of this evil[469].

Every child should receive a complete primary education, followed by a preoccupational education, which will complete the general studies and prepare the child technically for an occupation. Without this, the child will never reach

467 [At this point the manuscript contains an incomplete sentence: «Female wages should be such that industry loses int. in taking…».]

468 [Hurtado intended to include a reference to Chilean data here. In the manuscript he states: «see Chilean».]

469 [Hurtado intended to include a reference to Chilean data here. In the manuscript he states: «Statistics?»]

a truly human level of life. The unskilled laborer is condemned to wages that are below the survival level.

Beginning at school, minors should receive thorough occupational guidance, based on the child's expression of his interests and natural tastes, which should be developed under the careful observation of parents, supervisors and teachers, supplemented if possible with more scientific inquiries such as testing to discover the child's qualities and deficiencies. One who administer tests cannot blindly trust them, but they could give a good indication that would serve to complete the declarations of the child himself and the systematic observation of the teachers.

The best way to raise up a people is through the appropriate education of its minors. It is difficult to make people of a certain age acquire new habits of thinking, of work and of life, but all possibilities are open in childhood. Well-confirmed experience, even among vagabond boys, demonstrates the immense influence of the environment, ordinarily greater than that of heredity, to form or deform children. In new countries like ours, where there are intelligent people, everything is undeveloped in childhood, and we should do everything possible not only to instruct but to educate children. This education, if it is to bear lasting fruits, cannot be secular but seriously religious, lest it rob the youngster of all the force of his deeper longings. Legislators should increasingly direct the national budget towards education at all levels. Occupational education is, regrettably, very much neglected and it is almost impossible for the vast majority of working children to receive specialized instruction[470].

470 [Hurtado intended to incorporate statistics into the text. In the manuscript he states here: «Chilean data».]

Chapter 13

The Organized Occupation. Trade Unionism. Corporatism

The redemption of the proletarian can only be accomplished by the proletarian. This is not to be expected from the spontaneous initiative of the employers, who look primarily to their own interests, or from the State without selling his freedom. The Church, no matter how much she desires redemption of the proletariat and insists on it to Christians, lacks adequate means, since her mission is primarily spiritual and she has no authority in the technical matters, which are indispensable for solving economic problems. Most political parties, before each election, will offer to solve all outstanding problems, but afterwards their electoral interests will prevail over the great cause of proletarian redemption.

The proletariat, once it is mature, must organize itself strongly around its occupational interests, without mixing them up with any other considerations. The workers live close to the factory: there they spend most of their time, there they form most of their friendships; there they find their livelihoods. Therefore, their groups must be arranged according to occupational interests: such is the Union.

Mass and people are two words that are clearly distinguished by Pius XII. The victory will be achieved not by the amorphous mass, but by the organized people. In an authentic union, laborers cease to be a defenseless mass of issolated individuals, and become well-organized groups that march like military cadres to the defense of their authentic interests.

1
What is a Union?[471]

The union is a stable association of those who belong to the same industry or to the same profession; who «work in the same company or workplace, or pursue the same trade or profession, or similar or related professions and trades, whether of an intellectual or manual character»[472].

Unions are united under the guidance of leaders who have been freely chosen from among the members.

471 [The following pages related to unions are taken from *Syndicalism*, which Hurtado himself cut and pasted into the present manuscript.]

472 Article 362 of the Labor Code of Chile.

We say that the union is a stable association; therefore, it is intended to last. It is not a group organized occasionally for a few weeks or months. Those who are part of it are people linked by the bond of common work. There may be unions of employers and of wage earners. Here we will refer mainly to unions of laborers and employees. We understand them to be those people who live mainly on a wage fixed in advance and who execute their tasks under the orders and supervision of their employers.

The primary purpose of the union is to study, promote and, if necessary, defend the common interests of the members in all matters relating to the employment contract: duration, salary, social benefits, etc. The union represents its members in discussions with employers and with public authorities in all that concerns the terms of work. It is very difficult for wage earners to discuss the terms of work if each individually has to negotiate with the employer or its representative. To be on a footing of less inequality, they need to present their requests collectively.

Union leaders, in order to deserve the full confidence of the wage earners, must be chosen from among them: from among those who know the work arrangements in all their complexity and have been able to experience the justice of the demands they present.

The union must also promote the development of its members. Technical education through qualifying courses and schooling for trainees; economic education to promote saving, the formation of cooperatives, individual property for members, compliance with and improvement of laws for social protection, etc; and moral education, emphasizing and defending the dignity of the human person, respect for freedom, etc. So far as religious development is concerned, it is not directly a responsibility of a non-confessional union, like those we have in Chile, but the union must give all kinds of opportunities to its members to obtain it; the conscience of the members demands religious development, which is a duty of all rational beings and the basis for their moral formation. In confessional associations, the associates also find in the union the means to promote their religious lives.

These aims do not, however, exhaust the mission of the unions; their leaders cannot stop only with short term achievements. With their eyes fixed on a new world that embodies the idea of harmony, which is internal equilibrium, the leaders will direct their actions towards replacing the current capitalist structures inspired by liberal economy with structures oriented to the common good and based on a human economy: «It is the whole society that needs to be repaired and improved, because its foundations are shaking»[473].

2

The Right to Organize[474]

Leo XIII wrote in 1895: «[n]ow, with regard to entering societies, extreme care should be taken not to be ensnared by error. And We wish to be understood as referring in a special manner to the working classes, who assuredly have the right to unite in associations for the promotion of their interests; a right acknowledged by the Church and unopposed by nature»[475].

For the solution of the social problem, «[t]he most important of all are workingmen's unions, for these virtually include all the rest. History attests what excellent results were brought about by the artificers' guilds of olden times. They were the means of affording not only many advantages to the workmen, but in no small degree of promoting the advancement of art, as numerous monuments remain to bear witness. Such unions should be suited to the requirements of this our age —an age of wider education, of different habits, and of far more numerous requirements in daily life. It is gratifying to know that there are actually in existence not a few associations of this nature, consisting either of workmen alone, or of workmen and employers together, but it were greatly to be desired that they should become more numerous and more efficient»[476].

473 [*Speech to the Italian Workers.*]

474 [This sub-chapter is taken almost literally from a document of the Congregation of the Sacred Council (its name today is *Sacred Congregation of the Clergy*). The document is a letter dated June 5, 1929 to Cardinal Liénart of Lille, which refers to the conflict between the consortium of northern employers and Christian trade unions. The French version of the document is at http://www.doctrine-sociale-catholique.fr/114-lettre-a-monseigneur-lienart-eveque-de-lille (hereinafter referred to as Congregation of the Sacred Council, Letter to Cardinal Liénart). The editors translated these passages from Hurtado's manuscript.]

475 [Leo XIII, Encyclical on Catholicism in the United States *Longinqua Oceani* (6 January 1895) §16, at The Holy See, http://w2.vatican.va/content/leo-xiii/en/encyclicals/documents/hf_l-xiii_enc_06011895_longinqua.html (hereinafter referred to as *Longinqua Oceani.*)]

476 [*Rerum Novarum* § 49.]

Pius X exhorted Count Medolago Albani[477], in a letter dated March 19, 1904, in these terms: «[c]ontinue, then, beloved son, as you have done up to now, promoting and directing not only institutions of a purely economic character, but also other related organizations: occupational unions of workers or of employers that tend to harmonize with one another; and a people's agency to give legal and administrative advice. You will not lack the most comforting encouragements»[478].

And to the directors of the «Italian Economic Union» he addressed these words: «[w]hich institutions should you primarily promote in your Union? Your industrious charity will decide. As for Us, those that are called unions seem very opportune»[479].

Benedict XV, on May 7, 1919, wrote to the cleric Murry of Autun, through the Cardinal Secretary of State, that he «wishes to see the formation of truly professional trade unions and the proliferation throughout French territory of powerful trade unions animated in the Christian spirit, bringing together, in vast general and fraternal organizations, men and women workers of different occupations»[480].

On December 31, 1922, Pope Pius XI wrote, through the Cardinal Secretary of State, to Mr. Zirnheld, president of the French Confederation of Christian Workers: «With the greatest pleasure the Holy Father has learned of the progress of this group, which tries to achieve the improvement of the working classes through the practice of the principles of the Gospel, which the Church has always applied to the solution of social questions»[481].

The Pontiff himself in his encyclical *Quadragesimo Anno* affirms the influence of the teachings of Leo XIII on the development of trade unionism:

> «These teachings were issued indeed most opportunely. For at that time in many nations those at the helm of State, plainly imbued with Liberalism, were showing little favor to workers' associations of this type; nay, rather they openly opposed them, and

477 [Stanislao Medolago Albani (1851-1921), Italian philosopher, theologian, Catholic leader and founder of *Saint Joseph Workers Club* in Bergamo, a mutual aid society. He was one of the organizers, at the request of Pope Pius X, of the Italian Catholic movement, together with Toniolo and Pericoli.]

478 [Translated from *Social Christian Order*, item 235.]

479 [*Id.*]

480 [*Id.*]

481 [*Id.*]

while going out of their way to recognize similar organizations of other classes and show favor to them, they were with criminal injustice denying the natural right to form associations to those who needed it most to defend themselves from ill treatment at the hands of the powerful. There were even some Catholics who looked askance at the efforts of workers to form associations of this type as if they smacked of a socialistic or revolutionary spirit.

The rules, therefore, which Leo XIII issued in virtue of his authority, deserve the greatest praise in that they have been able to break down this hostility and dispel these suspicions»[482].

Faithful to the above principles, in every case the Holy See has reaffirmed wage earners' rights to union organization. A French employers' consortium lodged an accusation with the Holy See against Christian workers because they associated in a union, and the response of the Congregation of the Sacred Council, issued at the special request of the Roman Pontiff, leaves no room for doubt as to the right to organize:

«To begin with, Christian workers cannot be denied the right to establish independent workers' unions, apart from those of their employers, and without being opposed to them. All the more so and in particular in the present case, such unions are desired by the Ecclesiastical Authority and receive from it encouragement as a rule of Catholic social morality, whose observance is imposed on the members in Statutes and applies to union activity, which must be inspired especially by the Encyclical *Rerum Novarum*. Furthermore, it is evident that the constitutions of such unions, other than the employers' unions, is in no way incompatible with social peace, since, on one hand they repudiate, on principle, class struggle and collectivism in all forms, and on the other hand, they allow for collective-bargaining agreements to establish peaceful relations between capital and labor»[483].

The employer consortium[484] had indicated that trade union activities were not in accordance with the Christian spirit and were impregnated with Marxism. «The Sacred Congregation considers that it is its duty to declare, supported

482 [*Quadragesimo Anno* §§ 30 -31.]

483 [Congregation of the Sacred Council, Letter to Cardinal Liénart, § 7.]

484 [Hurtado is referring to the Employers Consortium of Roubaix-Tourcoing, as he explains further along in this text.]

by irrefutable documents and the testimonies that have been collected, that some of the employer consortium's motives are exaggerated, and that others, the most serious —those attributing to the unions a Marxist spirit and a State socialism— are entirely groundless and unjust»[485].

The Chilean Episcopate, in a collective pastoral letter on January 1, 1947, clearly reaffirms the legitimacy of union organization:

> «The Church, faithful to her history and doctrine, sees in trade associations an effective means of solving the Social Question, and, even more in the current state of affairs, considers it necessary to establish such union associations.
>
> Employers and workers have the right to form separated or mixed associations and unions.
>
> The Church desires union associations to be established and to be governed by the principles of Christian faith and morality.
>
> The Church loves and blesses workers' unionization, when it seeks the spiritual and material development of the members, their economic redemption and social peace.
>
> The union must be an organism for the defense of legitimate rights, for general improvement and for social harmony, possesing freedom within the organized occupation.
>
> Therefore we approve those who, within these principles and for the purposes indicated, promote unionization whether of workers or professionals. For the same reasons, we point out the dangers and damages of the union, used as a weapon of class struggle, political penetration or social unrest»[486].

The same right that the Pontiffs recognize in the workers to join a union is equally recognized in the employers. But Pius XI states, with pain, that such employers' associations «are so few —the condition is not wholly due to the will of men but to far graver difficulties that hinder associations of this kind which We know well and estimate at their full value. There is, however, strong hope that these obstacles also will be removed soon, and even now We greet with the deepest joy of Our soul, certain by no means insignificant attempts in this direction, the rich fruits of which promise a still richer harvest in the future»[487].

485 [*Id.*]
486 [*Syndicalism.* This book, on the page cited, contains the following footnote: «Call of the Chilean Episcopate to the Faithful, January 1, 1947».]
487 [*Quadragesimo Anno* § 38.]

3

Unionism and Social Peace

The Church desires unions to be instruments of concord and social peace.

«All who glory in the name of Christian, either individually or collectively, if they wish to remain true to their vocation, may not foster enmities and dissensions between the classes of civil society. On the contrary, they must promote mutual concord and charity»[488].

«The rights and duties of the employers, as compared with the rights and duties of the employed, ought to be the subject of careful consideration. Should it happen that either a master or a workman believes himself injured, nothing would be more desirable than that a committee should be appointed, composed of reliable and capable members of the association, whose duty would be, conformably with the rules of the association, to settle the dispute»[489].

These same ideas were reiterated by the Holy See years later through the Sacred Congregation of the Council, in the conflict between Catholic unions and the Employers Consortium of Roubaix-Tourcoing, to which we have already alluded:

«Catholic Associations must not only avoid but also combat class struggle as essentially contrary to the principles of Christianity... It is timely, useful and very consistent with Christian principles to continue, in principle, so far as practically possible, the simultaneous and distinct foundation of employers' and workers' unions»[490].

«The Sacred Congregation would be pleased to establish a regular mode of relations between the two unions through a permanent Joint Commission. The mission of this commission would be to address common interests in periodic meetings, and to ensure that occupational organizations are not organisms of struggle and antagonism

488 [*Singulari Quadam* § 3.]
489 [*Rerum Novarum* § 58.]
490 [Congregation of the Sacred Council, Letter to Cardinal Liénart § 5. The document cited has a footnote at this point which states: «*Lettre du cardinal Gasparri à l'Union économique sociale, 25 février 1915*».]

but, as they should be according to the Christian view, the means of mutual understanding, benevolent discussion and peace»[491].

But note that, as Pius XI says in *Quadragesimo Anno*, «[f]or if the class struggle abstains from enmities and mutual hatred, it gradually changes into an honest discussion of differences founded on a desire for justice, and if this is not that blessed social peace which we all seek, it can and ought to be the point of departure from which to move forward to the mutual cooperation of the Industries and Professions»[492].

4
Confessionality of Unions

«Catholics should preferably associate with Catholics, unless necessity compels them to act differently. This is an important point for the safeguarding of the faith»[493].

5
History of the Trade Union Movement

5.1. THE FIRST ASSOCIATIONS

In the history of ancient peoples, especially Egyptian, Hebrew, Greek and Roman, there are facts that highlight the awakening of the guild spirit. In all of them there were joint efforts aimed at defending the rights of workers and artisans.

The Old Testament mentions a guild of goldsmiths and of perfumers, that existed in Jerusalem 500 years before Jesus Christ[494].

491 [*Id.* § 7.]

492 [*Quadragesimo Anno* § 114.]

493 [Congregation of the Sacred Council, Letter to Cardinal Liénart § 6. That document states at this point: «(Léon XIII aux évêques des États-Unis, 6 janvier 1895)».]

494 [Nehemiah 3:8 states: «Next to them the work of repair was carried out by Uzziel, son of Harhaiah, a member of the goldsmiths' guild, and at his side was Hananiah, one of the perfumers' guild».]

Among the Romans since the time of Paul Servilius, there had been a «merchant's school». In the time of Tiberius there was a «school of sailors». In general, in Rome, the guilds were called «Collegia Opificum». These associations required the approval of the Emperor or the Senate; they had a mutualist character but they were languishing owing to the fact that the Romans despised manual labor, which they considered typical of slaves.

5.2. MEDIEVAL GUILDS

In the Middle Ages guilds reach a condition of splendor. They began their development in the eighth century, but their apogee arrived in the thirteenth century. The guilds had an intense life and united in their bosoms the best workers and artists. To belong to a guild at that time was an accomplishment of a goal much appreciated even by those who held administrative positions in the cities.

To appreciate the picture of medieval life, it is necessary to remember the destruction by the barbarians in the countries ruled by the Romans. Bishops, clergy and monks began the material and spiritual reconstruction of those countries. Around the churches schools were formed, then brotherhoods, which soon took on an economic character and formed the guilds, uniting those who practiced the same trade. These guilds developed technical education and organized the production and distribution of products. The guilds were not an artificial creation, but were born of the needs of the time and were the fruit of the Christian genius that inspired their members. In the countryside, the serfs worked the common property in addition to their family allotments, which gave rise to the principle of peasant democracy. In the cities, guild workshops were the cells of all economic activity. Workshops of the same trade formed a guild, which had a headquarters and was placed under the patronage of a saint. The guild completely satisfied the necessities of its members, both material and spiritual ones, and made its workers a great family, in an atmosphere of authentic economic democracy.

The internal constitution of the guilds was very simple. Three categories formed their basic elements: apprentices, workers or fellows and masters or employers.

The apprentices needed a period of up to twelve years to qualify as workers permitted to engage in the trade. Their employers were obliged to provide them with bread, roof and clothing.

The fellows or workers received a salary determined by a jury. They could not engage in trades other than that of their guilds. The extent of their work was regulated according to the type of trade and according to the time of year. Sunday rest, and sometimes even a Saturday afternoon rest (our current English Saturday), was rigorously protected. The economic situation of the workers of that time was much superior to that of the majority of current workers. In the days when the true guild spirit flourished, workers had a guarantee that they could ascend to the level of masters, once they completely knew the craft, which they demonstrated by producing a «masterpiece», «*a chef d'oeuvre*;» they also had to make contributions and swear an oath to be faithful to the statutes of the guild.

The master established his own workshop, which was at the same time the shop, and worked in it surrounded by his workers and apprentices subject to inspection by delegates of the guild. Each master, as an assurance to the customers, had to place his distinctive sign on the objects that he manufactured and was responsible for their quality. Rarely in history has respect for rights been better established than in that period of the flourishing of the guilds.

At the head of the guilds, there was a body of jurors or prudent men, who were elected every year. They were responsible for ensuring compliance with the statutes of the guild and representing it in commercial transactions or administrative matters. They constituted a court not subject to appeal in all labor conflicts between employers, workers and apprentices: an anticipation of our arbitration commissions. The jurors were chosen by the guild, to which they had to give account of their authority. The guilds were in charge of the purchase of raw materials and their distribution among employers. They regulated prices and production to avoid abuses and unemployment among their workers. A good number of contemporary social achievements were incorporated into the life of the medieval guilds. These associations not only served economic interests, but also cared for the creation and development of primary and occupational schools, for the care of the sick, orphans, widows, elders and invalids.

The degree of technical perfection reached by the workers within this regime can be observed even now when contemplating the wonderful works of architecture, painting, embroidery, knitting, jewelry: many of them never equaled despite current technical perfection. The medieval guilds were inspired by a mystique that elevated and dignified the work of the hands, valuing the spiritual significance of human effort and creating among the workers a fraternity inspired by Christian love.

The great postulates of social Catholicism, which struggles for a human economy, were understood by the medieval guilds. In them production was subordinated to consumption, thus preventing usury and speculation, so common in today's economy. This was true both of the production of finished goods and of raw materials.

Profit was subordinated to morality and not, as in the liberal economy, morality to interests. In short, profit was intended to put the economy at the service of man and not man at the service of economic interests.

In order to regulate production and prices, the guilds formed General Councils, called «Merchant Universities», which related to different guilds and made possible a policy of sound intervention, in the hands of the producers themselves. Guilds became an organized force within their own countries and also had their delegates, with consular powers, in various nations. Permanent concern for the common good harmonized the interests of the various professional and economic communities.

The decline of the guilds was an unfortunate fact that had its first origin in the tendency of the political power to take away their privileges in order to eliminate intermediaries between the central power and the subjects. Politics intervened in the internal affairs of the guilds and sovereigns conditioned the achievement of the rank of master on the payment of exhorbitant fees for military purposes; then sovereigns appointed inspectors from outside the guilds and ended up by selling their functions. All these actions distorted the original spirit of the guilds. When the Renaissance came, the guilds forgot more and more the spirit of Christian fraternity, and instead of considering themselves servants of the common good, they preferred to seek individual goods. In many guilds the worker was impeded in being promoted to master; the promotion examination was deferred for a long time; and even the title of master was entirely reserved to the children of masters. Little by little, the original democratic spirit was lost and a professional oligarchy was formed, careful of its own privileges. The workers were forced to unite in defense of their rights against the masters and a social struggle began, as bitter as the one of our days.

The abolition of the guilds, furthered by the abuses we have pointed out, was completed pursuant to the liberal ideology of the eighteenth century. Already in 1776, Turgot[495] tried to extinguish them using the pretext that «liberty balances supply and demand». The guilds defended themselves: they showed how their abolition would ruin the craftsmen, harm the consumers, and encourage the Jews to abuse the public. The danger was momentarily avoided, but the triumphant Revolution of 1789 put an end to the guilds. The Chapelier Act of 1791 formally prohibited the establishment of any guild of members of the same trade, because such guilds damaged the freedom that the Revolution had come to establish[496]. And curiously, these ideas caught on so widely in that environment that even the craftsmen themselves believed that they found in them liberation from the abuses of the guilds. They forgot, to their own harm, that «between the strong and the weak, it is freedom which oppresses and the law which sets free», as Lacordaire would later say[497].

336 5.3. ABOLITION OF THE GUILDS

In 1891, one hundred years after the Chapelier Act, Leo XIII sadly said: «for the ancient workingmen's guilds were abolished in the last century, and no other protective organization took their place. Public institutions and the laws set aside the ancient religion. Hence, by degrees it has come to pass that working men have been surrendered, isolated and helpless, to the hardheartedness of employers and the greed of unchecked competition. The mischief has been increased by rapacious usury, which, although more than once condemned by the Church, is nevertheless, under a different guise, but with like injustice, still practiced by covetous and grasping men. To this must be added that the hiring of labor and the conduct of trade are concentrated in the hands of comparatively few; so that a small number of very rich men have been able to lay upon the teeming masses of the laboring poor a yoke little better than that of slavery itself»[498].

495 [Anne Robert Jacques Turgot (1722-1781), French economist and politician, known for his work *Réflexions sur la Formation et la Distribution des Richesses* (*Reflections on the Formation and Distribution of Wealth*) (1770).]

496 [*Loi Le Chapelier*, issued on June 14th, 1791 by the French National Constituent Assembly, banned guilds and declared strikes unlawful. Its first article stated : «[i]n that the abolition of any kind of citizen's guild in the same trade or of the same profession is one of the fundamental bases of the French Constitution, it is forbidden to re-establish them under any pretext or in any form whatsoever».]

497 [«Between the strong and the weak, between the rich and the poor, between the master and the servant, it is liberty which oppresses, and the law that sets free. Right is the sword of the powerful, duty is the buckler of the lowly». *Dieu et l'homme* in *Conférences de Notre Dame de Paris* (*God and Man: Conferences Delivered at Notre Dame in Paris by the Rev. Père Lacordaire*) (1870). For Lacordaire, see footnote 37.]

498 [*Rerum Novarum* § 3.]

The French example was soon followed by other countries. The defenseless workers, guided by the natural instinct to unite for the defense of their rights, took timid steps to form new associations that soon gave rise to the unions.

5.4. TRADE UNIONISM IN THE MODERN ERA

Everywhere, trade unionism passes through an evolution in which we can distinguish three phases: 1) a coalition of the State and capital to place unions outside the law; 2) the State takes a passive role and capitalism makes concessions to unionism; 3) the State decides to intervene in favor of the unions, legally recognizes them, and regulates their existence.

There is no contemporary civilized country, with the exception of totalitarian ones whose clearest example is Russia, in which trade unionism does not constitute a formidable organized force, perhaps the main strength of each country.

The book *Syndicalism* sets forth the history and balance of forces in the world's most important countries[499].

A look at the strength of existing large international associations will allow us to notice the presence of trade union groups at the present moment. The World Federation of Trade Unions, controlled by the communists, declared in 1949 that it comprised 40 national centers with 71,580,890 members. In this enormous figure all Russian workers are included as members, but they cannot really be called that; the same for workers in countries behind the iron curtain, because there trade unionism is merely nominal: it is a framework that brings together the work force to receive and act on the slogans of the State, which is the only employer.

The International Confederation of Free Trade Unions promoted mainly by the British trade unions, and the C.I.O.[500] and A.F.L.[501], the two main American organizations, comprise some 50,000,000 workers from 34 countries.

The International Confederation of Christian Trade Unions, C.C.T.U.[502], currently has some 4,000,000 mostly Catholic members, but there are also Protestant and even Mohammedan federations.

499 [*Syndicalism.*]
500 [Congress of Industrial Organizations.]
501 [American Federation of Labor.]
502 [*Confédération des Syndicats Chrétiens* (Confederation of Christian Trade Unions) was created in Belgium in 1904, and evolved from the Anti-Socialist Cotton Workers' Union founded in 1886. It has now more than one million members. More information here: https://www.csc-en-ligne.be/csc-en-ligne/La-CSC/S-affilier/affiliation.html]

Anarchists have formed an International Association with headquarters in Berlin.

In Latin America two international associations compete for the predominance: the C.T.A.L., affiliated with the World Federation of Communists, and the C.I.T.[503], affiliated with the International Confederation of Free Trade Unions.

6
The Mission of Trade Unionism according to Various Social Schools

The mission of trade unionism has been conceived differently by various social schools. The main points of divergence relate to the purpose of trade unionism's action and the means to be used, to trade unionism's relations with political parties and to parliamentary action, the use of strikes, sabotage and other means of direct action.

The main approaches can be reduced to four antagonistic points of view, depending on the type of trade unionism they advocate: a) revolutionary; B) reformist; C) opportunist; D) realistic.

6.1. REVOLUTIONARY TRADE UNIONISM

There is no simple or homogeneous doctrine that characterizes the principles of this group. Trade unionism can be said to have been born revolutionary, because the first unions were violently persecuted by the public authorities, which forced them to organize illegally and encouraged the creation of a doctrine that would justify violence. Thereafter they were influenced, on the one hand, by the need to affirm positions that entailed the rejection of the purely reformist compromises of the socialists, and on the other hand, by the writings of revolutionary intellectuals such as Sorel, who tried to make a philosophy of revolution and violence[504].

In general terms, we can say that the purpose of revolutionary trade unionism is to destroy capitalism, the employers' regime, the salary system and the political State.

503 [*Confederación Interamericana de Trabajadores* (*Inter-American Confederation of Workers*).]

504 [Georges Sorel (1874-1922), French philosopher and writer, who developed the concept of «social myth». The trade union movement that arose around 1900 inspired Sorel to write *Réflexions sur la Violence* (Reflections on Violence) (1908), in which he developed his ideas about social myths and the virtues of violence.]

Instead of a political State there would be an economic State: that is a government of producers. The unions would be the only political and administrative bodies of this future society. At the base, the unions; at the second level, the federations; and at the summit, a national association which would bring together all federations. How would this new world be constituted? The militant workers have not bothered to describe it: they only know that it would be a free society, and work would also be free.

Members will be free in the union; the union will be free in the federation and the federation will be free in the national association. Work will cease to be an obligation and will become recreation. Everyone will work wherever he pleases; the work of a few hours will suffice to cover basic necessities. The capitalist market, with its price regime, will disappear and will be maintained only for luxury objects. Revolutionary trade unionists are sure about obtaining these results because they believe that the modification of the social environment will infallibly bring about a modification of individual psychology. To think that in such a society one might not work is for the revolutionaries a «blasphemy», a fruit of our ideas distorted by misery and by the rude struggle for life. Some, even among the most died-in-the-wool revolutionaries, do not share this optimism, and think that the only freedom that could be left to the trade union members is that to choose their work, but the work would be mandatory.

The way to reach this new society is nothing other than direct revolutionary action by the wage-earners themselves. They absolutely reject political and parliamentary action, because it would divide the workers and sterilize their efforts. Motivated by this same fear, they reject all immediate reform and accept only the general strike, the only thing that could immediately achieve for them the desired end: «*le Grand Soir*»[505] of the new society. Nothing through parliamentary action; all through the direct action of the union. Direct action means action by the workers themselves: action directly taken by the interested parties on their own. By direct action the workers create the struggle that will liberate them, and they will not rely on others but only on the forces of the working class: the struggle must be daily and must grow until it becomes a social conflagration: «the general strike» that will *be* the social revolution. The union, says a revolu-

505 [«The Great Evening»-*Le Grand Soir*-a metaphor of the revolution, is a term used by communists, anarchists and most of the revolutionary organizations to refer to the precise and concrete moment in which the transformation of society will take place. See footnote 383.]

tionary, «is a group of integral struggles that aspires to break down the legal regime that suffocates us, in order to give birth to a new legal order».

Before the general strike there are other procedures that also fall within the «direct action» plan: partial strikes, boycotting all products not authorized by the union so as to injure capitalism in the «cash box», sabotage. These measures, in the revolutionary plan, serve to awaken the masses and arouse public opinion. The strike, the main means of revolutionary trade unionism, educates, mobilizes, creates.

The ultimate solution, thinks Marx, will come as a result of an excess of misery. Some among the less intransigent claim, however, that successive reforms make people want new ones and thus prepare the revolution. Integral revolutionaries not only do not fight for improvements, they even reject them, as they did in France where they opposed the laws about trade unions which, they charged, were intended to break the revolutionary spirit of the working class, making them comfortable with a property regime. The legal personality of trade unions and their ability to contract rights and obligations appear to revolutionaries to be insidious means for attracting to the union those people who seek profit and distancing the ones who consider the union to be only an organ of resistance. The establishment of trade union funds serves as a pretext for the State to monitor the life of the union and give unions a bourgeois and capitalist mentality.

Revolutionary trade unionism is characterized today by anarchism and communism. Speaking of communism, we should note the difference between Marxism, Leninism and Stalinism, which are different and progressive orientations of what we call communism.

By the term Marxism, we refer to the social, materialist and dialectical philosophy elaborated by Marx and Engels. For them the capitalist regime has been a necessary stage in economic development, but it must disappear, victim of its own contradictions, and give rise to a new society without classes, prepared by a period of dictatorship of the proletariat.

Communist is the name that has been taken by the parties that adhere to the Third International.

Leninism points to the doctrinal contribution of Lenin in the maturation of Marx' and Engels' philosophy, and especially its strategic plan of proletarian revolution. Lenin is the great strategist of Marxism.

Stalin adds to his predecessors doctrines that tend to consolidate the revolution in Russia and to extend it from there to the universal proletariat. The consolidation of communism in Russia and support for its policy is, according to Stalin, the great step that has to precede the implantation of communism in the world.

Marxists, in order to obtain their end to replace private ownership of the means of production with collective property, actively use the trade union movement: they infiltrate all trade unions, form their cells, prepare the shock troops. They will use boycott, sabotage, strikes, and violent demonstrations until they have enough strength to seize power and expel the bourgeoise.

Marxism, once it comes to power, as is the case in Russia, ceases to consider trade unionism as a means of vindication and uses it as a framework that gives a structure to the working masses, disciplines them and directs them towards more intensive production. Then, its trade unionism is no different that of totalitarian countries.

Anarchism fights for the independence and complete freedom of the individual and is a sworn enemy of authority, in particular that of the State.

The Revolutionary Movement of Intellectuals: Berth[506], Lagardelle[507] and, above all, Georges Sorel created the doctrine of revolutionary syndicalism: «a metaphysics of syndicalism».

Sorel had a curious ideological line of development: first, he was a revolutionary syndicalist, then a monarchist committed to the Movement of the French Action and, finally, a communist. His most important work is «Reflections on Violence», which reconciles the doctrines of Marx and Proudhon[508].

Sorel demands, first of all, the education of the proletariat so as to raise it to a higher level. What is the mission of syndicalism in this educational work? That of reinforcing the moral values of the working class, the only one that still remains healthy, since the bourgeoisie and the intellectuals have deserted their missions. The first capitalists to organize industry were hardworking men. Their successors have become bourgeois. Nothing good can come of the bourgeoise

506 [Édouard Berth (1875-1939), French socialist thinker, author of several books and a disciple of George Sorel. Berth proposed a synthesis of revolutionary syndicalism and corporatism.]

507 [Hubert Lagardelle (1874-1958), French politician and writer, pioneer of French revolutionary syndicalism, author of several books including *La Confédération du Travail et le Socialisme* (*The Confederation of Labor and Socialism*)(1907) and *Syndicalisme et Socialisme* (*Unionism and Socialism*)(1908).]

508 [See footnote 504.]

and the intellectuals; therefore Sorel—an intellectual himself—puts the workers on guard against the intellectuals. The labor movement, he repeats, must consist purely of workers.

This ardent revolutionary has, however, a pessimistic soul. For him, the liberation of the working class «is a dream or an error». The victory of the proletariat is unattainable, since it presupposes a set of conditions almost impossible to bring together. However, the trade union movement must not abandon its unquenchable revolutionary attitude, because it keeps the working class willing to act, excites and stimulates energy, and has an educational and moral value in itself.

The general strike, Sorel thinks, is without value in its external aspects and moreover, is violent, brutal and useless, but it is fruitful in its internal effects: it keeps the will aligned towards the end and it elicits acts of value and sacrifice. More than violence itself, we must maintain a feeling of violence. Acts of violence will have to be carried out from time to time to remind militants of the state of war and struggle between classes.

For Sorel, the general strike is an organization of images that instinctively evokes the feelings of war against modern society. It has the value of a myth.

A «myth», according to Sorel, «is the expression of the convictions of a group in language of movement;» «is that which leads men to prepare to fight to destroy that which exists». The myth has no logical, cerebral character, but is a force that drags the will. Therefore, it is useless to attempt rebuttal. «Utopia», however —the product of intellectual conception—leads people to obtain reforms[509].

The general strike, conceived as a myth, will be the emblem of the working class that will prevent it from falling into the temptations of a soft reformism, and save the proletariat from the seductions of the decadent bourgeoisie.

In light of these principles, one must judge Sorel's attitude towards sabotage: he condemns it because he does not think it suitable as a guide to the worker along the path of his emancipation: it destroys his professional conscience. Future society will derive its rights from good practices in the workshop ... a workshop that functions with order, without loss of time, without caprice. «It is necessary to lead the people to love their work, to consider everything they do as a

509 [These ideas and the excerpts quoted above are presented in Sorel's book *Réflexions sur la Violence* (*Reflections on Violence*) (1908). Sorel stated that myths are «expressions of a will to act» and are the very antitheses of utopias. Through myths we can understand «the activity, the sentiments and the ideas of the masses as they prepare themselves to enter on a decisive struggle».]

masterpiece that could never be sufficiently protected; we should make them artists, learned people, councious of everything that concerns production»[510]. Jaurès[511] has the same conception as Sorel regarding sabotage: it conflicts with the technical value of the worker and degrades his professional value. As is to be expected, these ideas are not accepted by revolutionary workers; one of their representatives states that «these are sentimental statements inspired by the morality of exploiters».

Sorel is unpatriotic and anti-militarist, but not because he believes that war is bad; on the contrary, he thinks that war is an element of moral progress. He is unpatriotic and anti-militarist because the working class' attitude towards the homeland and the army would lead it to an understanding of its need to fight permanently against the ruling classes and against the State. This is a clear way to affirm the international solidarity of the working class and the absence of solidarity among the different classes of the same nation.

Sorel's doctrine, in short, states that trade unionism must keep the proletariat in a state of healthy violence, which is neither ferocity nor brutality, but a paroxysm of exaltation, heroism and sacrifice.

The purpose of violence, according to Sorel, is not to destroy the bourgeoisie, but to regenerate it. Violence will force capitalism to recover its warlike virtues so as to defend and regenerate itself. Sorel's doctrine is not aimed at bringing about immediate improvements for the proletariat but «to save the world from barbarism»[512] so as to avoid moral and economic decline. Sorel is a revolutionary who does not want the revolution.

If the workers were to take Sorel's doctrine seriously, they would have to renounce any immediate improvement of their situation and sacrifice themselves indefinitely for an end which Sorel himself declared unachievable; but he has never been taken seriously. Trade unionists fight for more tangible ends and in more immediate situations.

On the other hand, totalitarians such as Mussolini, Hitler and Rosenberg took advantage of Sorel's concept of myth. Hitler redirected it to race; Rosen-

510 [*Id.*]
511 [Jean Jaurès (1859-1914), French socialist politician, one of the great figures of the French left.]
512 [Sorel, *Réflexions sur la Violence*, supra.]

berg declared: «the mission of our century is to bring forth a new concept of life from a new myth»[513].

6.2. REFORMIST TRADE UNIONISM

For revolutionaries, trade unionism is the means to destroy modern society; for reformists it is a means to improve it: trade unionism is a policy rather than a doctrine. Reformist trade unionism does not have the sharp edge of revolutionary syndicalism: it looks, rather, to the immediate, without worrying about transformations that require a long time. It does not embrace mysticism or dogmatism: it aims, above all, to be realistic, and to concern itself with the immediate; it seeks to remain legal.

Reformist action is often paralyzed by the resistance of employers who do not want to be confined by narrow contractual obligations, and by the resistance of the State, which confuses order with immobility and is not affected except when the demands of workers lead to disturbances. In addition, in many nationalized industries, the State is both a judge and an interested party, since it acts as employer. Reformists reject, as a vain illusion, the new society that revolutionaries dream of. Man's heart and brain cannot be transformed, as can his passions and vices, in the blink of an eye. It would be childish to think that this is going to change entirely because the economic regime of society changes. A transformation of man is required first: a work of education and of technical skills that cannot be acquired on the fly.

The means employed by the revolutionaries seem to trade-union reformists to be contradictory, wrong and to be based only on illusion. Contradictory, because if any improvement of conditions makes the working class less fierce, there would be no other way but to be uninterested in obtaining any relief for their condition even by direct struggle; it would even be necessary to aggravate the misery of the worker to make him more combative. Can this honestly be affirmed in the face of an agonized working class? Wrong, because direct action either fails or succeeds. If it fails, it will only produce bloody repression and aggravate the situation of the worker. If it succeeds, this would undoubtedly be because the labor movement had matured and become strong enough to impose itself without brutal and illegal means. It is an illusion to think that an en-

513 [Probably taken from *Mythus des XX. Jahrhunderts* (*The Myth of the 20th Century: An Evaluation of the Spiritual-Intellectual Confrontations of Our Age*) by Alfred Rosenberg (1893 -1946), German intellectual who was one of the most influential ideologues of the National Socialist Party.]

tirely new society can be erected on a *tabula rasa* and the capitalist regime suddenly transformed. It is a fatal error to believe that all abuses, all private property, can be abolished by a revolution and no less wrong to believe that a revolutionary movement, although momentarily triumphant, can solve the social problem and transform national economic conditions at a stroke without taking into account international forces and influences: in a word, to establish a new society directed by federations of unions. Anarchists and revolutionary Marxists are victims of the same illusion: believing in the creative force of destruction. Thus think the leading reformers.

The Positive Aspect of Reformist Trade Unionism: Reformists accept, in principle, that the existing order: the political situation and the current economic regime—must be improved. They are neither anti-militaristic nor anti-patriotic. Anti-militarism seems to them a new source of division among the working class between patriots and anti-patriots; they lament that the army is used against the workers in social conflicts.

Reformist unionism seeks an understanding with the employers to improve the proletarian condition; it tries to humanize the existing regime in a constant, positive way, leaving to the future the responsibility to carry out social renewal.

Violent means: boycott and sabotage—are formally excluded, and the strike is only allowed as a last resort provided it is not general but confined to one industrial sector. The strike is considered by the reformists to be a means of forcing employers to deal with unions and the State to serve as arbitrator in the conflict.

Legal reforms are reformist unionism's great aspiration, which does not imply that it seeks the alliance of trade unionism with a political party, but that it do not close its doors to the use of political parties' services in the legislature. It is interventionist, first in social and then in economic issues.

Reformists accept working councils, and even apply for positions of responsibility in them in order influence them.

6.3. OPPORTUNISTIC TRADE UNIONISM

We can consider a third group composed of what we might call «opportunists», because although they declare themselves revolutionaries in their principles, their behavior brings them closer to the reformists[514].

514 Jouhaux, General Secretary of the C.G.T. French expounds this doctrine in his pamphlet «*Le syndicalisme, ce qu'il est, ce qu'il doit étre*», Flammarion, Paris, 1937. [The author is referring to Léon Jouhaux (1879-1954), a French trade union leader who received the Nobel Peace Prize in

They continue to use the revolutionaries' vocabulary, their ideology, their tendency to improvise, but the opportunists' action has only immediate purposes.

Trade union practice is pulled by contradictory temptations. At base, militants retain nostalgia for the formulas of revolutionary trade unionism, from which they demand a rejuvenation of the spirit. All the components of opposition to the political regime or to the incumbent government further this trend. But when trade union leaders feel attached to the responsibilities of power in any form, they slip insensibly into courses similar to those of Soviet syndicalism: this occurred in the Weimar Republic, in liberated France in 1945 and in the Laborite Great Britain of Attlee and Bevin. Trade unionism, then, tries to discipline the spontaneous reactions of the masses.

The failure of the 1920 strike led Jouhaux to declare that the general strike can only be the decisive manifestation of a proletariat capable of rebuilding the world. Another of the *Cégétiste*[515] leaders affirmed «that the general strike is not worth anything until popular education is completed». As can be seen, these attitudes accord more with reformist thinking than with that of the primitive revolutionary.

Direct action, conceived at first as a break with the methods and with the men of parliamentarism, and as involving the multiplication of industrial strikes to prepare for the general strike, has come to mean, according to Jouhaux, that the workers have resolved to arrange their affairs by their own means, even through political alliances. This new conception of direct action brings to an end all opposition between itself and political action. In contrast, revolutionary syndicalism has tried to achieve parliamentary representation and its leaders have held positions in government, even as ministers of state. In order to be able to influence affairs from a position of power, revolutionary syndicalism aspires not to be a nucleus of fervent individuals, but to have a mass as large as possible in order to get votes.

Technical workers in industry and directors, excluded at first as nonlaboring elements, are now invited into the trade union movement. «Your place is among us, not in a secondary place or as an accessory . . . but in a place similar to

1951, and was the General Secretary of the *Confédération Générale du Travail* (*General Confederation of Labour*) (the C.G.T.).]

515 [This term refers to the *Confédération Générale du Travail* (General Confederation of Labor): the C.G.T.]

that of the other elements and in proportion to the social mission they have to perform among us».

From time to time, the old principles reappear and the general strike is advocated; today they are still trying to organize one, as in November of 1947 to January of 1948 in France, and in the same period in Italy and Chile; but repeated failures have compelled them to return to a more opportunistic attitude that, although it remaines faithful to the final goal of action, in the use of means very close to those of reformism.

The morality of Marxism fully justifies this conduct; moreover, it demands it. For Marxism, everything that leads to the liberation of the proletariat, to the abolition of capitalism, is good; the means are indifferent: the important thing is that they conduce to the end sought. It cannot be said that Marxism has no morality: it has that of opportunism. An immoral morality, a morality based on a principle that cannot be the ultimate norm of morality, but one which gives its adherents a point of view for all their actions.

6.4. REALISTIC TRADE UNIONISM

There is a fourth orientation of the trade union movement, unlike the revolutionary, reformist and opportunist tendencies, which we might call «realistic» because, although it is radical in its demands for a new world, it adjusts its immediate demands to real possibilities, without signifying an opportunistic abandonment of its principles. It is not satisfied with a simple social reform, but aspires to change the structures to create a new order, but conceives of matters differently from revolutionary syndicalism: different in the very end that is sought to be achieved and different in the means of action.

This realistic trend can take many forms. We are going to present one that is in accord with Catholic thought and which is inspired by the principles of what we can call «Christian Social Order». The Catholic Church does not have a practical programmatic doctrine of the trade union, since it is outside her line of action. She is content to defend the trade union movement and to give it basic principles to inspire its action. Movements of Catholic inspiration, on their own and exercising their own responsibility, will develop the most detailed programs to fulfill the requirements of the Christian Social Order. The Church will not intervene in them except to remind them of the requirements of dogma and morality, to point out to them an accomplishment required by the common good, or to coordinate their forces in a situation requiring urgent action. The program outlined in the next chapter is generally accepted by trade union movements of a Christian inspiration.

The realistic unionism that we advocate, although it goes much further than reformist unionism because it favors a new order and a change of social structures, fully agrees with its principle of fighting for any reform that improves the condition of the wage-earner and makes it more human.

Technical workers have a decisive importance in realistic trade unionism, since they are called to look for the most suitable methods of elevating the proletariat from its subordinate position.

7
The Great Priciples of Realistic Trade Unionism

7.1. AT THE SERVICE OF MAN

The supreme aspiration of trade union activity is to achieve and ensure respect for the person and his complete spiritual, intellectual, physical and economic development: in a word, the fulfillment of man in himself and in his family and social life.

The end of the trade union is the man and not the class. It is an error, therefore, to subordinate the good of man to the good of any class whatsoever. This is what Marxist trade unionism does: it sacrifices man to the aggrandizement of the proletarian class. Man has dignity and sacred rights that no one—neither capital nor the State nor the working class—can sacrifice.

The end of the trade union is man and not the State. The State has been created for man and not man for the State. Fascism and all totalitarianism subordinate the trade union to the State, which they conceive as omnipotent: the people of the trade unions are simply gears for the greatness of the State.

Capitalism committed the serious crime of putting production and profit first among its aspirations, disregarding the personhood of the worker. Trade unionism can commit the same mistake and focus its aspirations on the working class or on the State. Its goal must be to redeem, to enhance, to perfect man in order to develop the fullness of his capacities and to obtain for him maximum satisfactions.

7.2. IN AN AUTHENTIC DEMOCRACY

Democracy is government of the people, by the people, for the people[516]. There are no privileged classes in it. There is no other title of superiority than personal merit.

Today's society recognizes men's equal political rights, but often denies their spiritual freedom: the basis of all democracy —and, furthermore, denies that which constitutes economic democracy, namely the opportunities to be prepared and educated and to act as a free and responsible man. Without a minimum of material well-being the practice of the virtues is impossible, taught St. Thomas. Political democracy is a mere chimera without a minimum of material welfare.

To reach this full democracy, the people must decide to think for themselves. Because they have not done so, people have seen their freedoms violated and have lost their economic independence. «The trade union must be fundamentally a group of men determined to take part intelligently and consciously in the elaboration of better conditions of life for the human person and consecrated to creating better times for better men»[517]. The trade union, thus conceived, educates for democracy.

7.3. FAITHFUL TO JUSTICE

Without social justice there can be no complete democracy. The trade union is called to fight for an order of social justice. There will be social justice when it is the common good and not the particular interest that regulates the distribution of goods. The economic world cannot be regulated either by free competition or by economic arrogance, but by justice and social charity. «The public institutions themselves, of peoples, moreover, ought to make all human society conform to the needs of the common good; that is, to the norm of social justice. If this is done, that most important division of social life, namely, economic activity, cannot fail likewise to return to right and sound order»[518].

Any union action must seek justice, whether it favors the worker or the employer. Justice has no parties, and acknowledges the rights of everybody.

516 [Abraham Lincoln, Gettysburg Address (1863).]

517 Núñez, ABC del Sindicalismo, p. 59. [The author is probably referring to Ignacio Núñez Soler (1891-1986), Paraguayan artist and anarchist trade union leader, founder, in 1916, of *Centro Obrero Regional del Paraguay* (*Regional Workers Center of Paraguay*). He is the author of the book *Evocaciones de un Sindicalista Revolucionario* (*Reminiscences of a Revolutionary Trade Unionist*) (1980).]

518 [*Quadragesimo Anno* § 110.]

A just social order cannot be created by committing injustices. True to this principle, the trade union will never be carried away by blind passions. It is necessary to react with equal courage before the injustice that oppresses and before the demagogy that destroys.

Sometimes a heroic personality is required to oppose decisions that are popular but unjust.

A social order mantains an inner equilibrium in which everyone is given what is appropriate. It is not «order» merely to preserve what we have. What we now call «economic order» involves a very serious disorder. Someone who shouts against the existing disorder is not a revolutionary; a revolutionary is someone who defends the disorder, although it has lasted many years.

The economic balance for several centuries has been too much inclined to the side of the employer, owing to the weight of his financial power. It is necessary to right the balance, and for this we will have to assert claims and press them with energy, and with even more energy when the rights that are asserted are especially important. These rights sometimes are related to the conditions necessary for a man to live as a man, to organize a family according to God's plan.

To be silent, in these cases, is not virtue but cowardice. Resignation to pain that one can and must remedy is a tremendous betrayal of God's plan and, when the common good has been violated, of the dignity of man, family and society. We have the right to resign ourselves only after we have spent the last cartridge in defense of truth and justice. Once we have exhausted our possibilities it is foolish to toss and turn without effect. A Christian joins his suffering to the redemptive suffering of Christ so that the kingdom of truth and justice may come into the world.

7.4. THE TIRELESS DEFENSE OF VESTED RIGHTS

The social achievements of workers have been codified in the Labor Code and in complementary social laws. Unfortunately, many such gains, granted to the people on the eve of elections or in difficult times for the country, may be distorted by legal measures that make them ineffective or fraudulent as applied. In addition, there is a large wage-earning sector that is completely ignorant of the social measures that favor it or that refrains because of timidity from applying to the agencies that can assist it.

The trade union has to know the established social legislation and the case-law perfectly. It must be linked to legal services that can defend the trade union and all its members; it must publicize the social laws so that everyone can take advantage of them; and, finally, it must draft all the provisions necessary to apply the laws so as to remedy their defects and to extend their benefits.

The workers cannot forget that if they do not urge the application and extension of the established social legislation it will remain a dead letter and will not progress. Without trade unionism, social legislation would be reduced to a minimum.

On the other hand, we must be careful not to think that social legislation will remedy all kinds of evils. It is only a legal framework, and can be rendered ineffective by multiple factors, for example, monetary inflation: subsidies that were sufficient ten years ago are now derisory and do not satisfy in any way the needs they were intended to cover.

The same thing can be said of the advantages obtained in a collective bargaining contract or by an arbitration award. After a short time, their results may be nil because of an increase in the cost of living that exceeds the gains obtained. Therefore, when discussing economic advantages, we must look at more than the increase in the number of pesos but also at the real and not just the apparent improvement they produce.

7.5. TO ELIMINATE THE CAUSE OF THE CLASS STRUGGLE: NOT TO EXACERBATE THE SOCIAL EVIL

The class struggle is a fact: just open your eyes to verify the permanent conflict between the economically and financially arrogant and those who have but a modest wage. To recognize this fact is to recognize a truth.

Some people lay the blame for the class struggle only on the proletariat, which wishes to shake off the oppressive yoke. The class struggle, in fact, is organized and directed by both sides: by capital and by labor.

Pius XI, among the social evils he points out, deplores «[i]n the first place, ... the war between the classes, a chronic and mortal disease of present-day society, which like a cancer is eating away the vital forces of the social fabric, labor, industry, the arts, commerce, agriculture —everything in fact which contributes to public and private welfare and to national prosperity. This conflict seems to resist every solution and grows worse because those who are never satisfied with the amount of their wealth contend with those who hold on most tenaciously to the riches which they have already acquired, while to both classes there is common the desire to rule the other and to assume control of the other's possessions»[519].

519 [*Ubi Arcano* § 12.]

Capital struggles to create,

> «[A]n immense power and despotic economic dictatorship [which] is consolidated in the hands of a few, who often are not owners but only the trustees and managing directors of invested funds which they administer according to their own arbitrary will and pleasure.
>
> This dictatorship is being most forcibly exercised by those who, since they hold the money and completely control it, control credit also and rule the lending of money. Hence they regulate the flow, so to speak, of the life-blood whereby the entire economic system lives, and have so firmly in their grasp the soul, as it were, of economic life that no one can breathe against their will.
>
> This concentration of power and might, the characteristic mark, as it were, of contemporary economic life, is the fruit that the unlimited freedom of struggle among competitors has of its own nature produced, and which lets only the strongest survive; and this is often the same as saying, those who fight the most violently, those who give least heed to their conscience.
>
> This accumulation of might and of power generates in turn three kinds of conflict. First, there is the struggle for economic supremacy itself; then there is the bitter fight to gain supremacy over the State in order to use in economic struggles its resources and authority; finally there is conflict between States themselves, not only because countries employ their power and shape their policies to promote every economic advantage of their citizens, but also because they seek to decide political controversies that arise among nations through the use of their economic supremacy and strength»[520].

It cannot be doubted, then, that when one speaks of class struggle, capital is among those who foment this struggle.

The worker, for his part, recalls the fact that, «a small number of very rich men have been able to lay upon the teeming masses of the laboring poor a yoke little better than that of slavery itself»[521], and also that «not only in the countries called new, but also in the realms of the Far East that have been civilized from antiquity, the number of the non-owning working poor has increased enormously and their groans cry to God from the earth. Added to them is the huge army of rural wage workers, pushed to the lowest level of existence and deprived of all hope of ever acquiring "some property in land", and, therefore, per-

520 [*Quadragesimo Anno* §§105-108.]
521 [*Rerum Novarum* § 3.]

manently bound to the status of non-owning worker unless suitable and effective remedies are applied»[522]. The worker also recalls that, as Pius XII warned in 1944, «on the one hand, immense wealth dominates public and private life, and often even civil life; on the other, there are countless numbers of those who are unprotected by any direct or indirect assurance with respect to their lives»[523]. The memory of these grievances and the perception of the present deplorable situation creates within a number of wage-earning sectors a spirit of struggle to improve their situation. These facts are undeniable.

Now, in view of this reality of the class struggle we can adopt two responses. First, to use it to carry out violent revolutions that lead to other injustices: such is the response of the Marxists, who exploit that energy of indignation to achieve the triumph of the proletariat, and the response of the fascists who, alarmed at what they call the danger of demagogy, suppress the freedom of the organs of popular expression in order to defend against the threat to capitalism. The second response is to fight to remove the cause of such struggles: such is the response of social Christianity. This recognizes the existence of the struggle and aims to end it, removing the cause of the conflict, which is social injustice and the exploitation of the worker. At the same time, social Christianity asks the worker for the conscientious fulfillment of his duties. There can be no capital without work or work without capital: both are called to mutual understanding and collaboration under the protection of justice.

If the possessors of wealth refuse the legitimate demands of the worker, they are the ones that ignite the social struggle: the true revolutionaries. In such a case, trade unions have a duty to defend the rights of trade unionists; but this in no case authorizes them to exaggerate their demands or to use means that injure the just interests of capital.

The response of social Christianity towards the class struggle is to demand justice for the oppressed. «The peace fought for is not the peace of the cemeteries, nor the harmony of the resignation by the weak to the great injustices of the strong. This justice and harmony demand the equal fulfillment of their reciprocal duties and respect for their mutual rights by employers and workers. When this has been accomplished, the cause of the class struggle will have ended. Then, cooperation among the different elements of production will arise, so there will be an equal sharing of the goods produced»[524].

522 [*Quadragesimo Anno* § 59.]
523 [Pius XII, *Radio Message Oggi al Compiersi on the Fifth Anniversary of the Beginning of the War* § 27.]
524 Núñez, *op. cit.*, p. 79.

«For if the class struggle abstains from enmities and mutual hatred, it gradually changes into an honest discussion of differences founded on a desire for justice, and if this is not that blessed social peace which we all seek, it can and ought to be the point of departure from which to move forward to the mutual cooperation of the Industries and Professions»[525].

«[T]he means of saving the world of today from the lamentable ruin into which a moral liberalism has plunged us, are neither the class-struggle nor terror, nor yet the autocratic abuse of State power, but rather the infusion of social justice and the sentiment of Christian love into the social-economic order»[526].

7.6. TO ACHIEVE THE COMMON GOOD AND TO SEEK NATIONAL GREATNESS

The trade union is not an instrument for a class dictatorship: its purpose is the

common good: justice for all social classes and for all nations of the earth. To this end the trade union's action takes on new nobility and acquires another motive for the sacrifices of its leaders and members: to contribute to creating a new world, not only for the workers but for the whole of society.

The trade union will therefore refrain from actions that undermine the normal development of national life. An increase in wages that may result in the bankruptcy of a company will be an injury to the national life, unless it can be remedied by other means. The welfare of the worker is the first concern of the trade union, but should not be sought apart from the national framework of which it forms part. The aims of a healthy trade unionism must not stop at the national borders, but must reach to the reconstruction of the whole world. Misery anywhere in the world endangers the stability of all nations. The social problem, as it is today, is an international problem. No national solutions will suffice to remedy it. There must be international associations aimed at obtaining for all wage earners in the world the well-being demanded by human dignity. To this end, trade union collaboration is required at the international level, beginning with those countries that are more closely related to our own or have similar conditions of life.

This international cooperation cannot in any case be a threat to the life and independence of each nation. Unions cannot be traitors to their homeland: they must help with the redemption of the world's proletariat, but safeguard national

525 [*Quadragesimo Anno* § 114.]
526 [*Divini Redemptoris* § 32.]

independence. This is to condemn energetically the attitude of those union agents who do not hesitate to destroy national industry so as to create a climate of disruption that facilitates revolt and Marxist domination of the nation. Before supporting an international movement we must know the ideology of its leaders.

To facilitate this international partnership, a trade union will support the International Labor Organization, which seeks to achieve humane living conditions in the countries where workers have joined it. Trade unions must effectively ensure that their representatives are able to convey the views and the real conditions of the workers in their countries to the International Office.

8
Relations of the Trade Unionism with other Societies

A trade union is called to have a well-defined attitude towards the State, politics, the Church and international movements.

8.1. THE TRADE UNION AND THE STATE

The State and the trade union movement are called upon to cooperate for the common good, respecting each other's freedom. The right to join a trade union is born ultimately not of the will of the State, but of the natural right that men have to associate. This right, therefore, cannot be ignored by the State, nor restricted in a way that makes it illusory. The State has the right to regulate it, to expedite its exercise, to monitor its actions so as to avoid the abuses that endanger the public good, and to punish its criminal actions; but in no case may the State absorb trade unions and make them instruments of its policy or permit the survival only of those which yield to its interests, as under totalitarian regimes.

The legitimate interests of the people require that organizations always retain the freedom to criticize and demand a change of conduct by a government that might be subject to the influence of the economic powers. Courageously, trade union leaders must overcome the temptation to surrender to the State in exchange for its support. «More than the favor of the State, it is the heart of citizenship and of the people that must serve as the basis of trade union organizations»[527].

527 Núñez, work cited, p. 67.

8.2. THE TRADE UNION AND POLITICS

An essential feature of trade unions, arising from their strictly economic-social function, is their apoliticism. This feature consists in the complete independence that trade unions must mantain in relation to political parties and to the affairs of electoral politics.

From the moment a trade union binds itself to a political party, it loses its special character in economic affairs and to becomes a group of workers who pursue the triumph of the party in which they believe they will find support for their interests. From this moment the union has to face these alternatives: to obtain the voluntary adhesion of all its members to the sponsored party or to betray the interests of those workers who do not want to adhere to that political party.

Given the impossibility of attaining the first alternative, the way is open for the betrayal of the working classes for the sake of partisan interests. A large number of workers would prefer to remain without the advantages offered by the union rather than covering up the mistakes and compromises that are often a necessary part of political juggling.

The great revolutionary trade unionists understood perfectly well that the politicization of trade unionism would destroy the unity of the proletarian class. Even reformers who have been closer to the political world have not fully sympathized with the fusion of trade unions and politics. Only Marxism and fascism, namely the totalitarianisms, of whatever their color, have wished to unite trade unionism and politics, because for them trade unionism is nothing more than an instrument for the conquest of political power.

A just harmony of trade union and political aspirations could be obtained on the basis of the following principles, adopted by the Chilean Trade Union Association:

I The movement respects the political ideology of all its members and can never employ political or electoral measures.

II The higher leaders of the movement should not be at the same time leaders of a political party, in order to show more clearly the independence of the two movements.

III In campaigns of proletarian redemption carried out by the Association it will ask for the support of all the country's living forces and the political forces that wish to join their campaigns, without implying any commitment on the part of the movement.

The Fr. D. Nuñez in the ABC *of Syndicalism*, explains this point:

> «An essential characteristic that emerges from the strictly economic-social function of the trade unions, is the absence of religious exclusiveness in the trade union movement.
>
> The trade union exists for the worker without distinctions of a religious nature. Every worker, whatever his religious position, has a series of problems that needs to be resolved and satisfied. He is a human being who has to live. From this truth it follows that the union must be open to any man who has a claim before the court of social justice. It cannot serve as an instrument of religious propaganda or for activities of a purely religious nature.
>
> This does not mean that trade unions become materialistic, conceiving man as an animal that needs to be fattened up. Nor does it mean that the trade union movement can dispense with the religious factor as an integral part of the harmonious development of the human person. Religious and moral values must enter into the concept of social welfare that has served as the basis for Christian civilization. The application and strengthening of moral and religious values can and should be a concern of the trade union movement. Actually, what this movement does, in promoting the well-being of the worker, is nothing else but to create the material conditions that make possible the maintenance and realization of moral and religious values worthy of the human person. The trade union movement tends to create a better world where the spirit lives more freely»[528].

9

Three Basic Problems: Freedom to Create Various Trade Unions; Freedom of Unions to Federate; and Free Versus Compulsory Organization

Once the right of workers to join trade unions has been recognized, the following three problems, which are closely related to each other, arise:

1) Does the law recognize the legal advantages accorded to a single association, which we might call privileged or unique, or does it recognize equal rights for the different unions that are formed within the same occupation or similar occupations?

528 Núñez, work cited, p. 72.

In other words, should workers who wish to enjoy the advantages of a trade union organization necessarily join a single association whatever its dominant ideology or the nature of its activities or may they establish several associations with equal rights?

2) Can these associations be federated within the same industry and occupation and confederate with other organized groups of workers, both within the country and within other countries?

3) Are workers free to join the trade union or must they necessarily be a member of it? Is trade unionism free or compulsory?

The defense of trade union interests requires a coordinated response to these three questions.

9.1. TRADE UNION UNITY OR PLURALITY

358 Faced with the first of the three problems raised above, we consider preferable, in theory, the principle of trade-union plurality, for the following reasons:

a) Because it gives wider respects to the right of association of the worker: it recognizes every human being's right to be part of any association that does not contradict the common good.

b) Because it fits better the principles of a healthy democracy respectful of the fundamental freedoms of the human being. For this reason the United Nations' Universal Declaration of Human Rights recognizes in Article 23, IV: «Everyone has the right to form and to join trade unions for the protection of his interests»[529].

c) Because no one can be forced to join a private association whose principles or actions seem incompatible with his; still less can he be compelled to participate, by his actions or through his membership fees, in activities that his conscience rejects.

d) Looking at the problem from the point of view of the socio-economic interests of the working class, the plurality of unions protects them more broadly: in a single association the energies of the components are directed primarily, and sometimes only towards obtaining political or personal dominance and to the neglect of strictly trade union activities.

529 [Universal Declaration of Human Rights, G.A. Res. 217 (III) A, U.N. Doc. A/Res/217(III)(Dec. 10, 1948), http://www.un.org/en/universal-declaration-human-rights/index.html.]

On the other hand, the competition of different organizations in the trade union field forces them to surpass their usual efforts for the benefit of the worker, which does not happen when there is only one trade union with full rights.

Associations gain in strength when their elements are homogeneous: when they are united by a common mystique and are not forced to consume much of their energies in internal disputes of an ideological type.

e) The single trade union is the formula adopted by all totalitarian countries or strongly centralized governments; such is or was the case of Russia, fascist Italy, Nazi Germany and Spain. This was the case in France and Belgium, under German occupation. The trade union in such cases is not an organ of free expression for the worker, nor an instrument for the legitimate defense of his social and economic interests, but the framework within which the working forces are held so as to receive the directives of the State in order that they may achieve a greater level of production and obtain a common ideology. In these countries, petitions are prohibited and, even more so, strikes.

In some Latin American countries, such as ours, union unification was adopted at the request of the employers' representatives to avoid the strength of the large occupational unions and in the hope that the employer's personal contacts with his workers would lessen the union's force.

Most democratic countries have preferred the formula of freedom of association: the United States, Canada, Switzerland, Holland, England, Germany before the war, France and Belgium before and after the German occupation.

f) The experience of Chilean trade-union life has shown all too clearly that most of the energies of our trade unions have been consumed by struggles for political dominance, and that too often the uncontrolled pressures of the boldest have imposed slogans which were rejected in their hearts by the majority of the workers, who have unfortunately been unable to defend their points of view owing to lack of proper preparation or owing to lack of necessary political experience that others possess to a high degree. The single trade union is always exposed to permanent manipulation and interventions by the right, the left or the government to the detriment of trade-union interests, the dignity of the worker or his freedom of conscience. Legislation allowing plurality, even in cases in which multiple trade unions have not been formed, always leaves a door open to a greater understanding owing to the fear of a schism that would divide forces.

g) The need to multiply the training possibilities for authentic trade union leaders is best satisfied within multiple trade unionism, which offers opportunities for more workers to have more direct contact with industry problems and enables them to gain managerial experience. The real reforms of the company that will de-proletarianize the worker will not be possible until there is a large group of workers capable of preparing to participate in the management of the company.

9.2. INTERNATIONAL NORMS ON FREE TRADE UNIONISM

The International Labor Conferences of 1947 and 1948, the International Labor Office and the United Nations Economic and Social Council have collaborated to adopt interesting international norms recognizing free trade unionism and the right of trade unions to federate.

Such norms were promoted by the World Federation of Trade Unions (WFTU), which proposed the following draft resolution:

«1. Trade Union Rights are recognized as an inviolable prerogative enjoyed by salaried workers for the protection of their professional and social interests.

2. Trade union organizations should be able to administer their own affairs, to deliberate and freely decide on all questions falling within their competence, in conformity with the law and with their constitution, without interference in their duties from governmental or administrative bodies.

3. There should be no obstacle to the federation of trade union organizations on the occupational or inter-occupational level, whether locally, regionally, nationally or internationally.

4. All legislation which places restrictions on the above-mentioned principles that are stated is contrary to the economic and social collaboration laid down by the Charter of the United Nations»[530].

In turn, the American Federation of Labor presented to the United Nations Economic and Social Council the following questionnaire:

1. To what extent do trade unions have the right to form professional or trade union organizations, to associate or to organize freely, without government intervention or coercion?

530 [The resolution proposed by the WFTU is contained in the following document of the Economic and Social Council of the United Nations, dated November 12, 1947: Second Session of the Commission on Human Rights, Trade Union Rights (Freedom of Association), Memorandum by the Division of Human Rights, section B. https://digitallibrary.un.org/record/561105/files/E_CN.4_31-EN.pdf.]

2. To what extent do trade unions have the freedom to carry out the decisions taken by their members at the national, regional or local level, without the intervention of public authorities?

3. To what extent are workers free to choose, to elect or to appoint representatives in their own unions?

4. To what extent do trade unions have freedom, without having to submit to government intervention, to raise funds and dispose of them in accordance with their statutes or according to the express agreement of their members?

5. To what extent are workers or their groups free to consult with other workers or other groups in their own countries or abroad?

6. To what extent can unionized workers belonging to local, regional or national organizations affiliate with international organizations, without having to suffer the intervention of public authorities?

7. To what extent can professional or trade-union organizations conduct discussions in full freedom with the employers of the workers they represent, enter into collective-bargaining agreements, and take part in their preparation?

8. To what extent is the right of workers and their organizations to strike recognized and protected?

9. To what extent are wage earners and their unions free to resort to voluntary arbitration to resolve a labor dispute, without fear that public authorities will influence or dictate its resolution?

10. To what extent are workers and their organizations entitled to request the government to take legislative or administrative measures in their interest?

The International Labor Office, by mandate of the Economic and Social Council of the United Nations, raised the issue of freedom of association at the Geneva Conference of 1947, securing agreements which were summarized in the following vote adopted by the General Assembly of the United Nations when it met in New York in November, 1947, by 45 votes to 6, with 2 abstentions:

> «The General Assembly considers that freedom of association is an inalienable right as well as other social guarantees essential for the improvement of workers' lives and economic well-being».

At the International Labor Conference in San Francisco, 1948, the declaration was supplemented by agreements on the following:

Article 2 of the Freedom of Association Convention. «Workers and employers, without distinction whatsoever, shall have the right to establish and, subject only to the rules of the organisation concerned, to join organisations of their own choosing without previous authorization»[531].

Scope of the agreement: 1) states that ratify it should refrain from contesting this right of the workers, either directly or indirectly; 2) no discrimination can be made as to trade-union matters; 3) it authorizes the organization of and membership in unions created for professional or political purposes.

Articles 3 of the Freedom of Association Convention:

Article 3

«1. Workers' and employers' organisations shall have the right to draw up their constitutions and rules, to elect their representatives in full freedom, to organise their administration and activities and to formulate their programs.

2. The public authorities shall refrain from any interference which would restrict this right or impede the lawful exercise thereof».

Article 4

Workers' and employers' organisations shall not be liable to be dissolved or suspended by administrative authority.

Article 5

Workers' and employers' organisations shall have the right to establish and join federations and confederations and any such organisation, federation or confederation shall have the right to affiliate with international organisations of workers and employers.

Article 6

The provisions of Articles 2, 3 and 4 hereof apply to federations and confederations of workers' and employers' organizations.

531 [Convention Concerning Freedom of Association and Protection of the Right to Organize (entry into force: Jul 4, 1950), Adoption: San Francisco, 31st ILC session (July 9, 1948), http://www.ilo.org/dyn/normlex/en/f?p=NORMLEXPUB:12100:0::NO::P12100_INSTRUMENT_ID:312232.]

Article 7

The acquisition of legal personality by workers' and employers' organisations, federations and confederations shall not be made subject to conditions of such a character as to restrict the application of the provisions of Articles 2, 3 and 4 hereof.

Article 8

In exercising the rights provided for in this Convention workers and employers and their respective organisations, like other persons or organised collectivities, shall respect the law of the land.

The law of the land shall not be such as to impair, nor shall it be so applied as to impair, the guarantees provided for in this Convention.

Article 9

1. The extent to which the guarantees provided for in this Convention shall apply to the armed forces and the police shall be determined by national laws or regulations.

2. In accordance with the principle set forth in paragraph 8 of Article 19 of the Constitution of the International Labour Organisation the ratification of this Convention by any Member shall not be deemed to affect any existing law, award, custom or agreement in virtue of which members of the armed forces or the police enjoy any right guaranteed by this Convention.

Article 10

In this Convention the term organization means any organization of workers or of employers for furthering and defending the interests of workers or of employers.

Article 11

Each Member of the International Labour Organization for which this Convention is in force undertakes to take all necessary and appropriate measures to ensure that workers and employers may exercise freely the right to organize»[532].

532 [*Id.*]

9.3. POSITION OF THE CHURCH TOWARDS TRADE UNION PLURALITY

The Catholic Church has repeated many times that the social problem «is first and foremost a moral and religious issue»[533]; that the end of working men's associations is «to furnish the best and most suitable means for attaining what is aimed at, that is to say, for helping each individual member to better his condition to the utmost in body, soul, and property. It is clear that they must pay special and chief attention to the duties of religion and morality, and that social betterment should have this chiefly in view»[534]. This same norm has been repeated by the Congregation of the Sacred Council in the controversy of Roubaix-Tourcoing, by Leo XIII in *Graves de Communi*, by Pius X in *Singulari Quadam*, and by Pius XI in *Quadragesimo Anno*, as can be read in numbers 230, 236 and 249 of *Social Christian Order*. «This is precisely the reason why we have never exhorted Catholics to enter into associations intended to improve the conditions of the people, or to undertake similar initiatives without first warning them that such institutions should have religion as an inspiration, partner and support. In any case, even in the temporal order of things, Christianity has no right to neglect supernatural interests; still more, the precepts of the Christian Doctrine impose on it the duty to orient all its work towards the Supreme Good and towards the last end»[535].

Although circumstances have changed greatly since Leo XIII wrote *Rerum Novarum* in 1891, it almost seems that the following paragraph was written in 1950:

> «Associations of every kind, and especially those of working men, are now far more common than heretofore. As regards many of these there is no need at present to inquire whence they spring, what are their objects, or what the means they imply. Now, there is a good deal of evidence in favor of the opinion that many of these societies are in the hands of secret leaders, and are managed on principles ill —according with Christianity and the public well-being; and that they do their utmost to get within their grasp the whole field of labor, and force working men either to join them or to starve. Under these circumstances Christian working men must do one of two things: either join associations in which their religion will be exposed to peril, or form associations

533 *Singulari Quadam.*
534 [*Rerum Novarum* § 57.]
535 [Congregation of the Sacred Council, Letter to Cardinal Liénart § 4, *supra* note 474. (See page 267, discussing this issue. That document cites at this point: «(Leo XIII, *Graves de communi*, 18 Janvier 1901 and Pius X, *Singulari quadam*, 24 September 1912)».]

among themselves and unite their forces so as to shake off courageously the yoke of so unrighteous and intolerable an oppression. No one who does not wish to expose man's chief good to extreme risk will for a moment hesitate to say that the second alternative should by all means be adopted»[536].

Faithful to these principles, Pius X, writing to the Bishops of Brazil on January 6, 1911, exhorts them «to establish among Catholic societies to safeguard interests in the social field». And the Congregation of the Sacred Council in 1929 reiterated that «Catholics should preferentially associate with Catholics unless necessity compels them to act differently»[537].

Pius X laid down rules for German Catholics «tolerating» their presence in non-confessional trade unions as long as they «refrain from everything that in theory or practice is not in accordance with the doctrine and laws of the Church or with her legitimate spiritual authority, and on this subject, nothing observed in their speech, writing or deeds should be unworthy of approval»[538].

Where Catholics cannot form confessional trade unions «because they are prevented by the State or certain practices of economic life, or by that lamentable discord of minds and wills which is so profound in modern society, as well as by the urgency of the need to resist with a union of forces and wills the tight phalanxes of those who devise novelties, Catholics see themselves forced to join neutral trade unions, always provided they intend to respect justice and equity and leave Catholic members free to examine their consciences and obey the Church's commands»[539]. If the Bishops recognize that such associations are necessary in some circumstances and present no danger to religion, they can approve Catholic workers' adherence to such associations, provided that along with these trade unions there are other groups that give their members a serious religious and moral formation.

From what has been said above, the Church's preference for free trade unionism, which best respects the natural right of association and the freedom of conscience of the citizen, flows clearly. That is why Leo XIII states in *Rerum Novarum* that the State or public authority has no right to prohibit the existence of freely formed trade unions:

536 [*Rerum Novarum* § 54.]
537 [Congregation of the Sacred Council, Letter to Cardinal Liénart § 6.]
538 [*Social Christian Order*, item 259.]
539 [There is no indication of the source of this quote.]

«For, to enter into a «society» of this kind is the natural right of man; and the State has for its office to protect natural rights, not to destroy them; and, if it forbids its citizens to form associations, it contradicts the very principle of its own existence, for both they and it exist in virtue of the like principle, namely, the natural tendency of man to dwell in society»[540].

Pius XI, when speaking in *Quadragesimo Anno* of this kind of association, reiterates once again the right to form free trade unions:

«Moreover, just as inhabitants of a town are wont to found associations with the widest diversity of purposes, which each is quite free to join or not, so those engaged in the same industry or profession will combine with one another into associations equally free for purposes connected in some manner with the pursuit of the calling itself... People are quite free not only to found such associations, which are a matter of private order and private right, but also in respect to them "freely to adopt the organization and the rules which they judge most appropriate to achieve their purpose"[541]. The same freedom must be asserted for founding associations that go beyond the boundaries of individual callings»[542].

Pius XI, criticizing Italian corporatism, points to the danger that «the State, instead of confining itself as it ought to the furnishing of necessary and adequate assistance, is substituting itself for free activity»[543].

Finally, the Chilean Episcopate, in a joint letter dated January 12, 1947, maintains that «the trade union must be a body defending legitimate rights of integral improvement and social harmony, with a free character within the organized occupation».

9.4. THE FREEDOM OF TRADE UNIONS TO FORM FEDERATIONS

At the beginning of this chapter we pointed to the right of citizens to form various trade unions and the power of trade unions to form federations within the confines of an occupation or industry as well as confederations of a national

540 [*Rerum Novarum* § 51.]
541 [The following footnote appears in the Encyclical: «Cf Encyclical, *On the Condition of Workers*, 76».]
542 [*Quadragesimo Anno* § 87.]
543 [*Id.* § 95.]

and even international character. This right cannot be denied by those who accept the principle of freedom of association because its foundation is the same.

However, the working class has been denied, in many cases, the right to federate by those who fear the strength of such federations. The freedom of association that we have defended previously would be a myth if the trade unions could not federate in the broadest sense of the word. The multiplicity of trade unions isolated from one another would expose the working class to the play of divisive maneuvers that would annihilate their power, and would divide those who, not because they have different ideologies, wish to be intimately united in the defense of their economic and social interests. The Church, in *Quadragesimo Anno*, clearly affirms, as we have just seen, the right to form such federations.

9.5. FREE OR COMPULSORY ORGANIZATION

The third problem that we presented at the beginning of this chapter is that of the free or compulsory nature of trade unionism. It cannot be doubted, unless there are special circumstances, that the citizen should not be forced to join a trade union, but such circumstances do exist and if trade unionism is not obligatory, there is a risk that all the gains obtained by them would be jeopardized. In many cases, the employers' pressure had prevented workers from being able to organize, and in others, the employers had threatened to retaliate against trade unions if they did not dissolve.

In sum, we affirm that the rights of the working class are better assured by free trade unionism, provided that trade unions can form federations and confederations as broad as seems necessary and that all workers are guaranteed the right to organize and to do so in the union of their choice.

The suspicions that are sometimes felt in the Chilean working class of multiple trade unionism stem from the fear that such multiplicity, unaccompanied by the right of federation and compulsory unionization, only serves to diminish the trade union's power and to divide the working class. Free unionism, with the guarantees indicated above, does not present such dangers, but rather is a powerful element of unity in diversity that cannot but exist among those who want to make use of their fundamental freedoms.

9.6. THE UNITY OF THE WORKING CLASS

Whatever the form of trade union organization, the proletariat can never lose sight of its need to attend to the unity of the working class.

This cannot be achieved by putting pressure on the consciences and freedoms of the members by forcing them into organizations that are not to their liking, or by imposing on them, sometimes by force and with acts of bullying, certain ideologies: such a unity is serious tyranny and is sometimes worse than the one that they try to shake off, and painfully damages the dignity of the worker.

In order to safeguard the achievements of the working class, unity of action must be obtained, while ensuring within the plurality of organizations the freedom of the individual. The working class must struggle together, but the workers should be free to choose the form of organization of their choice.

The French C.G.T., which has been closely linked in national campaigns with the F.C.C.W. (the French Confederation of Christian Workers), considering the great similarity of their programs for immediate action, has repeatedly proposed a merger with Catholic trade unions. They have always responded: unity yes, uniformity no. To achieve this unity they have organized liaison committees. They might also consider forming confederations that respect the internal independence of their associations.

10

Trade Unions' Means of Action

Trade union action is called to bring about an improvement of the conditions of the wage earner and even a reform of social structures. What means will it have to carry out its purposes? It can use peaceful or violent means: the main example of the first is the collective bargaining agreement; of the second, the strongest instance is the strike.

10.1. PEACEFUL MEANS

Collective-bargaining agreements are the result of an understanding between organized employees and capital about the principal terms of the employment contract.

Collective-bargaining agreements originated in negotiations between employers and workers to end strikes. Both groups realized that it was better to try to understand each other before starting a strike, leaving this as a last resort in case talks failed.

Industrialization, which brings together large populations of workers, and the rise of unionization, have multiplied collective-bargaining agreements. The value of these agreements depends on the strength of contracting occupational groups and on their discipline.

The influence of collective-bargaining agreements in transforming the capitalist regime is great: in the first place, they suppress the painful situations of isolated workers who negotiate helplessly with capital; such agreements modify the operation of the capitalist enterprise, which had been previously subject only to the will of the employer, so that it now is under the control of groups of workers jealous as to compliance with the pacts. Collective-bargaining agreements have led the capitalists to unite their forces to present a united front to organized labor.

Some have placed great hope in collective-bargaining agreements, as if they alone were sufficient to correct the defects of the capitalist regime: confronted with the worker's insecurity, his inequality as against the employer and class antagonism, wide spread collective-bargaining agreements would bring about security, equality and harmony.

Such hopes are not illusory but exaggerated. A job without a contract, or with a contract renewable every week or every month, exposes the worker to dismissal and the employer to a lack of workers. The collective-bargaining agreement, however, covering longer periods of six months or a year, gives greater stability to employment. Its defect is a lack of the elasticity which would permit modifications of the conditions of work, which in periods of economic instability demand constant readjustment. A just wage today may be insufficient three months later. In periods of depression prevalent conditions favor mainly workers because they maintain relatively high salaries that otherwise would tend to descend; on the contrary, in times of prosperity conditions deprive the workers of a constant rise in wages because they have agreed to wages during a time of less prosperity. Perhaps this defect could be avoided by more frequent readjustments. In any case it seems clear that a covenant freely agreed upon by the parties is more effective than a general legal measure, which often lacks the necessary realism.

The collective-bargaining agreement ameliorates the inequality of workers who deal with the employer alone, and even in isolation the agreement creates a «natural coalition;» and it defends the worker against an individual weakness that may tempt him to accept any condition so as not to starve.

The search for better means of production, for a greater rationalization of labor, is stimulated by collective bargaining-agreements: in times of economic depression or strong competition they do not leave the employer the easy resort of reducing the sale prices of their goods by lowering wages. As wages are fixed in advance, the capitalist will have to find other means of reducing cost without affecting wages, which is a great social advantage.

Liberal-minded bosses view collective-bargaining agreements very negatively, because such agreements diminish their absolute dominance in business. They miss the old days during which they could dispose at whim of that which was «exclusively theirs». Revolutionary workers also regard these agreements in a bad light as weakening the spirit of total struggle against the capitalist regime and making it appear acceptable to the workers.

It is a fact in normal times that violent conflicts are greatly diminished by collective-bargaining agreements. In abnormal times, such as during the Great Economic Depression that followed the war of 1914, it was almost impossible to speak of lasting collective bargaining agreements, because the abrupt change of conditions caused disputes and criticisms to arise every day about what had been agreed. But in general, such agreements are a step towards social harmony; and if they contain clauses that prepare for a renewal of social structures, they constitute a very effective weapon of progress.

Trade unionism could also achieve the redemption of the proletarian through other peaceful means, such as by intervening, at least in an advisory role, in official labor and economic organizations.

Pure revolutionary unionism rejected such intervention and it sought to stay away, not only from all politics, but from any approach to the government so as not to weaken revolutionary ardor and to prevent the absorption of unionism into established units and their formulas. Revolutionaries did not want to accommodate themselves to the existing formulas, but to destroy them.

However, subsequently, despite their declarations, they accepted the positions that were offered to them in politics and in government; moreover, they sought and clung to the positions they achieved.

In every organization in which the fate of workers is discussed, in which legislative plans concerning them are studied or economic problems of a national scope are analyzed, organized labor must make its voice heard through delegates chosen by the workers themselves. This should be done in a way that represents the living forces of the country and not by people designated by the executive power of the Republic, which «are supposed» to represent the workers: that would produce really absurd situations, such as when the same person is named on one occasion as representative of the workers and, in the following period, as an employer representative.

10.2. VIOLENT MEANS

The main means is the strike, a real act of war between capital and labor. It requires, if it is to be succesful, a violent demonstration, a complex coordination, a specific tactic: extralegal procedures, sometimes violent, are often used; mediators intervene to stop it. There is an extreme resemblance between strike and war.

Strikes have a political or a unionist character. Their cause is usually excessive duration of work, low salaries, excessively strict discipline, etc. The technique of strikes has changed radically. The first were spontaneous movements provoked by the miserable situations of the workers in certain industries. The lack of unions made understanding among the strikers difficult. The spontaneity of the movements easily led to acts of violence against people and property. Ordinarily they were led by the most impassioned preachers of extremism.

During strikes in former times, sabotage, destruction of the machines, which were blamed for unemployment, and acts of violence against technical workers accused of being «yellow» were frequent.

Trade unionism has greatly changed the nature of strikes. These are not now spontaneous, but carefully organized by the trade union, which studiously develop a detailed tactic to launch it, extend it, terminate it; the trade union pays strikers and organizes pickets to carry out its orders and maintains discipline and defends itself from the «strike-breakers». For these reasons strikes are less violent. They often seem like silent protests, accompanied by parades, declarations, speeches and efforts to influence public opinion, create interest within the government and demonstrate social impact.

On the other hand, there is a general opinion that the capitalist regime is responsible for the workers' situation rather than some specific capitalists, or the invention of this or that machine. This makes acts of violence decrease, but it does contribute to strikes' readily shaping public policy.

Modern strikes are complex. Faced with a workers' organization a strong employers' organization has been formed. In the last century it was not uncommon for an industrialist to rejoice at a strike that made his competitor's situation difficult; nowadays the employer class realizes that all are put at risk by a strike. That is why employers tend to unite in strong associations of farmers, industrialists or mine owners, which, in cases of strikes, can call on economic reserves; in extreme cases they go so far as to implement a lock-out. This procedure consists of responding to a staggered strike that shuts down sections of one or many industries by a total closure that automatically leaves all the workers in that or some other industries without work. The workers have hoped to win a battle in one section by starting a fight in another; the employer defends himself by forestalling the possibility of such a war by total closure.

Among the different forms that strikes take, the simplest is that which paralyzes the work of an isolated industry. Solidarity strikes are motivated not by a demand for improvements but by support for fellow strikers. The staggered strike is characterized by a successive presentation of petitions, first in one sector or industry, so that the strikers can be sustained economically by their comrades who still work: once a victory is obtained, the fight continues in another sector, so resources are not lacking. The slowdown strike consists, as its name implies, not in the cessation of work but in the reduction of its pace so as to force the employer to accept the conditions. Finally, the most intense form of strike is the one that is accompanied by occupation of the factory. This is declared after the workers have come to work, which is paralyzed; nobody leaves his post; ununionized workers are prevented from entering to resume the work. In Italy before the fascist regime, in France in 1936 and even recently, several strikes of this type have been declared. Ordinarily, the employers appeal for government forces to break the strike.

The damages of a strike are great: great in lost wages, diminished production for the country, misery and sometimes hunger in many households, but especially in the climate of bitterness and resentment that they easily leave behind. Trust between employers and workers declines; the discipline of work is relaxed; if the strike is lost, the ascension of the working class is delayed. Acts of sabotage and violence are possible on both sides. In spite of everything, there are times when there is no other way to obtain justice.

10.3. IS THE STRIKE LEGITIMATE?

The strike itself is not intrinsically bad. It is a means of pressure that can be legitimate.

Trade union leaders must first consider whether a strike is prohibited by a just law, as it would be in time of war or owing to the serious damage it would cause to the common good, or prohibited by a previous agreement freely entered into by the parties, for example, in an enforceable collective-bargaining contract.

If such a prohibition does not exist, those promoting a strike should consider the goods that are certain or seriously likely to be obtained. Remember that it is not licit to cause serious harm for futile and illusory reasons: compare the benefits that can be obtained with the real damages that the strike may cause. Thus, a strike that would endanger the security of the nation or lead the country into chaos would not be licit. Then consider whether there is a real probability of success, because it would be criminal to bring hunger to many homes and then leave them in an even more miserable situation. Be careful to attempt all peaceful means before resorting to a strike. If all these conditions are satisfied, the strike is legitimate. In such a case the worker can and in some circumstances must participate in order to fight for a more dignified life for himself or for his co-workers.

The means employed during the strike must show the workers' awareness and responsibility. Any unjust or false accusation, even any exaggeration which departs from the strict truth, all provocation to hatred, to revenge, must be avoided. Strikers should be urged to respect authority and its officials. If they are wrong, point out the defects to your superiors, but do not proceed to violence.

Trade unions must exercise extreme caution in electing their strike committees: they must be made up of prudent, experienced, strong-willed men, who have real prestige among the workers and are not corruptible. They should be able to consider the situation of the industry and not allow themselves to be carried away by demagogy and a desire for applause when they draft their petitions, but guided by the common good. In their speeches they should express themselves without hatred, with dignity, so that the justice of their cause becomes clearer and they win the support of public opinion.

What has been said about the strike is also valid for the lock-out. Let the employers meditate on these principles before declaring the closure of a factory, which is a serious evil.

The statements of the French Episcopate on the occasion of the great strikes of 1947, and in particular of Cardinal Suhard[544] on that subject, are of real inter-

544 [Emmanuel Célestin Suhard (1874-1949), French Cardinal, Archbishop of Paris, founder of the Mission of France and the Worker-Priest movement, which aimed to bring priesthood closer to the people.]

est. These statements are the best illustration of the right to strike. When the country was in extreme agitation, they were read in the French parliament and listened to by all parliamentarians with the utmost respect[545].

«In the presence of serious and threatening events for the life of the Nation, which are taking place at the present time, the Archbishop of Paris deems it his duty to make his voice heard.

For some days, the strikes continue to multiply, especially in the Paris region. Their breadth puts at stake the very life of the Nation: for each household, life becomes even more difficult and the working class asks how it will eat tomorrow.

The strike is a real right recognized by our Constitution. One hundred years of history has taught us that it has been the only effective weapon of the workers to make their just claims succeed. At a time when so many wages are clearly insufficient to support a family, it is not surprising that workers in the most diverse categories in the world of work resort to striking. In particular, the Archbishop of Paris wants and must openly say that he regards as legitimate the claims of those who request a minimum living wage, below which a man is not capable of feeding his wife and children. However, we must remember that it is not permissible to use the right to strike with injustice or recklesness, because the strike is a dangerous weapon. That is why it should be used only in the last instance, and it is convenient to leave the assessment of its necessity to the workers themselves with complete freedom.

We ask with concern whether in the present conflicts this is always the case.

We wholeheartedly hope that these strikes, that are new blows to our national economy and terrible obstacles to the way towards recovery, will cease. But we wish, just as strongly, that the just demands of the workers be heard and we ardently ask those responsible to spare no effort to satisfy them.

The Archbishop of Paris appeals to the good sense and the spirit of solidarity of all, whether believers or not, and reminds Catholics that they must be the first to understand the urgency of social problems and must try everything to solve them. For in this matter, they will know how to accept, with generous hearts, the sacrifices demanded by social justice and the general interest. Let them meditate on St. Paul's command: "Help one another to bear your burden, and thus you will have fulfilled the Law of Christ". [Gal. 6:2]»[546].

545 Paris, November 24, 1947.

546 Cardinal Suhard, Bishop of Paris.

Following this statement, the Assembly of Cardinals and Archbishops of France declared,

> «At the time of the strikes of last November, the Bishops of France were unanimous in expressing their sympathy for workers who were disoriented and wounded by the passions unleashed on that occasion. Knowing of the daily suffering of the working classes in a directed economy, they have affirmed that it is a right for every family to find in the remuneration of their labor enough to decently secure their food and life»[547].

10.4. CONCILIATION AND ARBITRATION

These are excellent means for resolving conflicts, so long as the arbitrators deserve and have the confidence of both parties.

Attempts to reconcile will begin before the strike has been declared and will be resumed when they bring a hope of success. Arbitration has no other sanction than that of public opinion, which disapproves of anyone who does not submit to it. It is very difficult to effectively punish those who violate it. Compulsory arbitration can be provided for by agreement, the breach of which would lead to a public complaint, but it is not possible to go further.

11 *Corporative Association*

An occupation is natural society formed by all the people who engage in a coherent set of activities directed to the satisfaction of a stable need of the community. In the same occupation are employers, technical workers, salaried employees and workmen.

Today, we only have to look at the occupational field to realize that it is totally disorganized, lacks a competent authority and a legislative framework to orient activities to the common good. Pius XI in *Quadragesimo Anno* made the corporative association one of the fundamental pillars of the new social order.

Trade unions could be the first elements used for corporative organization. In fact, they are organizations sharing some common interests, and offering the advantage of bringing together different elements as parts of the association.

547 (March 4, 1948.)

Parallel trade unions could be coordinated under a superior authority to pursue the common good of the corporative association.

11.1. THE CORPORATIVE ASSOCIATION'S CHARACTERISTICS

A corporative association is a unitary occupational society; that is one integrated by all who participate in the same occupation or activity regardless of the social class to which they belong. It is mandatory, as membership is required and exclusive for all of the same occupation.

It is a public-law entity with respect to the State but autonomous as to all matters relating to the occupation.

Its end is the common good of the corporative association, and therefore it is called to coordinate the class interests within the occupation, to discipline economic relations within it, and to protect the rights of the occupation in the society.

As for its authority, it would be constituted by representatives of the different constituents.

There will be as many corporative associations as there are branches of economic activities existing in each country.

The ideological pluralism reflected in parallel trade unions will also be reflected in the corporative associations, proportionally to the number of members that each trade union has. This is the consequence of the Catholic formula: free trade unionism means organized corporative association.

Authority within the occupation consists of a joint council, which represents the interests of the social classes and reflects the different tendencies of the various unions in each sector. This council is chaired by a person that is neutral with regard to the interests of the parties. The corporative council will issue regulations, impose sanctions, administer the assets, and require contributions by members of the occupation. It will also arbitrate labor disputes and represent the interests of the occupation, in relation to other occupations, before the State.

11.2. MISSION OF THE CORPORATIVE ASSOCIATION

The corporative association is called upon to exercise the *social function* of harmonizing the different interests of the classes that work together in the same occupation. In addition to the contact between employers and workers, which ameliorates many difficulties, the corporative association will offer necessary social services, the regulation of working conditions, the resolution of conflicts and the provision of those social services which are appropriate to the occupational field, such as social security and social assistance, professional education, etc.

The corporative association has an *economic function* which consist of the organization of production and the regulation of prices and exchange. Free competition and capitalist hegemony would thus be subject to a higher standard based on justice and charity. The State would withdraw from functions which involve dangerous interventions. The *political function* of corporative associations would be to represent the rights of the occupation in society and contribute to the government of the State.

The threefold mission of the corporative association that we just reviewed must be legally recognized by the State, which will defend its rights and coordinate its activities.

The corporative association may not carry out its mission if it is not imbued with a deep moral sense that puts the dignity of the human person first and places social justice and charity at his service. The corporative association cannot be satisfied with immediate temporary achievements, unless it has transformed the purpose of the occupation and reestablished social solidarity.

In modern times, corporative arrangements have been attempted in Italy and Portugal under regimes with strong centralized administrations. In Italy, the corporative association was not an autonomous entity but it was directly subjected to the State, as was the trade union that served as its foundation. Referring to the Italian corporative association, Pius XI said that «some who fear that the State, instead of confining itself as it ought to the furnishing of necessary and adequate assistance, is substituting itself for free activity; that the new syndical and corporative order savors too much of an involved and political system of administration; and that (in spite of those more general advantages mentioned above, which are of course fully admitted) it rather serves particular political ends than leads to the reconstruction and promotion of a better social order»[548].

Portuguese corporatism is based on union associations of employers and workers and affords greater freedom than the now-extinct Italian regime.

In some other countries there are corporative arrangements being developed and some have already dissappeared, such as those devised in Austria and Poland.

548 [*Quadragesimo Anno* § 95.]

Chapter 14

Private Property

1

The Notion of Private Property

Social doctrines reach a point of great antagonism when they address the problem of private property. Let us begin with a definition of «property right» which is in line with the Christian thesis that we are going to develop later: it is the right to enjoy, use and consume, consistently with reason, some economic good. We call limited useful material things «economic goods» or «wealth»; distinguishing them from non-economic or unlimited goods such as air and space.

Roman law spoke of *ius utendi et abutendi.* Ordinarily the word *abutendi* has been misunderstood, as synonymous with abuse, and in fact that is the meaning that the proponents of unlimited property have in fact wished to give it. However, the word *abutendi* means total consumption, which is what occurs with consumer goods such as comestibles.

2

Various Forms of Property

The study of social institutions and legislations shows the multiplicity and complexity of forms of property. As Pius XI states, «history proves ownership, like other elements of social life, to be not absolutely unchanging, We once declared as follows: "What divers forms has property had, from that primitive form among rude and savage peoples, which may be observed in some places even in our time, to the form of possession in the patriarchal age; and so further to the various forms under tyranny (We are using the word tyranny in its classical sense); and then through the feudal and monarchial forms down to the various types which are to be found in more recent times"»[549]. The Quiritarian law of the Romans[550], and the one established by the Napoleonic Code assigned a very indi-

549 [*Quadragesimo Anno* § 49. The encyclical here has a footnote as follows: «Encyclical, *On the Condition of Workers*, 14».]

550 [The *Quiritarian Law* defined ownership (*dominium*) as an absolute: a man is either the owner of a thing or he is not. This ancient law defined different methods and titles that allowed Roman citizens to acquire Roman property. Later, ownership split: one person could be the owner (*dominus*) of a thing *ex jure Quiritium*, and another might have the thing *in bonis* (*Bonitarian ownership*), giving him an equitable title.]

vidualistic character to property. Feudal property was characterized by the reciprocal coexistence and limitation of the rights of lords and vassals. The notion of property is diminished in limited liability entities in which the owners have lost control of management and lack responsibility, and only the production of goods for consumption is emphasized. Private property exists along with public property, as in the time of the Incas, in Egyptian collectivism or in modern nationalized industries.

In our present civilization different forms of property coexist: agricultural property, that in some places is very familial, whereas in others it is more individual; the crafts and the capitalist enterprise; state monopoly or state ownership; nationalized property—of which it has been paradoxically said that it is a company without an owner; easements; literary or artistic property, etc.

Hence, the existence of several great forms of property through all ages can be deduced:

- Property which is private and personal;
- Property which is private and familial, which remains undivided among members of the same family;
- Property which is private and communal, such as that of a religious community or a work community;
- Public property, which may be either municipal, national or state property.

To these different regimes must be added that which the sixteenth-century juridical theologians called the State's «political property», that is, the right of control exercised by the public powers over the management and use of private property, taking into consideration the common good.

The combinations of these different types of property give each regime its original character, according to the modalities that predominate. These are closely related to the evolution of techniques of production and circulation, to labor regimes and to the way of life that prevails within a group at a given time.

> «From the above, the relative and analogical nature of the concept of property is revealed according to historical circumstances and geographical areas. This concept is neither univocal, nor equivocal, but analogous. It contains permanent and essential elements, mainly the power of management and disposition, but it has different nuances depending on the social context in which it is found. The abstract and general concept of property is applied to realities so different that it can lead to misunderstandings, which have not been lacking. This concept must therefore be considered as

a necessary instrument, but its use, in order not to be dangerous, requires precautions, and above all, precision»[551].

3 *Doctrines about Property*

In speaking of social doctrines, the points of view of different schools on the social problem have been indicated, and greatly affect their concepts of property. Here we will briefly summarize these ideas.

The *individualistic* doctrine perceives property as an exclusive right or as predominantly individual. The owner can use the property at his own discretion and for his exclusive benefit. It is not necessary to take into account moral norms in the use of goods. The intervention of the State must be reduced to a minimum and restricted almost exclusively to laws about general public policies. Collective and State property are only allowed in rare instances of strict necessity. This doctrine, much in vogue since the French Revolution, has been the soul of modern capitalism and is largely responsible for the excessive concentration of wealth, for pauperism and class struggle.

The *collectivist* doctrine goes to the opposite extreme, because it perceives property only in its social function and not in its individual one. Goods must be attributed to the community: this is the only way to avoid injustice, inequality and the existence of social classes, which must be abolished.

Leaving aside the purely theoretical systems —utopian ones such as those of Plato, Morus, Campanella and Saint Simon— collectivism had many expressions in contemporary times: anarchists like Bakunin and Kropotkin desire all means of production to be collectively owned and not owned by the State, which must disappear, but by local municipal or free associations. Marxist communists, with different shades in the doctrines of Marx and Engels, of Lenin, Trotsky and Stalin, desire the means of production to be collective, owned by the State, the sole organizer of the production and distribution of the goods produced. Consumer goods are handed over to private property. *Socialism*, in many of its forms, aspires not to collectivization but to nationalization of the most powerful companies, and to the public management of the main social activities. *Agrarian so-*

551 *Notes Doctrinales à l'usage des prêtres du Ministère*, written by the Priestly Committee of the Archbishopric of Lyon, 1951 N 23, p.190.

cialism, advocated by Henry George[552], desires the land to become collective property by expropriation or seizure through heavy taxes.

4
The Catholic Doctrine of Property

The Catholic doctrine of property has a great richness of nuance and reconciles the demands of the individual with the social function without being a compromise between extremes. It has very unique characteristics and is based on the very nature of economic goods and of the human person and society, on the notion of personal good and of common good. We will analyze its theoretical foundation, immediate bases, characteristics and limitations.

4.1. THE FOUNDATIONS OF PROPERTY RIGHTS

Positive law bases its authority on natural law. We must go beyond history and sociology to find the principles of natural law and morality. Once these principles are found, they receive their clarity from the light of the Gospel.

The Fathers of the Church, recalling the natural right of property and the prohibition of robbery, have insisted on the fact that, strictly speaking, there is only one owner: God the creator and governor of the world, who has entrusted the earth not to this or that person, but to all men. In this perspective the owner does not appear as an absolute master who can use his property capriciously, but as a custodian, a trustee for God, in charge of administering, for the good of all, what God has entrusted to him. For this reason the Fathers of the Church have vehemently insisted on the duties accompanying private property and have strongly denounced the selfish use of the goods of the earth. Pius XI makes this doctrine his own when he says, «[t]he rich should not place their happiness in things of earth nor spend their best efforts in the acquisition of them. Rather, considering themselves only as stewards of their earthly goods, let them be mindful of the account they must render of them to their Lord and Master, and value them as precious means that God has put into their hands for doing good»[553].

552 [Henry George (1839-1897), American journalist and economist, author of *Progress and Poverty* (1879). George advocated land reform which would have made land common property.]

553 [*Divini Redemptoris* § 44.]

The scholastics who have commented on the thinking of the Fathers and have integrated it into their philosophical synthesis are divided into two tendencies. For the Franciscan school, property derives from original sin: once human nature was wounded by hardness and selfishness, it became necessary to create property rights in order to obtain an appropriate administration of goods, but this has occurred «*propter duritiam cordis*», because of the hardening of the human heart. The doctrine of St. Thomas is more social and more humanistic. It is based on the distinction between the administration of goods and their use: private administration and common use[554].

> «The private administration of property is the best condition for the common good, because the coincidence among law, duty and interest ensures the good administration of wealth, and, by stabilizing society, also ensures social peace. The use of wealth reestablishes the necessary community by bringing goods back into the universal circuit by commercial exchanges, by liberality, by the virtues of great lords and by alms. Almsgiving is an *obligation* of charity: it is an absolute duty of every owner to deposit his wealth in the lap of the poor once his legitimate needs are met, both essential needs and those that correspond to the specific situation in which he finds himself: *necessarium vitae, et necessarium personae.*
>
> For those who follow St. Thomas, property is linked not to natural law itself, but to *ius gentium*, which is derived from natural law: namely from the great principles of natural law completed, specified and applied by reasoning, social experience and positive law. This means that property rights are respectable like all other rights, and that they have nothing particularly sacred about them; in case of conflict, property rights must bow to prior and higher rights, starting with the right to life on which they are based, because property is not, after all, anything but a means to protect individuals and groups. This clearly appears in the case of *extreme necessity*, foreseen by the whole theological tradition: property rights dissapear in the face of the right to life»[555].

The Thomist argument had its point of departure in an agricultural and artisanal society in which there was neither machinery nor a concentration of capital, so the argument can be applied only with considerable difficulty to certain contemporary circumstances which raise new issues: for example, the large industry.

554 S. Th. II-II, q. 66.
555 Priest Committee of Lyon, ib. [See footnote 551.]

Recent Popes, in their encyclicals and messages, have added important complements to traditional thinking. Leo XIII in his encyclical *Rerum Novarum*, bases property rights on a consideration of the human person. Private property is legitimate because it emanates from the person who, with his work, leaves his mark on wealth. Then the Pope adds: private property is also legitimate because it exists for the person. On the one hand, it derives from the intelligent and free character of the person, who must anticipate his needs; what he gets by work and savings flows into property. In addition, private property guarantees the person's freedom, surrounding him with a zone of security that protects him against the abuses of other people, groups or the State. Private property also guarantees the freedom and security of the family, thus satisfying the most intimate desires of the father[556].

4.2. THE DIVINE SANCTION

Private property, within the limits that constitute it, is inviolable, because it is sanctioned by the law of God, which prohibits us from stealing and even coveting the property of others.

Private property is therefore based on natural law in the sense indicated above, is socially useful and is recognized by divine law. This is why Catholic social morality defends it with zeal.

4.3. THE FUNCTIONS OF PRIVATE PROPERTY

Defending private property does not mean, in any way, to speak of «the Supreme Pontiff, and even the Church herself, as if she had taken and were still taking the part of the rich against the non-owning workers»:[557] that would be to misunderstand the full character of private property and its mission.

Pius XI has clearly taught, and before him Leo XIII and St. Thomas, that property has two functions: an individual and a social one.

556 [Hurtado here includes the following fragment: «Here are some texts of the Roman Pontiffs in which they propose these arguments». Then Hurtado directs one to cut and paste some portions of his book *Social Christian Order*, which include the following Papal documents that refer to private property: *Rerum Novarum* §§ 5 -15, *Radio Message Oggi al Compiersi on the Fifth Anniversary of the Beginning of the War*, and Christmas Message of 1942. The editors could not determine which parts were to be copied and so decided only to mention them here and not to include them in the text.]

557 [*Quadragesimo Anno* § 44.]

Property, in its *individual function*, must serve the development of the person of the owner and the members of his family, in order to enable them to satisfy their immediate needs and the creation of a family estate to provide for family freedom and stability. For this function to be fulfilled, the owner must manage his assets with prudence, spend them with temperance and sobriety, and distribute them equally among the members of his family according to their needs.

In its *social function*, property must serve the common good, which is done first by its own existence, which provides social benefits by ensuring the freedom of individuals, the autonomy of families and greater productivity and involvement in economic and social life; but it must also serve the common good directly.

This service to the common good is realized, according to St. Thomas, when the owner *uses as common* the goods he owns:

> «Two things are competent to man in respect of exterior things. One is the power to procure and dispense them, and in this regard it is lawful for man to possess property [...] The second thing that is competent to man with regard to external things is their use. In this respect man ought to possess external things, not as his own, but as common, so that, to wit, he is ready to communicate them to others in their need»[558].

This common use of goods consists in making the goods available to those who lack them so that they can meet their needs. Common use affects superfluous goods. We call *necessary goods* ones that are indispensable to maintain the physical and moral life of the owner and his family within a standard of living according to their social situation: these properties can be used exclusively by the owner for himself and his family, except in case of the extreme necessity of an individual or the society. We call *superfluous goods*, those that are left after satisfying the vital and appropriate needs of the owner and his family: these belong to the owner, not by natural law, because they are not indispensable, but by social convenience. Their owner must conduct himself as a simple administrator of these goods for the service of his brothers. These ideas are developed extensively by Leo XIII, Pius XI and Pius XII in several documents, among which we note: *Quadragessimo Anno* 44-48 and *Rerum Novarum* 22.

558 [*Summa Theologica*, IIa-IIae, q. 66, art. 2, corpus.]

4.4. CONCRETE WAYS OF REALIZING THE SOCIAL FUNCTION OF PROPERTY

a) Alms.

The concrete forms of performing this social function are various: *alms*, provided they are given with respect for the poor and proportionally to the needs of the recipient and the capacity of the giver. True almsgiving is a gift to a brother in whom a Christian sees the living image of Christ: if they are given in this spirit, they will not degrade the recipient or the one who gives them. Bestowed in a spirit of faith, alms should be given on one's knees or at least with an attitude of equality, rejoicing that the recipient receives it in a spirit not servile but of healthy dignity. Alms can also be moral: those who put their intelligence, energy and knowledge at the service of others give precious alms no less than those who seek work for the unemployed; those who prevent a youth from committing a crime and those who work to replace an unjust social order with one based on justice confer important social alms.

Alms can never be understood to be a palliative for the nonfulfillment of the duties of justice. When alms multiply, it means that the social machine is not working. It is abnormal and immoral that hundreds and sometimes thousands of healthy men and women should have to beg in order to subsist or to be able to educate their children when they are willing and able to work. In a well constructed society, almsgiving is only conceived of as something totally extraordinary and for those who are in difficulties because of their physical or moral deficiencies. Such people will always exist, and even if the State were to take responsibility for all social evils—which seems very unlikely—it would still be possible to show respectful affection, to console the sad and encourage those who are tired of life. Official almsgiving, in practice at least, is more humiliating because of the lack of tact and discernment with which it is usually done. Almsgiving must always be completed with something that cannot be imposed by law: true love.

Almsgiving, in Christian morality, is *obligatory* for all who have superfluous goods. The distinction between superfluous and necessary goods is not easy to define, but this must be done with Christian honesty. Pope Innocent XI condemned this proposition: «[y]ou will scarcely find among laymen, even kings, things that are superfluous to their states. And so, there is scarcely anyone who is obliged to give alms for the sole reason that goods are superfluous to his state»[559]. In today's world one need only open one's eyes to see the immense quantity of purely superfluous goods that coexist with immense misery.

559 Azpiazu, 145. [Hurtado is referring to Azpiazu's book *Economic Professional Morality*.]

In *extraordinary* circumstances of misery, the obligation to give alms can include the goods necessary for the dignity and maintenance of the rich, but under ordinary circumstances moralists require the giving only of relatively superfluous goods. To what extent this obligation extends, moralists argue at length: Fr. Vermeersch[560] establishes a scale which he constructs by considering income surpluses and family burdens, establishing rates that reach 40% for those who do not have such burdens and much lower percentages for those who have several children. Fr. Azpiazu estimates, as a minimum level of obligatory alms in the current circumstances, 10% of disposable income defined broadly, and this percentage must rise progressively as the amounts of disposable income rise and as the needs of the people increase[561].

We wish that Christians not ask themselves how much they are obligated in the matter of alms, but that they raise the problem of how much they can give without detriment to their other obligations. Almsgiving, the fruit of love, leads to donation with sacrifice, even to total donation. However, the person's sacrifice is less the greater the income he has, because money is not worth the same in different situations; it worth less the more a person has. In order to consider the obligation to give alms, one must also consider the situation of those who have to be attended to: the obligation to give alms to a needy person who is dying of hunger is very grave; and is much greater in circumstances of unemployment, earthquakes, etc. than in normal times. Rich people who live in poor countries have, under similar circumstances, greater obligations than those who live in countries of greater wealth and well-being.

The obligation to give alms belongs to the field of charity and, in a certain sense, to social justice, inasmuch as the rich man is obliged to give back to society the welfare and progress that he possesses and which he owes to society in large part. When saying that alms belong to the field of charity and social justice, one does not affirm in any way that it is only a matter of the Lord's simple advice and not a strict precept. Moralists agree in affirming that the obligation —the grave precept requiring the giving of alms— does not oblige in a particular case, except in extraordinary circumstances. «[T]he Sacred Scriptures and

560 [Arthur Vermeersch, S.J., (1858-1936) Belgian priest, law professor and moral theologian. He taught moral theology and Canon Law at the University of Louvain for more than 25 years. Between 1922 and 1924 he completed his *summa* of moral theology, *Theologiae Moralis Principia, Responsa, Consilia* (*Principles of Moral Theology, Answers, Advice*) and was a contributor to the Catholic Encyclopedia.]

561 Azpiazu, 148. [Hurtado is referring to Azpiazu's book *Economic Professional Morality*.]

the Fathers of the Church constantly declare in the most explicit language that the rich are bound by a very grave precept to practice almsgiving, beneficence, and munificence»[562]. St. Thomas says: «[W]hatever certain people have in superabundance is due, by natural law, to the purpose of succoring the poor»[563]. The well-known classic moralist, Cardinal Cajetan, affirms, «The rich man who does not give what is superfluous, but accumulates it to buy more and more goods, from a mere desire to rise and grow ... sins mortally by using and having superfluous goods that are owed to the poor, for the very reason that they are superfluous»[564].

One cannot speak of an obligation of commutative justice, and in this sense it is improper to say that our superfluous goods belong to the poor: if this were so, we would be obliged to give back to them whatever is superfluous, which no moralist has affirmed. The duty of almsgiving is not a right of the poor to the goods themselves, but a personal obligation of the rich.

If such contributions are not sufficient to meet the needs of the poor, the State can, as manager of the common good, establish the amount of superfluous goods which each person must contribute, and that is what is done by taxes, especially progressive ones[565].

> «Christian perfection asks that whoever gives alms, goes beyond the obligation and reaches as far as possible, as long as he does not violate other obligations. That is why, not by duty, but by a sincere aspiration to perfection, he gives everything superfluous and with holy ingenuity, restricts his personal expenses so as to give more. This is the Christian tradition that goes back to the Old Testament, as seen for example in the advice of Tobiah to his son: "Give alms from your possessions. Do not turn your face away from any of the poor, so that God's face will not be turned away from you. Give in proportion to what you own. If you have great wealth, give alms out of your abundance; if you have but little, do not be afraid to give alms even of that little. You will be storing up a goodly treasure for yourself against the day of adversity". [Tob. 4:7-9] This

562 [*Quadragesimo Anno* § 50.]

563 [*Summa Theologica*, IIa-IIae, q. 66, art. 7, corpus.]

564 [At this point Hurtado handwrote something that was not totally legible but which seems to read as follows: «Commentaria in S. Thomam, II-II, q.118 a.4, Edit Antwerp, 1567, volume 2, p. 409- quoted by Azpiazu p.163».]

565 [At this point Hurtado cites a portion of his book *Social Christian Order* that sets out *Quadragesimo Anno* § 49. The editors decided not to copy that section, because it was already copied at least two times previously in this book, see footnotes 248 and 549.]

is the example left us by Christ, who had no place to lay his head; the example of the saints who have had the sublime ambition to give and believed the thought of the Master, who said: "It is more blessed to give than to receive". [Acts 20:35]»[566].

b) Magnificence and Social Justice.

In addition to almsgiving, property fulfills its social function owing to the virtue of magnificence[567], the virtue of the noble souls, who employ their property in great works of public utility: in churches, missions, shelters, schools and universities, road works, scientific discoveries. These works are a source of employment, and allow others to take advantage of the fruits of such works once they are accomplished.

All that contributes to the common good, to the realization of social justice through a more equitable distribution of income, to a better standard of living for the people, to the construction of popular housing, to compensation of funds to establish the family wage, etc.: all of these things are accomplishments of the social function of property.

«Expending larger incomes so that opportunity for gainful work may be abundant, provided, however, that this work is applied to producing really useful goods, ought to be considered, as We deduce from the principles of the Angelic Doctor, an outstanding exemplification of the virtue of munificence[568] and one particularly suited to the needs of the times»[569].

These words of the Pope cannot serve as an excuse for those who think that they fulfill their social obligations by the mere fact of giving jobs. If they have superfluous incomes, they are still obliged to give alms. Also consider that there is no magnificence if they arrange useful jobs for their own benefit and not for the

566 [The source of this quote is is not identified in the manuscript.]

567 [Aristotle's *Nicomachean Ethics*, book VI, chapter 2, refers to Magnificence, Vulgarity, Niggardliness. Saint Thomas Aquinas also explained the virtue of magnificence: «According to De Coelo i, 16, "we speak of virtue in relation to the extreme limit of a thing's power", not as regards the limit of deficiency, but as regards the limit of excess, the very nature of which denotes something great. Wherefore to do something great, whence magnificence takes its name, belongs properly to the very notion of virtue. Hence magnificence denotes a virtue». Saint Thomas Aquinas, *Summa Theologica*, IIa-IIae, q. 134, art. 1, corpus.]

568 [According to the Oxford English Dictionary online-en.oxforddictionaries.com-magnificence is the quality of being magnificent, and munificence is the quality or action of being extremely generous. Translators of *Nicomachean Ethics* have translated that virtue in both ways.]

569 [*Quadragesimo Anno* § 51.]

people. In that case, there will be nothing but utility for themselves. It is a common error to think that the virtue of magnificence is fulfilled by the organization of sumptuous feasts, which have no other justification than the satisfaction of personal vanity and the display of riches and are an echo of other times when social inequality offended less. Such parties are continually discouraged in papal documents, which call for a more sober life. Social ostentation should not be called virtue; therefore it does not fulfill the virtue of magnificence. (Note: *L'Osservatore* Romano protested the scandal of the Festival of Venice...).

5
State Intervention in Private Property

392 «As far as necessity demands it, public authority, taking into consideration the common good, has the right to determine in the light of natural and divine law, what use owners may or may not make of their possessions»[570].

The State's right to intervene in matters of private property flows from its direction of the common good and results in benefits in the private sector, strengthening and preventing its ruin.

The scope of State intervention must be such as to avoid certain extremes:

1) In establishing the property regime, as is within its authority, the State cannot damage the natural right of property or the right to bequeath property: «these are rights which the public authority may not abolish. Nor has it the right to extinguish private property by excessive burdens and taxation»[571].

2) Do not confuse the right of property with its use, nor make it dependent on use. Pius XI clearly warned against this when he said, «[t]he right of property is distinct from its use[572]. That justice called commutative commands sacred respect for the division of possessions and forbids invasion of others' rights through the exceeding of the limits of one's own property; but the duty of owners to use their property only in a right way does not come under this type of justice, but under other virtues, obligations of which "cannot be enforced by legal action"[573]. Therefore, they are in error who assert that ownership and its

570 [*A Code of Social Principles* §96.]
571 [*Id.* §97.]
572 [The following footnote appears in the Encyclical: «Encyclical, *On the Condition of Workers*, 35».]
573 [The following footnote appears in the Encyclical: «Encyclical, *On the Condition of Workers*, 36».]

right use are limited by the same boundaries; and it is much farther still from the truth to hold that a right to property is destroyed or lost by reason of abuse or non-use»[574].

The State has several means to induce the owner to make correct use of his property, such as taxes, without violating his rights. Only when it is evidently required does the public interest imply the right to expropriate the property of those who do not use or abuse it, upon payment of just compensation.

Different Kinds of State Intervention: The State may intervene:

1) *To assure that wealth*, constantly increased by social and economic growth, *be distributed in such a way that common profit remains beneficial to all.* Social justice forbids one class to exclude another from sharing in benefits.

«Hence the class of the wealthy violates this law no less, when, as if free from care on account of its wealth, it thinks it the right order of things for it to get everything and the worker nothing, than does the non-owning working class when, angered deeply at outraged justice and too ready to assert wrongly the one right it is conscious of, it demands for itself everything as if produced by its own hands, and attacks and seeks to abolish, therefore, all property and returns or incomes, of whatever kind they are or whatever the function they perform in human society, that have not been obtained by labor, and for no other reason save that they are of such a nature»[575].

(Pius XII in his speech of September 1, 1944, reinforces these ideas and applies them to the disorders introduced by capitalism. Cf. *Orden Social Cristiano* (*Social Christian Order*) 205, p. 276.)

2) *To multiply the number of owners.*

«Many excellent results will follow from this; and, first of all, property will certainly become more equitably divided. For, the result of civil change and revolution has been to divide cities into two classes separated by a wide chasm. On the one side there is the party which holds power because it holds wealth; which has in its grasp the whole of labor and trade; which manipulates for its own benefit and its own purposes

574 [*Quadragesimo Anno* § 47.]
575 [*Quadragesimo Anno* § 57.]

all the sources of supply, and which is not without influence even in the administration of the commonwealth. On the other side there is the needy and powerless multitude, sick and sore in spirit and ever ready for disturbance. If working people can be encouraged to look forward to obtaining a share in the land, the consequence will be that the gulf between vast wealth and sheer poverty will be bridged over, and the respective classes will be brought nearer to one another. A further consequence will result in the great abundance of the fruits of the earth. Men always work harder and more readily when they work on that which belongs to them; nay, they learn to love the very soil that yields in response to the labor of their hands, not only food to eat, but an abundance of good things for themselves and those that are dear to them. That such a spirit of willing labor would add to the produce of the earth and to the wealth of the community is self evident. And a third advantage would spring from this: men would cling to the country in which they were born, for no one would exchange his country for a foreign land if his own afforded him the means of living a decent and happy life. These three important benefits, however, can be reckoned on only provided that a man's means be not drained and exhausted by excessive taxation. The right to possess private property is derived from nature, not from man; and the State has the right to control its use in the interests of the public good alone, but by no means to absorb it altogether. The State would therefore be unjust and cruel if under the name of taxation it were to deprive the private owner of more than is fair»[576].

This same idea is repeated by Pius XII in his Christmas Message of 1942:

«Those who are familiar with the great Encyclicals of Our predecessors and Our Own previous messages know well that the Church does not hesitate to draw the practical conclusions which are derived from the moral nobility of work, and to give them all the support of her authority. These exigencies include, besides a just wage which covers the needs of the worker and his family, the conservation and perfection of a social order which will make possible an assured, even if modest, private property for all classes of society, which will promote higher education for the children of the working class who are especially endowed with intelligence and good will, will promote the care and the practice of the social spirit in one's immediate neighborhood, in the district, the province, the people and the nation, a spirit which, by smoothing over friction arising from privileges or class interests, removes from the workers the sense

576 [*Rerum Novarum* § 47.]

of isolation through the assuring experience of a genuinely human, and fraternally Christian, solidarity»[577].

3) *To procure material conditions*, such that citizens' individual lives may achieve their complete development:

«Likewise the national economy, as it is the product of the men who work together in the community of the State, has no other end than to secure without interruption the material conditions in which the individual lives of the citizens may fully develop. Where this is secured in a permanent way a people will be in a true sense economically rich because the general well-being and consequently the personal right of all to the use of worldly goods is thus actuated in conformity with the purpose willed by the Creator»[578].

4) *To expropriate*, when public necessity requires it, particular items of property subject to payment of compensation.

5) *To nationalize* some public utility companies.

«By nationalization is meant that an undertaking belongs to the national community, represented by the political power. It may be limited to ownership, or extend to management and profits. It cannot be condemned in principle on grounds of Christian ethics.

Where undertakings already worked by private persons are concerned, their taking over is subject to just compensation.

Nationalization, taken in its widest sense and applied to all industries or the majority of them, amounts by force of circumstances to collectivism, which was condemned by the Encyclical, *Rerum Novarum*.

Nationalization, if applied generally, still runs the risk of arriving at the same result even when limited to mere ownership or management.

Not even a system of more or less self-governing public undertakings would seem to be acceptable, if it includes the majority of undertakings.

Private initiative of individuals or groups can only be limited to the extent that the common good manifestly requires. It is very needful to preserve the two great stimulants to production, viz.: the prospect of acquiring property and lawful competition.

577 [*Christmas Message of 1942.*]
578 [*La Solennità.*]

Considerations of public interest may in particular cases demand or suggest public management, either national, provincial or municipal. In that case, the setting up of autonomous bodies, carrying on industrially under under the control of public authorities and for the benefit of the community, can be recommended in preference to wholly official administration.

It is understood that the right of supervision by the State is to be exercisable when private organizations are entrusted with the maintenance of public services, and whenever the public interest calls for it.

In undertakings which are subject to concessions placed with private organizations, it is desirable that agreements shall contain clauses securing liberty of contract and fair wages to the workpeople, and providing for family allowances.

In case of war, famine, or serious and manifest abuse, the State has not only the right, but the duty to set up a special organization for checking monopoly and usurious speculation in necessary articles of consumption»[579].

6) *To regulate rights of hereditary succession*, which, however legitimate they may be, are subject to the common good.

«The State, therefore, cannot directly or indirectly suppress inheritance, without gravely injuring social interest and attacking the inviolable rights of the family. Nevertheless, it has the right to adapt the degrees of relationship that may inherit to the actual organization of the family.

It is desirable that the State should reduce the duty as much as possible, and even abolish it, in the case of succession in the direct line.

It is, moreover, desirable that testamentary rights should be allowed to the head of the family sufficient to ensure the passing on of small undertakings intact within the family»[580].

7) *To establish maximum limits on agricultural possession.* It should be noted that excessive subdivision, far from increasing production, decreases it. There are maximum limits as well as minimum limits to property holdings. Small property holdings also call for cooperative organization to assist them[581].

579 [*A Code of Social Principles* §§ 103-111.]
580 [*Id.* §§ 101-102.]
581 Cfr. *A Code of Social Principles* § 98.

The Popes fought bravely to end the abuse, in their own domains, of uncultivated large estates. Clement IV, in the thirteenth century, authorized every stranger to cultivate up to one-third of an uncultivated domain. Sixtus IV decreed:

«It shall be permitted in future and for ever, to each and every one, within the territory of Rome and the Patrimony of St. Peter, to cultivate and sow, when convenient and in normal times, uncultivated fields of his choice, whoever the owner might be: a monastery, chapter, church, consecrated place, or a public or a private person of any state or condition —provided permission is requested, even if not obtained»[582].

8) In addition to these specific charges, the State is responsible for the control of economic and public activities required by the common good, such as the legal fixing of the prices for some merchandise, especially when there is a special danger of speculation, but always tending to minimize such interventions so as not to deprive commerce of its private character.

«[T]he State in the field of private property is not a weapon for an unhealthy collectivism, since it does not deny the natural right of private property, but only regulates its use, harmonizing it with the common good: on one hand, it sets the just limits of private property and, on the other hand, it ensures full compliance with its social function»[583].

The State's mission is to foster progressive evolution.

«It is not by revolution but by evolution and concord that salvation and justice are obtained. Violence has never served but to destroy, never to build; it does not calm, but excites the passions; does not reconcile adversary groups, but builds up hatred and destruction. Violence leads men and parties to confront the difficult task of slowly rebuilding, after sad experiences, the ruins of discord. Only by means of a progressive and prudent evolution, with all courage and according to nature, enlightened and guided by Christian laws and equity, can the fulfillment of the desires and needs of the workers be achieved.

582 Valsecchi, o.c. pp. 88-89. [See note 185.]
583 *Id.* p. 93.

Not to destroy them, but to consolidate them. Not to abolish private property, the foundation of family stability, but to work for its extension as a reward for the toil of every worker, man and woman, so that, little by little, the masses of discontented and aggressive beings that at some times, through sullen despair —or at others through rude instinct— let themselves be carried away by false doctrines or by the cunning wiles of agitators devoid of any moral sense.

Not to dissipate private capital, but to promote its regulation, under careful surveillance, as a means and assistance to the achievement and increase of the genuine well-being of the whole people. Not to hinder industry, but instead to grant exclusive preference to it, while striving for a harmonious linkage to small trades and to agriculture, which brings about multiple and necessary production on national lands.

Not only to seek, with the use of technical progress, maximum profits, but to use the advantages they provide to improve the personal conditions of workers, making their work less arduous and difficult, and strenghtening the ties that unite their families in the homes they inhabit and in the work by which they live.

Not to claim that the lives of individuals depend entirely on the whims of the State, but rather to ensure that the State, which has a duty to seek the common good, can, through social institutions like insurance and social security, provide assistance and complement everything that helps to strengthen the associations of workers and, especially, the fathers and mothers of families, who work to earn their own subsistence, on which they depend.

Perhaps you will say that it is a beautiful vision of the true state of things, but how can all this become a reality and a fact in daily life? First of all, great uprightness of will and perfect loyalty to the end and to the action is required for the development and regulation of public life, both by the citizens and by the authorities that govern them. We need a spirit of true concord and fraternity to encourage all: superiors and subjects, employers and workers, great ones and little ones, in all social classes»[584].

584 [*Speech to the Italian Workers.* Translation by the editors from Hurtado's book *Social Christian Order*, item 211, p. 286, comparing it with the Italian version at the Vatican website. See footnote 305.]

6
Legal Titles and Property Acquisition

Property rights, abstract as they are, require legal titles in order to attached themselves to specific property. Legal titles may be *original* when they confer the ownership of something not previously possessed: for example, by *occupation* and *work*; or *derivative*, when ownership is transferred from one owner to another: for example, by prescription, inheritance, contract.

6.1. OCCUPATION

Occupation consists in the taking of visible possession of an economic good that does not belong to anyone with the intention of making it one's own. All properties have begun this way, as can still be observed in a new country in which migrants settle and establish the boundaries of their land. The act of taking possession has to be manifested externally, either by visible signs or by recording in a registry of property. Occupation also implies a certain permanence and activity—at least one that is manifested by care and vigilance— and a minimum of work performed by the occupant or by his or her dependents. Effective occupation is not the foundation of property: that is based on the nature of man and on the other arguments set forth just above, but occupation establishes the specific title of a particular right that can be asserted against others.

6.2. WORK

Besides occupation, work or specification[585] establishes a right over goods that have been transformed by one's own labor: a trunk turned into a statue, stones transformed into buildings, an empty field transformed into agricultural land. In the case of work, a kind of incorporation of the work into the worker's own being is accomplished.

> «Now, when man thus turns the activity of his mind and the strength of his body toward procuring the fruits of nature, by such act he makes his own that portion of nature's field which he cultivates —that portion on which he leaves, as it were, the im-

585 [*Especificación* in Spanish. Hurtado is probaby using the word in the legal sense, according to which it refers to the formation of a new species. (The word in this sense is similar to the word «accession» in American law.).]

press of his personality; and it cannot but be just that he should possess that portion as his very own, and have a right to hold it without any one being justified in violating that right.

So strong and convincing are these arguments that it seems amazing that some should now be setting up anew certain obsolete opinions in opposition to what is here laid down. They assert that it is right for private persons to have the use of the soil and its various fruits, but that it is unjust for any one to possess outright either the land on which he has built or the estate which he has brought under cultivation. But those who deny these rights do not perceive that they are defrauding man of what his own labor has produced. For the soil which is tilled and cultivated with toil and skill utterly changes its condition; it was wild before, now it is fruitful; was barren, but now brings forth in abundance. That which has thus altered and improved the land becomes so truly part of itself as to be in great measure indistinguishable and inseparable from it»[586].

6.3. PRESCRIPTION

Prescription establishes a title derived from dominion by which a person acquires a right of property over an economic good practically abandoned by its previous owner. It requires physical possession of that property for the number of the years that the statute specifies and the intention to hold dominion over the property. The abandonment of the good by the first possessor justifies a presumption that he intended no longer to possess it. Equity demands that those who in good faith occupy and work a piece of property as their own for a long period of time not be deprived of the fruits of their labors. It is, furthermore, the only way to avoid endless litigation.

6.4. INHERITANCE

This consists of the transmission of the ownership of certain property from one person to another upon the death of the first. The intention of the testator can be manifested expressly by a will, or tacitly, by prescription in case of intestate death.

Inheritance is the legitimate consequence of the right of property: a man works not only for himself, but also for his wife and children, or for those persons or institutions to which he wishes to give the legitimate fruit of his labors.

586 [*Rerum Novarum* §§ 9-10.]

The most honorable forms of inheritance are those that occur in the direct line, in which the children and, similarly, the spouse receive the benefits from the efforts of the testator; and thereafter, according to other express testamentary provisions. When the testator does not provide for them, the rights of distant relatives are less clear.

6.5. CONTRACTS

Contracts of sale, donation and exchange represent the agreement of the parties, and are in daily use.

7
Contemporary Evolution of and Options about Forms of Property

Owing to social and economic evolution, people today judge the capitalist and liberal notion of property severely, as too exclusive and as ignoring its social aspect almost entirely.

However State direction or at least economic control, State planning, and union and professional organizations, limit every aspect of the right to property. Taxes, social security or family-allowance systems aim to bring about a redistribution of national income. The separation between the notions and the realities of property grows larger every day.

New forms of property appear, most of them collective, whether publicly owned, such as State-owned companies, or privately owned, such as large capitalist or community companies; or property halfway between private and public, still badly explored in law, such as nationalized companies. The various socialisms tend to suppress at once, as in Russia, or progressively, as in other countries, all private property in the means of production, which leads many people to deny the legitimacy of such private property.

This development is based, on the one hand, on the needs of modern technology. The cost of certain instruments of production, for example of a power plant, surpasses the means of every individual owner and even of any private collectivity. In addition, modern technology's economic importance gives such power to its possessors that they can obstruct the actions of the public powers. The number and importance of large holdings steadily increases, with the consequent diminution of the importance of small private personal property holdings and also of individual responsibility, which appears to be diluted in a collective.

The comparison of principles and facts shows some immediate practical conclusions:

1a) Private property in *consumer goods* is not seriously denied by anyone, not even by socialists. It is legitimate insofar as these goods are the product of work or inheritance and remain subject to the traditional duties of private property which we have set forth above.

The State has a right to control consumer goods and has the authority to make a more equitable distribution in cases of serious need, such as war, crisis, hunger or the existence of a large number of needy people. It also has the right to collect the taxes necessary for the common good.

The State should not suppress opportunities of personal or family savings, but rather should favor and guarantee this kind of savings.

Regarding inheritances, the State has the right to prevent an accumulation of assets that could have harmful social consequences, but it cannot suppress the right of inheritance, especially when it comes to spouses or descendants in the direct line.

2a) Regarding the property in productive assets, it is necessary to distinguish between the following cases:

a) The forms of property that establish an almost complete coordination among the person, the family, the work and the property: for example the craft company, the cultivated family farm, the small commercial enterprise: if these companies present us technical and economic problems, they do not offer moral problems. The traditional notion of property is fully justified. This does not prevent the State from exercising over these companies its right of supervision and control insofar as the common good requires it.

b) The forms of property in which there is a partial coincidence between ownership and work, such as companies that have personal and family capital, are equally legitimate and conducive to the realization of the common good. However, the owner's right is not absolute: it must be combined with the rights of the workers, those who provide funds, and corporative groups and with the right of the State to control and harmonize particular activities, taking into account the common good. The liberal notion of the «master by divine right» —the only master in his company after God— cannot be sustained before the facts or before the law.

c) In the large industrial, capitalist type of company, the notion of property disappears. Theoretically the property belongs to a multitude of shareholders. In fact, these shareholders are uninterested in their rights and the true economic power falls *de facto* upon individuals or groups of people who do not have a real mandate. Here we have a difficult, often insoluble problem that calls for a change of legal structure.

«In legal terms, property belongs to the shareholders and the authority is exercised by the delegates of the general assembly. The head of the company, called the director, is nothing but a salaried employee, sometimes in no way interested in the profits. This conception of property fuels curious paradoxes: suppose a company from the Paris region, with a shareholder residing in Chicago as the co-owner, while a worker who has worked for twenty-five years in it has no property rights. The technical director, who is a specialized man, has to bow to the decisions of some financiers who do not understand anything but the pecuniary interest. It is in this case, above all, that we must rectify the deviations of contemporary capitalism and transform the work contract into an association contract. The economic city should not continue to be exclusively owned by capital that governs as an absolute and irresponsible master, but by all the hierarchical elements of the company: directors, labor and capital»[587].

d) Something similar happens to nationalized companies, whose owner is not strictly the State. In them it can be seen that several rights over the same object coexist: rights that carry with them real and effective responsibilities.

Public authorities have the right to nationalize companies when, owing to their size and importance, they can prevent the State from promoting the common good. Such a case involves a political operation. Such nationalization can also take place when private initiative is not capable of securing the common good. Such a case involves a social decision. In both cases nationalization is not a punishment and must be accompanied by the payment of just compensation to the rightful owners. It should be noted that nationalization does not solve structural problems inside companies and leaves pending as many problems as it solves. Therefore, it cannot be considered a panacea.

587 [Joseph Folliet, *Morale Sociale* (*Social Morality*) (1937), Volume II, Chapter XI, p. 105. The quoted passage was translated by the editors from the French original.]

e) In the State-owned company, the State is both the owner and the head of the company and, therefore, has the duties of every owner and every manager. The nationalization of companies does not appear to be convenient except when it directly concerns the State's function, as is the case, for example, with national defense.

8

General Conclusions

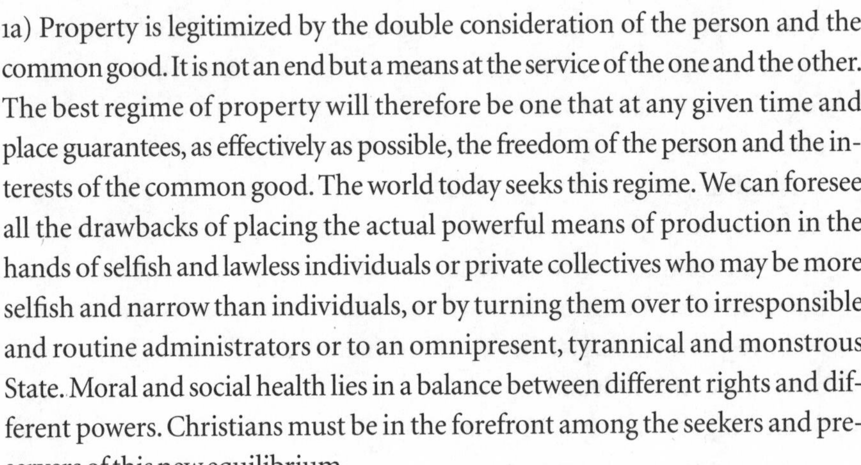

1a) Property is legitimized by the double consideration of the person and the common good. It is not an end but a means at the service of the one and the other. The best regime of property will therefore be one that at any given time and place guarantees, as effectively as possible, the freedom of the person and the interests of the common good. The world today seeks this regime. We can foresee all the drawbacks of placing the actual powerful means of production in the hands of selfish and lawless individuals or private collectives who may be more selfish and narrow than individuals, or by turning them over to irresponsible and routine administrators or to an omnipresent, tyrannical and monstrous State. Moral and social health lies in a balance between different rights and different powers. Christians must be in the forefront among the seekers and preservers of this new equilibrium.

2a) All property is characterized by a certain exclusivity as to its objects, but liberalism transformed this exclusivity into something absolute. It seems necessary to evolve towards a more complete conception of property, to coordinate different rights that are exercised over the same object and are limited by one another: labor rights, capital rights, consumer rights, State rights. This legal agility will allow us to establish institutions that tend towards a new social equilibrium. Principles remain stable, since they correspond to the demands of human nature and divine revelation, but the applications to be made under certain historical circumstances are now in doubt.

3a) The moralist must bear in mind with vigor the Christian ideal: in particular he must insist on the requirements of social justice, equity and charity. Christian morality must be presented to the faithful as a morality of love rather than as a static casuistry or an excessively mechanical legalism.

The moralist will avoid confusing the Christian notion of property, which in its foundations is very simple and according to common sense, with some historical form of property. He will avoid making property the myth that led certain Christians of the last century to put it at the same level as family and homeland, a myth that concealed many hypocrisies and oppressions.

We have all been more or less contaminated by the liberal notion of property. We have to free ourselves of its annoying consequences and fight for the Christian conception of property by which it acts as a safeguard for the person, serves the common good and holds us accountable before God, author of all the wealth of which we are nothing more than administrators and distributors[588].

588 These reflections have been closely followed in the note on property, No. 23 of the Priestly Committee of Lyon. [The author is referring to *Notes Doctrinales à l'usage des prêtres du Ministère.* See footnote 551.]

Chapter 15

Commercial Life

1

Purchase and Sale

A sale consists in the transfer of the ownership of an object through its equivalent payment in money. Commutative justice normalizes these operations and tends to establish an approximate price for the object. This price cannot be more than an approximation, because the variations of the currency, the merchandise available and the cost of production make it impossible to fix an absolute price. A sale supposes good faith on the part of both parties and excludes, of course, fraud either in word or deed: if that exists, there is an obligation to make restitution.

In the case of falsification as to foods, we must distinguish what is sinful and what is criminal. Adulterated oils that can poison a population; products mixed in the flour to make it absorb more water and give greater weight to the bread but that produce intestinal disorders; the mixture of copper peroxide with the cigarette paper made with all kinds of old clothes in order to take away the flavor: some mixtures can, in a certain minimum amount, be allowed, but in greater doses will make the merchant responsible for the lives of the consumers.

In the matter of commercial deception, there are some lies that are harmless, because in fact nobody believes them and everyone knows that they are typical of the seller's occupation. On the other hand, there are other lies that are grave: for example, the falsification of the books in selling a business; the falsification of damages of an accident in order to exaggerate a claim for insurance compensation. These frauds violate commutative justice and oblige to restitution.

An unjustified price increase, especially for basic necessities, only for the purpose of obtaining a greater profit, causes a great social evil, as it contributes to an increase in living costs. This measure is greatly feared, because it can be imitated by others with serious damage to social justice. To the extent that the new price is totally unfair there is an obligation to make restitution.

In sales, there are unfortunately a series of practices that are at least dirty business and very often offend social justice and also, in not a few cases, offend commutative justice. A system of bribes or commissions exists in many forms: when selling a property for 500,000 people request a receipt for 600,000; a matter is not dealt with or a favorable vote is not achieved in a council except upon the payment of a commission. All these extra charges, in the case of articles for resale to the public, are paid for by the consumer, who has to bear all these expenses. The one who demands such a commission clearly violates the interests entrusted to him; the situation is different when the person simply accepts, without requiring it, such a commission as a «tip», especially if his economic situation is very bad. The saddest part of this is that honest people, who would not wish to use fraudulent procedures in any way, are compelled by such practices to use the system of bribes in order to be able to exercise their right to sell, otherwise they could not do so. Fathers Müller and Azpiazu, while lamenting such practices, do not venture to state that a salesman, confronted with serious harm, may not employ them[589].

In dealing with so-called «purely criminal» laws, we touched upon making a mockery of taxes and other tax burdens, and we established a rule in this respect[590].

Fr. Azpiazu, using excellent criteria, points out the fundamental remedy for these corrupt acts: the improvement of the professional conscience:

> «The doctrine is clear, but the practice is dangerous. Avarice can easily lead, in order to avoid State regulations, to the use of unjust procedures, and thus it falls squarely into the illicit.
>
> External reasons —that others do the same— are worth nothing; other reasons —that the good are always the ones who pay and that this puts them in a worse condition than the bad people who use all kinds of means— are more meritorious, because of exact distributive justice, which is something the State is suppose to desire above all. In general, these reasons are not too strong; but they are based on reality as well as justice.
>
> In general, today there is an widespread tendency to say that the professional conscience is relaxed, especially as regards the fulfillment of duties towards the State; and at the same time, there is an enormous tendency to defraud the State by all possible means, just or unjust. It is a characteristic contradiction of our times.[…][591]

589 [*Economic Professional Morality*, p. 268.]

590 [See chapter 4.9.4. Criminal Laws, page 97.]

591 [Here the *Economic Professional Morality* text states: «Pero nótese que el sistema de las leyes penales deja más cauce abierto al fraude que el que niega su existencia y trata de interpretar las leyes fiscales con el criterio que hemos hecho, introduciéndoles dentro del concepto corriente de la ley verdadera». The text is not clear in Spanish, so the editors have excluded it.]

The reader has supposed that we speak in this chapter only and always of the industrialists and private merchants, not of the State officials who either teach the means of defrauding individuals or invite bribes to examine accounts and balances. They are slaves to their commutative injustice to the State and have, in general, an obligation to make restitution for what they have stolen from the State or unjustly taken»[592].

2
Just Price

In every sales contract, the price of what is sold must be just. But what is the just price?

Liberal economists are not concerned with determining a just price, first because it is almost impossible to do so because of the imprecision of the elements involved, and then because any price determined by the law of supply and demand is just. But such a doctrine is morally false, because ethics must intervene in fixing the price as in other economic matters that affect the common good. It is also economically false, because there is often no free price, since the combined action of trusts and *kartells* arbitrarily establishes prices when the State does not do that. Supply and demand influence price, without determining it; but they do not establish the just price!

In the Marxist conception, the just price is confused with the amount of labor put into the execution of a work. This conception is simplistic because it fails to take into account other values, such as the quality of the worker or the artist: a painting by Michelangelo is not worth the same as the painting by a beginner although each has spent twenty hours on painting, nor are eight hours of labor by a laborer equal to those of a specialized worker or technician.

The just price includes *cost price*, namely, the just remuneration of labor and capital, the cost of raw materials, the general expenses of the company, amortization of the material: in a word, all the expenses necessary for production. It also supposes a *just profit* or just benefit: this is the profit that the seller is entitled to add to the cost as compensation for his activity, for his service and for the risks. As a commodity circulates, it establishes for itself a cascade of just prices, each of which has repercussions for the next, adding a just profit.

592 [*Economic Professional Morality*, pp. 272-273.]

3

Just Profit

The right to profit has a double foundation. First, the fact that the producer brings the customer the goods he needs: the grape from a distant region is brought to his table or even better is transformed into wine; the clay soil is brought to him transformed into bricks that he will employ in construction. This service deserves a recompense. The second foundation is the risk of the producer: risks of the bad agricultural year, or the sinking of his ship, or losing his capital to cheaters, or the risk of accidental injuries to his operators for which the employer will be liable. The proof that the risk is real is that an insurance company can appraise it and charge for taking it upon itself by covering the insured. As the risk to a man is the basis of his compensation, so also the risk of capital justifies the profit. From this it follows that in businesses in which there is no risk or no movement of products closer to the consumer, there is no justification for profit. Profit may, morally, be higher or lower depending on the service provided to the client and the risk that it involves. There are times, such as wartime, when the circumstances of danger are extraordinary, and therefore extraordinary gains appear justified. As regards risk, the shareholder's is much greater than that of the simple lender to the same company, because lenders have priority over shareholders.

When establishing the amount of profit that the producer has the right to receive, it is necessary to distinguish among several particular profits:

- *The profit attributable to the businessman.* If he is both a capitalist and the chief executive, he will receive a just amount of return for what he has invested as capital and a return for his managerial work. If he is not a capitalist but only a chief executive, the salary corresponds to his work, and takes into account, besides compensation for the hours he works, the amortization of his more or less lengthy and expensive training, his responsibility for a more or less complicated company, the risks of failure, the need to seek new capital and bank loans, etc. The amount of legitimate profit for such a businessman cannot be determined mathematically but by the application of an honest conscience.

Together with the businessman are his *collaborators* —employees and workers— who are owed a just salary according to the rules set forth above. Wage factors include the risks to their life, health, security of employment, etc.; their responsibilities and the amount of their technical training. Any extraordinary profits of the business, which in a capitalist regime go only to suppliers of capital and to executives in the form of bonuses, must also be shared among all the collaborators in production.

- *Return on the capital* invested in shares, whose rate is not fixed. (Today in Chile banks charge 10 and 12%. This is necessary to take into account the depreciation of the currency, because if somebody lends a thousand pesos and receives back, a year later, a thousand pesos depreciated by 15 or 20%, this amounts to one thousand pesos with which he can buy 15 or 20% less in value than the year before; that depreciation can legitimately enter into consideration when determining the requested interest.). As with just interest, the producer is entitled to a dividend justified by the risk that shares involve, provided that his obligations of social justice towards workers and consumers have been faithfully fulfilled. What should be the ceiling on this dividend? The German economist Adolph Wagner[593] stated that the amount that represents twice the legal interest on a loan, according to legislation and current use, should not be considered an exaggerated benefit. In France, when the profits made in commerce during wartime were discussed, it was estimated that an interest rate of over 15% should be considered abusive. Father Vermeersh[594] speaks of an interest rate of 10 to 12%; Fr. Prümmer, O.P.[595], does not consider a profit of 30% unjust. As can be seen, in determining profit it is necessary to remember the factors that justify it: the risk to capital (a much greater danger in times of inflation, which does not allow for a constant purchasing power); the service rendered to the individual, to the common good and to society. It is not licit to put capital at risk or to serve individuals, if to do so would harm the nation, for example by introducing harmful drugs, narcotics, etc.

- *The fixing of the product's price* is another element that must be taken into account in establishing the just profit. For many goods today, prices are determined nationally and internationally, especially when influenced by large companies that control them, but in many cases there is anarchy, especially when it comes to products that are new, rare, recent inventions, etc. Ancient moralists said that the just price was fixed by consensus and had variations: maximum

593 [Adolph Wagner (1835-1917), German economist, one of the leaders of the school of economics and social policy, called *Staatssozialismus* (State Socialism). *Wagner's Law*, named after him, holds that for any country, public expenditure rises constantly as income growth expands.]

594 [See footnote 530.]

595 [Dominic Prümmer (1866-1931), Professor of Theology at the University of Fribourg. Author of *Vademecum Theologiae Moralis* (*The Handbook of Moral Theology*) (1923).]

and minimum prices. They admitted the existence of a margin between those prices that was commonly estimated at 10%; Cardinal Toledo estimated it at up to 25%. The price within those margins was considered to be just.

The price of products in modern life undergoes tremendous oscillations between periods of economic crisis and those of temporary prosperity, oscillations which distort every calculation. In luxury industries, benefits that seem excessive may be normal, given the immensity of the risks that the producer runs. Therefore, to fix the price of a product one would have to rely on the estimate of those that have a reputation for prudence and honesty in the field.

- *The conventional price.* The fact that a price is agreed by both parties does not mean that it is just, because it can be the result of extortion: a worker without a job will accept any wage, even a starvation wage, but nevertheless it will be unjust; a sick person will pay any price for a medicine that he needs, but nevertheless the price will be unjust. If an object is going to bring great profit to the buyer, the seller may not improperly increase its price for that reason: that would be extortion. The conventional price is only just, based on convention, when the parties stipulate a price they consider just in view of the risk to both parties.

Therefore, in the ordinary course of work people can set the just price based on the usual approach, determined today by what honest and prudent merchants in the particular area do. When it comes to large operations that can significantly impact the national economy, we must bear in mind the national common good. If that is harmed, an operation that is beneficial to a private individual can be allowed only if prohibiting it would result in damage as grave as that which the national economy would suffer.

4
Consequences of the Legality of «Individual Benefit» and Competition

Some do not consider permissible a regime in which individual gain is allowed. Certainly such a regime is not the best that can be conceived, and it must be totally rejected if it concedes primacy of profit over morality, but if the regime conforms to morality, it is the duty of the moralist to examine it and establish its standards, rather than to reject it in a closed-minded way. The sociologist seeks the social systems that are appropriate to an era; the moralist only judges them.

From the moral point of view, the personal gain of an employer and the collective profit of a company will be acceptable if they take into account the roles of all the collaborators who produced it and if they do not unduly burden the consumer.

The profit that each company can obtain, once it has adhered to standards of justice, will be a stimulus for a better technical and commercial organization, for closer attention to the customers, for a better spirit of work and of healthy competition, which are absolutely necessary for the progress of science and economics.

Between two social systems, one founded on self interest and another on fear, as in the Russian system, the former is immensely superior to the latter, as the regime of liberty is superior to that of slavery. It is undeniable that the profit system involves a great danger: bitter and sometimes unfair competition between producers and merchants and a tendency to reduce costs by reducing the remuneration for work. This is why we must always be wary about this system. But, what incentive can be applied in a rather interconnected world that might replace the profit motive? In small, harmonious communities that are unified in spirit, profit is not the incentive, but in the great world of work and commerce there is still no other. When the day comes that a better system appears and is accepted, we will greet it with joy.

Competition is also a necessity of commerce: it has the same advantages as those we pointed out when speaking of the system of individual profit and is in any case inevitable. If the suppression of competition within a country were achieved, it would survive internationally in an even more vivid and violent form.

The fact that competition cannot be suppressed does not mean that it cannot be rationalized and moralised. Justice will prevent unfair competition: deception about the quality of merchandise, plagiarism, usurpation of technical secrets, price cutting to destroy a competitor and then dominate a market in which there is no longer any competition, the spread of slander and false news to raise one price or to lower another. Charity will also remind merchants that, although they are in competition, they are brothers and have common interests that must lead them to assist one another.

To channel competition, new institutions are needed, such as associations that embrace all those who are part of the same occupation and regulate their occupational interests in combination for the common good.

Channeled competition is a good formula, because it stimulates private initiative, fueled by self interest, which encourages innovation which avoids routine. Competition must be humanized to prevent it from becoming a field of intrigue for the enrichment of a few, even at the price of the misery of the many. The struggle is stimulating and healthy so long as it is subordinated to the common good.

5
Some Sales Procedures that are Used in Our Days

Merchants' wits have sharpened so as to acquire new customers and have discovered several new systems to attract them.

- *Installment sale* is a system very commonly used to sell parcels of land, furniture, radios, etc. The total price, including interest, is much higher than would have been charged in cash. In the present situation, unfortunately, this is the only system that can be used by many customers, especially young married couples, to clothe themselves and acquire certain goods: if the total price were kept within the bounds of justice, there would be nothing to criticize, except for the fact that if he is not able to pay, the buyer forfeits the object and also his previous payments, which is unjust. One hopes that this system will be replaced by a personal credit system that would allow, through reasonable amortization and interest, the acquisition of certain objects, excluding luxury ones.
- *Sale with Gift Coupons.* Each purchase entitles the buyer to a certain number of coupons which can be use to acquire certain products. This system fascinates many buyers who believe that they will be able to acquire certain products free of charge, when in reality the products are paid for by the consumers, as their value is included in the sale price. There is, then, a kind of deception, and unfair competition with those merchants who cannot employ such a procedure.
- *Department stores* are places where everything is sold, from books to sandwiches, pets and dining room furniture; some department stores have *branches* in all towns and neighborhoods. In each case they depend on a strong, centralized capitalist system, and they have the defect of artificially stimulating a desire for acquisition, often using a sales staff which is not well paid. They

also compete ruinously with small stores —the main livelihood of the middle classes— who are so important to the life of a country.

- *Advertising*, as a means of sale. Commercial advertising is everywhere: on posters and placards, in illuminations, through skywriting, in the press and brochures. It has become a way of life for thousands of men. Advertising is paid for in full by the consumer of the products.

  The advertising system deserves several observations of a moral order: a man of conscience can never devote his artistic skills or allow the use of his printing presses for immoral advertising: movies, the sale of contraceptives, advertisements for houses of ill repute, etc.; nor can he advertise products that, while not doing harm, do not achieve any good, and therefore, should be controlled: pharmaceutical products that have no more value than their packaging and their false prestige, drinks offered at a high price, which includes the extensive advertising that makes them penetrate the markets. Advertising should be subject to sensible control within corporative organization that would keep it within the limits of what is just and reasonable.

  One system that should be supported: Consumer Cooperatives.

The consumer cooperatives have a very simple operation: several future buyers associate, they contribute an initial capital through shares to acquire facilities and make the first purchases. They appoint a manager or an administrator in charge of sales, who is paid a salary or a participation in profits. Interested parties choose a council that advises and oversees the operations of the cooperative. Purchases are made by shareholders, either at the acquisition cost plus the operating costs of the warehouse or at the market price, and they then distribute the profits pro rata according to shares or pro rata according to the purchases made.

To work properly, this system requires the creation of a cooperative spirit that is acquired through serious formation. Without this, it is dangerous to institute cooperatives.

The cooperative is a precious assistance to the common good, because in addition to benefiting its associates through lower prices, it benefits society by serving as a testimony to the just price, and introduces into society an element of mutual aid beyond simple utilitarianism. In countries such as Sweden, Denmark, England and Canada, consumer cooperatives and other forms of cooperatives are precious structures which prepare a new order[596].

596 [At this point Hurtado added headings that were not developed: «Loan and Interest. F. 97» and «Game and Speculation. F.103».]

Chapter 16

Currency and Business

1
Currency

Currency emerged as a complement to economic life, as a complement to barter. A measure for valuing was needed—an instrument of exchange, and that was currency.

From the beginning, currency tended to be metallic, of high value, lightweight and easily divisible. Gold was recognized as the most important, then silver, copper and nickel for coins of lesser value.

Since the last century, gold as a currency has been supplemented with other means of exchange: gold certificates and paper currency backed by gold and then bills secured, not directly by gold deposits, but by national wealth.

Complications of currency exchange have produced a situation in which one currency may have two values: one inside the country (where the currency may not be backed by gold), and another outside the country, which depends on the regime of the particular trading partner. If the gold standard applies in that country, the bills will be valued based on the gold that supports them; if the paper regime applies, they will be valued according to their real purchasing power.

In modern times only states coin money; previously, money could also be coined by princes and important corporations.

If more money is issued than is supported by the gold reserve at the time, this can effect a real plundering of private individuals. This procedure, which regrettably has often been used surreptitiously, amounts to a real taking of peoples' wealth, because it lowers their purchasing power and is also a disruptive element in national economic harmony: it destroys the credit of the State, it deceives wage earners and all those who have contributed their time, their money, their products in exchange for an agreed value. This phenomenon is what is called *inflation*: excessive quantities of the means of payment with respect to commercial goods, which translates into a decrease in the purchasing power of money. *Devaluation* consists in officially varying the ratio between the gold reserve and the note that represents it. England, Italy, France and Russia have repeatedly devalued their currencies. This procedure sometimes appears to be an extreme resort: a sacrifice demanded of the people as a whole, but in no way can it be approved except in extreme cases. Currency, to have value on national and international currency exchanges, requires a minimum of stability and security. The best regime, in terms of the quantity of currency in circulation, is that in which there is an amount of currency equal to the volume of goods in commerce, multiplied by the speed of circulation of the currency, according to the quantitative theory of currency of the American professor Irving Fisher[597]. This theory is widely accepted as an explanation of the relationship between the value of money and the price of goods: high prices correspond to a low value of currency; low prices, to a high value of currency.

Circulating currency, national and international credit, the banking system, public trust, and social and international tranquility are nowadays more influential than are isolated efforts to fix prices or than the general state of the economy. The extent of these problems exceeds the current capacities of most businessmen and even large financiers who have proved powerless to solve the economic problems of the postwar world.

Since the last war, problems of international exchange have worsened. Speculation has added to this problem, and concerted offensives have artificially raised or lowered the value of national currencies. The first duty of the State is to ensure the stability of its currency. Then one could consider an international action to create an international currency that would facilitate and regularize exchanges, although for the moment it seems that nobody seriously thinks about that.

2
Banking Morality

The bank in modern economic life has a multiple mission: its main one is to receive deposits from customers, manage them prudently and facilitate credit. Unfortunately, the tendency to become a merchant has dominated the modern bank. Some countries, such as the United States, have tried to fight against the tendency of depository banks also to become commercial banks, and hence to become managers of the economy.

Leaving aside many technical aspects linked to banking life, let us point out only a few considerations as to issues that make contact with morality:

597 [Irving Fisher (1867-1947), American economist, one of the first American neoclassical economists. He wrote about utility and general equilibrium, and developed a theory of capital and interest rates which he explained in his book *The Theory of Interest* (1930).]

- The *investment of funds* deposited by clients at least seems equitable when they are invested in a way which serves the interests or the business purposes of the depositors: for example by benefitting commerce or industry if the customers are commercial or industrial. This especially concerns the more specialized institutions such as savings banks, which have been created to benefit the economic situation of the poor classes. It disserves this purpose when such funds go to build luxury buildings, to rent appartments or to lend money to institutions that have nothing to do with the welfare of the needy classes.
- The *granting of bank loans* greatly contributes to the process of commercial inflation if they are readily given, or the process of deflation, if they are restricted abruptly, with a resulting procession of bankruptcies and unemployment. These measures have, therefore, to be carefully considered.
- The *mission to promote economic life*: the bank has a grave responsibility in the use of the assets it has available that can serve to promote businesses of real value for the life of the country. There are businesses that may sink if they are denied credit, or could not even be started for the same reason. On the other hand, there are other businesses more lucrative for industrialists, but that do not produce anything necessary; businesses which obtain credit for reasons of friendship or by «pulling some strings». A bank aware of its mission cannot proceed arbitrarily in these matters, which concern the common good.

  The secrets that a bank manager receives from the merchants, or from industrialists who entrust him with their projects or urgent needs, bind him most strongly to professional confidentiality.
- *Bank intervention in other companies.* Banking influence on the entire economic life of the country is greater every day, since all industries and commerce need credit, and thus banks often becomes the masters of life and death. Moreover, banks often invest their funds in the shares of the companies that they try to control. For that reason, beyond their own share ownership, banks manage to obtain from their clients the rights to represent them at shareholders' meetings, and sometimes they come to dominate those meetings. Thus we have the problem that an entity that owns relatively few shares, thanks to powers given arbitrarily, can impose its own policy on the company, elect directors and exert a fundamental influence on its businesses, which end up becoming those of the bank.

- *Directorship.* There is a great ambition to join banks' boards of directors because of the compensation directors receive and for the enormous power conferred by such positions. Thus, there are people who are directors on ten and even twenty different boards, because the bank is a major shareholder in or has influence over many entities that are controlled or overseen by it. The directors of the bank ordinarily select directors of the other companies they control. This can lead to moral concerns for a number of reasons: first, because of the enormous economic power concentrated in a few entities and people; next, as a result of the accumulation of positions in a few hands, which is contrary to distributive justice; third, because little or no close attention can be given to such a variety of positions—positions that must involve weighty national and international economic problems, beyond the problems of the entity itself. Many directors attend meetings but remain entirely passive, which could constitute a very grave moral offense, and they can become complicit, by their omissions, in all the injustices that may be committed and that they may not even be interested in knowing about[598].

As a solution to these evils, the same Pontiff proposes:

«No genuine cure can be furnished for this lamentable ruin of souls, which, so long as it continues, will frustrate all efforts to regenerate society, unless men return openly and sincerely to the teaching of the Gospel, to the precepts of Him Who alone has the words of everlasting life[599], words which will never pass away, even if Heaven and earth will pass away[600]. All experts in social problems are seeking eagerly a structure so fashioned in accordance with the norms of reason that it can lead economic life back to sound and right order. But this order, which We Ourselves ardently long for and with all Our efforts promote, will be wholly defective and incomplete unless all the activities of men harmoniously unite to imitate and attain, in so far as it lies within human strength, the marvelous unity of the Divine plan. We mean that perfect order which the Church with great force and power preaches and which right human reason itself demands, that all things be directed to God as the first and supreme end of all

598 [At this point Hurtado added: «All this Pius XI seemed to have in mind when he wrote: copy *Social Christian Order* p. 21 -22». Those pages included portions of §§ 105-108 of *Quadragesimo Anno*. The editors are not copying those paragraphs here because they have been included three times previously in this book (see pages 155, 178 and 295).]
599 [The encyclical here includes a footnote as follows: «Cf. John 6:69».]
600 [The encyclical here includes a footnote as follows: «Cf. Matt. 24:35».]

created activity, and that all created good under God be considered as mere instruments to be used only in so far as they conduce to the attainment of the supreme end. Nor is it to be thought that gainful occupations are thereby belittled or judged less consonant with human dignity; on the contrary, we are taught to recognize in them with reverence the manifest will of the Divine Creator Who placed man upon the earth to work it and use it in a multitude of ways for his needs. Those who are engaged in producing goods, therefore, are not forbidden to increase their fortune in a just and lawful manner; for it is only fair that he who renders service to the community and makes it richer should also, through the increased wealth of the community, be made richer himself according to his position, provided that all these things be sought with due respect for the laws of God and without impairing the rights of others and that they be employed in accordance with faith and right reason. If these principles are observed by everyone, everywhere, and always, not only the production and acquisition of goods but also the use of wealth, which now is seen to be so often contrary to right order, will be brought back soon within the bounds of equity and just distribution. The sordid love of wealth, which is the shame and great sin of our age, will be opposed in actual fact by the gentle yet effective law of Christian moderation which commands man to seek first the Kingdom of God and His justice, with the assurance that, by virtue of God's kindness and unfailing promise, temporal goods also, in so far as he has need of them, shall be given him besides»[601].

3
Some Aspects of Stock Market Morality

The purposes of the stock exchange are to regularize, facilitate and give greater formality to commercial operations, reflecting the actual condition of the national economy, which constitute very real advantages. Public exchanges, whether of securities or commodities, are the marketplaces for such items. Purchase and sale transactions are carried out by brokers. There are spot and forward transactions. In addition to transactions motivated by a desire to invest capital or the need to exchange values for money, there are other transactions motivated by speculation, by the hope of rapid profit. There are those who bid

601 [*Quadragesimo Anno* § 136. The encyclical here has a footnote as follows: «Cf. Matt. 6:33».
Hurtado directed the citation of Azpiazu's book *Economic Professional Morality*, pp. 301-307, which refers to the encyclical passage just quoted.]

on stock that might rise, hoping to buy below market value, waiting for the price to rise and to gain on the difference; or the opposite, selling stock which is above market value in the hope of profiting. Stock sales have a fixed date. These transactions are involved with others that are called *report* and *déport*. The *report* is a bank loan transaction requested by those who bid on rising stock, and which is secured by the securities to be purchased. This loan is given for interest and commissions. The *déport*, on the other hand, is ordinarily resorted to by those who bid on a stock which is going down and borrow some of it, returning it with the payment of interest. Forward transactions are of a speculative nature and are for a rapid profit. Many times people bid uncovered and lacking funds or assets, seeking only to gain based on a change in price. Such transactions involve the danger that speculators may arrange with third parties to raise or lower prices artificially, doing serious and unjust damage. The price of a security must be determined by the situation of the company. To vary the price of the stock artificially by circulating news about good or bad business developments is absolutely wrong. This does not prevent those who have an accurate knowledge of business and foresee a good or bad development from taking advantage of their information to buy or sell the stock. In such a case, the operation is lawful.

Deals that are conducted on the stock market are complicated and greatly varied, but in terms of morality the central problem comes down to the fairness of the price of what is bought and sold: the stock market is nothing more than a market for buying and selling.

In most cash transactions between private individuals who in good faith want to invest their capital or exchange their stock for money, there is no great problem, but in speculation there are several dangers.

The first is that of fraudulent manipulation of prices by means of false news, using inside information. The second is to make speculation a way of life, since that would be tantamount to living from gambling with all its disastrous consequences: for family assets, which sometimes have been entrusted to a person and who will not be able to restore them, and by way of disruption of the national economy and the stability of companies. The trader, like the gambler, usually ends up losing. Easy profits excite the desire of simple people to make money in this way and to risk with one bid that they believe to be safe, savings accumulated by years of work. In speaking of the practice of speculation, we are not referring to isolated cases, but to general fraud and deception, which are common ways to alter just prices. The duty of the State will be to preserve the order of the stock market and to closely regulate its operations so as to protect the customers and the general economy.

4

Gambling and Specullation

Gambling and speculation consist essentially of seeking a profit not justified by a work or a service. Gambling is the effect of chance. When small amounts are risked, it cannot be condemned without falling into rigorism. Beyond a certain level it becomes immoral and the State should not tolerate such an invitation to laziness and disorder.

In speculation, chance and foresight are mixed in varying proportions. Speculation is mostly conducted in commodity markets. In the current state of the economy, speculation cannot be completely prohibited as morally wrong. Moreover, it would be impossible to prohibit it since in any forward transaction there is a certain amount of speculation, as there is in any transaction in stock.

Morality does not allow manipulation that disrupts the relationship of supply and demand, such as false news, hoarding or certain ficticious market transactions effected to obtain only better prices. In the matter of speculation, all honest merchants must unite.

Chapter 17

Loans with Interest

1

The Current Frequency of Loan

The great instrument of the capitalist world for carrying on its business is the loan. The cost of a loan is the interest that has to be paid for it. In modern economic life a price is paid for the service of temporarily using other people's money, as for any other service, like going to a theater or for a railroad ticket. Is this practice justified? How has this been considered in different times?

2

The Concept and the Use of Money in the Precapitalist Era

Until the nineteenth century, the purpose of money was almost exclusively as a medium of exchange: it was used to buy consumer goods or to make investments in agriculture or small industry, the development of which did not require credit. Only the capital invested in farms or in artisanal industries bore interest. All other money remained inactive, locked up and unproductive.

Credit was given on a small scale. Consistent with this situation, moralists did not imagine that money that remained inactive could itself produce fruits or interest. Since Aristotle it had been affirmed that money was barren. The goat breeds a goat, but money does not generate money.

The usual loan at that time was for the requirements of consumption and ordinarily was offered to persons in need or to acquaintances or friends to whom one was bound by ties of kinship or friendship.

Usurers, nevertheless, did exist: men dedicated to getting people out of trouble in times of necessity, especially kings and those who organized armies; usurers' services were very expensive. Their attitude clashed strongly with the Christian spirit of the times, and that is why moralists considered the problem of whether it was permissible to charge interest on loaned money.

Various official acts of the Church discuss this problem. The Council of Vienna[602] and the 3rd, 4th and 5th Lateran Councils prohibit usury[603]; Innocent XI in 1679[604] and especially Benedict XIV in the constitution *Vix Pervenit* of 1745[605] return to this subject. What are their resolutions, and what are the arguments on which they are based?

Benedict XIV says: «[t]he nature of the sin called usury has its proper place and origin in a loan contract. This financial contract between consenting parties demands, by its very nature, that one return to another only as much as he has received. The sin rests on the fact that sometimes the creditor desires more than he has given. Therefore he contends some gain is owed him beyond that which he loaned, but any gain which exceeds the amount he gave is illicit and usurious»[606].

Innocent XI condemned some scandalous propositions, but stated: «[b]eing present money of greater value than the future one, the creditor may demand for that something of the debtor and thus be free from usury»[607].

These statements are based on a condemnation of the loan based on a «*contrato de mutuo*»[608]. This contract is one by which a good which is consumed when first used is transferred to another subject to an obligation to return another one equivalent to that consumed.

When lending money to another person, I transfer it to him, since he cannot use it without ownership. The money is no longer that of the lender. If the money produces fruits owing to the work of the new owner, I cannot claim a part of

602 [The Council of Vienna was the fifteenth ecumenical council of the Catholic Church, and met between 1311 and 1312 in Vienna. This council made it clear that princes should at least not protect usurers and no authority should pass laws permitting usury.]

603 [The Third Lateran Council was the eleventh ecumenical council of the Catholic Church, and met in 1179. Canon 25 excommunicates those who engage in usury. The Fourth Lateran Council was the twelfth ecumenical council of the Catholic Church, and met in 1215. Canon 67 prohibits the charging of extortionate interest.]

604 [Innocent XI, in his Bull «*Sanctissimus Dominus*», issued on March 2nd, 1679, condemned sixty-five propositions which favored laxism in moral theology.]

605 [See footnote 23.]

606 Folliet. [Hurtado is referring to Joseph Folliet book's *Morale Sociale* (*Social Morality*) volume II, Chapter IX, p. 97 (1937). At that point Folliet is quoting *Vix Pervenit*, § 3, I. The editors used the translation available at http://www.papalencyclicals.net/ben14/b14vixpe.htm.]

607 Azpiazu, p. 96. [The quoted phrase in Azpiazu's book, *Economic Professional Morality*, refers to Innocent XI's papal bull *Sanctissimus Dominus Noster* of 1679, which condemned 65 propositions that favored moral laxism in moral theology.]

608 [*Mutuo* is a contract by which a person is obliged to transfer ownership of a sum of money or other fungible things to another person called a borrower, who is obliged to return another of the same kind and quality.]

them, because he worked with his own money: *res fructificat domino*. In the same way, if the object is lost while in his power: for example, if the money is stolen, the lost falls on him, the owner, and I retain my right to recover the equivalent of the money borrowed.

In the simple «*contrato de mutuo*», the Church forbids asking for interest, for the reasons indicated above. The loan is not a lease, because in a lease the same property must be repaid, whereas in the case of a loan, only an equivalent amount must repaid because the thing lent has been consumed. Neither is such a contract a deposit, because it effects a transfer of ownership.

The proposition Innocent XI condemned was based on the idea that the simple passage of time does not change the value of the money that has to be returned, but even the more severe commentators of that period agreed that something could be asked if, in addition to the passage of time, there was an extrinsic reason, such as damage to the lender.

These resolutions must be strictly interpreted with an eye to what was condemned, as was set out above, and in the economic context of the times, when money was really unproductive and was simply an instrument of exchange, expended at its first use.

Even during those times, however, moralists like Saint Thomas admitted the licity of interest when intervening extrinsic circumstances applied to the *contrato de mutuo* itself. They reduced these entitlements mainly to three: *actual damages*, which relate to the losses suffered by the lender; *consequential damages*, which relate to the gains that the claimant forfeited; and *the risk* that the money will not be returned. According to great moralists of the precapitalist period, like Lugo and Lessio in their treatises *De Justitia et Jure*[609], these circumstances, when they occur, justify interest.

3
Lending at Interest in the Capitalist Era

The external conditions are totally different. The growth of large industry requires credit, and an immense demand for capital leads to the formation of banks that offer credit which can be immediately transformed into machinery, land and raw materials. Today, idle capital is not conceivable.

609 [See footnote 20.]

The purpose of the loan in present times is also different: it is not mainly for consumption, but for production. The very nature of money has changed in the present age, not because it has esentially changed, but because of the new economic circumstances. In antiquity, money had no value other than that of an instrument of exchange which was consumed at its first use, but today it is understood that money is capital that represents all other sorts of capital: it can be transformed immediately into machines, lands, ships...

Hence, modern moralists arrive at the conclusion that in an economy like ours in which the ownership of the means of production belongs to the individual (as distinct from a Marxist economy, in which production would be reserved to the State) money has ceased to be unproductive. It is eminently productive, because it is nothing but accumulated work converted into an intangible good, for example through a machine, because with it man can produce much more than without it. Money itself, while it is pure money—while it has not been transformed— is a pure instrument of exchange, but once it has been transformed it becomes everything that it is capable of producing. And no one keeps money today except in small quantities (maybe a rare miser does in a corner of his house), but ordinarily money is in company shares, bonds, machinery, buildings or the securities of urban companies; is always invested in something productive: unproductive money is a phenomenon that has disappeared from the modern economy. This transformation of the nature of money is a fact typical of our economy and makes money something that can be rented, because it is rented so as to be transformed into purchased goods one can affirm that money is a productive good not one expendable in its first use, and that therefore it can be rented like a house. Money is unproductive only when it is not exchanged for something valuable; but the moment it is exchanged for anything valuable it becomes capital, and when joined to labor, it becomes productive. Loans for production are made to be transformed into machines and land, and to be productive. If a lender does not lend, he will make an analogous investment. Entitlement to interest owing to the risk of consequential damages, rare in ancient times, has become frequent in modern economies, and is a normal condition.

Beyond these justifications —the fecundity of capital, typical of a capitalist economy and justifications based on actual damages, consequential losses and risk— there are others acknowledged by Benedict XIV: the *association contract* by which the owner of money does not give up his ownership, he keeps it; and while others contribute work, technical competence or management he contributes the money and participates in the risks of the company, which entitles him to a part of the benefits. Benedict XIV also acknowledges the legitimacy of the contract of rent, which is another form of the association contract: the lender delivers the money to another to buy a good, in whose fruits the lender will participate, as he is taking all the risks in the matter.

This justification of the right to receive interest in the capitalist economy does not imply an approval of the way such an economy works, distant as it is for so many reasons from the Christian spirit. Today, financial capital controls industry like a master; industrial capital is imposed on technology and work. When drawing up a balance sheet, companies assign an interest to capital —its regular remuneration— and a dividend reflecting participation in the benefits obtained with the capital: a participation in profits that overlooks the main factor in production, which is work. Similarly, there are other objections to capitalism as mentioned above. But notwithstanding all these concerns, in this economy —which is not strictly unjust— it is lawful to receive interest. It is also licit for Christians to seek another, more just, economic regime.

4
Interest Rates

The value of the service rendered must be accommodated. The rate of interest must be, like every price, first of all just and must also reflect equity and charity. The amount of interest will therefore depend on the service that money renders to production. Interest on a consumer loan is justified by the opportunities afforded by the capitalist economy—by the benefit of which the lender is deprived, which he would normally have obtained with his money— but the rate of interest on this kind of loan, especially, must reflect equity and charity. What is lawful can often be unjust and opposed to equity and charity. The legal or current rate, provided it is not proven to be unjust, may serve as a standard for the interest that may be charged.

Canon Law, in Canon 1543, provides that if money is extended in the form of a *mutuo*, nothing else may be required by the same contract, but that other things may be requested by other instruments and as set forth in them:

«If a fungible thing is given to someone in such a way that it becomes his and later is to be returned only in the same kind, no gain can be received by reason of the contract itself; but in the payment of a fungible thing, it is not in itself illicit to contract for the gain allowed by law, unless it is clear that this is excessive, or even for a greater gain, if a just and adequate title be present»[610].

610 [Code of Canon Law of 1917, canon 1543 (English version). The Code of Canon Law promulgated in 1983 abrogated the 1917 Code.]

Chapter 18

Social Reform

1

The Urgency of a Social Reform

If we compare the principles of social morality with our daily lives, we can see that we are far from living by those principles. The need for a social reform is urgent.

> «A great part of mankind, and, let Us not shirk from saying it, not a few who call themselves Christians, have to some extent their share in the collective responsibility for the growth of error and for the harm and the lack of moral fiber in the society of today»[611].

> «These conditions of social security must be fulfilled if we do not want society to be shaken, every moment, by ferments of turbulence and dangerous rebellions, but to be calm and progress in harmony, in peace and in mutual love»[612].

2

Moral and Religious Reform

> «For, it is the opinion of some, and the error is already very common, that the social question is merely an economic one, whereas in point of fact it is, above all, a moral and religious matter, and for that reason must be settled by the principles of morality and according to the dictates of religion … Take away the instinct which Christian wisdom has planted and nurtured in men's hearts, take away foresight, temperance, frugality, patience, and other rightful, natural habits, no matter how much he may strive, he will never achieve prosperity»[613].

> «And if human society is to be healed now, in no other way can it be healed save by a return to Christian life and Christian institutions»[614].

611 [*Christmas Message of 1942.*]
612 [*Speech to the Italian Workers.*]
613 [Leo XIII, Encyclical on Christian Democracy *Graves de Communi Re* (18 January 1901) §§ 11-12, at The Holy See, https://w2.vatican.va/content/leo-xiii/en/encyclicals/documents/hf_l-xiii_enc_18011901_graves-de-communi-re.html (hereinafter referred to as *Graves de Communi Re*).]
614 [*Rerum Novarum* § 27.]

Pius XI repeats the same ideas insistently:

«... we shall clearly perceive that, preceding this ardently desired social restoration, there must be a renewal of the Christian spirit, from which so many immersed in economic life have, far and wide, unhappily fallen away, lest all our efforts be wasted and our house be builded not on a rock but on shifting sand»[615].

«All experts in social problems are seeking eagerly a structure so fashioned in accordance with the norms of reason that it can lead economic life back to sound and right order. But this order, which We Ourselves ardently long for and with all Our efforts promote, will be wholly defective and incomplete unless all the activities of men harmoniously unite to imitate and attain, in so far as it lies within human strength, the marvelous unity of the Divine plan. We mean that perfect order which the Church with great force and power preaches and which right human reason itself demands, that all things be directed to God as the first and supreme end of all created activity, and that all created good under God be considered as mere instruments to be used only in so far as they conduce to the attainment of the supreme end. Nor is it to be thought that gainful occupations are thereby belittled or judged less consonant with human dignity; on the contrary, we are taught to recognize in them with reverence the manifest will of the Divine Creator Who placed man upon the earth to work it and use it in a multitude of ways for his needs. Those who are engaged in producing goods, therefore, are not forbidden to increase their fortune in a just and lawful manner; for it is only fair that he who renders service to the community and makes it richer should also, through the increased wealth of the community, be made richer himself according to his position, provided that all these things be sought with due respect for the laws of God and without impairing the rights of others and that they be employed in accordance with faith and right reason. If these principles are observed by everyone, everywhere, and always, not only the production and acquisition of goods but also the use of wealth, which now is seen to be so often contrary to right order, will be brought back soon within the bounds of equity and just distribution. The sordid love of wealth, which is the shame and great sin of our age, will be opposed in actual fact by the gentle yet effective law of Christian moderation which commands man to seek first the Kingdom of God and His justice, with the assurance that, by virtue of God's kindness and unfailing promise, temporal goods also, in so far as he has need of them, shall be given him besides»[616].

615 [*Quadragesimo Anno* §127.]
616 [*Id.* § 136.]

«As in all the stormy periods of the history of the Church, the fundamental remedy today lies in a sincere renewal of private and public life according to the principles of the Gospel by all those who belong to the Fold of Christ, that they may be in truth the salt of the earth to preserve human society from total corruption.

With heart deeply grateful to the Father of Light, from Whom descends "every best gift and every perfect gift"[617], We see on all sides consoling signs of this spiritual renewal. We see it not only in so many singularly chosen souls who in these last years have been elevated to the sublime heights of sanctity, and in so many others who with generous hearts are making their way towards the same luminous goal, but also in the new flowering of a deep and practical piety in all classes of society even the most cultured, as We pointed out in Our recent Motu Proprio *In multis solaciis* of October 28 last, on the occasion of the reorganization of the Pontifical Academy of Sciences»[618].

The renewal of life, according to the principles of the Gospel, is a transformation of individuals, taken one by one, according to the principles of Christ, to look at life with His eyes, to judge it with His judgment, to do on earth what He would do if he were in our place. This ideal is lofty—it is the purest sanctity— but only with such men, of any state and social condition, can one think of carrying out a social reform. Christianity, lived entirely by a large group of Christians, will be the yeast that will raise the dough and will also transform public institutions.

The world, almost without realizing it, is anxious to find men determined to realize an absolute ideal: men who, when the world finds them, will attract many to follow them. The human soul is «*naturaliter christiana*».

«... let us strive with all our strength to help those unhappy souls who have turned from God and, drawing them away from the temporal cares in which they are too deeply immersed, let us teach them to aspire with confidence to the things that are eternal. Sometimes this will be achieved much more easily than seems possible at first sight to expect. For if wonderful spiritual forces lie hidden, like sparks beneath ashes, within the secret recesses of even the most abandoned man — certain proof that his

617 [The encyclical here has a footnote as follows: «St. James, 1, 17».]
618 [*Divini Redemptoris* §§ 41-42.]

soul is naturally Christian — how much the more in the hearts of those many upon many who have been led into error rather through ignorance or environment»[619].

Life according to the precepts of the Gospel requires the practice of all the virtues: we will only dwell on those which have a more eminently social character, although in fact all do, even those that some contemptuously call «passive», such as mortification, prayer, purity and obedience. A Christian apostle, without them, cannot be conceived, and their absence constitutes the root of regrettable evils.

2.2. CHRISTIAN LOVE

Christianity is entirely summarized in the message of love:[620]

This pre-eminence of charity in the mind of Christ and in those who were immediate repositories of his doctrine makes charity the primary virtue that calls for social reform. Leo XIII asks bishops to instill above all, by authority and example:

> «... charity, the mistress and the queen of virtues. For, the happy results we all long for must be chiefly brought about by the plenteous outpouring of charity; of that true Christian charity which is the fulfilling of the whole Gospel law, which is always ready to sacrifice itself for others' sake, and is man's surest antidote against worldly pride and immoderate love of self; that charity whose office is described and whose God-like features are outlined by the Apostle St. Paul in these words: "Charity is patient, is kind, ... seeketh not her own, ... suffereth all things, ... endureth all things"»[621].

> «How completely deceived, therefore, are those rash reformers who concern themselves with the enforcement of justice alone—and this, commutative justice— and in their pride reject the assistance of charity! Admittedly, no vicarious charity can substitute for justice which is due as an obligation and is wrongfully denied. Yet even supposing that everyone should finally receive all that is due him, the widest field for charity will always remain open. For justice alone can, if faithfully observed, remove the causes of social conflict but can never bring about union of minds and hearts. In-

619 [*Quadragesimo Anno* §139.]

620 [Hurtado added at this point: «text of *Social Humanism*». It is not clear to which part of his book *Humanismo Social* (*Social Humanism*) he is referring to.]

621 [*Rerum Novarum* § 63. The encyclical here has a footnote as follows: «1 Cor. 13:4-7».]

deed all the institutions for the establishment of peace and the promotion of mutual help among men, however perfect these may seem, have the principal foundation of their stability in the mutual bond of minds and hearts whereby the members are united with one another. If this bond is lacking, the best of regulations come to naught, as we have learned by too frequent experience. And so, then only will true cooperation be possible for a single common good when the constituent parts of society deeply feel themselves members of one great family and children of the same Heavenly Father; nay, that they are one body in Christ, "but severally members one of another"[622], so that "if one member suffers anything, all the members suffer with it"[623]. For then the rich and others in positions of power will change their former indifference toward their poorer brothers into a solicitous and active love, listen with kindliness to their just demands, and freely forgive their possible mistakes and faults. And the workers, sincerely putting aside every feeling of hatred or envy which the promoters of social conflict so cunningly exploit, will not only accept without rancor the place in human society assigned them by Divine Providence, but rather will hold it in esteem, knowing well that everyone according to his function and duty is toiling usefully and honorably for the common good and is following closely in the footsteps of Him Who, being in the form of God, willed to be a carpenter among men and be known as the son of a carpenter»[624].

«But when on the one hand We see thousands of the needy, victims of real misery for various reasons beyond their control, and on the other so many round about them who spend huge sums of money on useless things and frivolous amusement, We cannot fail to remark with sorrow not only that justice is poorly observed, but that the precept of charity also is not sufficiently appreciated, is not a vital thing in daily life. We desire therefore, Venerable Brethren, that this divine precept, this precious mark of identification left by Christ to His true disciples, be ever more fully explained by pen and word of mouth; this precept which teaches us to see in those who suffer Christ Himself, and would have us love our brothers as Our Divine Savior has loved us, that is, even at the sacrifice of ourselves, and, if need be, of our very life. Let all then frequently meditate on those words of the final sentence, so consoling yet so terrifying, which the Supreme Judge will pronounce on the day of the Last Judgment: "Come, ye blessed of my Father ... for I was hungry and you gave me to eat; I was thirsty and you

622 [The encyclical here has a footnote as follows: «Rom. 12:5».]
623 [The encyclical here has a footnote as follows: «1 Cor. 12:26».]
624 [*Quadragesimo Anno* §137.]

gave me to drink ... Amen, I say to you, as long as you did it to one of these my least brethren you did it to me"[625]. And the reverse: "Depart from me, you cursed, into everlasting fire ... for I was hungry and you gave me not to eat; I was thirsty and you gave me not to drink ... Amen, I say to you, as long as you did it not to one of these least, neither did you do it to me"»[626].

2.3. HUNGER AND THIRST FOR JUSTICE

«But charity will never be true charity unless it takes justice into constant account. The Apostle teaches that «he that loveth his neighbor hath fulfilled the law» and he gives the reason: "For, *Thou shalt not commit adultery, Thou shalt not kill, Thou shalt not steal* ... and if there be any other commandment, it is comprised in this word: *Thou shalt love thy neighbor as thyself*"[627]. According to the Apostle, then, all the commandments, including those which are of strict justice, as those which forbid us to kill or to steal, may be reduced to the single precept of true charity. From this it follows that a "charity" which deprives the workingman of the salary to which he has a strict title in justice, is not charity at all, but only its empty name and hollow semblance. The wage-earner is not to receive as alms what is his due in justice. And let no one attempt with trifling charitable donations to exempt himself from the great duties imposed by justice. Both justice and charity often dictate obligations touching on the same subject-matter, but under different aspects; and the very dignity of the workingman makes him justly and acutely sensitive to the duties of others in this regard.

Therefore We turn again in a special way to you, Christian employers and industrialists, whose problem is often so difficult for the reason that you are saddled with the heavy heritage of an unjust economic regime whose ruinous influence has been felt through many generations. We bid you be mindful of your responsibility. It is unfortunately true that the manner of acting in certain Catholic circles has done much to shake the faith of the working-classes in the religion of Jesus Christ. These groups have refused to understand that Christian charity demands the recognition of certain rights due to the workingman, which the Church has explicitly acknowledged. What is to be thought of the action of those Catholic employers who in one place succeeded in preventing the reading of Our Encyclical *Quadragesimo Anno* in their local churches? Or of those Catholic industrialists who even to this day have shown themselves hos-

625 [The encyclical here has a footnote as follows: «St. Matthew, xxv, 34-40».]
626 [*Divini Redemptoris* § 47. The encyclical here has a footnote as follows: «St. Matthew, xxv, 41-45».]
627 [The encyclical here has a footnote as follows: «Romans, xiii, 8, 9».]

tile to a labor movement that We Ourselves recommended? Is it not deplorable that the right of private property defended by the Church should so often have been used as a weapon to defraud the workingman of his just salary and his social rights?»[628]

«The soul of peace, worthy of that name, and its life-giving spirit, can only be one: a justice that, in an impartial way, gives to each one what corresponds to him, and obtains from each one what he owes; a justice that does not give all things to all, but that gives love to all and does no harm ... a justice that is daughter of the truth, and mother of a healthy freedom and sure greatness»[629].

«...the rules, even the best that can be established, will never be perfect and will be doomed to failure if those who govern the destinies of the peoples, and those same peoples, are not impregnated with a spirit of good will, hunger and thirst for Christian idealism»[630].

2.4. SOBRIETY OF LIFE[631]

In the encyclical on atheistic communism, the Pope urges us:

«... to return to a more moderate way of life; to renounce the joys, often sinful, which the world today holds out in such abundance; to forget self for love of neighbor. There is a divine regenerating force in this "new precept" (as Christ called it) of Christian charity[632]. Its faithful observance will pour into the heart an inner peace which the world knows not, and will finally cure the ills which oppress humanity»[633].

2.5. SPIRIT OF POVERTY

The poverty to which the Gospel promises happiness is not misery, begging or the proletarian condition, but the knowledge of how to reduce one's possessions to what is necessary, to shed what is superfluous, to detach oneself from

628 [*Divini Redemptoris* §§ 49-50.]

629 [*Radio Message Oggi al Compiersi on the Fifth Anniversary of the Beginning of the War.*]

630 [Pius XII, Address *In Questo Giorno* to the Sacred College of Cardinals and members of the Roman Curia for Christmas (24 December 1939), https://w2.vatican.va/content/pius-xii/es/speeches/1939/documents/hf_p-xii_spe_19391224_questo-giorno.html. This document is only in Italian and Spanish at that website. This quoted passage is translated by the editors.]

631 [At this point Hurtado states: «Cfr. Humanismo Social». Hurtado is referring to his book *Humanismo Social* (*Social Humanism*) (1947).]

632 [The encyclical here has a footnote as follows: «St. John, XIII, 34».]

633 [*Divini Redemptoris* § 48.

At this point in the text Hurtado placed the phrase «Damage of luxury». This idea remains undeveloped. Hurtado set forth a plan for writing on this topic in the following fragments: «Social Humanism. When talking about the current social life. Austerity in all social classes. When people squander, races, wine, statistics. Chile Poblete Troncoso».]

earthly goods. In fact, the poor man who generously accepts his poverty, insecurity and dependence will be happy in the next world and even in this world, because he enjoys the true peace that is based in the soul. He renounces everything, possesses everything and passes through life with a free, pure and detached attitude.

The Lord tells the rich man, if he wants to be happy he has to become poor. He may possess his wealth as one who is not an owner but a mere administrator. He cannot serve two masters: the service of God is incompatible with the service of wealth. The spirit of poverty will not be achieved by a rich man unless he accepts a minimum of effective poverty, which will be reduced his property to what is necessary and will deposit his superfluity in the bosom of the poor.

In our times of high culture and high standards of living, it is necessary for men to have the courage to embrace poverty, so that others can escape misery. If the kingdom of abundance ever comes to be established, men will need poverty and a spirit of sacrifice as never before if they want to remain free men and not slaves.

This is the truth that Pius XI inculcates when he says:

> «All Christians, rich or poor, must keep their eye fixed on heaven, remembering that "we have not here a lasting city, but we seek one that is to come"[634]. The rich should not place their happiness in things of earth nor spend their best efforts in the acquisition of them. Rather, considering themselves only as stewards of their earthly goods, let them be mindful of the account they must render of them to their Lord and Master, and value them as precious means that God has put into their hands for doing good; let them not fail, besides, to distribute of their abundance to the poor, according to the evangelical precept[635]. Otherwise there shall be verified of them and their riches the harsh condemnation of St. James the Apostle: "Go to now, ye rich men; weep and howl in your miseries which shall come upon you. Your riches are corrupted, and your garments are moth-eaten; your gold and silver is cankered; and the rust of them shall be for a testimony against you and shall eat your flesh like fire. You have stored up to yourselves wrath against the last days"»[636].

634 [The encyclical here has a footnote as follows: «Hebrews, XIII, 14».]
635 [The encyclical here has a footnote as follows: «St. Luke, XI, 41».]
636 [*Divini Redemptoris* § 44. The encyclical here has a footnote as follows: «St. James, V, 1-3».]

Pius XI, as very powerful methods, recommends to us:

«...the spirit of prayer joined with Christian penance. When the Apostles asked the Savior why they had been unable to drive the evil spirit from a demoniac, Our Lord answered: "This kind is not cast out but by prayer and fasting"[637]. So, too, the evil which today torments humanity can be conquered only by a world-wide crusade of prayer and penance. We ask especially the Contemplative Orders, men and women, to redouble their prayers and sacrifices to obtain from heaven efficacious aid for the Church in the present struggle. Let them implore also the powerful intercession of the Immaculate Virgin who, having crushed the head of the serpent of old, remains the sure protectress and invincible "Help of Christians"»[638].

The same Pontiff points out a special fruit of prayer:

«In addition, prayer will remove the fundamental cause of present day difficulties, which We have mentioned above, that is the insatiable greed for earthly goods. The man who prays looks above to the goods of heaven whereon he meditates and which he desires; his whole being is plunged in the contemplation of the marvelous order established by God, which knows not the frenzy of earthly successes nor the futile competitions of ever increasing speed; and thus automatically, as it were, will be re-established that equilibrium between work and rest, whose entire absence from society today is responsible for grave dangers to life physical, economic and moral. If, therefore, those, who through the excessive production of manufactured goods have fallen into unemployment and poverty, made up their minds to give the proper time to prayer, there is no doubt that work and production would soon be brought within reasonable limits, and that the conflict which now divides humanity into two great camps struggling for transient interests, would be changed into a noble and peaceful contest for goods heavenly and eternal.

In like manner will the way be opened to the peace we long for, as St. Paul beautifully remarks in the passage where he joins the precept of prayer to holy desires for the peace and salvation of all men: «I desire, therefore, first of all, that supplications, prayers, intercessions and thanksgivings be made for all men; for kings and all that are in high station, that we may lead a quiet and peaceful life in all piety and chastity.

637 [The encyclical here has a footnote as follows: «St. Matthew, XVII, 20».]
638 [*Divini Redemptoris* § 59.]

For this is good and acceptable in the sight of God our Savior, who will have all men to be saved, and to come to the knowledge of truth» (I *Tim.* ii. 1-4). Let peace be implored for all men, but especially for those who in human society have the grave responsibilities of government; for how could they give peace to their peoples, if they have it not themselves? And it is prayer precisely, that, according to the Apostle, will bring the gift of peace; prayer that is addressed to the Heavenly Father who is the Father of all men; prayer that is the common expression of family feelings, of that great family which extends beyond the boundaries of any country and continent»[639].

«Let your thoughts and the feelings of your heart stimulate your faith, Christian laborers and workers, renewing the life of your faith, strengthening it with daily prayer. Let prayers begin and end your days of work. Let your thoughts and the feelings of your heart enlighten and energize your souls, especially during the Sunday rest and at holy days, allowing them to accompany you and guide you when you attend the Holy Mass.

Our Savior, a worker like you, in His earthly life was obedient to the Father until death, and now, on the altar, unbloody Calvary, perpetually renews His Sacrifice, for the good of the world, thus completing the work of redemption and becoming the Giver of Grace and the Bread of Life, for those souls who love Him and who, in their weaknesses, turn to Him seeking remedy.

May every Christian renew, before the altar of the Church, his promise to work obediently to the Divine Precept of work, whether it be intellectual or manual, in order to gain with his fatigue and sacrifices the bread that nourishes those he loves, always remembering the moral end of earthly life and eternal life, conforming his intentions to those of the Savior and turning his work into a hymn of praise to God.

In every circumstance and occasion, beloved sons and daughters, uphold and defend your personal dignity. The materials with which you work were created by God from the beginning of the world and, in the laboratories of the centuries, were molded by Him, on earth and deep in its entrails, by cataclysms, natural evolution, eruptions and transformations, to prepare an abode for man and for his work. Let these materials then become a perennial memory of the Creator's Hand of God, and let your souls be elevated to Him, the Supreme Lawgiver, whose precepts must be observed even in the life of the factories»[640].

639 [*Caritate Christi Compulsi* §§ 18-19.]
640 [*Speech to the Italian Workers.*]

2.7. SOCIAL FORMATION[641]

«To give to this social activity a greater efficacy, it is necessary to promote a wider study of social problems in the light of the doctrine of the Church and under the aegis of her constituted authority. If the manner of acting of some Catholics in the social-economic field has left much to be desired, this has often come about because they have not known and pondered sufficiently the teachings of the Sovereign Pontiffs on these questions. Therefore, it is of the utmost importance to foster in all classes of society an intensive program of social education adapted to the varying degrees of intellectual culture. It is necessary with all care and diligence to procure the widest possible diffusion of the teachings of the Church, even among the working classes. The minds of men must be illuminated with the sure light of Catholic teaching, and their wills must be drawn to follow and apply it as the norm of right living in the conscientious fulfillment of their manifold social duties. Thus they will oppose that incoherence and discontinuity in Christian life which We have many times lamented. For there are some who, while exteriorly faithful to the practice of their religion, yet in the field of labor and industry, in the professions, trade and business, permit a deplorable cleavage in their conscience, and live a life too little in conformity with the clear principles of justice and Christian charity. Such lives are a scandal to the weak, and to the malicious a pretext to discredit the Church»[642].

Note that the Pope desires formation on social rights and duties to be given to all social classes, including workers. Some people think it is imprudent[643].

2.8. SOCIAL ACTION

Leo XIII demanded social action with great urgency,

«Every one should put his hand to the work which falls to his share, and that at once and straightway, lest the evil which is already so great become through delay absolutely beyond remedy. Those who rule the commonwealths should avail themselves of the laws and institutions of the country; masters and wealthy owners must be mindful of their duty; the working class, whose interests are at stake, should make every lawful and proper effort; and since religion alone, as We said at the beginning, can avail to

641 [Hurtado stated at this point: «Cfr. Hum. Soc». Refering to his work *Social Humanism.*]
642 [*Divini Redemptoris* § 55.]
643 [Hurtado added at this point: «Hear how this is well answered by Pildain, Bishop of the Canaries».]

destroy the evil at its root, all men should rest persuaded that [the] main thing needful is to re-establish Christian morals, apart from which all the plans and devices of the wisest will prove of little avail»[644].

This urgency has been renewed by the most recent popes in the face of the growth of evils.

«To ward off such great evils from human society nothing, therefore, is to be left untried; to this end may all our labors turn, to this all our energies, to this our fervent and unremitting prayers to God! For with the assistance of Divine Grace the fate of the human family rests in our hands.

Venerable Brethren and Beloved Sons, let us not permit the children of this world to appear wiser in their generation than we who by the Divine Goodness are the children of the light[645]. We find them, indeed, selecting and training with the greatest shrewdness alert and resolute devotees who spread their errors ever wider day by day through all classes of men and in every part of the world. And whenever they undertake to attack the Church of Christ more violently, We see them put aside their internal quarrels, assembling in fully harmony in a single battle line with a completely united effort, and work to achieve their common purpose»[646].

«We trust that our faithful sons and daughters of the Catholic world, heralds of the social-Christian idea, will contribute—even at the price of considerable sacrifices — to a progression towards that social justice, in search of which all the true disciples of Christ must suffer hunger and thirst»[647].

2.9. ACTION OF THE PRIEST

In the first place, the Pope asks priests, who are responsible for lighting the beacon of faith, to go to the people.

«To priests in a special way We recommend anew the oft-repeated counsel of Our Predecessor, Leo XIII, to go to the workingman. We make this advice Our own, and faithful to the teachings of Jesus Christ and His Church, We thus complete it: "Go to the workingman, especially where he is poor; and in general, go to the poor". The poor

644 [*Rerum Novarum* § 62.]
645 [The encyclical here has a footnote as follows: «Cf. Luke 16:8».]
646 [*Quadragesimo Anno* §§ 145-146.]
647 [Radio Message *Oggi al Compiersi* on the Fifth Anniversary of the Beginning of the War.]

are obviously more exposed than others to the wiles of agitators who, taking advantage of their extreme need, kindle their hearts to envy of the rich and urge them to seize by force what fortune seems to have denied them unjustly. If the priest will not go to the workingman and to the poor, to warn them or to disabuse them of prejudice and false theory, they will become an easy prey for the apostles of Communism.

Indisputably much has been done in this direction, especially after the publication of the Encyclicals *Rerum Novarum* and *Quadragesimo Anno*. We are happy to voice Our paternal approval of the zealous pastoral activity manifested by so many Bishops and priests who have with due prudence and caution been planning and applying new methods of apostolate more adapted to modern needs. But for the solution of our present problem, all this effort is still inadequate. When our country is in danger, everything not strictly necessary, everything not bearing directly on the urgent matter of unified defense, takes second place. So we must act in today's crisis. Every other enterprise, however attractive and helpful, must yield before the vital need of protecting the very foundation of the Faith and of Christian civilization. Let our parish priests, therefore, while providing of course for the normal needs of the Faithful, dedicate the better part of their endeavors and their zeal to winning back the laboring masses to Christ and to His Church. Let them work to infuse the Christian spirit into quarters where it is least at home. The willing response of the masses, and results far exceeding their expectations, will not fail to reward them for their strenuous pioneer labor. This has been and continues to be our experience in Rome and in other capitals, where zealous parish communities are being formed as new churches are built in the suburban districts, and real miracles are being worked in the conversion of people whose hostility to religion has been due solely to the fact that they did not know it»[648].

This is the same doctrine that Pope Pius XI set forth in his letter to the Philippine episcopate:

«Your paternal solicitude should take care with singular attention to both the industrial workers and the peasants: they are the favorites of our heart, because they are in the social situation that Our Lord chose for Himself during his earthly life, and because the conditions of their material lives are subject to great suffering, since they are often deprived of means sufficient for a life worthy of a Christian and that tranquility of spirit born of security about the future. Most, unfortunately, lack the spiritual and

648 [*Divini Redemptoris* §§ 61-62.]

moral comforts that could sustain them in their anguish. In addition, their very situation exposes them to being more easily penetrable by those doctrines which are said to be true, inspired by the good of the worker and the humble in general, but which are full of fatal errors, since they combat the Christian faith, which secures the bases of law and social justice, and reject the spirit of fraternity and charity instilled in the Gospel, the only thing that can guarantee a sincere collaboration between the classes. On the other hand, such communist doctrines, based on pure materialism and the unbridled desire for earthly goods, as if they were capable of fully satisfying man, disregarding his ultimate purpose, have shown themselves in practice full of illusions and incapable of giving the worker a true and lasting material and spiritual well-being»[649].

The priest's main means of action must be his poor and disinterested life:

452 «But the most efficacious means of apostolate among the poor and lowly is the priest's example, the practice of all those sacerdotal virtues which We have described in Our Encyclical *Ad Catholici Sacerdotii*[650]. Especially needful, however, for the present situation is the shining example of a life which is humble, poor and disinterested, in imitation of a Divine Master Who could say to the world with divine simplicity: "The foxes have holes and the birds of the air nests, but the Son of Man hath not where to lay His head"[651]. A priest who is really poor and disinterested in the Gospel sense may work among his flock marvels recalling a Saint Vincent de Paul, a Cure of Ars, a Cottolengo, a Don Bosco and so many others; while an avaricious and selfish priest, as We have noted in the above mentioned Encyclical, even though he should not plunge with Judas to the abyss of treason, will never be more than empty "sounding brass' and useless "tinkling cymbal"[652]. Too often, indeed, he will be a hindrance rather than an instrument of grace in the midst of his people. Furthermore, where a secular priest or religious is obliged by his office to administer temporal property, let him remember that he is not only to observe scrupulously all that charity and justice prescribe, but that he has a special obligation to conduct himself in very truth as a father of the poor»[653].

649 [Quoted in *Social Christian Order*, item 334. Hurtado is citing a letter to the Phillipine Episcopate.]
650 [The encyclical here has a footnote as follows: «Dec. 20, 1935, A.A.S., vol. XXVIII (1936), pp. 5-53. 42. St. Matthew, VIII, 20».]
651 [The encyclical here has a footnote as follows: «Lk 9, 58».]
652 [The encyclical here has a footnote as follows: «1 Corinthians, XIII, 1».]
653 [*Divini Redemptoris* § 63.]

Special qualities of character and preparation are required for such priests:

«A difficult task, certainly, is thus imposed on priests, and to meet it, all who are growing up as the hope of the Church, must be duly prepared by an intensive study of the social question. Especially is it necessary that those whom you intend to assign in particular to this work should demonstrate that they are men possessed of the keenest sense of justice, who will resist with true manly courage the dishonest demands or the unjust acts of anyone, who will excel in the prudence and judgment which avoids every extreme, and, above all, who will be deeply permeated by the charity of Christ, which alone has the power to subdue firmly but gently the hearts and wills of men to the laws of justice and equity. Upon this road so often tried by happy experience, there is no reason why we should hesitate to go forward with all speed»[654].

When presenting doctrine, the priest will remember the immense damage that Marxism brings to souls and civilization:

«But the Church cannot ignore or overlook the fact that the worker in his efforts to better his lot, is opposed by a machinery which is not only not in accordance with nature, but is at variance with God's plan and with the purpose He had in creating the goods of earth.

In spite of the fact that the ways they followed were and are false and to be condemned, what man, and especially what priest or Christian, could remain deaf to the cries that rise from the depths and call for justice and a spirit of brotherly collaboration in a world ruled by a just God? Such silence would be culpable and unjustifiable before God, and contrary to the inspired teaching of the Apostle, who, while he inculcates the need of resolution in the fight against error, also knows that we must be full of sympathy for those who err, and open-minded in our understanding of their aspirations, hopes and motives»[655].

«As a protection for the dignity of the human being, it may be necessary at times to denounce and to blame boldly unjust and unworthy living conditions; at the same time, however, care must be taken to guard against either making violence legitimate with the pretext of applying a remedy to the ills of the people, or admitting and favoring those

654 [*Quadragesimo Anno* § 142.]
655 [*Christmas Message of 1942.*]

rapid and violent changes of temporal conditions of society which may lead to effects that are more harmful than the evil itself which is intended to be corrected»[656].

The priestly mission is to form men, to educate them

«by teaching youth, forming Christian organizations, and founding study groups guided by principles in harmony with the Faith. But above all, let them hold in high esteem and assiduously employ for the good of their disciples that most valuable means of both personal and social restoration which, as We taught in Our Encyclical, *Mens Nostra*, is to be found in the Spiritual Exercises. In that Letter We expressly mentioned and warmly recommended not only the Spiritual Exercises for all the laity, but also the highly beneficial Workers' Retreats. For in that school of the spirit, not only are the best of Christians developed but true apostles also are trained for every condition of life and are enkindled with the fire of the heart of Christ. From this school they will go forth as did the Apostles from the Upper Room of Jerusalem, strong in faith, endowed with an invincible steadfastness in persecution, burning with zeal, interested solely in spreading everywhere the Kingdom of Christ»[657].

The priest's mission is to serve the spiritual needs of the worker, in particular through specialized exercises, and not least his material needs through economic and social institutions[658].

«If you truly love the laborer (and you must love him because his conditions of life approach nearer to those of the Divine Master), you must assist him materially and religiously. Materially, bringing about in his favor the practice not only of commutative justice but also of social justice, that is, all those provisions which aim at relieving the condition of the proletarian; and then, religiously, giving him again the religious comforts without which he will struggle in a materialism that brutalizes him and degrades him.

656 [Pius XI, Encyclical on the Religious Situation in Mexico *Firmissimam Constantiam* (28 March 1927) §15, at The Holy See, http://w2.vatican.va/content/pius-xi/en/encyclicals/documents/hf_p-xi_enc_19370328_firmissimam-constantiam.html (hereinafter referred to as *Firmissimam Constantiam*).]

657 [*Quadragesimo Anno* § 143.]

658 [Hurtado states at this point: «Cfr. Letter from Pius XI to the Philippine Episcopate, *Social Christian Order*, item 334.]

No less grave and no less urgent is another duty: that of the religious and economic assistance of the *campesinos* (peasants), and in general of that not small portion of your sons forming the population, mostly agricultural, of the Indians. There are millions of souls, they too redeemed by Christ, entrusted by Him to your care and for whom He will some day ask you to render an account; there are millions of individual men often in such sad and miserable living conditions that they have not even that minimum of well-being indispensable to protect their very dignity as men. We conjure you, Venerable Brethren, in the bosom of the charity of Christ to have particular care for these children, to encourage your clergy to devote themselves with ever-increasing zeal to their assistance, and to interest the whole Mexican Catholic Action in this work of moral and material redemption»[659].

2.10. WORK OF CATHOLIC ACTION

Pius X had already established that «[s]uch, Venerable Brethren, are the characteristics, the aim and conditions of Catholic Action, considered in its most important function, namely, the solution of the social question. For that reason it demands the most energetic attention of all the Catholic forces»[660].

Pius XI exhorts his beloved children enrolled in Catholic Action and who share with him the care of the social question:

«All these We urge in the Lord, again and again, to spare no labors and let no difficulties conquer them, but rather to become day by day more courageous and more valiant. Arduous indeed is the task which We propose to them, for We know well that on both sides, both among the upper and the lower classes of society, there are many obstacles and barriers to be overcome. Let them not, however, lose heart; to face bitter combats is a mark of Christians, and to endure grave labors to the end is a mark of them who, as good soldiers of Christ, follow Him closely»[661].

The social work of Catholic Action must be preceded by:

«This task of formation, now more urgent and indispensable than ever, which must always precede direct action in the field, will assuredly be served by study-circles, con-

659 [*Firmissimam Constantiam* §§ 16-17.]
660 [Pius X, Encyclical on Catholic Action in Italy *Il Fermo Proposito* (11 June 1905) §20, at The Holy See, http://w2.vatican.va/content/pius-x/en/encyclicals/documents/hf_p-x_enc_11061905_il-fermo-proposito.html (hereinafter referred to as *Il Fermo Proposito*).]
661 [*Quadragesimo Anno* § 138.]

ferences, lecture-courses and the various other activities undertaken with a view to making known the Christian solution of the social problem.

The militant leaders of Catholic Action thus properly prepared and armed, will be the first and immediate apostles of their fellow workmen. They will be an invaluable aid to the priest in carrying the torch of truth, and in relieving grave spiritual and material suffering, in many sectors where inveterate anti-clerical prejudice or deplorable religious indifference has proved a constant obstacle to the pastoral activity of God's ministers. In this way they will collaborate, under the direction of especially qualified priests, in that work of spiritual aid to the laboring classes on which We set so much store, because it is the means best calculated to save these, Our beloved children, from the snares of Communism.

In addition to this individual apostolate which, however useful and efficacious, often goes unheralded, Catholic Action must organize propaganda on a large scale to disseminate knowledge of the fundamental principles on which, according to the Pontifical documents, a Christian Social Order must build.

Ranged with Catholic Action are the groups which We have been happy to call its auxiliary forces. With paternal affection We exhort these valuable organizations also to dedicate themselves to the great mission of which We have been treating, a cause which today transcends all others in vital importance.

We are thinking likewise of those associations of workmen, farmers, technicians, doctors, employers, students and others of like character, groups of men and women who live in the same cultural atmosphere and share the same way of life. Precisely these groups and organizations are destined to introduce into society that order which We have envisaged in Our Encyclical *Quadragesimo Anno*, and thus to spread in the vast and various fields of culture and labor the recognition of the Kingdom of Christ.

Even where the State, because of changed social and economic conditions, has felt obliged to intervene directly in order to aid and regulate such organizations by special legislative enactments, supposing always the necessary respect for liberty and private initiative, Catholic Action may not urge the circumstance as an excuse for abandoning the field. Its members should contribute prudently and intelligently to the study of the problems of the hour in the light of Catholic doctrine. They should loyally and generously participate in the formation of the new institutions, bringing to them the Christian spirit which is the basic principle of order wherever men work together in fraternal harmony»[662].

662 [*Divini Redemptoris* §§ 64-69.]

Of workers, in a special way, the Pope asks for an apostolate among those in the same condition: «The first and immediate apostles to the workers ought to be workers; the apostles to those who follow industry and trade ought to be from among them themselves»[663].

Pius XI says to Catholic Action that social work is among its tasks:

> «more particularly, urgently to respond to the more extensive and strongly felt needs ... with assistance not only spiritual, which must always occupy the first place, but also material, through those institutions which have the specific purpose of putting into practice the principles of social justice and evangelical charity ... Today the Church, with very special solicitude, goes in search of the mass of the most humble workers, not only so that they may enjoy those goods to which they are entitled according to justice and equity, but also to protect them from the pernicious work of communism ... For this reason the Church invites all her children, priests as well as lay people, especially those who fight in Catholic Action, to help her in this most urgent undertaking of safeguarding, before such a terrible threat, the spiritual and material benefits that the redemption of Christ has produced for all humankind and especially the humble classes»[664].

3
Economic and Social Action

> «The so-called social works, in the meantime, are not to escape the activities of Catholic Action, inasmuch as they aim at putting into practice the principles of justice and charity, and inasmuch as they are means of approaching the multitudes; since often souls are not reached except through the relief of corporal miseries and economic needs. And this We, Ourselves, as did Our predecessor of blessed memory, Leo XIII, recommended several times. But it is also true that, if Catholic Action has the duty of preparing men fit to direct such works, and of pointing out the principles which must guide them, with norms and directions drawn from the genuine sources of Our Encyclicals, it must not nevertheless assume the responsibility in that part which is purely technical, financial, economic, which is outside its competency and outside its purpose»[665].

663 [*Quadragesimo Anno* § 141.]

664 [This paragraph is translated from Hurtado's manuscript, which cites Hurtado's book *Social Christian Order*, ítem 369, which refers to *Pius XI*, Apostolic Letter to Cardinal Cerejeira Concerning Catholic Action in Portugal *Ex Officiosis Litteris* (10 November 1933).]

665 [*Firmissimam Constantiam* § 13.]

In *Quadragesimo Anno* Pius XI again reminds us that:

> «Catholic Action excludes strictly syndical or political activities from its scope but has influence over them and imbues with Catholic principles those sons of Ours whom Catholic Action trains for carrying on an apostolate under the leadership and teaching guidance of the Church»[666].

The Pope, in several documents, reiterates the idea that «economic and social institutions do not pertain to Catholic Action itself, because they operate directly in the economic and professional field. For this reason, they alone are responsible for their initiatives in purely economic matters … they must be inspired by the principles of charity and justice taught by the Church and must follow the directives laid down by the ecclesiastical authority in such a delicate matter»[667].

4 *Political Action*[668]

Civic duty is most grave and no Catholic can neglect, in conscience, to fulfill it[669]. The law of social charity requires that the life of the Republic be regulated by Christian principles.

Since Leo XIII the Pontiffs, as well as recalling the gravity of this duty, have left innumerable documents to indicate that the Church and Catholic Action are entirely different from political parties and cannot be contained within the narrow bounds of factions. This does not prevent «any Catholic from belonging to organizations of a political nature when they give, in their programs and in their activities, guarantees necessary to protect the rights of God and the conscience. It is necessary to add that participation in political life corresponds

666 [*Quadragesimo Anno* § 96. The editors translated this paragraph from Hurtado's Spanish rather than using the English translation at the Vatican website.]

667 [Hurtado states at this point: «Letter from Pius XI to the Philippine Episcopate, Social Christian Order item 334». The editors translated this passage from this book.]

668 [Here the manuscript states: «(Cfr. previous chapter in dealing with civic duty)».]

669 Cfr. *Firmissimam Constantiam* § 28.

to a duty of social charity, since every citizen must contribute according to his abilities to the welfare of his own nation»[670].

The attitude of Catholics towards the vindication of civil rights and freedoms is set forth in the courageous document of Pius XI to the Mexican Episcopate:

> «For the rest, once this gradation of values and activities is established, it must be admitted that for Christian life to develop itself it must have recourse to external and sensible means; that the Church, being a society of men, cannot exist or develop if it does not enjoy liberty of action, and that its members have the right to find in civil society the possibility of living according to the dictates of their consciences. Consequently, it is quite natural that when the most elementary religious and civil liberties are attacked, Catholic citizens do not resign themselves passively to renouncing those liberties. Notwithstanding, the revindication of these rights and liberties can be, according to the circumstances, more or less opportune, more or less energetic.
>
> You have more than once recalled to your Faithful that the Church protects peace and order, even at the cost of grave sacrifices, and that it condemns every unjust insurrection or violence against constituted powers. On the other hand, among you it has also been said that, whenever these powers arise against justice and truth even to destroying the very foundations of authority, it is not to be seen how those citizens are to be condemned who united to defend themselves and the nation, by licit and appropriate means, against those who make use of public power to bring it to ruin.
>
> If the practical solution depends on concrete circumstances, We must, however, on Our part recall to you some general principles, always to be kept in mind, and they are:
>
> 1) That these revindications have reason (the ratio) of means, or of relative end, not of ultimate and absolute end;
>
> 2) That, in reason (ratio) of means, they must be licit actions and not intrinsically evil;
>
> 3) That, if they are to be means proportionate to the end, they must be used only in the measure in which they serve to obtain or render possible, in whole or in part, the end, and in such manner that they do not cause to the community greater damages than those they seek to repair;

670 Pius XI, *Ex Off Officiosis Litteris*, 7 o.s.c. 376, c.f.r. also 371 -375 o.s.c., other documents about the same subject, c.f.r. Letter to Card. Pacelli to the Chilean Episcopate in Bulletin of Chilean C.A. [Hurtado is referring to the following documents, many of them cited in his book *Social Christian Order*: Pius XI, Apostolic Letter to Cardinal Cerejeira Concerning Catholic Action in Portugal, *Ex Officiosis Litteris* § 7 (10 November 1933); Pius X's *Motu Proprio*, Pius X's Letter to the French Episcopate (25 August 1910), Pius XI's *Qua Nobis* number 9, Pius XI's *Laetus Sane* number 4 and Letter of the Honorable Cardinal Eugenio Pacelli to the Chilean Episcopate (1934).]

4) That the use of such means and the exercise of civic and political rights in their fulness, embracing also problems of order purely material and technical, or any violent defense, does not enter in any manner in the task of the clergy or of Catholic Action as such, although to both appertains the preparation of Catholics to make just use of their rights, and to defend them with all legitimate means according as the common good requires;

5) The clergy and Catholic Action, being, by their mission of peace and love, consecrated to uniting all men *in vinculo pacis* (*Ephesians* iv. 3), must contribute to the prosperity of the nation, especially encouraging the union of those social initiatives which are not opposed to dogma or to the laws of Christian morals»[671].

5
Joint Action by All Men of Good Will

In view of the immense gravity of contemporary problems there is a fundamental universal question: either for God or against God! Before this problem:

«...[H]ere, again, is a debate in which the fate of the whole world is concerned; for in every matter, in politics, in economics, in morals, in discipline, in the arts, in the state, in civic and domestic society, in the East and in the West, everywhere we meet with this debate, and its consequences are a matter of supreme moment. And so it comes to pass that even the masters of that sect which foolishly says that the world is nothing but matter, and boasts that it has already shown for certain that there is no God—even these are constrained, again and again, to institute discussions about Him, though they thought they had done away with Him altogether.

Wherefore, We exhort all, private individuals as well as states, in the Lord, that now when such grave matters are agitated, critical questions concerning the welfare of all mankind, to lay aside that sordid and selfish regard for nothing but their own advantage, which blunts even the keenest minds, and cuts short even the noblest enterprises if they go the least bit beyond the narrow bounds of self-interest. Let all, then, join together, if need be even at the cost of serious loss, so that they may save themselves and all human society. In this union of minds and of forces, those who glory in the Christian name ought surely to take the foremost place, remembering the illustri-

671 [*Firmissimam Constantiam* §§ 26-28.]

ous examples of the Apostolic age, when "the multitude of believers had but one heart and one soul" (*Acts* iv. 32), but besides these, all whoever sincerely acknowledge God and honor Him from their heart should lend their aid in order that mankind may be saved from the great peril impending over all. For since all human authority must needs rest on the recognition of God, as on the firm foundation of any civil order, those who would not have all things overturned and all laws abrogated, must strive strenuously to prevent the enemies of religion from giving effect to the plans which they have so openly and so vehemently proclaimed»[672].

«But in this battle joined by the powers of darkness against the very idea of Divinity, it is Our fond hope that, besides the host which glories in the name of Christ, all those —and they comprise the overwhelming majority of mankind—, who still believe in God and pay Him homage may take a decisive part. We therefore renew the invitation extended to them five years ago in Our Encyclical *Caritate Christi*, invoking their loyal and hearty collaboration "in order to ward off from mankind the great danger that threatens all alike". Since, as We then said, "belief in God is the unshakeable foundation of all social order and of all responsibility on earth, it follows that all those who do not want anarchy and terrorism ought to take energetic steps to prevent the enemies of religion from attaining the goal they have so brazenly proclaimed to the world"»[673].

«The clarity of vision, the dedication, the energy, the inventive genius and the sense of brotherly love in all just and honest men, will determine that Christian thought will succeed in maintaining and supporting the gigantic work of restoration of social, economic and international life through a plan that is not in conflict with the religious and moral content of Christian Civilization.

In accordance with this, We make all our sons and daughters throughout the vast world, as well as those who while not belonging to the Church feel united to Us in this time of irrevocable decisions, the urgent call to weigh the extraordinary gravity of the moment and consider that, above and beyond all cooperation with other ideological tendencies and social forces suggested by purely contingent reasons, fidelity to the patrimony of Christian civilization and its strenuous defense against atheistic and anti-Christian tendencies, should be a cornerstone that should never be sacrificed for a transitory benefit or because of any temporary situation»[674].

672 [*Caritate Christi Compulsi* §§ 11-12.]

673 [*Divini Redemptoris* § 72. The encyclical here has a footnote as follows: «Encycl. *Caritate Christi*, May 3, 1932 (A.A.S., vol. XXIV, p. 184)».]

674 [*Radio Message Oggi al Compiersi on the Fifth Anniversary of the Beginning of the War* §§ 13-14, translated by the editors from the Spanish version at Vatican.va.]

Chapter 19

Supernatural Life

1

The Church

The Church is a spiritual society founded by Jesus Christ to lead man to his eternal destiny. Christ could have helped each soul directly to realize this end and established only individual relations between men and God, but He wanted man to achieve his supernatural life *socially*, that is, by means of the visible institution which is the Church. Just as in the natural order man does not reach his development and progress except through the family, the occupation and State, in the supernatural order God has established a society that offers man the means of his salvation and perfection.

The Divine Founder wished this society to be universal. To be a member, it is enough to be a man, regardless of race, nationality or social class. In Christ there is neither Jew nor Greek, there is neither slave nor free person, there is not male and female; for you are all one in Christ Jesus. (Ga. 3: 28).

In no society other than Church are equality and fraternity arranged so perfectly, as is the consequence of the identity of nature and of the supernatural vocation to be a child of God in Jesus Christ. God calls all men without exception and offers them His grace to pattern their lives on the life of Jesus.

This call is universal. God will not deny his grace to any man who does his part to follow the truth and the good manifested by the testimony of his conscience. The baptized are part of the Church. Besides those who have visibly received baptism, who constitute what is commonly called the visible body of the Church, those who have adhered to the Church —invisibly to our eyes but known to God— are also part of it. It is said that they are part of the *soul* of the Church, because of the invisible nature of their adherence. In this category are the righteous souls who have honestly followed their consciences and, without their fault, have not been able to know the revealed truth. God, in his infinite mercy, will not deny them the graces required to know what is necessary to believe and to do what is necessary to obey.

The Intimate Nature of the Church: Seen in its essence, the Catholic Church is a *perfect society*, that is, she has, by divine gift, all the necessary means to lead man to his supernatural end, as the State has, through the Creator, all the means necessary to provide man with temporal common good.

«But Catholicism is not limited to the sanctification of individuals, of individual consciences: it includes also in its supernatural and divine task social organizations and public institutions.

What is often called "the social reign of Jesus Christ" does not consist in writing his Holy Name at the head of the constitution of a country, or in the placing the image of the Sacred Heart on the national flag. These exterior acts, excellent and desirable in themselves, are rather, at the present day especially, a result than a cause, and the world would not be changed on the day that the strong hand of authority performed these great acts. Indifference and irreligion will scarcely be lessened by them.

The true social reign of Jesus Christ exists when His holy law of justice and love pervades all social organisms. The best possible work nowadays is indeed to make that law sink deeper therein by the worthiest means, which are also the best adapted to the condition of men's minds, their weakness and their possibilities.

There is neither ambition, nor jealousy, nor meddling in that, but the fulfillment of a mission that respects the autonomy and lawful functions of other organizations, and desires only to instil into them more of justice and of charity»[675].

2
The Communion of Saints

As we reach the end of this discussion of Catholic Social Morality, it is convenient for us to shift our attention to the great reality that stimulates all our works. The concept communion of saints has a double meaning: the union of all the members of the Church, whom the Christian tradition since Saint Paul calls *saints*, and also participation in the same supernatural benefits, in the same *holy* things. The two realities are comprised in the communion of saints, a supernatural community of life that unites us in the same body, circulates among us the same divine grace, as merited by the redemptive blood of Christ so as to make us participate in the very life of God: «to share in the divine nature». (2 Pet. 1:4). It is the realization of that mystic union between us and Christ revealed by Jesus and explained by St. John and St. Paul: Christ is the head that vivifies the whole body and communicates grace to us, and we, the multitude of members, each with his own function coordinated among us and subordinated to Christ, the source of our grace.

675 [*A Code of Social Principles* § 176.]

The first Adam dragged the entire human race into its fall owing to the community of nature within it; Christ, the second Adam, superabundantly repairs the work of Adam, offers the Father, in the name of the human race, a sacrifice of infinite value, and offers each of us effective redemption and divine adoption if we wish voluntarily to adhere to his Mystical Body. By our union with Christ we have all the treasures of divine grace.

The communion of saints makes us understand the eminently social aspect of the Church. In her reality, she embraces all men who are now struggling in her lap and men whose lives have already been embedded in God, whether they are in glory or temporarily purifying their faults. Those who are part of this immense community are bound not only by moral but also by physical bonds and by sanctifying grace: a participation created of the divine being that comes to us from Christ acting as its source. This grace establishes, among those who participate in it, bonds much superior to those of blood and communicates to all of them the spiritual goods of each.

The suffering Church: the souls in purgatory—receive the assistance of our prayers, and we receive aid through their intercession. The infinite merits of Christ and the merits of the Virgin and the saints are applied to us in the measure that God determines, by assuring us of a union with Christ that is greater every day. Each of us benefits from the good of all. There is no act of a Christian in a state of grace that does not benefit his brothers who struggle and who suffer, and in turn he is permanently helped by the actions of unknown brothers who make him a participant in their merits. Through sacraments, through indulgences and through works carried out in a state of grace the Church always maintains and enriches the circulation of supernatural life in the world. Hence, there is a need to live in a state of grace, without which our actions have no supernatural value whatsoever. Those who have departed from this world continue to be equally united with us and to take an interest in our good and in obtaining favors for us—favors whose source we ignore.

But also, the communion of saints imposes upon us an immense duty: the fate of the Church is in our hands. The Church is not Christ alone, but Christ and the faithful. We are responsible for the Church: collaborators with God in the great building up of the Body of the Lord, in the redemption and sanctification of humanity.

«Marvelously, Karl Adam develops this idea when he says: "The essential being of the Church must be realized and expressed not without the faithful, but by them. In their members and for them the Body of Christ must be affirmed and perfected. For the faithful, the Church is not only a gift, she is also a duty. They have to prepare and cultivate good soil in which the seed of the Kingdom of God can germinate and prosper. In other words, the life of the Church, the development of her faith and her charity, the elaboration of her dogma, her morality, her worship and her rights, are all closely dependent on the faith and the personal charity of the members of the Body of Christ. By the elevation and the abasement of his Church on earth, God rewards the merit or punishes the demerit of the faithful. It can be said with Saint Paul (Eph. 2: 21-22) that the Church, founded by Christ, is also built up by the common work of the faithful. Let us always work in building the temple of God and precisely here, on earth, let us work in His house, that is, the Church, as St. Augustine says. God would want a Church whose full development and perfection are the fruit of the personal supernatural lives of the faithful, of their prayer and charity, of their fidelity, of their penitence, of their self-denial. That is why God has not established her as a finished institution, perfect from the beginning, but as something incomplete that always leaves room for improvement and always invites us to work for her perfection»[676].

676 [*Social Humanism*, p. 278.]

Index

Albani, Stanislao Medolago
PAGE 328

Amunategui Solar, Domingo
PAGE 79

Antoine, Charles
PAGE 139

Aquinas, St. Thomas
PAGES 76, 77, 78, 102, 103, 152, 153, 156, 186, 222, 280, 282, 285, 349, 385, 386, 387, 390, 391, 433

Aristotle
PAGES 76, 77, 109, 151, 269, 391, 431

Augustine of Hippo
PAGES 75, 88, 129, 151, 194, 221, 286, 468

Azpiazu Zulaica, Joaquin
PAGES 87, 155, 156, 157, 280, 282, 303, 388, 389, 390, 410, 425, 432

Balmes y Urpia, Jaime Luciano
PAGE 86

Basil of Caesarea
PAGES 74, 75

Bastiat, Claude-Frederic
PAGE 223

Bellarmino, Roberto
PAGE 146

Bigo, Pierrre
PAGE 212

Blum, Leon
PAGES 239, 243, 244

Buchez, Philippe-Joseph-Benjamin
PAGE 81

Bureau, Paul
PAGE 82

Burke, Edmund
PAGE 80

Burnham, James
PAGE 202

Capitalism
PAGES 50, 51, 77, 132, 199, 230-238, 251, 253, 337, 343, 348, 369, 370, 383, 401, 403, 413, 433, 434, 435

Catholic Social Action movement
PAGES 33, 81, 83, 84, 85, 86, 87, 89, 92, 153, 230, 449

Children
PAGES 23, 30-32, 81, 87, 89, 109-199, 121, 125, 126, 129, 132, 133, 134, 168, 273, 287, 293, 306, 307, 316, 321-322, 394, 400-401,

Chile
PAGES 25, 26, 27, 28, 31, 32, 33, 46, 78, 79, 90, 91, 94, 111, 121-123, 125, 172, 173, 184, 205, 213, 295, 296, 297, 303, 321, 325, 326, 330, 347, 356, 359, 366, 367, 413, 445, 459

Christmas Message of 1942 (*Internal Order of States and People*)
PAGES 70, 93, 126, 273, 386, 394, 395, 439, 453

Chysostom, John
PAGE 75

Claro Vásquez, Miguel
PAGE 91

Clement of Alexandria
PAGE 74

Code of Canon Law
PAGES 111, 432

Code of Social Principles of Mechlin
PAGES 59, 100, 109, 114, 118, 147, 187, 304, 305, 306, 307, 316, 319, 320, 392, 396

Common good
PAGES 51, 67, 100, 101, 102, 103, 105, 111, 112, 139, 140, 142, 145-150, 153, 154, 155, 156, 159, 161, 164, 167, 170, 171, 176, 182, 187, 188, 201, 202, 221, 228, 233, 236, 237, 280, 282, 286-288, 292, 294, 303, 306, 308, 309, 310, 326, 335, 349, 350, 354, 355, 358, 382, 384, 385, 387, 390, 391, 392, 395, 396, 397, 398, 402, 403, 404, 414, 415, 414

Communism
PAGES 37, 91, 93, 111, 117, 163, 170, 214, 217, 229, 245, 246, 247, 251, 252, 254, 255, 256, 257, 258-261, 266, 337, 340, 341, 445, 451, 456, 457

Cyprian of Carthage
PAGE 74

De Bonald, Louis
PAGE 80

De Cepeda y Márques, Rafael Rodríguez
PAGE 86

De Coux, Charles
PAGE 81

De Lamennais, Hugues-Felicite Robert
PAGE 80

Del Valle, Florentino
PAGE 87

De Man, Henri
PAGE 240

De Molina, Luis
PAGE 77

Demolins, Edmond
PAGE 82

De Mun, Adrien Albert Marie
PAGES 82, 85, 86

De Rosales, Diego
PAGE 79

De Torres Bollo, Diego
PAGE 79

De Tourville, Henri
PAGE 82

De Valdivia, Luis
PAGES 63, 79

De Vitoria, Francisco
PAGE 78

Didache, The
PAGE 74

Durkheim, Emile
PAGES 239, 240

Education
PAGES 26, 30, 32, 90, 93, 104, 105, 109, 110, 113, 114-119, 120, 123, 124, 126, 131-134, 140, 150, 170, 201, 204, 205, 240, 243, 258, 270, 273, 291, 316, 317, 321-322, 341, 342, 344, 349, 388, 394, 454

Einstein, Albert
PAGE 204

Employers Consortium of Roubaix-Tourcoing
PAGES 329, 331, 364

Encomienda
PAGES 79, 295, 296

Family wage
PAGES 81, 85, 122, 306, 307, 308, 310, 311, 320, 321, 391, 394, 396, 398

Fascism
PAGES 88, 158, 348, 353, 356, 359

Fernández Pradel, Jorge
PAGE 303

Fisher, Irving
PAGE 422

Folliet, Joseph
PAGES 157, 159, 160, 165, 279, 284, 403, 432

French Revolution
PAGES 80, 336, 341, 383

Freppel, Charles-Emile
PAGE 85

Gaillard, Emilio
PAGE 233

Gandia, Isidro
PAGE 282

Gide, Andre
PAGE 260

George, Henry
PAGE 384

Gregory of Nyssa
PAGE 75

Guilds
PAGES 76, 80, 163, 186, 202, 295, 298, 327, 332-337

Hauriou, Maurice
PAGE 233

Housing
PAGES 36, 57, 88, 113, 123-128, 140, 204, 209, 296, 299, 316, 391

Hume, David
PAGE 223

Inquilinaje
PAGE 296

International Catholic Conversations of San Sebastian
PAGE 87

Jannet, Claudio
PAGE 85

Jocists (J.O.C., Jeunesse Ouvriere Chretienne or Young Christian Workers)
PAGES 83, 90, 93

Joliot-Curie, Frederic and Irene
PAGE 204

Joseph-Marie, Comte de Maistre
PAGE 80

Koestler, Arthur
PAGE 260

Kravchenko, Viktor
PAGE 260

Lacordaire, Jean-Baptiste Henri-Dominque
PAGES 80, 81, 336

Lacroix, Jean
PAGES 247, 251

L'Action Populaire
PAGES 83, 84, 212, 239

Lallement, Daniel-Louis
PAGES 153, 177, 193, 388

Lassalle, Ferdinand
PAGE 304

La Tour de Pin, Charles Humbert Rene
PAGES 82, 85

Lebret, Louis-Joseph
PAGES 84, 203, 204, 207, 214, 230

Leo XIII
PAGES 68, 69, 85, 86, 89, 91, 92, 93, 99, 100, 120, 144, 154, 159, 164, 239, 244, 245, 295, 298, 305, 311, 315, 327, 328, 336, 364, 365, 386, 387, 439, 442, 449, 450, 457

Le Play, Pierre Guillaume Frederic
PAGE 82

Le Sillon movement
PAGES 83, 92, 147

Lessius, Leonardus
PAGES 77-78

Lombard, Peter
PAGE 76

Malthus, Thomas
PAGES 223, 304

Marriage
PAGES 74, 91, 110-113, 119, 120, 130, 258, 321

Marx, Karl
PAGES 80, 304, 340, 341, 383

Marxism
PAGES 26, 49, 88, 200, 212, 214, 230, 237, 243, 247-255, 261, 271, 278, 288, 329, 330, 340, 341, 347, 353, 355, 356, 383, 416, 434, 453

Mill, John Stuart
PAGE 223

Montalembert, Charles Forbes Rene

PAGE 81

Mounier, Emmanuel

PAGE 292

Orti y Lara, Juan Manuel

PAGE 86

Ownership

PAGES 309, 352, 381, 386, 387, 392, 393, 395, 396, 397, 398, 399, 402, 434, 445

Ozanam, Antoine-Frederic

PAGES 80-81

Pemán, José María

PAGE 292

Perin, Charles

PAGE 85

Perozzi, Antonio

PAGE 269

Perroux, Francois

PAGE 230

Philip, Andre

PAGE 239

Pinero Carvallo, Bernardino

PAGE 297

Pius X

PAGES 83, 87, 92, 315, 328, 364, 365, 455, 459

Pius XI

PAGES 68, 69, 70, 76, 86, 88, 90, 93, 104, 121, 172, 184, 210, 212, 213, 255, 256, 280, 298, 302, 307, 309, 310, 312, 319, 328, 329, 330, 332, 351, 353, 364, 366, 375, 377, 381, 384, 386, 387, 392, 424, 440, 446, 447, 451, 454, 455, 457, 458, 459

Pius XII

PAGES 33, 70, 76, 93, 94, 121, 122, 136, 173, 209, 273, 300, 325, 387, 393, 394, 445

Pottier, Antoine

PAGES 85, 89

Priestly Committee of the Archbishopric of Lyon

PAGES 383, 385, 405

Quadragesimo Anno

PAGES 69, 70, 86, 93, 100, 120, 121, 125, 159, 165, 168, 184, 187, 201, 210, 211, 212, 213, 217, 228, 229, 230, 231, 234, 238, 245, 255, 257, 281, 284, 286, 291, 299, 302, 310, 312, 319, 328, 329, 330, 332, 352, 353, 354, 364, 366, 367, 375, 377, 381, 386, 387, 390, 391, 393, 424, 425, 440, 441, 442, 443, 444, 450, 451, 453, 454, 455, 456, 457, 458

Reducciones (Reductions)

PAGES 78, 79

Renard, Georges

PAGE 233

Rerum Novarum (*On the Condition of Workers*)
PAGES 50, 68, 82, 85, 86, 87, 88, 89, 90, 91, 93, 94, 99, 102, 120, 125, 127, 128, 159, 160, 162, 163, 168, 210, 212, 244, 291, 298, 299, 305, 329, 331, 336, 352, 364-366, 381, 386, 387, 392, 394, 395, 400, 439, 442, 450, 451

Revolt or revolution
PAGES 145, 169, 170, 206, 218, 243, 244, 247, 248, 250, 252-255, 272, 300, 315, 329, 338, 339, 340-346, 347, 349, 350, 353, 355, 356, 370, 383, 393, 397

Ricardo, David
PAGE 309

Rossi, Pellegrino
PAGE 223

Rostand, Jean
PAGE 205

Rousseau, Jean-Jacques
PAGES 101, 141, 145, 147, 219

Rucker Sotomayor, Martín
PAGE 91

Salas, Rafael Edward
PAGES 25, 91

Say, Jean-Baptiste
PAGE 223

Silone, Ignacio
PAGE 260

Slavery
PAGES 73, 74, 75, 78, 91, 141, 193, 202, 210, 269, 272, 274, 285, 292-295, 298, 333, 415, 446

Smith, Adam
PAGE 304

Social Weeks (Semaines Sociales de France)
PAGES 83, 159, 227, 239

Social Code of Mechlin or Mechelin
PAGES 59, 100, 109, 114, 118, 147, 187, 304, 305, 306, 307, 316, 319, 320, 392, 396

Sorel, Georges
PAGES 338, 341-343

Sturzo, Luigi
PAGE 88

Suárez, Francisco
PAGES 78, 146, 147

Taparelli, Luigi
PAGE 87

Taylor, Frederick Winslow
PAGE 320

Tertullian
PAGE 74

Trade Unions

PAGES 33, 67, 83, 85, 87, 89, 90, 92, 95, 103, 104, 163, 181, 225, 240, 266, 287, 301, 304, 316, 317, 325-330, 337-351, 353, 354, 355, 356-361, 365, 367, 370, 373, 375, 376, 377

Toniolo, Blessed Guiseppe

PAGES 87, 88, 328

Turgot, Anne Robert Jacques

PAGE 336

Unions, trade and labor

PAGES 33, 67, 83, 85, 87, 89, 90, 92, 95, 103, 104, 163, 181, 225, 240, 266, 287, 301, 304, 316, 317, 325-330, 337-351, 353, 354, 355, 356-361, 365, 367, 370, 373, 375, 376, 377

Union of Fribourg

PAGES 82, 85, 100

United States

PAGES 31, 78, 85, 93, 100, 144, 205, 207, 212, 311, 327, 422

Urey, Harold

PAGE 205

Versailles Treaty

PAGES 192, 317

Veuillot, Louis

PAGE 81

Vicent, Antonio

PAGES 86, 87

Villain, Jean

PAGE 84

Villeneuve-Bargemont, Jean-Paul-Alban

PAGE 81

Vives Solar, Fernando

PAGE 91

Vix Pervenit (On Usury and Other Dishonest Profits)

PAGES 78, 432

Vermeersch, Arthur

PAGE 389

Von Ketteler, Wilhelm Emmanuel

PAGE 89

Von Kopp, Georg

PAGE 92

Wagner, Adolph

PAGE 413

Walter Lippmann Colloquium

PAGE 224

Wealth distribution

PAGES 383-393, 401, 402, 405, 440, 446

Wilbois, Joseph

PAGE 82

Wright, Richard

PAGE 260

Women

PAGES 87, 90, 93, 128-136, 358, 320-321

Social Morality

This book was printed on *thin opaque smooth white Bible paper,* using the *Minion* and *Type Embellishments One* font families. This edition was printed in Panamericana Formas e Impresos, S.A., in Bogotá, Colombia, during the last weeks of the ninth month of the year two thousand and eighteen.

Ad publicam lucem datus mense septembre in nativitate Sancte Marie